AN INTRODUCTION TO

# GREENHOUSE PRODUCTION

ROBERT W. McMAHON

Ohio Agricultural Education Curriculum Materials Service

## FOREWORD

This student manual, *An Introduction to Greenhouse Production,* is intended to provide a very readable basic text for those preparing for greenhouse and floriculture work. This manual replaces *The Greenhouse Worker Student Manual* with comprehensive, current material and statistics about greenhouse production.

At the beginning of each chapter, competencies are listed that can be achieved as the result of studying information in that chapter. These competencies have been suggested by the author and verified by industry experts. At the end of each chapter, a self-check can be made of the information learned by using the review questions. Page references are included for locating information that answers the questions. Related math and science concepts are also included at the beginning of each chapter. The list of terms to know provides familiarity with the industry terms used in that chapter and thus improves communication. The terms are included in a glossary at the end of the manual that gives fairly simple definitions relating to greenhouse production.

**Robert D. Sommers II, Assistant Director**
Vocational and Career Education
Agricultural Education Service
Ohio Department of Education

**Roger D. Roediger, Project Consultant**
Ohio Agricultural Education
Curriculum Materials Service
The Ohio State University

ISBN Number: 1-56502-002-2



**Ohio Agricultural Education Curriculum Materials Service**
**The Ohio State University**
**Room 254, 2120 Fyffe Road**
**Columbus, Ohio 43210-1010**

**1992**

## ACKNOWLEDGMENTS

The author is grateful to the many individuals and greenhouse businesses who assisted in the preparation of this book. Foremost is the horticultural advisory committee that helped to develop the text outline and contributed suggestions to the final draft of the text. These advisory committee members (who met with the author) and the organizations in Ohio that they represent, either in the greenhouse industry or in academia, are the following:

Ms. Lily Felder, Hehn's Wholesale Greenhouse, Akron
Mr. Tom Machamer, Cedar Lane Farms, Inc., Wooster
Mr. Erik Mayer, Ashland High School, Ashland
Mr. Danny Missler, Green Circle Growers, Inc., Oberlin
Mr. Erik Munson, Montgomery County JVS, Clayton
Dr. Roger Roediger, Curriculum Materials Service, Columbus
Mr. James Scott, Agricultural Education Service, Columbus
Mr. Jeffrey Schaffstall, Hehn's Wholesale Greenhouse, Akron
Mr. Richard Waggoner, Penta County JVS, Perrysburg
Mr. Rick Webb, Tri-County JVS, Nelsonville

Most of the photographs used in this book were taken by the author. There are, however, some photographic contributions from other individuals and businesses. Their cooperation in supplying photographs is sincerely appreciated.

Dr. Gary Anderson
Blackmore Company, Inc. (Belleville, Michigan)
Mr. Dale Bradshaw
Paul Ecke Poinsettias (Encinitas, California)
Mr. Michael Fulton
Ms. Janet Kellner
Dr. Richard Lindquist
Mr. Timothy Pfaffel
Ms. Marilyn Riese
Dr. Roger Roediger
Dr. Ted Short
Mr. Thomas Taylor
Ms. Alison Witt
Yoder Brothers, Inc. (Barberton, Ohio)

Photographs were taken in the following businesses or organizations. Their cooperation is also acknowledged.

The Ohio State University Agricultural Technical Institute, Wooster, Ohio
Architectural Greenery, Akron, Ohio
Bernecker's Nursery, Homestead, Florida
Cedar Lane Farms, Inc., Wooster, Ohio
Costa Nursery, Homestead, Florida
Endres Floral Company, New Philadelphia, Ohio
Epcot Center and Walt Disney World, Lake Buena Vista, Florida
Green Circle Growers, Oberlin and Columbia Station, Ohio
Hehn's Wholesale Greenhouse, Akron, Ohio
Interior Plant Specialists, Inc., Westlake, Ohio
Moore's Greenhouse, Shreve, Ohio

*(continued)*

**Acknowledgments** *(continued)*

Natural Beauty of Florida/Greiling Farms, Inc., Apopka, Florida
Ohio Agricultural Research and Development Center, Wooster, Ohio
Phil's Greenhouse, Homeworth, Ohio
Plantasia, Canal Winchester, Ohio

The author would also like to thank the following individuals for their important and varied contributions.

Dr. Gary Anderson
Mr. Dale Bradshaw
Ms. Teresa Lanker
Dr. Ted Short
Ms. Ladonna Whitt

Dr. Roger Roediger, Director of the Ohio Agricultural Education Curriculum Materials Service of The Ohio State University, was Project Director. Dr. Roediger's many helpful comments and suggestions are greatly appreciated. Muriel N. King, project editor, did an outstanding job of editing the text and implementing the layout of the book. The cover design was by Eric D. King.

---

## About the Author

Robert W. McMahon is an assistant professor in the Horticultural Industries Division of The Ohio State University's Agricultural Technical Institute (ATI). He teaches courses in floriculture production, commercial interior plantscaping, greenhouse environment control, and practicum. He also manages ATI's five greenhouses and the conservatory.

McMahon did his undergraduate work at St. Olaf College (Minnesota) in biology. He received the M.S. and Ph.D. degrees from Iowa State University (Ames, Iowa) in horticulture. McMahon holds membership in the Ohio Florists' Association and the International Carnivorous Plant Society. Several research publications and presentations bear his name as author and presenter.

---

## CONTENTS

**Chapter 1 Overview of the Greenhouse Industry** ........ 1
History of the greenhouse industry ........ 3
Major greenhouse crops and production statistics ........ 3
International floriculture production ........ 9
The greenhouse business ........ 13
Careers in floriculture ........ 16
Chapter 1 review ........ 24

**Chapter 2 Greenhouse Structures** ........ 25
Suitable greenhouse locations ........ 26
Greenhouse structures and glazing materials ........ 29
Greenhouse framing materials ........ 39
The headhouse ........ 41
Chapter 2 review ........ 44

**Chapter 3 Controlling the Greenhouse Environment** ........ 45
Heating principles ........ 46
Heating fuels ........ 48
Heating systems ........ 50
Greenhouse energy conservation ........ 61
Greenhouse ventilation and cooling equipment ........ 64
Air cooling methods ........ 68
Greenhouse shading ........ 71
Carbon dioxide generators ........ 72
Chapter 3 review ........ 75

**Chapter 4 Greenhouse Equipment and Lighting** ........ 77
Greenhouse benches ........ 78
Supplemental lighting ........ 87
Chapter 4 review ........ 91

**Chapter 5 Greenhouse Irrigation Systems** ........ 93
Watering systems ........ 94
Water quality ........ 103
Intermittent mist systems for propagation ........ 106
Greenhouse environment control computers ........ 108
Chapter 5 review ........ 113

**Chapter 6 Root Media and Containers** ........ 115
Introduction to soils ........ 116
Root media ........ 118
Containers for floriculture crops ........ 131
Propagation materials ........ 134
Chapter 6 review ........ 139

**Chapter 7 Nutrition** ........ 141
The seventeen essential elements ........ 142
Effect of pH on nutrient availability ........ 143
Fertilizers ........ 144
Fertilizer calculations ........ 149
Nutritional problems ........ 153
Chapter 7 review ........ 158

*(continued)*

**Contents** *(continued)*

**Chapter 8 Integrated Pest Management** .... 159
Definition of IPM .... 160
Principles of IPM .... 160
Setting up an IPM program .... 165
Chapter 8 review .... 167

**Chapter 9 Plant Height Control by DIF** .... 169
Definition of DIF .... 170
Effects of DIF on plant growth .... 170
Applications of DIF .... 173
Chapter 9 review .... 175

**Chapter 10 Bedding Plant Production (including Geraniums)** .... 177
**Bedding plants** .... 178
Overview of the bedding plant industry .... 178
Seed germination in flats and plug trays .... 181
Seedling growth stages .... 189
Finishing the crop .... 191
Schedules for bedding plant crops .... 201
Marketing bedding plants .... 203
**Geraniums** .... 205
Chapter 10 review .... 217

**Chapter 11 Flowering Potted Plant Production -**
Poinsettias, Chrysanthemums, and Easter Lilies .... 219
Introduction - Statistics .... 220
**Poinsettia production** .... 222
Poinsettia review .... 238
**Potted chrysanthemum production** .... 239
Chrysanthemum review .... 260
**Easter lily production** .... 261
Easter lily review .... 270

**Chapter 12 Minor Potted Crops** .... 271
African violets .... 273
Cineraria .... 274
Cyclamen .... 275
Holiday cacti .... 276
Kalanchoe .... 277
Foliage plants .... 279
Chapter 12 review .... 294

**Chapter 13 Cut Flower Production** .... 297
Introduction and statistics .... 298
Roses .... 298
Carnations .... 300
Alstroemeria .... 303
Freesia .... 304
Snapdragons .... 305
General cultural guidelines .... 306
Harvesting .... 307
Chapter 13 review .... 309

**References** .... 311
**Glossary** .... 312

# CHAPTER 1

# OVERVIEW OF THE GREENHOUSE INDUSTRY

## Competencies for Chapter 1

As a result of studying this chapter, you should be able to do the following:

1. Describe the history of the floriculture industry worldwide.
2. Describe the impact of international trade policies on floriculture products worldwide.
3. Describe the economic importance of floriculture.
4. Identify the major segments of the floriculture industry.
5. Name the leading states in floriculture production in the U.S.
6. Categorize the major costs of a greenhouse business.
7. Describe available careers in floriculture.
8. Identify continuing education opportunities.
9. Summarize the trends in cut flower production.
10. Consult reference manuals and reports that relate to the greenhouse industry.

## Related Math Concepts

1. Read, interpret, and construct charts, graphs, and tables.
2. Apply basic operations to whole numbers, decimals, and fractions.

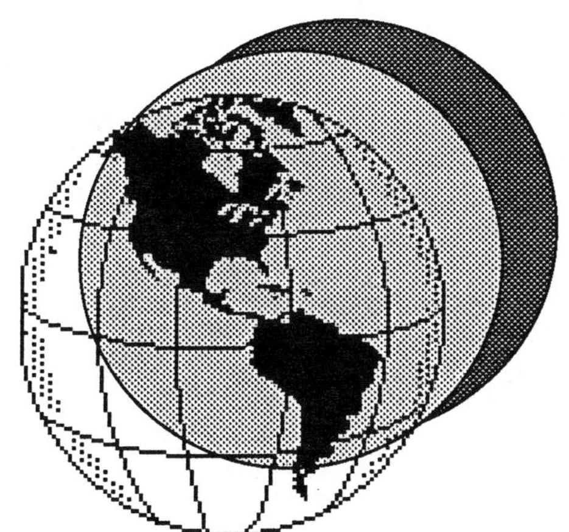

## Terms to Know

environmental
fertilize
**floriculture**
foliage plant
greenhouse
growing media
irrigation
liners
pesticide
propagation
quarantine

# INTRODUCTION

Welcome to the exciting and dynamic floriculture industry! By choosing a career in the floriculture industry, you are stepping into a field that is growing and constantly changing. Exciting new technologies have been developed; they enable the industry to bring new and improved floriculture products to the American consumer. You will be involved in new methods of production and marketing. You will experience changing trends in consumer demands. This will always be challenging, but you will reap great rewards as you meet each challenge, and you will grow with the industry.

**Floriculture** is defined as the growing and marketing of bedding plants, flowering potted plants, cut flowers, and foliage. The floriculture industry fills a basic need in people. It supplies us with beautiful plants and flowers. In our often "sterile" world of concrete, plaster, and limited yard space, we need something living and beautiful to lift our spirits and satisfy the desire many of us have to grow something. For these reasons, gardening is the number one hobby in the United States, and indoor foliage plants are very popular.

Therefore, floriculture is an important part of the agriculture industry. Greenhouse workers, growers, shippers, wholesalers, and retail florists are all involved in the floriculture industry (Figure 1.1). Your choosing to study floriculture greenhouse production is a sound career decision for your future.

**Figure 1.1**

Organization of the commercial greenhouse industry

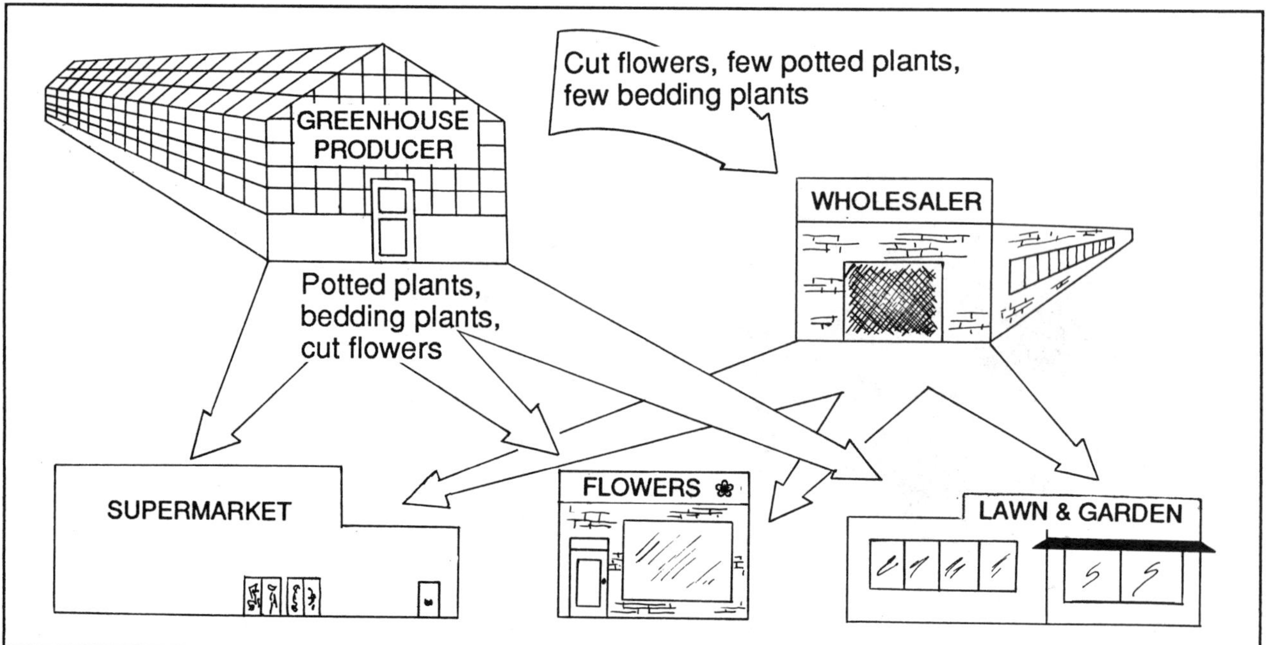

## HISTORY OF THE GREENHOUSE INDUSTRY

The modern greenhouse industry had its origins in the Netherlands in the 1600s. At that time, dormant lilac bushes were first dug and brought in from the field. Lilacs thus became the first crop to be forced into bloom in lean-to glass greenhouses. The industry prospered in the Netherlands. Today this small country has the largest greenhouse industry in the world, due to automation and efficient production techniques.

The greenhouse industry in the United States was started in the early 1700s mainly to serve the wealthy. At a time when this country's population was concentrated in the original thirteen colonies, the greenhouse industry was located in the population centers of Boston, New York, and Philadelphia. Fresh flowers were a luxury; only the upper class could afford them. As the population of the United States expanded west, the floriculture industry followed. Before the 20th century, the industry was located in or near the major population centers. At that time, perishable flowers and plants could not be shipped long distances because of slow transportation and no refrigeration.

The 1800s saw the floriculture industry expand virtually across the country, thanks in part to the transcontinental railroad. It opened the West to settlement and greatly improved the transportation of floriculture products. No longer were wealthy people the sole recipients of flowers and plants. The market expanded to include the average citizen, thanks to more efficient production techniques. Also, improved transportation lowered production costs.

In the 1900s the floriculture industry has mushroomed into a multibillion-dollar industry. Refrigerated trucks and jet transportation are two technological advancements that have enabled the floriculture industry to ship its product virtually anywhere in the United States or around the world within 24 hours. (See Figure 1.2.) Thus, growers do not have to locate in or near their market. They can build their greenhouses in locations that are the most favorable not only for the crops they want to grow, but also for tax rates, water quality, etc. Today, many wholesale greenhouses are located in rural areas as much as hundreds or thousands of miles from their markets. They rely on the rapid transportation systems that are available.

## MAJOR GREENHOUSE CROPS AND PRODUCTION STATISTICS

Floriculture is one of the largest parts of the horticulture industry. There are four major segments of the floriculture industry: bedding plants, flowering potted plants, cut flowers and foliage plants. The ***Floriculture Crops 1990 Summary*** produced by the USDA (United States Department of Agriculture) surveys all commercial growers that produce and sell at least $10,000 worth of floriculture crops in the top 28 states. This summary reports that the wholesale value of the 28 crops included in the survey totalled an impressive $2.77 **billion**, an increase of 10 percent from 1989.

**Figure 1.2**
The commercial greenhouse industry (floriculture) encompasses a worldwide network of growers, propagators, wholesalers, brokers, shippers, retail florists, mass market outlets, etc.

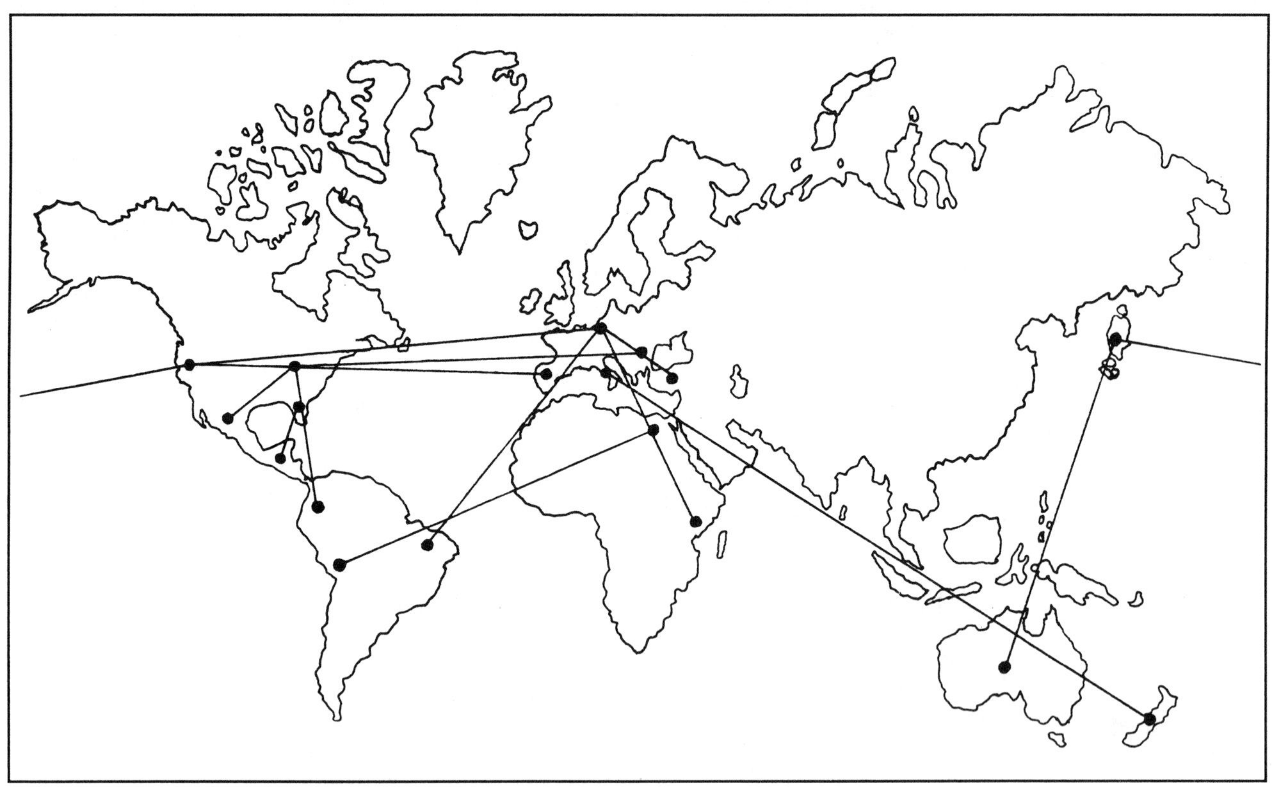

Bedding plants make up the largest segment of the floriculture industry. The 1990 wholesale value of bedding plants was $971 million, or 35 percent of the $2.77 billion total (Table 1.1). This is an increase of 8 percent from 1989. Potted flowering plants were second at $673 million, or 24 percent of the total value. This is an impressive increase of 25 percent from 1989. Foliage plants came in third place and cut flowers fourth. Cut cultivated greens came in fifth, at a distant last place.

**Table 1.1** Wholesale value of the floriculture industry in 1990

| Crop | Wholesale Value (millions $) | Percent Wholesale Value |
|---|---|---|
| Bedding plants | 971 | 35.1 |
| Potted flowering plants | 673 | 24.2 |
| Foliage | 512 | 18.5 |
| Cut flowers | 503 | 18.2 |
| Cut cultivated greens | 111 | 4.0 |
| Total | 2,770 | 100 |

Source: *Floriculture Crops 1990 Summary.* United States Department of Agriculture, National Agricultural Statistics Service, Agricultural Statistics Board, Washington, DC, April 1991

California, in first place, and Florida, second, lead all other states in floriculture production (Table 1.2). Together these two states account for nearly **half** of the wholesale floriculture production in the United States. The generally mild to tropical climates of these states favor floriculture production, and their large populations supply the needed labor. Rounding out the top five states are New York, Texas and Ohio. Ohio alone produces 4.5 percent of the floriculture crops in the United States.

Since 1960, there has been a shift in some segments of the floriculture industry to the South and West. Over 80 percent of foliage is produced in Florida, California, and Texas (Table 1.3). Nearly 70 percent of the cut flowers produced in the United States are produced in California, Florida, and Colorado (Table 1.4).

---

**Table 1.2** Top five states in floriculture production in 1990

| State | Wholesale Value (millions $) | Percent Wholesale Value |
|---|---|---|
| 1. California | 717.5 | 26.0 |
| 2. Florida | 528.8 | 19.1 |
| 3. New York | 221.0 | 8.0 |
| 4. Texas | 135.3 | 4.9 |
| **5. Ohio** | **125.7** | **4.5** |

**Table 1.3** Top five states in foliage production in 1990

| State | Wholesale Value (millions $) | Percent Wholesale Value |
|---|---|---|
| 1. Florida | 280.8 | 54.8 |
| 2. California | 109.2 | 21.3 |
| 3. Texas | 21.5 | 4.2 |
| 4. Hawaii | 13.1 | 2.6 |
| **5. Ohio** | **11.6** | **2.3** |

**Table 1.4** Top five states in cut flower production - and Ohio's ranking - in 1990

| State | Wholesale Value (millions $) | Percent Wholesale Value |
|---|---|---|
| 1. California | 293.7 | 59.0 |
| 2. Florida | 29.8 | 5.9 |
| 3. Colorado | 22.3 | 4.4 |
| 4. New York | 21.6 | 4.3 |
| 5. Hawaii | 19.4 | 3.9 |
| **12. Ohio** | **8.7** | **1.7** |

Source of Tables 1.2, 1.3, 1.4: *Floriculture Crops 1990 Summary*. United States Department of Agriculture, National Agricultural Statistics Service, Agricultural Statistics Board, Washington, DC, April 1991

The major floriculture production areas in the United States are given in Table 1.5. In bedding plant production, California was the leading state in 1990 with a wholesale value of $164 million or nearly 17 percent of the total value of $971 million (Table 1.6). Michigan, Texas, New York, and Ohio round out the top five states. Ohio produced $71 million (wholesale) worth of bedding plants, or 7.3 percent of all bedding plants produced.

California also was the top producer of potted flowering plants in 1990. Nearly 21 percent of the total wholesale value, or $138 million worth, was grown in California (Table 1.7). New York, Florida, Ohio, and Texas make up the rest of the top five states in this category. Ohio produced $34.3 million or 5.1 percent of the total wholesale value for flowering potted plants.

The *Floriculture Crops 1990 Survey* found that there were 9,185 growers in the top 28 states, an increase of 398 from 1989. Florida had the most growers with 1,313, followed by California, New York, Ohio, and Pennsylvania (Table 1.8). The number of growers in Ohio in that year increased by 35 to 560.

The total greenhouse-covered area in 1990 was 404 million square feet, an increase of 3 million square feet from 1989 (Table 1.9). Film plastics accounted for nearly 56 percent of the covered area, followed by fiberglass/rigid plastics at 24 percent, and glass at 20 percent. California had the largest area under greenhouse cover with 123 million square feet (Table 1.10). Florida was second with 48.5 million square feet. Michigan was third with 25.8 million square feet. Ohio was fourth with 23.1 million square feet of greenhouse cover. Texas was fifth with 19.7 million square feet of covered greenhouse growing area.

**Table 1.5** ⇨
Major floriculture production areas in the United States

| Crop | Major Areas |
|---|---|
| **Cut flowers** | |
| Carnations | Colorado and California |
| Pompon mums | Florida and California |
| Standard mums | California |
| Roses | California |
| **Potted plants** | Throughout the United States |
| **Bedding plants** | Throughout the United States |
| **Foliage plants** | California, Florida, and Texas |

**Table 1.6** ⇨
Top five states in bedding plant production in 1990

| State | Wholesale Value (millions $) | Percent Wholesale Value |
|---|---|---|
| 1. California | 164.2 | 16.9 |
| 2. Michigan | 84.0 | 8.6 |
| 3. Texas | 78.6 | 8.1 |
| 4. New York | 71.5 | 7.4 |
| **5. Ohio** | **71.1** | **7.3** |

Source: *Floriculture Crops 1990 Summary.* United States Department of Agriculture, National Agricultural Statistics Service, Agricultural Statistics Board, Washington, DC, April 1991

**Table 1.7** Top five states in flowering potted plant production in 1990

| State | Wholesale Value (millions $) | Percent Wholesale Value |
|---|---|---|
| 1. California | 138.3 | 20.6 |
| 2. New York | 122.6 | 18.2 |
| 3. Florida | 68.1 | 10.1 |
| **4. Ohio** | **34.3** | **5.1** |
| 5. Texas | 34.1 | 5.1 |

**Table 1.8** Top five states in number of growers in 1990

| State | Number of Growers |
|---|---|
| 1. Florida | 1,313 |
| 2. California | 1,130 |
| 3. New York | 675 |
| **4. Ohio** | **560** |
| 5. Pennsylvania | 551 |

**Table 1.9** Greenhouse-covered area* in 1991 by covering material

| Covering | Square Feet (millions) | Percent of Total |
|---|---|---|
| Glass | 79.6 | 19.7 |
| Fiberglass/Rigid plastic | 98.6 | 24.4 |
| Film plastic (single and double layer) | 226.0 | 55.9 |
| Total covered area | 404.2 | 100.0 |

* This does not include shade and temporary cover

**Table 1.10** Top five states in 1990 in greenhouse-covered growing area*

| State | Covered Growing Area (millions of square feet) | Percent of Total |
|---|---|---|
| 1. California | 123.0 | 30.4 |
| 2. Florida | 48.5 | 12.0 |
| 3. Michigan | 25.8 | 6.4 |
| **4. Ohio** | **23.1** | **5.7** |
| 5. Texas | 19.7 | 4.9 |

* This does not include shade and temporary cover

Source of Tables 1.7, 1.8, 1.9, 1.10: *Floriculture Crops 1990 Summary.* United States Department of Agriculture, National Agricultural Statistics Service, Agricultural Statistics Board, Washington, DC, April 1991

## Ohio Production Statistics

These statistics show us that Ohio is a major state for floriculture production. On a national level, in 1990, Ohio ranked fourth by wholesale value for producing flowering potted plants and fourth for covered greenhouse growing area. Ohio ranked fifth in several categories, including bedding plant production, foliage production, and overall floriculture production wholesale value. More detailed Ohio production statistics are given in Table 1.11.

**Table 1.11** Ohio floriculture production statistics of selected crops for 1990

| Crop | Wholesale Value (millions $) | National Rank | No. of Ohio Growers |
|---|---|---|---|
| CUT FLOWERS | | | |
| Mums | | | |
| Standard | 0.27 | 6 | 45 |
| Pompon | 0.31 | | |
| Roses | | | |
| Hybrid tea | 5.99 | 7 | 12 |
| Sweetheart | 0.71 | 9 | 11 |
| FLOWERING POT PLANTS | | | |
| African violets | 5.49 | 1 | 26 |
| Azaleas | 4.90 | 5 | 75 |
| Easter lilies | 2.41 | 4 | 133 |
| Mums | 3.20 | 9 | 73 |
| Poinsettias | 12.85 | 2 | 278 |
| BEDDING PLANTS | | | |
| **Flats** | | | |
| Geraniums | 3.02 | 2 | 245 |
| Other flowering/foliar | 31.00 | 4 | 477 |
| Vegetable | 4.84 | 5 | 407 |
| **Potted** | | | |
| Cutting geraniums | 6.39 | 3 | 364 |
| Seed geraniums | 3.28 | 3 | 250 |
| FLOWERING HANGING BASKETS | 10.15 | 1 | 470 |

Source: *Floriculture Crops 1990 Summary.* United States Department of Agriculture, National Agricultural Statistics Service, Agricultural Statistics Board, Washington, DC, April 1991

Other impressive statistics of Ohio's floriculture industry are as follows. Ohio produces more African violets and flowering hanging baskets than any other state. Ohio is second in production of geraniums in flats (behind Texas) and behind only California in poinsettia production. Ohio ranked third for seed and cutting geraniums and ranked in the top ten for the other crops listed in Table 1.11. Note that potted poinsettias, flowering/foliar bedding plants in flats, and flowering hanging baskets were the three most valuable crops grown in Ohio. These accounted for nearly $54 million in wholesale value. The smallest segment of Ohio's floriculture industry is cut flower production, which had a wholesale value of $7.3 million for mums and roses.

## INTERNATIONAL FLORICULTURE PRODUCTION

The United States certainly is not the only country in the world with a thriving floriculture industry. Worldwide, the floriculture industry is linked together by modern, intercontinental jet transportation. Delivery anywhere on earth in a refrigerated environment is possible within 24 hours. Thus, cut carnations harvested in Colombia, South America can be delivered to the United States in excellent condition in a matter of hours. This is also true for cut orchids harvested in Thailand and cut roses harvested in Israel.

The United States floriculture industry is obviously no longer isolated. Its market here is greatly influenced by foreign floriculture markets, especially in regards to cut flower production. Our floriculture industry is influenced from abroad, not only economically but also technologically and culturally. For example, much of our new greenhouse technology came from the Netherlands. Also, new cultivar introductions have come from abroad. It is to our advantage to interact and even compete with foreign countries to improve our floriculture industry at home.

Examples of greenhouses from Europe and the Middle East are shown in Figure 1.3, A-E. Parts of the Netherlands, for example, are literally covered with greenhouses (Figure 1.3A). Other countries too have a thriving greenhouse industry. In Egypt, greenhouses or "tunnels" are built in the desert and used successfully to raise crops (Figure 1.3B). Even where greenhouses are more primitive in structure, fine crops can be produced, such as shown in Portugal (Figure 1.3C, D) and in Turkey (Figure 1.3E). Every country has its own methods for greenhouse production, but the end result is the same: a high quality, beautiful product that adds beauty and joy to our lives.

Centers of floriculture production are found throughout the world. In the northern hemisphere, major producing areas are in Europe, Japan, and the United States. In the southern hemisphere, dominant producing areas are located in Central and South America, Africa, Australia and New Zealand. Table 1.12 lists the major floriculture-producing countries by continent.

**A** Aerial view of greenhouses in the Netherlands

**B** "Tunnel" greenhouses of Egypt

**C & D** Greenhouses in Portugal - wooden frames before and after covering with single-layer polyethylene

**E** Ridge and furrow greenhouses in Turkey

**Figure 1.3**

Greenhouses of Europe and the Middle East

Photos courtesy of Ted Short, Agricultural Engineering Department, OARDC, Wooster, Ohio

| Continent | Major Producing & Exporting Countries |
|---|---|
| Europe | Netherlands<br>Italy<br>Spain |
| Africa & Near East | Israel<br>Kenya<br>Turkey |
| Central & South America | Brazil<br>Colombia<br>Costa Rica<br>Ecuador<br>Mexico<br>Peru |
| Far East (Asia) | Japan |

**Table 1.12**
Major countries for floriculture production in 1991

Source: *Worldwide Production and Distribution of Floriculture Crops.* Jan Van Doesburg. International Short Course presentation, Ohio Florists' Association, Cincinnati, Ohio. 15 July 1991.

## Imported Cut Flowers

Cut flower imports to the United States have increased dramatically since 1970. Sixty-seven percent (67%) of the major cut flower crops sold in this country in 1990 were imported from foreign countries, compared to only 4 percent in 1971 (Table 1.13). In other words, only one-third of the roses, carnations, standard mums, and pompons sold in the United States were actually grown here. In 1971, no cut flower crop imports accounted for more than 10 percent of the stems sold. Now, nearly 80 percent of the carnations and pompons, 56 percent of the mums, and 42 percent of the roses sold in the United States are imported.

The large volume of cut flower exports from these countries is possible for two reasons: 1) labor is very inexpensive and overhead costs low; and 2) the climate is ideal for cut flower production. The result is an inexpensive, high quality product that can be sold in the United States at prices that are very competitive or considerably lower than those of domestically grown cut flowers.

A positive trend since 1970 is the increase in the yearly per capita consumption (stems purchased per person). Overall, it increased from slightly less than 7 stems per person in 1971 to over 13 in 1990 (Table 1.13). Carnations and roses account for most of this increase in per capita consumption. Pompon consumption also increased from 1 to 2.6 stems per person. Mum consumption, however, decreased from 0.75 stem to 0.23 stem per person in the same period of time.

Besides cut flowers, unrooted cuttings are also imported into the United States. Major exporting countries to the United States include several in Central and South America for carnations and chrysanthemums, and Netherlands and Israel for roses (Table 1.14). Freesia and alstroemeria and unrooted cuttings are exported from a number of areas around the world.

**Table 1.13** Cut flower import statistics of selected crops

| Crop | Year | % imported | % U.S. grown | Stems purchased per person |
|---|---|---|---|---|
| Carnations | 1971 | 5.2 | 94.8 | 3.08 |
| | 1981 | 58.2 | 41.8 | 3.98 |
| | 1990 | 78.9 | 21.1 | 6.19 |
| Mums | 1971 | 7.3 | 92.7 | 0.75 |
| | 1981 | 19.9 | 80.1 | 0.47 |
| | 1990 | 56.0 | 44.0 | 0.23 |
| Pompons | 1971 | 5.6 | 94.4 | 1.06 |
| | 1981 | 54.8 | 45.2 | 2.12 |
| | 1990 | 80.5 | 19.5 | 2.61 |
| Roses | 1971 | 0.2 | 99.8 | 2.08 |
| | 1981 | 14.6 | 85.4 | 2.15 |
| | 1990 | 41.7 | 58.3 | 4.10 |
| **Totals** | 1971 | 4.0 | 96.0 | 6.97 |
| | 1981 | 44.5 | 55.5 | 8.72 |
| | 1990 | 67.2 | 32.8 | 13.13 |

*Source:* ***Flower Marketing Information*** newsletter, June 1991. Alvi O. Voigt, Agricultural Economist, The Pennsylvania State University - Cooperative Extension Service

**Table 1.14** Major floriculture crops imported from other countries

| Crops Imported | Exporting Countries |
|---|---|
| CUT FLOWERS | |
| Carnations | Central and South America |
| Pompon mums | Colombia |
| Standard mums | Ecuador |
| Roses | Guatemala |
| | Netherlands |
| | Israel |
| UNROOTED FOLIAGE PLANT CUTTINGS | Central and South America |
| | Europe |
| | Africa |
| | Japan |
| | Australia |
| | New Zealand |

At present, potted plants are banned from import into the United States (Figure 1.4) by Quarantine 37, a policy mandated by the Animal and Plant Health Inspection Service. Soil in the pots and the potted plants themselves often contain disease-causing organisms and pests. This ban reduces the possibility of introducing these harmful organisms into the United States. (Cut flower imports do not have as much foliage as do flowering potted plants, nor is there any soil involved.) Amendments to Quarantine 37 which have recently been proposed would allow many species of potted plants to enter the United States. However, before these amendments will be passed, suitable inspection procedures to protect our floriculture industry will have to be developed.

## THE GREENHOUSE BUSINESS

### The Business Structure

Greenhouse businesses are generally classified in one of three types: grower, grower-wholesaler, or grower-retailer.

**Figure 1.4** Plant materials imported from overseas. Plants growing in soil or potting media may not enter the United States.

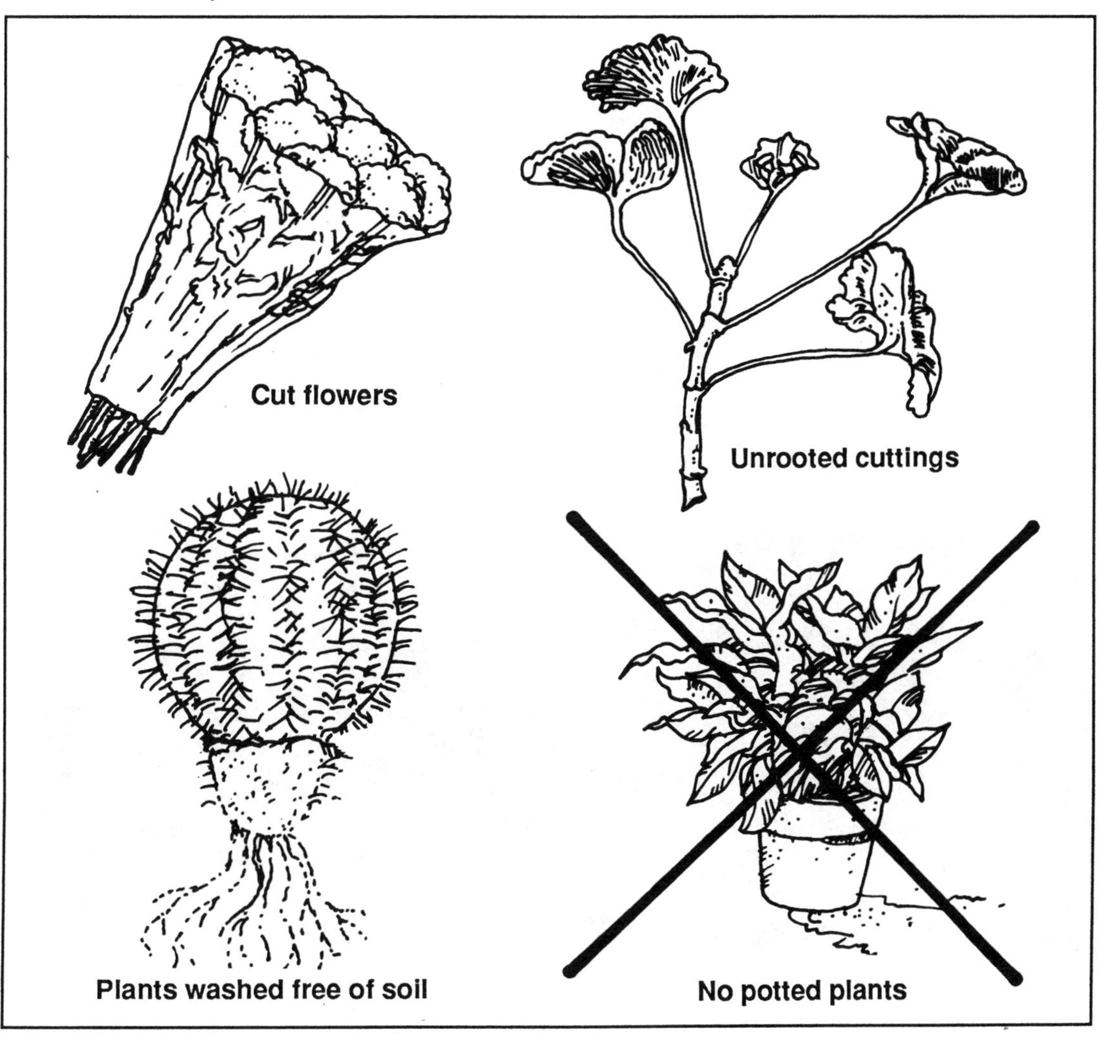

**Growers** usually produce crops which are marketed by a wholesale or retail florist outlet. They often specialize in one crop or a limited number of crops. Growers concentrate on production. They leave the marketing of their crops to wholesalers.

**Grower-wholesalers** also specialize in a limited number of crops. However, they purchase products from other producers in order to provide retailers with a full line of floral products (Figure 1.5). In addition to plant material, grower-wholesalers may provide a line of "hard goods" such as vases, pots, planters, ribbon, florist tape, etc.

**Grower-retailers** generally produce a variety of crops for sale through their own retail outlets (Figure 1.6). Some of their crops may be sold to other wholesale or retail florists. In effect, grower-retailers eliminate the "middle man" to increase profits. However, they are then responsible for growing many crops expertly.

Some growers specialize in the production of seeds, bulbs, cuttings, small plants, or "liners," which they market through brokerage firms or directly to other growers. Propagation of disease-free plant material requires special expertise. Plant propagators are the experts in the early part of the production program. They provide growers with the "clean" plant material that is essential for quality production.

**Brokerage firms** function as "middle men" between greenhouse producers and customers. Brokers usually handle only the marketing transaction, not the product. They collect a commission (percentage of the profit) for acting as sales agents. Brokers take orders from greenhouse customers. Products ordered are shipped directly from the producer to the customer. In many cases, brokers also provide greenhouse customers with valuable advice, such as information on crop scheduling, cultivars, etc.

**Figure 1.5**
This large grower-wholesaler produces a wide range of potted plants.

**Figure 1.6**
This grower-retailer produces many of the potted plants sold through this retail store.

## Greenhouse Costs

Greenhouse costs are extremely variable. They are influenced by many factors, including climate, size and location of the business, and strength of the local economy. It is difficult, therefore, to make broad generalizations. However, when determining costs of production, four categories should be considered (Figure 1.7).

1. **Direct materials costs.** These include the cost of plant materials, pots, growing media, chemicals, and other items that are **directly** related to the production of the crop.

2. **Direct labor costs.** These costs are based on production activities such as preparing growing media, planting crops, spacing crops, spraying pesticides, and watering and fertilizing. The cost of labor should include not only wages, but also benefits, such as health insurance, paid vacations, and sick leave.

3. **Overhead costs.** These are the indirect costs of production, such as heating fuels, secretarial support and office management, depreciation, taxes, insurance, and utility services.

4. **Marketing costs.** These costs include advertising, packing the product for shipping, shipping, and billing.

Figure 1.7 diagrams the cost of a typical bedding plant producer. Ranges are given for each category because production costs vary considerably across

**Figure 1.7** Relationship of major costs to the total cost in the greenhouse bedding plant industry

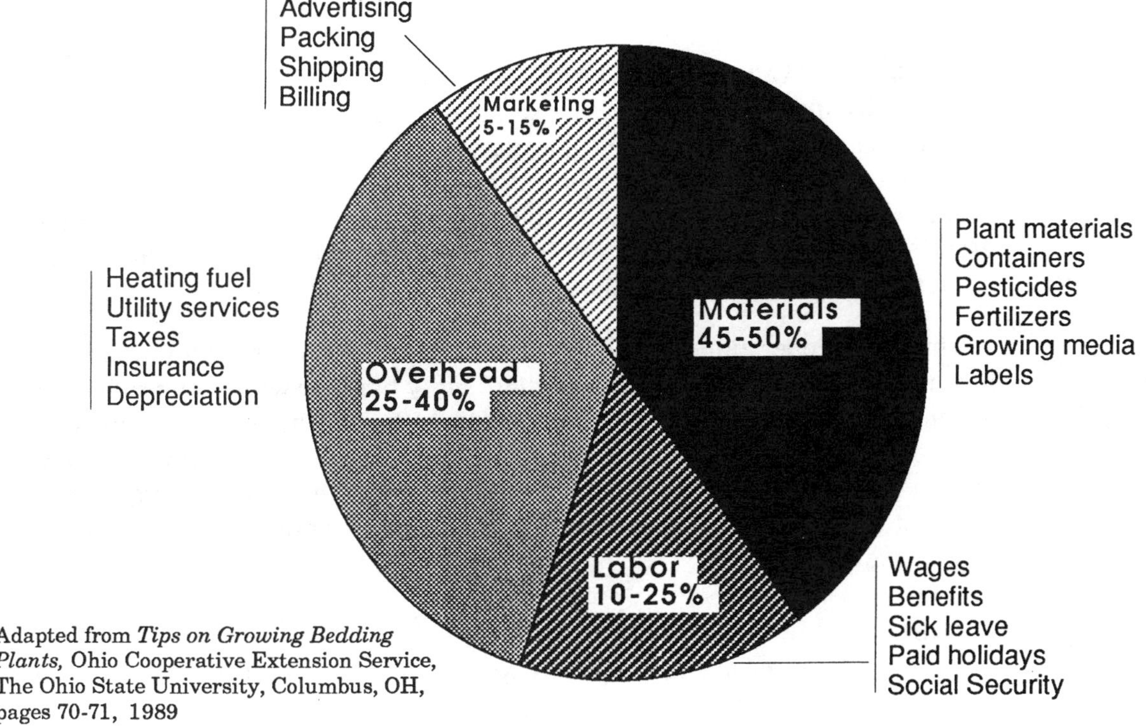


Adapted from *Tips on Growing Bedding Plants,* Ohio Cooperative Extension Service, The Ohio State University, Columbus, OH, pages 70-71, 1989

the country and even within Ohio. Labor is still the largest **single** cost for a greenhouse operator. For bedding plant production, labor can account for 10 to 25 percent of the total production costs. Heating fuel makes up a significant portion of the overhead costs, usually from 15 to 20 percent. In northern climates with severe winters, the cost of heating fuel can be as high as 25 percent of the production costs. Costs for crops other than bedding plants will vary from these figures because of different environmental requirements, labor required, etc. However, these figures will give you a general idea of the production costs that are involved.

# CAREERS IN FLORICULTURE

## Greenhouse Careers

Regardless of the size of a greenhouse operation, there are certain specific jobs that must be done for the operation to run smoothly. Someone must be assigned the responsibility of seeing that these jobs are done when necessary and as efficiently as possible. In a large operation, one person may be responsible exclusively for propagating plants, another for scheduling crops, another for watering and fertilizing, and so on. In a small operation, the same person may have all of these responsibilities and others.

Knowing who is responsible for what and establishing a chain of command is essential for any business. As a student of floriculture, you should have a general knowledge of job titles/careers and the responsibilities involved. Following are some generalized descriptions of the careers in a greenhouse operation and the responsibilities associated with each. Any given greenhouse business may have more or fewer positions than those listed here. However, someone must be responsible for all the activities described. Figures 1.8 and 1.9 outline typical business structures for a large and a small greenhouse business.

### Greenhouse Manager or Owner/Manager

In many instances the greenhouse manager also owns the business. The manager is responsible for the total greenhouse operation. This person outlines and assigns duties and coordinates the activities of various working groups. He or she must deal with the problems related to the various individuals' work. The manager's job is to make sure the business achieves its production and marketing goals.

In a small operation, managers directly supervise all production, marketing, and maintenance. They must be thoroughly familiar with crop production techniques, business principles, and personnel management. A two- or four-year college degree (B.S. or Associate degree) in floriculture is highly desirable, though graduates of a strong high school or post high school vocational program might qualify. Regardless of education, several years of practical experience are required.

### Production Manager

The production manager's job is to plan and supervise the growing of crops which the management has decided to produce. Responsibilities include

**Figure 1.8**
Typical chain of command in a **large** greenhouse operation

MANAGER
or
Owner/Manager
Marketing Manager
Production Manager
Maintenance Manager
Office Staff
Section Foreman
Maintenance Staff
Growers
Grower's Assistants

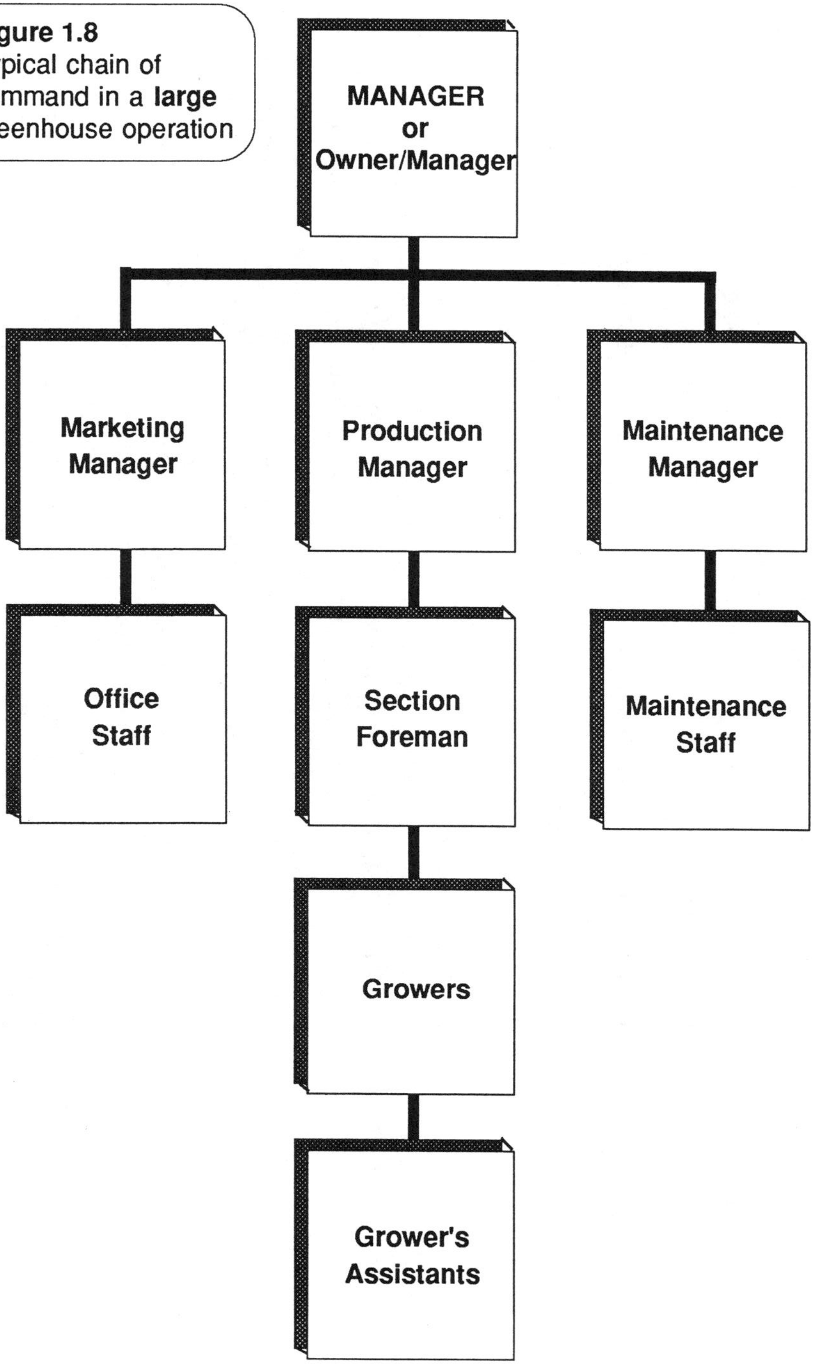

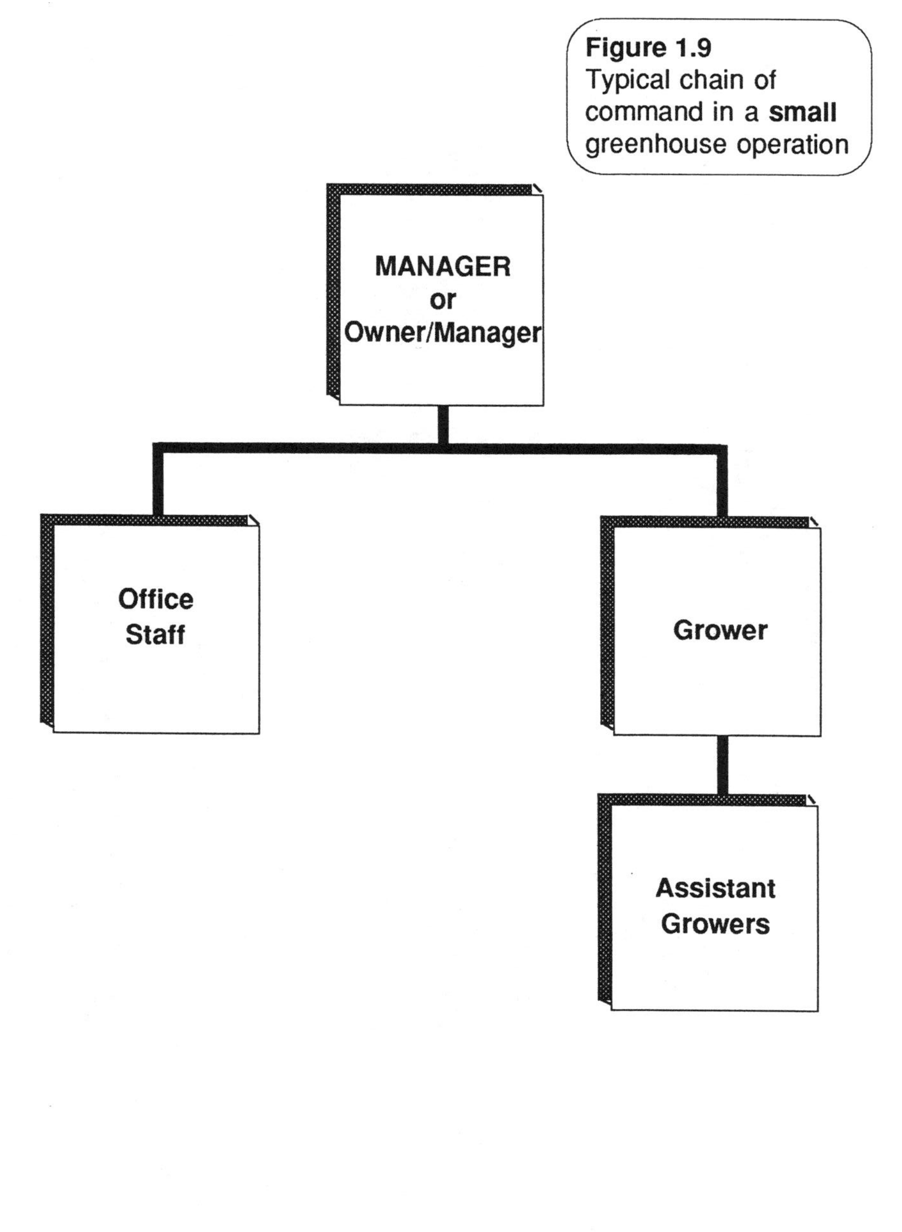

**Figure 1.9**
Typical chain of command in a **small** greenhouse operation

MANAGER
or
Owner/Manager
Office Staff
Grower
Assistant Growers

crop scheduling, ordering cuttings, seeds and supplies, and preparing work schedules. Production managers should have detailed knowledge of current cultural techniques and familiarity with current market trends. The production manager reports directly to the greenhouse manager. The production manager should also have an Associate or B.S. degree in floriculture. Vocational high school graduates with training in floriculture may also qualify for this position. Several years of practical experience is another important qualification.

### Marketing Manager

The marketing manager oversees sales, supervises shipment of products, and handles advertising and pricing. This person works closely with the greenhouse manager and production manager in planning the types, quantity, and timing of crops. Sales records are an important part of the job of the marketing manager. Sales records often determine which crops will continue to be grown and which discontinued. A major job of the marketing manager has to do with customers: finding new prospects and maintaining contact with established customers. Marketing managers also work closely with the business office; they often supervise business office personnel.

The marketing manager often has a B.S. degree in business, marketing, or business administration. Previous business experience and familiarity with the greenhouse industry are desirable.

### Maintenance Manager

The maintenance manager is responsible for maintaining all physical facilities of the business and for attending to routine maintenance problems. This manager supervises maintenance crews, plans work schedules, orders materials, and keeps record of regularly scheduled jobs. Maintenance managers should have a strong background in mechanical and agricultural engineering. They also need a practical knowledge of the structures and equipment used in the greenhouse business. A knowledge of crop production methods is useful, but not essential. The maintenance manager usually reports directly to the greenhouse manager. Qualifications for this job include a high school degree with vocational and/or technical training combined with practical experience.

### Section Foreman

The foreman oversees a section of a greenhouse range. In a large range, this individual may be responsible for a single crop. A foreman schedules crop rotations, takes inventories, orders supplies, and supervises and trains growers. The foreman helps growers plan their work schedules and assists in solving production and personnel problems. Foremen are directly responsible to the production manager. Typically, a foreman supervises two to six growers.

A greenhouse foreman should have an Associate or B.S. degree in floriculture; many are also graduates of high school programs in horticulture. Greenhouse foremen must be well educated and knowledgeable about current cultural techniques for their crops. Further, foremen must also be skilled in personnel relations. Several years of experience in greenhouse production are required.

### Grower

The grower is responsible for doing the physical work involved in growing a greenhouse crop, following directions given. The individual grower is often responsible for a limited number of large crops or for several small crops. Growers prepare soil, plant crops, fertilize, water, pinch and prune crops, and apply pesticides. They frequently harvest cut flowers and potted plants and transport them to grading and shipping areas. The grower reports to the greenhouse foreman.

Growers typically are graduates of a high school program in floriculture and/or graduates of a two-year technical college in greenhouse production. Usually one or more years of practical experience are also required.

### Grower's Assistant

A grower's assistant helps the grower perform his or her responsibilities. In addition to jobs directly involved in growing plants, this person may work at maintenance and repair of facilities and equipment during off-peak periods in the summer. In large operations, some assistants are involved only in grading, packing, and shipping. Other assistants are employed on a seasonal basis during periods of heavy work loads or when certain crops, such as bedding plants, demand a lot of work like transplanting.

Most grower's assistants are graduates of horticulture high school programs. The training for a grower's assistant is a good solid foundation for entry into the greenhouse business. Employers look for productive and reliable assistants - those who are willing to learn, accept responsibility, and get along well with fellow employees. Such grower's assistants can expect increased responsibilities and pay during the first year of employment. An interest in plants and in people and some knowledge of mechanics are all important for a successful employee in a greenhouse business.

## Academic Careers in Floriculture

In addition to actually working in the greenhouse business, there are two floriculture careers available in the academic world: teaching and research.

### Teaching

Teaching floriculture at either the high school or the college level is a demanding career. Instructors teach a wide variety of courses ranging from general introductory floriculture, which covers all aspects of greenhouse production, to advanced, detailed courses such as bedding plant production, flowering pot plant production, or greenhouse equipment and construction (the more advanced, detailed courses). The generalized courses usually are taught at the high school level and the more specialized courses at the college level (in two- and four-year programs).

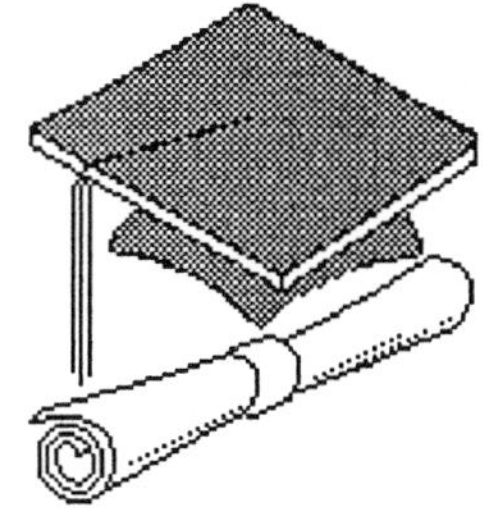

Regardless of the level, floriculture instructors and students should have access to at least one sizeable greenhouse for laboratory exercises and practicum. Only in greenhouses can students obtain the valuable hands-on experience they need for growing floriculture crops and operating greenhouse equipment.

The educational qualifications include a B.S. teaching degree with experience in floriculture for the high school level and an M.S. degree in floriculture (minimum) for college level teaching, with experience in greenhouse production. Many instructors at the college level also have a Ph.D. degree in floriculture.

### Research

Careers in floriculture research require advanced training in some aspect of floriculture. A Ph.D. degree is usually required. Researchers are hired by universities, colleges, and private industry. They usually work on solving problems of floriculture production such as height control, pest/disease management, nutrition, irrigation, etc. The results of their research are then translated into procedures that greenhouse producers can implement in their production practices. A career in floriculture research requires the most specialized training and education.

## Career Ladders in Floriculture

The floriculture career ladder generally has a place on it for anyone with an interest and desire to develop job skills in floriculture (Figure 1.10). The usual procedure for climbing the ladder is to start at the bottom. While not everyone reaches the top, every job along the way is essential. Floriculture offers all levels and types of careers. What you choose will depend on your interests, experience, educational level, and abilities.

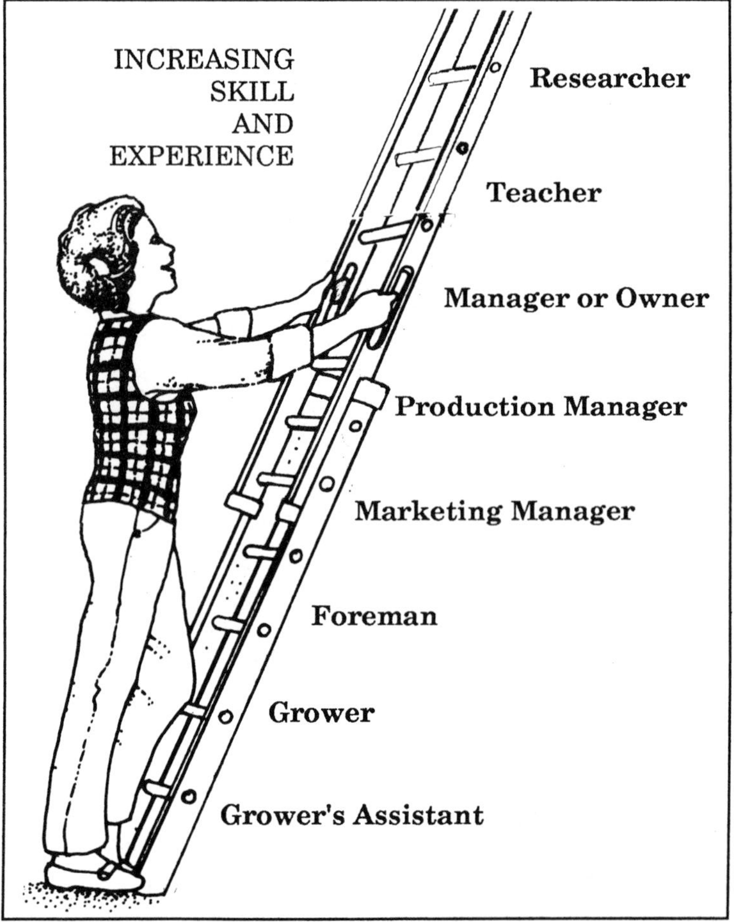


**Figure 1.10**
Career ladders are available in the floriculture industry.

## Entry Level Positions in Floriculture

Your vocational horticulture program has been designed to give you two choices: 1) prepare for an entry level position in the horticulture industry, or 2) prepare for advanced education at a two- or four-year institution of higher learning. The vocational horticulture program typically includes several instructional areas besides floriculture (Figure 1.11). Your school may provide training in one, several, or even all of these areas. As you consider training for any of the entry-level positions in horticulture, you may have questions about the nature of each job, expected income, job skills, and experience or educational requirements. One way to learn about a job is to develop a "job profile" chart. Table 1.15 on the next page profiles careers that are available in floriculture.

With successful completion of your vocational training program, you will have the skills needed for an entry-level job in floriculture such as grower's assistant. Even if your school offers training in only one of the instructional areas (Figure 1.11), you will still be prepared for entry into several jobs in that employment area. You will also have had opportunity to explore horticulture as a career before you enroll in a college program.

---

**Figure 1.11** Vocational horticulture instructional areas

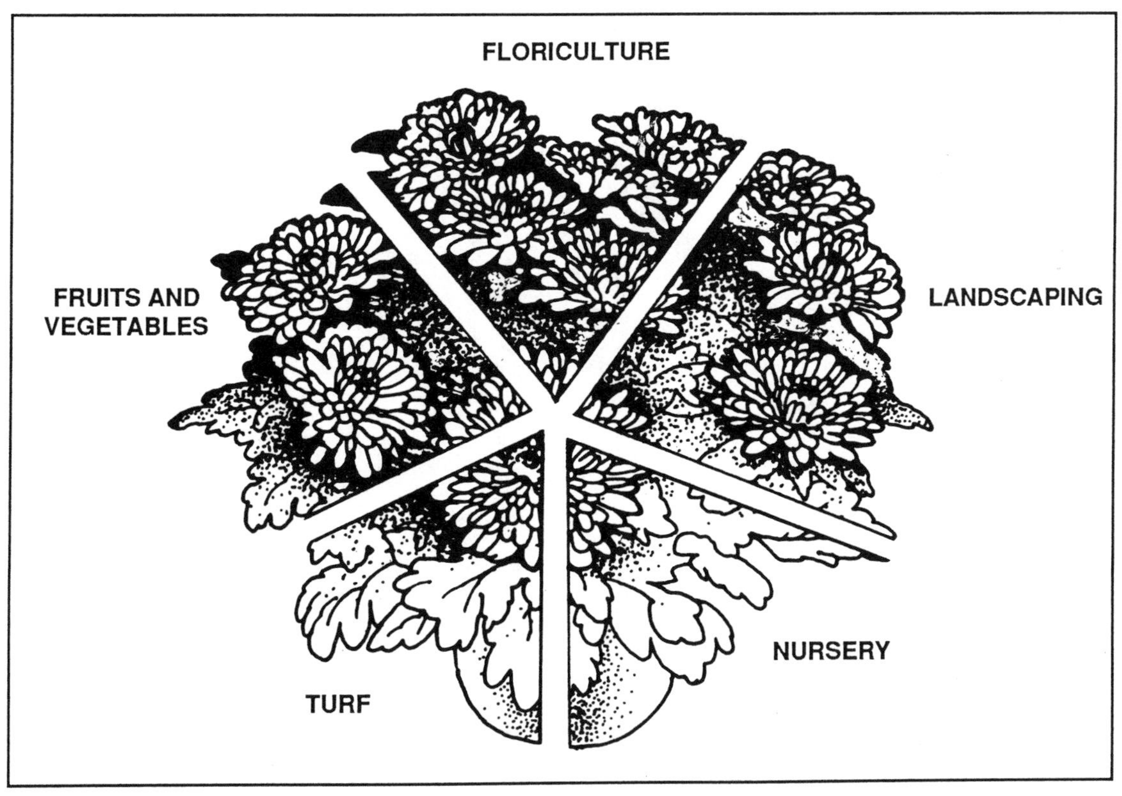

Table 1.15 Job profile chart

| Job | Regular Income | Regular Hours | Offers Variety in Work | Much Travel Required | Work in One Place | Fringe Benefits | Work with Others | Minimum Educational Requirements |
|---|---|---|---|---|---|---|---|---|
| Manager or Owner/Manager | Yes | Generally, but some overtime required | Yes | No | Yes | Yes | Yes | Two- or four-year college degree in floriculture |
| Production Manager | Yes | Yes, but there are peak seasons | Yes | No | Yes | Yes | Yes | Two- or four-year college degree in floriculture |
| Marketing Manager | Yes | Yes, but there are peak seasons | Yes | No | Yes | Yes | Yes | College degree in marketing or business |
| Maintenance Manager | Yes | Yes | Yes | No | Yes | There may be some | Yes | High school with course in agriculture, horti-culture, or mechanics |
| Section Foreman | Yes | Yes, but there are peak seasons | Yes | No | Yes | There may be some | Yes | Two- or four-year college degree in floriculture |
| Grower | Yes | Yes, but there are peak seasons | Sometimes | No | Yes | There may be some | Yes | Two-year degree in greenhouse production and management |
| Grower's Assistant | Some-times | Sometimes | Sometimes | No | Yes | Not to any good extent | Not necessarily | High school with course in agriculture or horticulture |
| Teacher | Yes | Usually | Yes | No | Yes | Yes | Yes | College degree (B.S.) in horticulture for high school level; M.S. or Ph. D. for college level |
| Researcher | Yes | Sometimes | Yes | Sometimes | Yes | Yes | Not necessarily | College degrees - B.S. & M.S., but Ph.D. preferred |

***In conclusion:***

In Chapter 1 we defined floriculture and explored the history of this exciting industry. The major segments of the floriculture industry are bedding plants, potted flowering plants, foliage plants, and cut flowers. The floriculture production statistics of wholesale value nationally and in Ohio are impressive. Floriculture as we know it started in Europe and is still greatly influenced by the overseas industry. Some of the careers that are available in floriculture include that of greenhouse manager, production manager, marketing manager, maintenance manager, section foreman, grower, and grower's assistant. Also, positions are available in teaching and research.

---

## CHAPTER 1 REVIEW

This review is to help you check yourself on what you have learned about an overview of the greenhouse industry. If you need to refresh your mind on any of the following questions, refer to the page number given in parentheses.

1. Define "floriculture." *(page 2)*
2. In what part of the world did the floriculture industry originate? *(page 3)*
3. What are the four major segments of the floriculture industry by order of their economic importance? *(page 3)*
4. What states rank first and second in the U.S. in each of these four major segments? *(page 5)*
5. What are your state's major contributions to the floriculture industry in the U.S.?
6. List the major floriculture-producing countries of the world today. Locate each country on a world map. *(page 9)*
7. Approximately what percent of the cut flowers sold in the United States today are imported? *(page 11)*
8. Why are growers concerned about proposed amendments to Quarantine 37? *(page 13)*
9. What are the three classifications of greenhouse businesses? *(page 13)*
10. What are the major costs of operating a greenhouse business? *(page 15)*
11. What are the major responsibilities of:
    greenhouse manager? *(page 16)*
    production manager? *(page 16)*
    marketing manager? *(page 18)*
    maintenance manager? *(page 18)*
    section foreman? *(page 18)*
12. What is the difference between a section foreman and a grower? *(pages 18-19)*
13. What entry-level position in the greenhouse will you be qualified for when you have graduated from a high school vocational program in horticulture? *(page 19)*
14. What academic careers are available in horticulture? *(page 19)*

# CHAPTER 2

# GREENHOUSE STRUCTURES

## Competencies for Chapter 2

As a result of studying this chapter, you should be able to do the following:

1. Identify suitable locations for greenhouses.
2. Determine soil and water table characteristics of the building site.
3. Determine space requirements.
4. List the types of greenhouse structures.
5. Determine the life expectancy of greenhouse structures.
6. Design plans for greenhouse structures.
7. Describe the major glazings used on greenhouses and the advantages and disadvantages of each.
8. Determine the importance of light to greenhouse crops.
9. Summarize the purposes of the headhouse; identify its location in relation to the greenhouse.
10. Follow zoning requirements.

## Related Science Concepts

1. Describe the make-up of light waves.
2. Determine temperature and wind velocity.
3. Estimate weight-holding capabilities of a greenhouse frame.

## Related Math Concepts

1. Apply measuring skills to calculate angles and distance in feet.
2. Apply basic operations to whole numbers, decimals, and fractions.
3. Apply basic operations to ratios and percents.
4. Read, interpret, and construct charts, graphs, and tables.
5. Read topography maps.

## Terms to Know

| | | |
|---|---|---|
| A-frame | footer | polyvinyl fluoride |
| acrylic | fossil fuel | purlin |
| aquifer | gable | quonset house |
| cold frame | glazing | sash bar |
| curtain wall | greenhouse range | side post |
| eave | light transmission | topography |
| energy conservation | nitrate | truss |
| even-span | pollutant | ultraviolet (UV) radiation |
| fiberglass | polyethylene | uneven-span |

## INTRODUCTION

This chapter will cover the basics of greenhouse design, glazings, and suitable locations. Choosing the greenhouse structure, glazing, and location will depend on many variables including economics, availability of supplies, and types of floriculture crops to be grown. In order to understand fully the concepts to be discussed, you need to know just what a greenhouse is. By definition, a greenhouse is a structure characterized by the following features:

1. The structure must be covered with a transparent glazing.
2. The structure must be artificially heated.
3. People working inside it must be able to stand upright without touching the roof.

A structure like a cold frame would not be considered a greenhouse. However, as we will see, there are many structures that ***are*** greenhouses by definition.

## SUITABLE GREENHOUSE LOCATIONS

In time, the decision as to the best location for a greenhouse or greenhouse range may be up to you. What are the factors that you should take into consideration? Building a greenhouse is a major, long-term investment. Careful site selection before construction will prevent many potential problems. The following guidelines should be helpful in this major decision.

### Land Area

When building a greenhouse or greenhouse range, allow room for expansion. Most greenhouse businesses begin on a small scale and enlarge as they become established. A rule of thumb is to purchase ***at least twice*** as much land as the growing area of the greenhouse structure (Figure 2.1). For example, if you plan to build a one-acre greenhouse range, buy at least two

**Figure 2.1** This grower purchased enough land for expansion. At the start, two 80' x 40' greenhouses were built. With available space, the size of the operation could be doubled in the future.

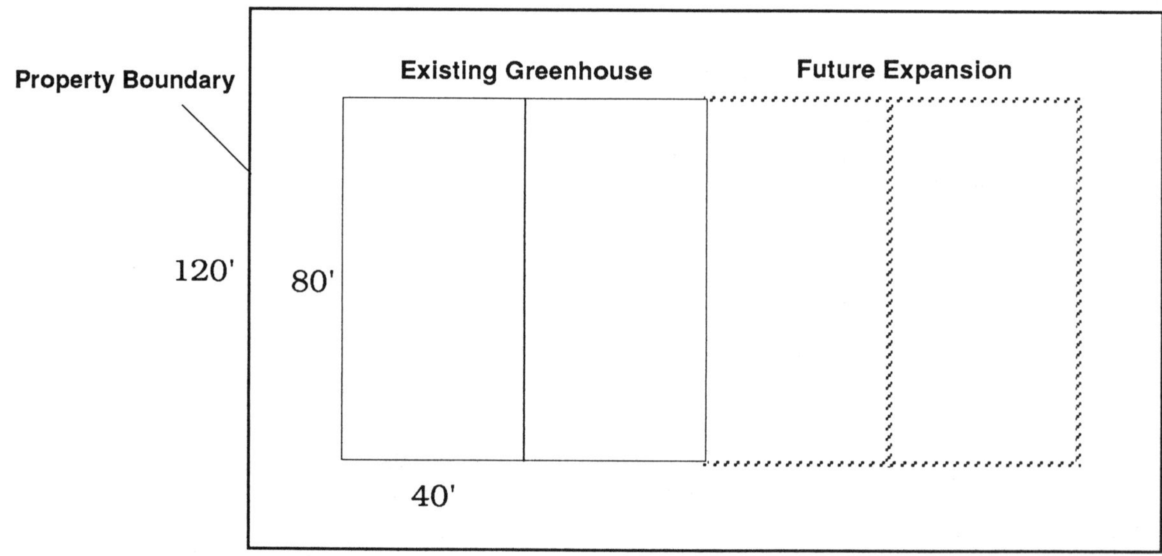

acres of land. That will give you enough room for future expansion. Don't limit the future growth of your greenhouse business by purchasing too small a plot of land. Be smart and plan for the future now!

### Topography

A second factor to consider is the topography or "lay of the land" on which the greenhouse will be built. Select a site as level as possible so that grading costs will be minimal. Also, a greenhouse built on level land rather than on a hillside is easier to automate. (Discussion of automation will come later.) Select a site with soil that drains easily - that is not located in a depression. (This is no longer critical for those growers who recirculate their irrigation water.)

### Windbreaks

If possible, build the greenhouse to the south or southeast of a hill or tree line. The hill or tree line will act as a windbreak, since the direction of the winter wind is usually from the north or northwest. This windbreak will significantly decrease heat loss. (See Chapter 3 on energy conservation.) There is one precaution, however. Be sure to locate the greenhouse ***at least*** 100 feet away from the hill or tree line (Figure 2.2). A natural windbreak will also act as a snow fence. A greenhouse built too close to a natural windbreak may be in trouble during a heavy snowfall. Snow will drift to the south of a windbreak just as it does by a snow fence. As a result, the greenhouse may become buried with snow.

### Zoning Permit

No matter where a greenhouse is constructed - in a city, town, or township- you must check with local zoning ordinances. First, make sure that greenhouses are permitted on the land you are considering buying. For example, ***residential zoning*** will not permit the building of a greenhouse on that land, as a greenhouse is considered a business.

---

**Figure 2.2** A treeline windbreak should be at least 100 feet to the north or northwest of a greenhouse.

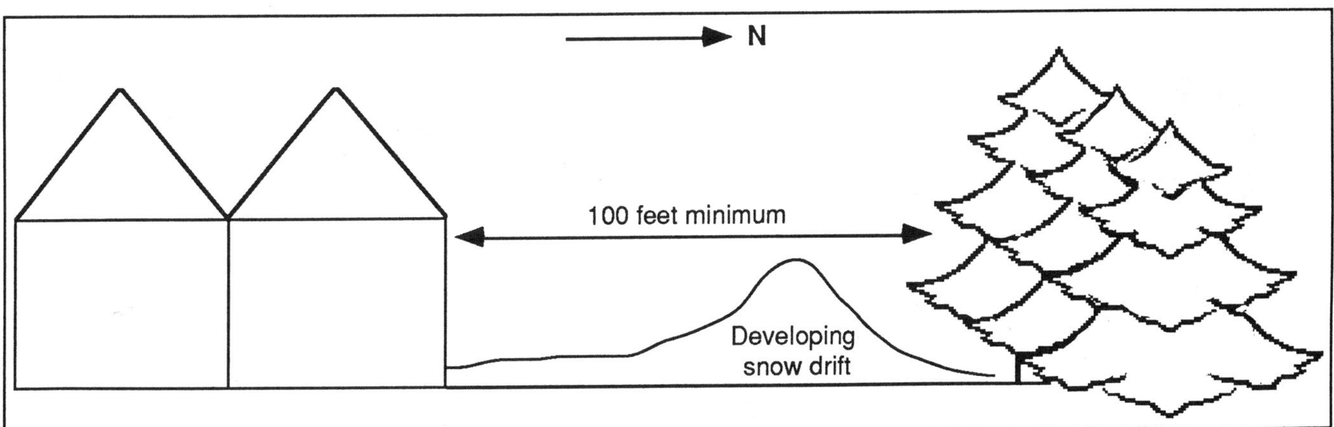

## Labor Availability

In spite of advances in automation, greenhouses still require substantial labor for smooth operation. Another consideration in locating a greenhouse is the potential labor supply in the vicinity. If possible, locate near an urban area or at least within easy commuting distance. Pay as high wages as possible to attract quality workers from the vicinity of the greenhouse. Offset the higher wages by automating as much as possible. It is a good policy to estimate labor requirements in advance, so that you will have an idea whether these requirements can be met in the local area.

## Transportation and Shipping

Wholesale growers should locate near major forms of transportation for easy access to shipping routes. Examples are interstate highways, commercial airports, and truck distribution centers. Ready access to any of these will minimize shipping costs. The grower will not have to transport plants long distances for shipment. Those not so located must pass the extra costs on to the consumer.

## Water Supply and Quality

One of the most important aspects to investigate before building a greenhouse is the quantity and quality of the water supply. Watering plants in a greenhouse is one of the most important tasks involved in floriculture; it requires an enormous amount of water. If no city water is available, the grower will have to rely on well water for irrigation needs. If a well must be dug, a geological survey should first be done on the land. This should include information about the quantity of water existing in aquifers and other subsurface sources of water.

Equally important to quantity is the quality of the water supply. If the water source for a greenhouse is a polluted well, the plants will probably be of poor quality no matter what other cultural measures the grower implements. The result will be a greenhouse doomed to failure. A thorough test of city and/or well water should be conducted to determine the levels of nitrate nitrogen, phosphorus, and other pollutants (including herbicides), as well as the pH and alkalinity of the water. The cost involved in such a survey and in having water tests done is a wise investment. A well that dries up or a water supply that is polluted will mean the end of your greenhouse business!

## Fuel Cost

The cost of fuel is one of the largest expenses of a greenhouse grower. Therefore, a potential greenhouse location must be carefully researched as to fuel availability and acceptability of fuel prices in that area.

## Market Accessibility

Locating near the market is very important for retail growers who rely on customers getting to the greenhouse. The market potential should be explored before building. The competition should be scouted out and surveys conducted (if possible) as to the greenhouse market demands of the local area.

Wholesale growers should consider locating in an area that is centrally located for the market area they serve. This will minimize transportation costs. A central location is especially important for growers of pot plants and bedding plants, as these products are more expensive to ship than are cut flowers.

## GREENHOUSE STRUCTURES AND GLAZING MATERIALS

Prior to 1950, all greenhouses in existence were made of glass. Plastics were not yet available for widespread commercial use. Today, mainly the older greenhouses are glazed (or covered) with glass. Sometimes, greenhouses are still constructed using glass because it does have some excellent advantages. But most greenhouses today are glazed with flexible or rigid plastics.

### Glass

Glass is a very transparent glazing material. It transmits approximately 90 percent of the sunlight striking its surface. Unlike plastics, glass is not affected by ultraviolet (UV) radiation from the sun. So its longevity runs from several decades to over 100 years. Glass also does not expand or contract like plastics do in response to changes in temperature. Glass does not have the warping problems sometimes encountered in plastic greenhouses. And, finally, glass is readily available. Pane width is typically 16 to 20 inches.

But there are certain disadvantages to glass. It is fairly expensive and it breaks easily. Also, its relatively heavy weight requires a substantial frame for support.

### Range Structure

Glass greenhouses usually are built using A-frame or even-span construction. With even-span construction, the two sides of the roof are equal in width and the pitch or angle of the two halves of the roof is the same (Figure 2.3). Rarely, a glass greenhouse is built as an uneven-span structure with one roof longer than the other (Figure 2.4). This type of construction is suitable for greenhouses built on the side of a hill. However, uneven-span construction makes automation difficult.

---

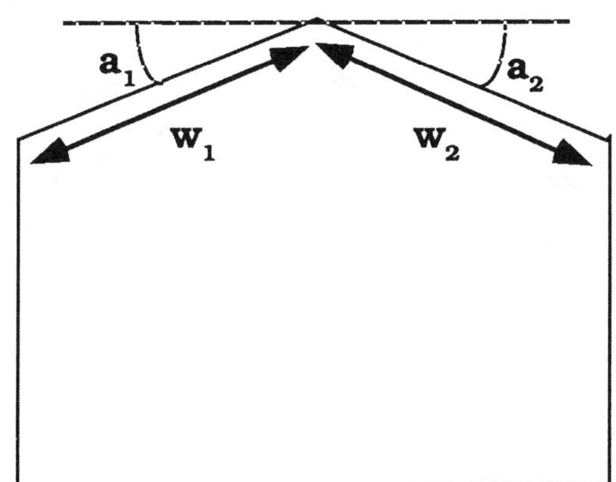


**Figure 2.3**

Even-span greenhouse frame. Roof angles, $\mathbf{a}_1$ and $\mathbf{a}_2$ are equal; roof widths $\mathbf{w}_1$ and $\mathbf{w}_2$ are equal.

**Figure 2.4** Uneven-span greenhouses are built primarily on hillsides.

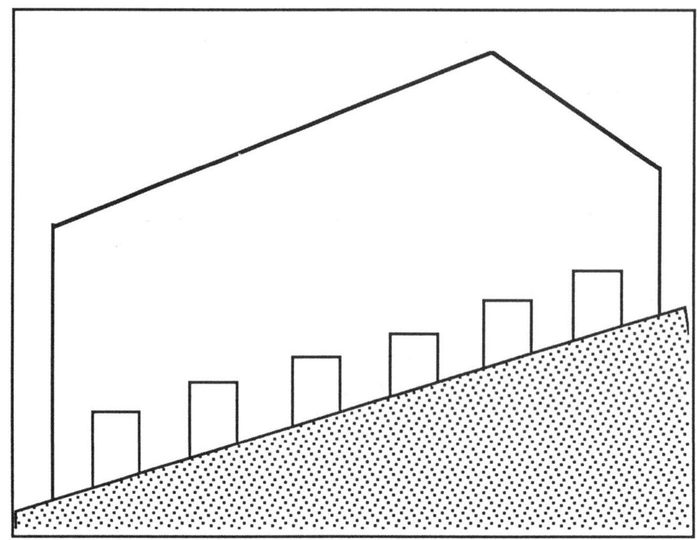

There are two basic types of even-span greenhouses: American or high profile (Figure 2.5) and Dutch or low profile (Figure 2.6). Dutch greenhouses are becoming popular because the gable and roof areas are much smaller. This reduced size means less heat loss, less framing materials required, and a more economical structure.

Even-span greenhouses can be built separately (detached) (Figure 2.7) or attached to other even-span greenhouses. The attached greenhouses are referred to as ridge-and-furrow greenhouses (Figure 2.5). These greenhouses have one large interior space that is conducive to automation. Compared to detached greenhouses, ridge-and-furrow greenhouses are more economical to heat on a per-square-foot basis. Where more than one greenhouse (detached or ridge-and-furrow) is situated at the same location, the greenhouses are called a **greenhouse range**.

**Figure 2.5** Ridge-and-furrow greenhouses, American style

**Figure 2.6**

End view of a low-profile or Dutch greenhouse. Note the small gables.

**Figure 2.7** Even-span, detached greenhouses

Several ridge-and-furrow greenhouses are less expensive to build than are an equivalent number of detached greenhouses. Ridge-and-furrow greenhouses are often used in the production of a single crop or several crops with similar environmental requirements. If widely varying environments must be maintained within a ridge-and-furrow greenhouse range, walls will have to be installed between the individual houses. When a ridge-and-furrow greenhouse range is compared with a similar-sized detached greenhouse range as to **usable square footage**, the ridge-and-furrow greenhouse comes out way ahead.

## Supporting Framework

The framework of an even-span greenhouse is basically the same for both glass and plastic glazings. Figure 2.8 shows the basic framing components of an even-span greenhouse. The **side posts** support the trusses and therefore bear most of the weight of the greenhouse; they are set in concrete footers that extend below the frost line. The **curtain walls** usually comprise the first two to three feet of the side wall above the soil line. They are made of concrete block, cement, and other non-transparent materials. Curtain walls do ***not*** support the weight of the greenhouse; the side posts carry out that function.

**Figure 2.8** End view diagram of even-span greenhouse construction

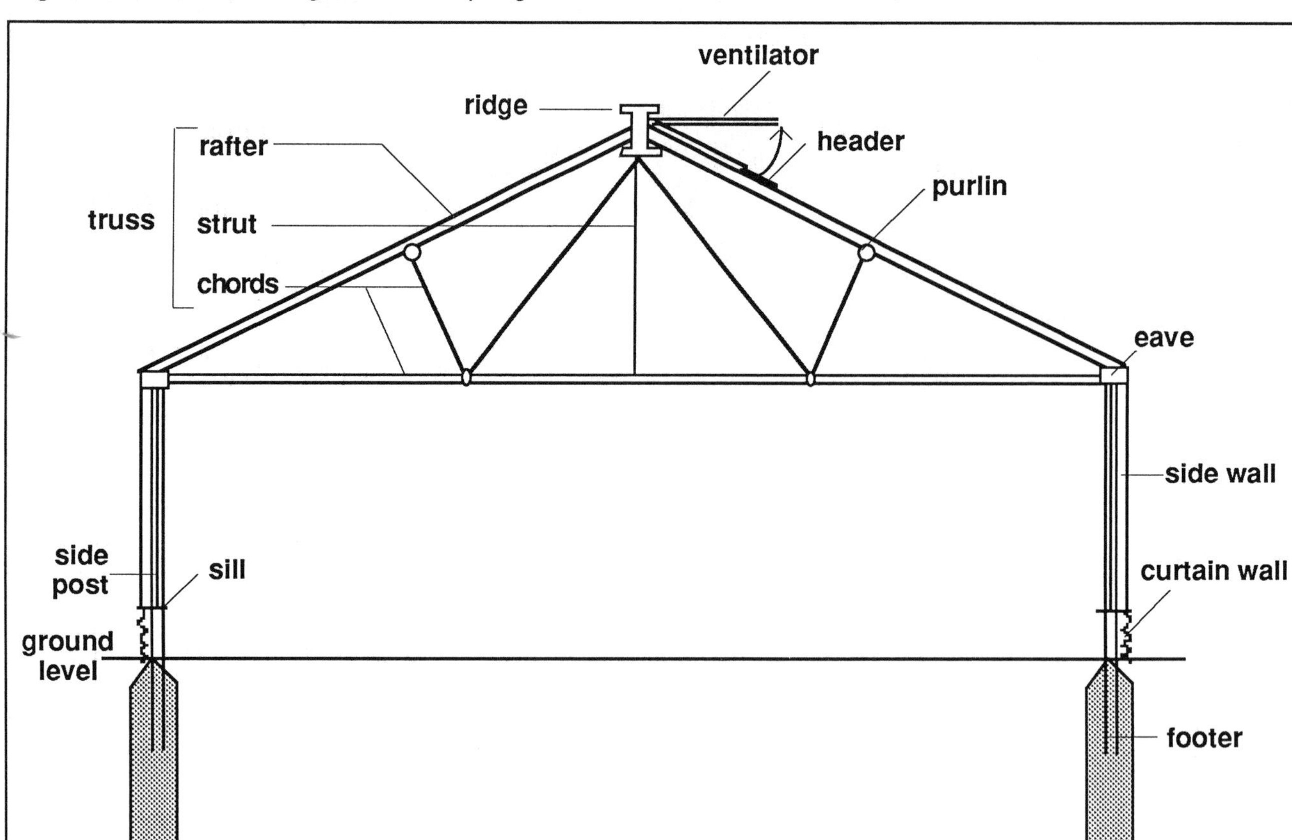


Curtain walls do help prevent heat loss, since heating pipes are commonly attached to them. The **glazing sill** covers the top of the curtain wall and serves as a support for the glazing of the side wall.

Side posts are placed approximately 10 feet apart with the roof trusses attached to them. The transparent side wall and the roof join at a point called the **eave**. Ridge and furrow greenhouses are joined along the length of the greenhouse; the eave now becomes the gutter. The gutter drains away rain water and water from melted snow. Columns are placed beneath the gutter every 10 to 20 feet for support.

The **truss** is made up of rafter, strut and chords (Figure 2.8.) It supports the weight of the roof. Trusses are connected by the roof ridge and the **purlins** which run the length of the greenhouse. Purlins are spaced 4 to 7 feet apart, depending on the glazing and the type of sash bars. The number of purlins required depends on the width of the greenhouse. Purlins also support the sash bars (or "roof bars") that hold the glass in place (as shown in Figure 2.9). The end wall portion of an even-span greenhouse outlined by the truss is called the **gable**. It is triangular in shape (Figure 2.8).

**Sash bars** can be wooden or metal. Figure 2.10 shows a wooden sash bar and Figure 2.11 shows a metal sash bar. Glass panes are installed between

**Figure 2.9**
Typical even-span construction showing a purlin running the length of the greenhouse, supporting the sash bars and connecting the trusses

**Figure 2.10**
Wooden sash bar with the glass being held in place by an aluminum bar cap

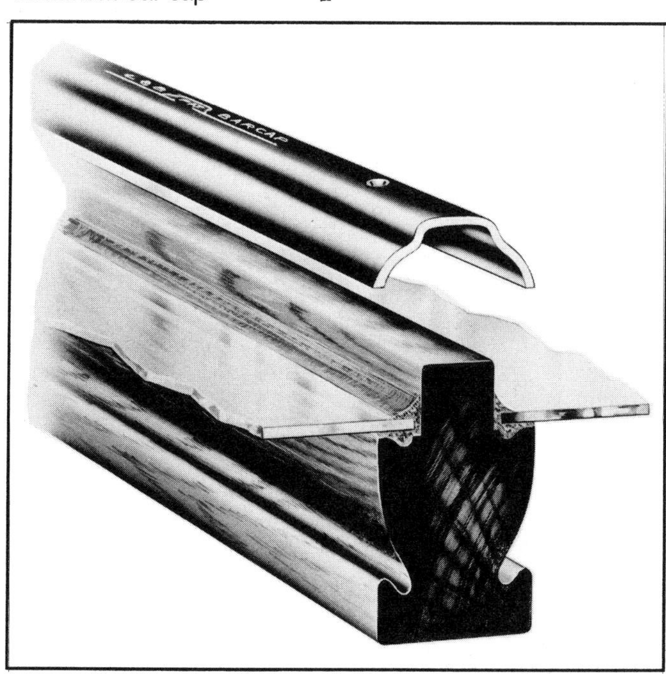

**Figure 2.11** Aluminum sash bar showing a drip groove to drain away water condensing on the glass pane

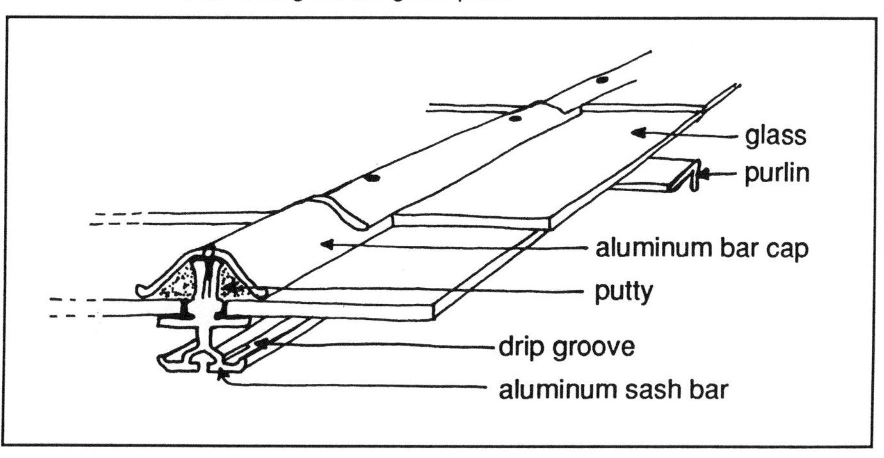

the sash bars (Figure 2.12). The upper panes overlap the lower panes by approximately 1/4 inch. A putty material is applied to the grooves of the bar before the glass is installed to form a weather-tight seal. More putty is applied on top of the glass. Aluminum **sash bar caps** are then screwed into place over the glass to hold it securely (Figure 2.13). Aluminum sash bar caps also increase the life of wooden sash bars. These caps lengthen the effectiveness of the putty holding the glass in place for both aluminum and wooden sash bars.

## Rigid Plastics

ADVANTAGE

Besides glass, several rigid plastics have been developed for use in glazing even-span greenhouses. Two of the most commonly used rigid plastics are acrylic and polycarbonate. They are available under many brand names and can be purchased in single or double layers. Double-layered acrylic and polycarbonate sheets are preferred because of the dead air space between layers that acts as an insulator (Figure 2.14). The two sheets or layers of plastic are held apart by evenly spaced plastic ribs. The result is dead air spaces that run the length of the panel. Figure 2.15 shows a greenhouse with side walls made of double-layer acrylic. Note the distance between sash bars. The use of double-layer rigid plastic glazing means energy savings to the grower. Research has shown that a double-layer rigid plastic greenhouse will use from 50 to 60 percent **less** fuel for heating than a conventional glass greenhouse. This is very significant with today's escalating fuel costs and depletion of fossil fuel resources.

**Figure 2.12**
Aluminum sash bar holding glass panes in place

**Figure 2.13** ⇨
Close-up view of an aluminum sash bar (Figure 2.12) showing the sash bar cap

**Figure 2.14** Cross section of a 16-mm thick, double-layer, rigid plastic glazing

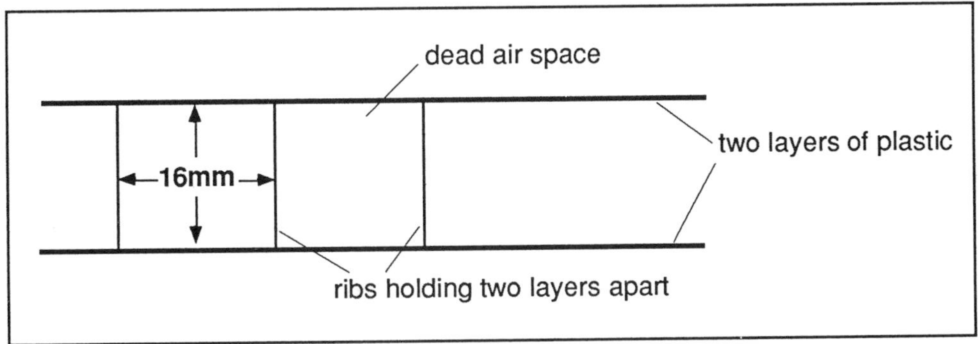


**Figure 2.15**

Greenhouse under construction using double-layer acrylic glazing. Note the wide spacing of the sash bars.

---

Other advantages of double-layer plastics are the following:

1. They have high light transmission (85 to 90 percent).
2. They are not easily broken.
3. They are lightweight compared to glass.

Therefore, the even-span greenhouse structure for double-layer plastic glazing can be less substantial than for glass. The plastic panes are lighter and larger, so the roof bars can be further apart than with glass panes of the same size. Larger panes mean less shadow cast by the frame on the crops below.

The primary disadvantage of acrylic and polycarbonate double glazings is their cost. These are the most expensive glazings available. However, since we discovered that they greatly reduce fuel consumption, these glazings will pay for themselves in a relatively short time. Acrylic glazings last approximately 25 years and polycarbonates last from 10 to 15 years.

Another disadvantage of acrylic and polycarbonate double glazings is that they contract and expand significantly in response to temperature changes. This "movement" must be taken into consideration when one is designing sash bars and other framing for these glazings.

### Semi-rigid Plastics - FRP

Fiberglass Reinforced Plastic or FRP can be classified as a semi-rigid glazing material. It is suitable for even-span greenhouses and quonset structures. This glazing consists of glass fibers embedded in acrylics. It is usually corrugated for added strength (Figure 2.16). Light transmission initially is almost equivalent to that of glass. After a few years, however, light transmission drops quickly if the FRP is not properly maintained. The surface of the plastic becomes etched and then collects dust and debris, which reduce the light passing through.

**Figure 2.16**
Corrugated FRP is stronger than flat FRP sheets.

Fiberglass surfaces can be treated with polyvinyl fluoride to lengthen the life of the glazing. This treatment should be done every five years. Light transmission through fiberglass is more uniform than through other plastics because light is scattered by the fibers as it passes through the glazing. FRP is a little less expensive than glass, but it lasts only 10 to 15 years because of weathering.

### Film Plastics

#### *Polyethylene*

One of the most common greenhouse types built today is the film plastic greenhouse. Polyethylene currently accounts for about 80 percent of all plastic sales. It is the least expensive material available. The greenhouse structure itself can be much simpler than for a glass or rigid plastic greenhouse. A common design for polyethylene greenhouses is known as a quonset house (Figure 2.17). It is a detached greenhouse with a simple frame. The frame consists basically of pipe bent into an arc, forming the truss and the quonset outline of the greenhouse. Depending on the width of the greenhouse, one

**Figure 2.17**
Quonset greenhouse covered with polyethylene glazing. The end wall is covered with FRP.

or more purlins are installed on each side, connecting the trusses (Figures 2.18 and 2.19). The end walls can be a variety of glazings: polyethylene, fiberglass, etc.

Quonset greenhouses can also be attached to each other like even-span, ridge-and-furrow greenhouses. As shown in Figure 2.20, the quonset greenhouses are elevated on sidewalls and attached to each other where the quonset structure would have touched the ground. This arrangement is called barrel vault ridge-and-furrow. It is one of the most popular greenhouse designs in use.

**Figure 2.18** Interior view of a quonset, polyethylene-glazed greenhouse. Trusses are pipes bent into an arc and connected by purlins.

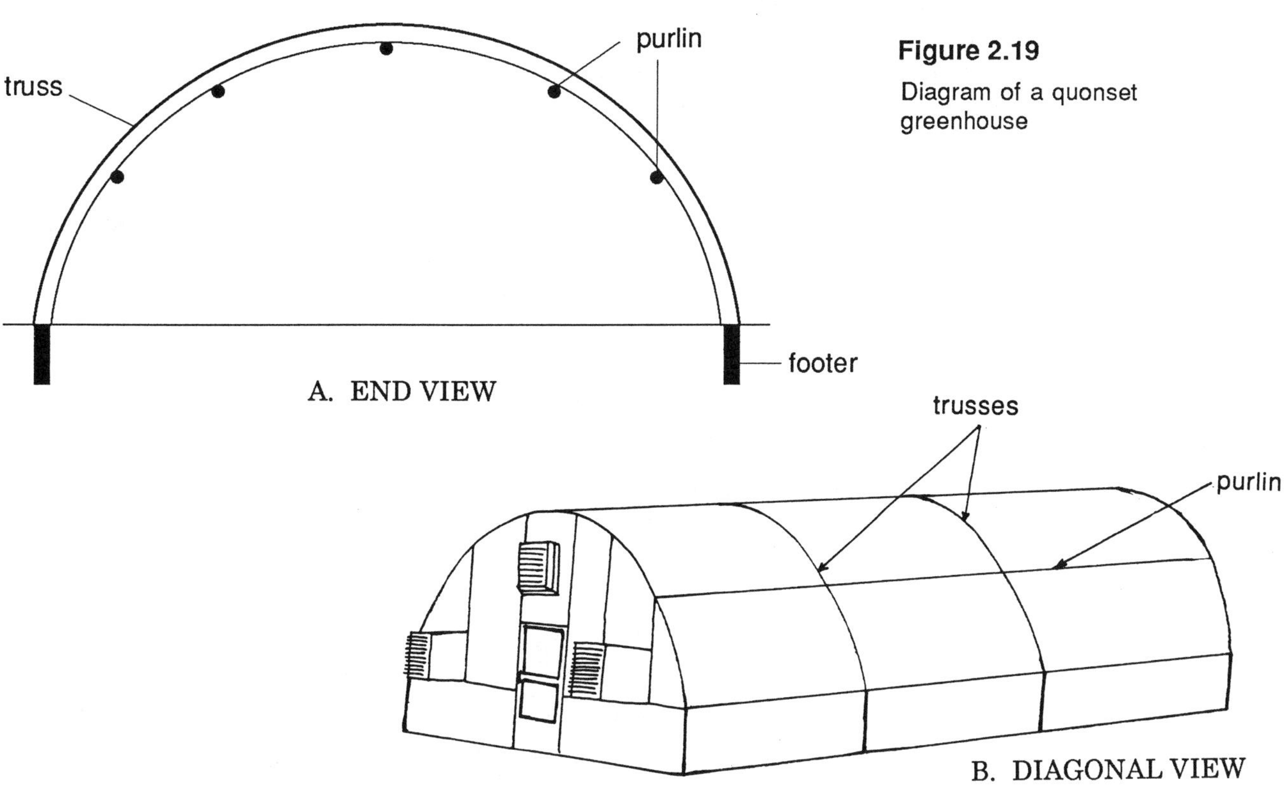


**Figure 2.19**
Diagram of a quonset greenhouse

**Figure 2.20** Barrel vault ridge-and-furrow greenhouse range

Not only is polyethylene inexpensive, but it is easy to install. It comes in large sheets which make covering the greenhouse much easier than if small pieces had to be spliced together. It is easily attached to the end walls and along the length of the base of the greenhouse. Figure 2.21 shows the rail and spindle and snaplock devices commonly used to attach polyethylene to the structure. The snaplock system is the easier of the two for installation.

Most polyethylene greenhouses are glazed with two layers of plastic that are inflated by a squirrel cage fan (Figure 2.22). As with rigid double-layer plastics, a dead air space is created, providing insulation for the greenhouse. Growers can enjoy a potential fuel savings of 40 percent compared to the cost for a glass greenhouse.

The main drawback of double polyethylene greenhouses is reduced light transmission through the glazing. Roughly 5 to 10 percent less light is transmitted through polyethylene than through glass. However, the simple framing of a polyethylene greenhouse casts much fewer shadows than an even-span

**Figure 2.21** Polyethylene glazing attachment devices: **A)** rail and spindle system, and **B)** snaplock system

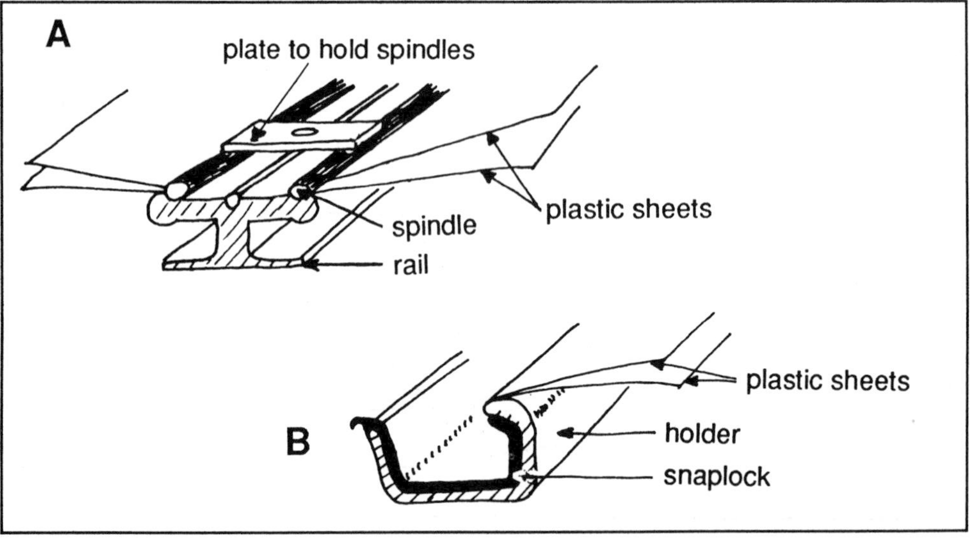

**Figure 2.22** Squirrel cage fan used for inflating double-layer film plastic greenhouses

greenhouse frame does. This partially offsets the lower light transmission of the double glazing.

The other disadvantage of polyethylene is its very short life span. The ultraviolet rays of the sun break down polyethylene; after two or three years the plastic becomes quite yellow and brittle. The result is reduced light transmission and tears in the glazing. Thus, this kind of glazing has to be replaced every two or three years. A lot of labor and time are involved in this procedure. These factors offsets the very low cost of the glazings. Several variations of polyethylene are available, including brands containing UV inhibitors. Even these have to be replaced every three years, however.

### *Polyvinyl Fluoride*

Another film plastic glazing material similar to polyethylene is polyvinyl fluoride. It can be used on the same frames as polyethylene. Polyvinyl fluoride is much more expensive than polyethylene. But it lasts up to 10 years because it is resistant to UV radiation. Polyvinyl fluoride has excellent light transmission, close to that of glass.

Table 2.1 on the next page summarizes the major greenhouse glazings we have discussed and lists some of their properties.

## GREENHOUSE FRAMING MATERIALS

Greenhouses are built to provide as much light as possible to the crops. Ideally, there is minimal casting of shadows from the frame to the crop below. There are basically two types of framing materials used in the greenhouse industry: wood and metal. Many of the older greenhouses are constructed with wooden frames, while most new greenhouses have metal frames. Both kinds have their advantages and disadvantages.

**Table 2.1** Characteristics of different greenhouse glazings

| Glazing | Relative Cost | Approximate Longevity | Average % Light Transmission | Durability | Heat Retention Ability |
|---|---|---|---|---|---|
| Glass | moderate | 25+ years | 90 | excellent | low |
| Double Acrylic | high | 20+ years | 83 | excellent | high |
| Double Polycarbonate | high | 7-12 years | 80 | good | high |
| FRP | moderate | 10-15 years | 88 (dropping rapidly after 3-5 years) | good | medium |
| Double-layer Polyethylene | low | 2-3 years | 84 | poor | high |
| Double-layer Polyvinyl Fluoride Film | low/ moderate | 10 years | 89 | fair | high |

## Wooden Frames

Wooden frames are less expensive than metal frames and are readily available. However, in time, wood will decay. It is also susceptible to attack from termites and carpenter ants. Precautions must be taken, therefore, to improve the longevity of the wood. Cedar or redwood should be used to construct wooden frames, as these woods are resistant to decay and insects.

To help preserve the wood and increase light intensity, the wood should be coated with a white **greenhouse paint**. Painting, of course, requires labor. It is a task that must be repeated periodically, since paint eventually will break down. ***Caution:*** **Never use mercury-based paints!** These paints are toxic to plants. They will ruin a greenhouse crop.

Some growers also treat the wood with an approved preservative before construction. This treatment adds more years to the life of the frame. However, avoid using creosote and pentachlorophenol because of their toxicity to plants. Sites on which wooden greenhouses will be built should be inspected for termites and carpenter ants. Extermination treatment should be done if necessary. All wood scraps and other potential sources of food for these pests should be promptly removed from the location.

Wooden frames are the most suitable for lightweight glazings such as polyethylene and other plastics. Heavy glazings such as glass require more sash bars spaced closer together to hold the glass panes adequately. The result is more shadows cast on the crop below.

### Metal Frames

With advances in metal technology, metal greenhouse frames have become more attractive. Prices have decreased and metal strength has increased. Early metal frames were mainly iron - strong and relatively inexpensive. But iron rusts easily. Iron frames required considerable maintenance because they needed frequent coats of white paint to prevent rust.

Aluminum frames, though the most expensive kind, offer several advantages over other frames. Aluminum is both lightweight and very strong. Sash bars and other framing components can be further apart, letting more light into the growing area. Furthermore, aluminum is rust resistant and requires little maintenance. Growers who paint the frames white do so to maximize light intensity inside the structure.

## THE HEADHOUSE

All greenhouse locations should have a headhouse or service building. Large operations may have two or more headhouses. When you plan a greenhouse layout, use this rule of thumb. Make the headhouse equivalent in size to at least 10 percent of the total greenhouse growing area. For example, a certain greenhouse contains 40,000 square feet of growing area. Its headhouse, then, should contain at least 4,000 square feet. This may seem like too much space for a service building, but many important functions are carried out in the headhouse.

Headhouses are used for planting crops, mixing soil, cold storage, housing boilers, and loading docks for shipping plants. Administrative offices are located here, too.

Figures 2.23 and 2.24 show two headhouses of a large, modern greenhouse grower. One headhouse contains the administrative offices for the managers and growers along with the support staff (Figure 2.23). The other headhouse has many different areas: a shipping area with loading docks, a planting area, cold storage for finished crops, and a worker break room (Figure 2.24).

**Figure 2.23**

Headhouse of a modern grower housing administrative offices

**Figure 2.24**
Large headhouse with loading docks

**A)** Outside view

**B)** Inside, the area is used for plant shipments, planting, mixing soil, and cold storage of finished crops.

Headhouses should be constructed with efficient and easy access. For example, a headhouse could be located in the center of a greenhouse range. This would be especially helpful for large greenhouse ranges (Figure 2.25). For a small greenhouse range or a single greenhouse, the headhouse should be located on the north side/end of the greenhouse. The building will serve as a windbreak from the prevailing north-northwest winter winds, helping reduce heat loss from the greenhouse (Figure 2.26).

---

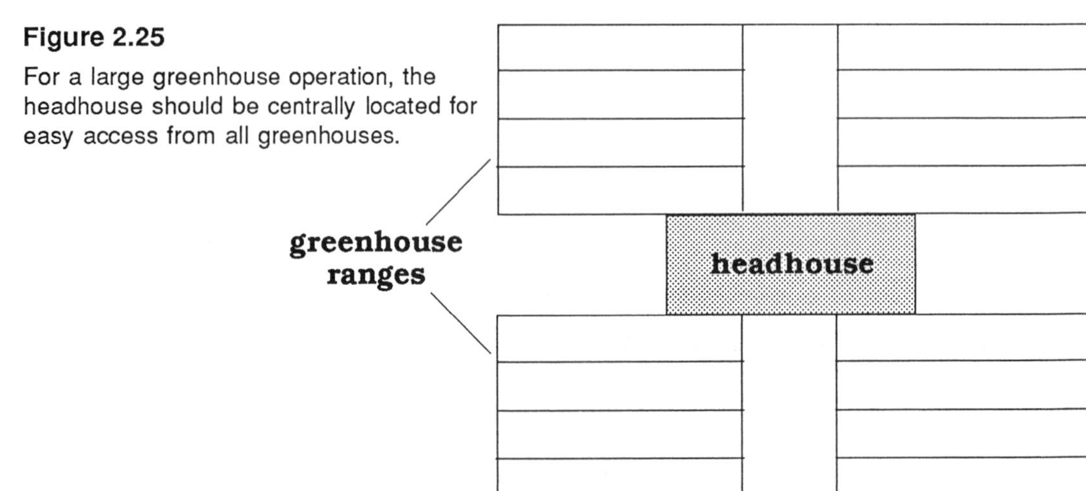


**Figure 2.25**
For a large greenhouse operation, the headhouse should be centrally located for easy access from all greenhouses.

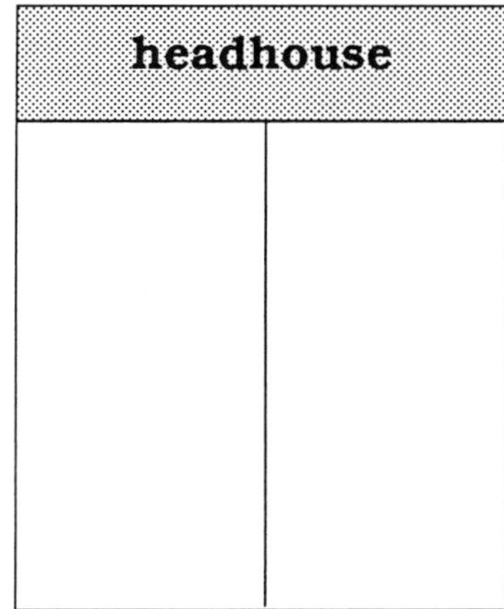


**Figure 2.26**
For a single greenhouse or small greenhouse range, locate the headhouse on the north end.

---

***In conclusion:***

In Chapter 2 you discovered what factors are important to consider when selecting the location for a greenhouse. The two types of glazing used on greenhouses are glass and plastic (of various kinds). Greenhouse frames are constructed out of wood or metal (more commonly metal today). The type of glazing and framing used depends on what crops are to be grown, the light transmission requirements, and economics. The headhouse of a greenhouse operation serves many important functions, including shipping and receiving, a potting room, storage, and administrative offices.

---

## CHAPTER 2 REVIEW

This review is to help you check yourself on what you have learned about greenhouse structures. If you need to refresh your mind on any of the following questions, refer to the page number given in parentheses.

1. Define "greenhouse." *(page 26)*

2. What factors should be considered in selecting a suitable greenhouse location? *(pages 26-29)*

3. Contrast the characteristics of an American style greenhouse with those of a Dutch style greenhouse. *(page 30)*

4. What is a greenhouse range? *(page 30)*

5. What are the three parts of an even-span greenhouse truss? What is the function of a truss? *(page 32)*

6. Sketch and label the major parts of an even-span greenhouse. *(page 32)*

7. Sketch and label the major parts of a quonset greenhouse frame. *(pages 36-37)*

8. What is the function of a sash bar cap? *(page 34)*

9. What is the main advantage of using rigid plastic glazing (considering its expense)? *(pages 34-35)*

10. Why must polyethylene be replaced every two or three years? *(page 39)*

11. What are two precautions that must be taken when using wooden greenhouse frames? *(page 40)*

12. List four activities that take place in a headhouse. *(page 41)*

# CHAPTER 3

# CONTROLLING THE GREENHOUSE ENVIRONMENT

## Competencies for Chapter 3

As a result of studying this chapter, you should be able to do the following:

1. Describe three forms of heat loss from a greenhouse.
2. Describe methods of controlling heat levels in a greenhouse.
3. Identify the common heating fuel sources.
4. List the major greenhouse heating systems and the advantages and disadvantages of each.
5. Describe heat conservation techniques for greenhouses.
6. Describe the major cooling equipment used in greenhouses.
7. Place and set a thermostat.
8. Describe the importance and functions of carbon dioxide generators.

## Related Science Concepts

1. Illustrate radiation, conduction, and air leakage.
2. Describe photosynthesis and its importance to plants.
3. Explain factors that affect heat flow rate.

## Related Math Concepts

1. Apply measuring skills to determine temperature and humidity.
2. Apply basic operations to whole numbers, decimals, and fractions.
3. Apply basic operations to ratios and percents.
4. Read, interpret, and construct charts, graphs, and tables.
5. Contrast Btu rating with cost of the major fuels.

## Terms to Know

biotherm
Btu
cellulose
combustion
condensation
conduction
ecosystem
evaporative cooling
excelsior
heat exchanger
infrared
louvers
pasteurization (soil)
photosynthesis
radiation
stomata
thermostat
ventilator
viscosity

# HEATING PRINCIPLES

## Introduction

Heating greenhouses in cold climates is a major expense for the greenhouse grower, second only to the cost of labor. Many heating systems are available for heating greenhouses. Choosing the right system for a particular greenhouse depends on a number of variables:

- ✩ climate
- ✩ expense of the equipment
- ✩ size of the greenhouse
- ✩ cost and availability of heating fuels

Once the heating system is functioning, the greenhouse grower must pay attention to two important items:

1) distributing heat in the greenhouse, and
2) conserving heat.

These concerns will be discussed later in this chapter.

## Solar Energy

The primary heat source of any greenhouse is the sun. Solar energy entering the greenhouse is converted into heat and trapped inside by the glazing. In southern states, little if any additional heat is required. In Ohio and other northern states, however, a significant portion of the year is cold. After sunset, the solar warmth accumulated in the greenhouse during the day dissipates, leaving the plants too cool at night. Cloudy weather also reduces the amount of solar energy the greenhouse collects during the day and makes artificial heating necessary.

## Rate of Heat Addition

When heating a greenhouse, the objective is to **add heat at the same rate at which it is lost**. Greenhouse air temperature should be maintained with no variation. If heat is added at a higher rate than it is lost, the air temperature in the structure will rise. In some cases, this is the desired goal, for example when raising night temperature to day temperature in the morning. However, usually the grower wants to avoid adding more heat than is needed, for the result would be needlessly high fuel bills.

## Measure of Heat

The unit of heat measurement used in the greenhouse industry is the British thermal unit or **Btu**. One Btu is the amount of heat required to raise 1 pound of water one degree Fahrenheit. For example, to heat 10 pounds of water one degree Fahrenheit would require 10 Btu's. Heating equipment is classified by the number of Btu's produced. The heating requirement of a greenhouse is stated in terms of Btu's needed per hour of heat to be supplied.

## Heat Loss

There are three primary ways that heat is lost in a greenhouse, by:

★ conduction
★ air leakage
★ radiation

### *Conduction*

Most heat is lost by the process of conduction, which is movement of heat through solid materials (Figure 3.1). Heat is conducted through framing materials, glazing, and other materials to the outside. Not all materials, however, conduct heat at the same rate. For example, metal greenhouse frames conduct heat faster than do wooden frames. Double-layer polyethylene glazing reduces conduction heat loss by providing dead air space for insulation.

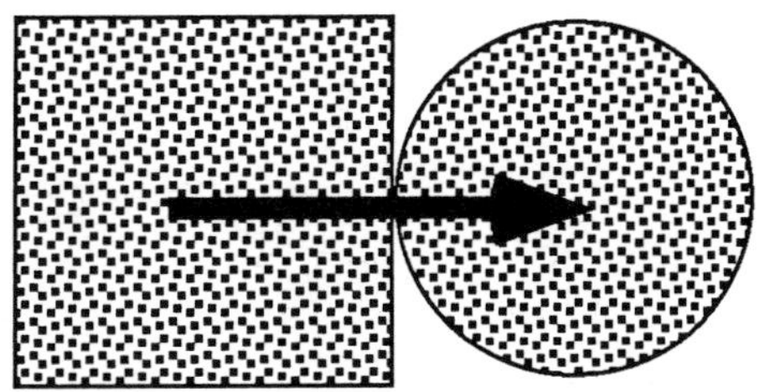

**Figure 3.1**
Heat transfer by conduction

### *Air Leakage*

Air leakage is escape of warm air through openings in the greenhouse frame. Heat loss by air leakage depends on the age, condition, and type of greenhouse. Air currents result from infiltration of natural air through cracks and openings in the greenhouse surface (Figure 3.2). Obvious greenhouse openings through which infiltration of air occurs are door frames, ventilation openings, and fans and louvers.

Even glass greenhouses in good condition allow infiltration through openings where the panes overlap. Older greenhouses or those in poor condition generally have cracked, slipped, or missing glass and excessive gaps where panes overlap. The use of larger glass panes or large sheets of fiberglass reduces infiltration. Greenhouses covered with double layers of film plastic have the least amount of heat loss by air leakage.

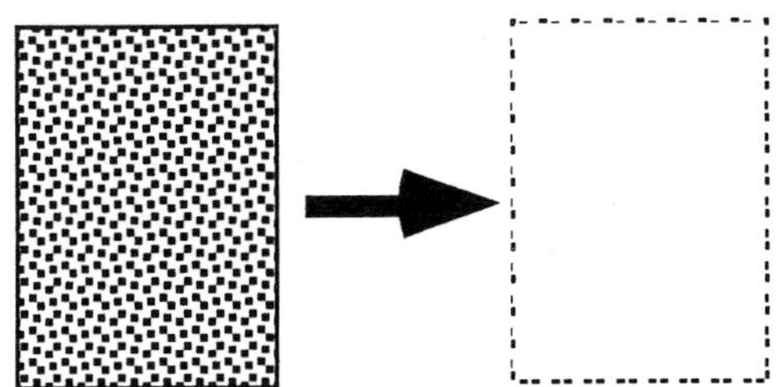

Warm air moves to a colder location. Greenhouse heat is lost by air leakage through greenhouse frame openings.

**Figure 3.2**
Heat transfer by air leakage

### *Radiation*

Radiation is the direct transfer of heat energy between objects not in contact (without warming the air between them). The amount of radiation heat loss (Figure 3.3) depends on the type of glazing on the greenhouse. Fiberglass and glass allow less than 4 percent of thermal (heat) radiation to pass through in contrast to 50 percent for polyethylene.

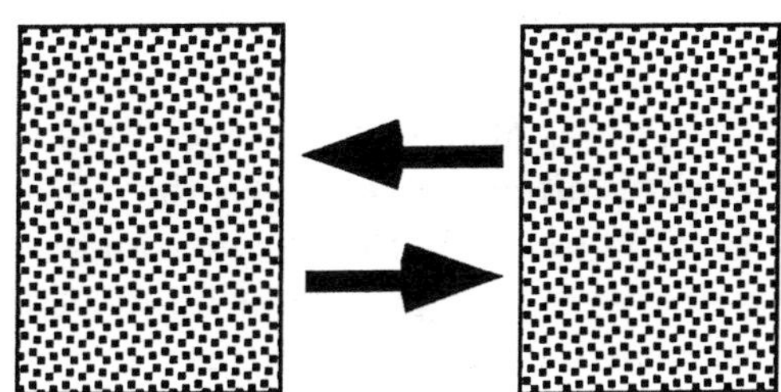

**Figure 3.3**
Heat transfer by radiation. Objects are not in contact.

Figure 3.4 depicts how heat is gained and lost by a greenhouse. Other heat loss factors are also important. The size of a greenhouse is significant. Small greenhouses have more surface area relative to the volume enclosed. So, they lose more heat per square foot and are more difficult (and more expensive per square foot) to heat than are larger houses. More heat is lost by conduction from corrugated fiberglass than from flat fiberglass because the corrugated fiberglass has a larger surface area.

**Figure 3.4** Types of heat exchange between the greenhouse and surroundings

conduction heat loss or gain
heat loss through ventilation
solar heat input
thermal radiation to sky
furnace heat
equipment heat
air leakage heat loss or gain
heat loss or gain to soil

Adapted from *Conserving Energy in Ohio Greenhouses*, Cooperative Extension Service Bulletin, The Ohio State University

## HEATING FUELS

The three most commonly used heating fuels in the greenhouse industry today are natural gas, fuel oil, and coal.

### Coal

Coal is the least expensive fuel, but also the least well adapted for greenhouse use. Coal is not easily stored. It has to be stockpiled at the site, taking up valuable land that could be used for greenhouse space. Then coal requires a great deal of labor for handling.

DISADVANTAGE

Coal is also a "dirty" fuel. It is very dusty to work with. Most important, coal significantly pollutes the air when burning. Coal must be burned in accordance with EPA regulations. When burned, it produces considerable amounts of ash that must be disposed of properly. Coal is sometimes used as a back-up fuel when there is a shortage of the primary fuel.

## Fuel Oil

Fuel oil is the second most commonly used fuel for heating greenhouses and is the prime back-up fuel. Like coal, fuel oil requires significant storage area, since it is contained in large tanks. It also produces ash when burned, but not as much as coal does.

Problems can arise because of the viscosity or thickness of fuel oil. Fuel oil viscosity increases as the temperature drops. Extreme cold can stop the flow of fuel oil from outside fuel tanks to the heaters with disastrous results. Fuel oils are available in grades 1, 2, 4, 5 and 6. Grade 1 has the least viscosity and grade 6 the most viscosity. Number 2 grade is used for small greenhouse heaters and grades 5 and 6 are used for large greenhouse boilers. Therefore, more severely cold weather will affect the operation of a large boiler before that of a small heater. The fuel for the large boiler is already thicker at the start; it will stop flowing before the grade 2 fuel oil does.

## Natural Gas

Natural gas is the most widely used fuel in greenhouse heating.

- ☆ It causes the least amount of air pollution.
- ☆ Natural gas heating equipment requires less cleaning.
- ☆ No storage area is required.
- ☆ Gas is relatively inexpensive.
- ☆ No fuel delivery system is needed (unlike coal and fuel oil).

Heating equipment is directly connected to the source of natural gas. Therefore, obviously a lot less labor is involved. Compared to the other fuels, natural gas is very economical.

### Summary

Table 3.1 gives the Btu output of the three main fuels and compares the cost of each per 1,000 Btu's. Clearly, the cost of coal per Btu is by far the lowest of the three fuels. However, as previously mentioned, the actual total cost of heating with coal may be considerably ***higher***, since 1) storage areas must be set aside; 2) much labor is involved in handling coal; 3) transportation and delivery costs must also be taken into account; and 4) additional air-cleaning equipment will be required by state and federal laws.

---

**Table 3.1** BTU output and cost per Btu of natural gas, fuel oil, and coal

| Fuel | Heat Value [a] | Average Cost [b] | Average Cost per 1000 Btu |
|---|---|---|---|
| Natural gas | 1,000 Btu/cubic foot | $ 4.80/1000 cubic feet | $ 0.0048 |
| Fuel oil (No. 2) | 140,000 Btu/gallon | $ 0.78/gallon | $ 0.0056 |
| Coal | 12,500 Btu/pound | $ 0.02/pound | $ 0.0016 |

a Information source: Erwin, John, and Mark Strefeier, ***Winterize your greenhouse to save fuel costs***. Grower Talks 55: 83.

b Average prices as of July 1991

Fuel oil is slightly more expensive per Btu than is natural gas, but, like coal, oil costs are increased because of the required storage tanks, delivery, and more maintenance of heating equipment. Natural gas is the best buy because it burns clean (and thus, cleaning heaters is not so time-consuming). Also, natural gas requires virtually no handling.

### Fuel and the Environment

Whatever fuel is chosen for heating a greenhouse, the effects of its combustion on the environment must be taken into consideration. Coal should be hard and as free of sulfur as possible to reduce air pollution. If high sulfur levels are present, scrubbers will have to be installed in the stack to reduce pollutants. Fuel oil and natural gas should be free of contaminants and of high enough quality to ensure efficient combustion (conversion to mostly heat) with minimal pollution. Heaters should be cleaned on a regular basis to ensure efficient combustion.

The location of the stack in relation to the greenhouse is an important factor, often overlooked. If the stack is located on the same side of the greenhouse as the prevailing winter wind, the exhaust is likely to infiltrate the structure. This polluted air can cause many problems including distorted foliage and flower growth, shattering of flowers (petals falling prematurely), and in some cases even worker discomfort. Therefore, the stack should be located on the opposite side of the greenhouse from the prevailing wind, so the exhaust fumes will be carried ***away*** from the greenhouse, not over it.

## HEATING SYSTEMS

There are several ways to supply heat to a greenhouse.

- ☆ steam
- ☆ hot water
- ☆ infrared
- ☆ solar

Generally, steam heating is the most commonly used system in large greenhouse ranges. Hot water heating is most often used in smaller greenhouse ranges and single greenhouses. Infrared heating is used infrequently in small greenhouse ranges and in single greenhouses. Solar heating is still largely experimental and can be considered only in areas of the country that experience mostly sunny winter weather. Each of these systems has its advantages and disadvantages.

### Steam

The use of steam heat in greenhouses is an ***advantage*** in many ways.

1. Steam heat takes smaller mains and heating lines because of the higher temperature of steam.
2. Steam heating lines can be heated or cooled more rapidly.
3. Steam can be transported very efficiently over long distances.
4. Steam used for heating is also available for pasteurization.

However, there are some ***disadvantages*** to using steam heat.

1. The temperature can not be adjusted. Typically, steam comes at temperatures of 212° to 215° degrees Fahrenheit, leaving no flexibility in "fine-tuning" desired temperatures.
2. Steam lines do not hold heat very long. They can not serve as a reservoir of heat in the event of boiler failure as hot water lines do.
3. A steam system must have steam traps installed with return lines. The condensed steam (water) is then reheated and circulated again as steam.

## Hot Water

Hot water heating has a number of distinct ***advantages.***

1. The water temperature can be adjusted as needed.
2. The temperature of the heating lines is more uniform.
3. No traps are needed.
4. Less water treatment is required, as no extra water is added.

However, the ***disadvantages*** are:

1. The expense of hot water heating is higher than for steam heating because hot water requires more extensive piping and larger diameter lines than steam does.
2. Hot water does not produce as many Btu's as steam does, so more piping is required to heat a greenhouse.
3. Response time for changing heat levels in the greenhouse is slower than with steam because of the lower temperature of hot water.
4. Hot water can not be used for pasteurization. If steam pasteurization is needed in a greenhouse heated by hot water, a separate steam source such as a portable steam generator must be purchased.

## Infrared

The ***advantages*** of infrared heaters are:

1. Infrared heaters are a clean and very efficient (90 percent) source of heat.
2. The infrared heater heats the plants, soil and benches directly without heating the air. The heat given off by these objects in turn warms the air. (The heating principle is the same as the sun heating the earth.)
3. Thus, air temperatures can be several degrees lower than in conventionally heated greenhouses.
4. Problems of condensation on plants are reduced.
5. Heat loss and heating cost are both reduced. Growers have found a 30-50 percent reduction in fuel bills.

The ***disadvantages*** of infrared heating are as follows.

1. In large greenhouse ranges, uneven heating is a common occurrence with infrared heating. Placement of the infrared heater must be directly over the plants to be warmed. Since the air is not heated to the extent of conventional steam and hot water heating, any plants that are not directly under the heaters may get too cold and decline in quality.

2. A great deal of overhead equipment is needed. Sometimes the reflectors reduce the amount of natural light reaching the crop.
3. As the crop grows larger, the canopy of vegetation may completely block infrared energy from reaching the soil. The result can be very cold soils which inhibit seed and plant growth; also, growth of root rot organisms is more likely.

### Solar

Solar heating has its ***advantages***:

1. Energy from the sun is theoretically at least an unlimited resource. Solar heating uses solar collectors to store the sun's energy by day and release it at night to heat the greenhouse.
2. Once established, solar heating actually lowers heating costs.
3. This non-polluting fuel decreases our dependency on fossil fuels.

However, using solar energy for heating purposes presents problems, as it is not very efficient at this time. The main ***disadvantages*** are:

1. Solar heating is very dependent upon and influenced by the weather. Periods of cloudy weather greatly diminish the usefulness of solar heaters. They are simply not practical in areas of the country where clouds are common.
2. Solar collectors take up considerable space and can be quite expensive. Research has shown that it takes a collector surface area of one half to one square foot to heat one square foot of greenhouse floor area.
3. With the use of solar heat, a back-up heating system is essential to take over during cloudy weather and severe cold.

**Summary** - Table 3.2 compares the advantages of each of these four systems of greenhouse heating.

## Thermostats

### *Types*

Heating systems in the vast majority of greenhouses today are automatically controlled. Very few manual systems still exist, requiring monitoring of greenhouse heat levels by greenhouse personnel and manual operation of heating valves in response to changes in greenhouse temperatures. Automatic control of heating systems is accomplished by a thermostat, a device that operates electric or pneumatic valves. Many thermostats measure greenhouse temperature by means of a strip made of two types of metal that expand and contract at different rates. Other thermostats, like those used in computer-controlled heating systems, are solid state. They measure air temperature electronically.

### *Placement*

Regardless of the type of thermostat in use, its placement in the greenhouse is of critical importance. For accurate measurement of the heat in a greenhouse, thermostats must be placed **at or near crop level** in a location

**Table 3.2** Comparison of several greenhouse heating systems

| Steam | Hot Water |
|---|---|
| ◆Very economical<br>◆Smaller mains and heating lines used<br>◆Rapid heating or cooling of heating lines<br>◆Steam easily transported over long distances<br>◆System also used for pasteurization | ◆Overall costs reasonable<br>◆Water temperature precisely adjustable<br>◆Temperature of heating lines quite uniform<br>◆Less water treatment required<br>◆No traps needed |
| **Infrared** | **Solar** |
| ◆Lower fuel bills<br>◆Heaters 90% efficient<br>◆Clean source of heat<br>◆Less heat loss; lower air temperatures<br>◆Direct heating of plants and so reduced condensation | ◆Lower operating costs<br>◆Unlimited energy source<br>◆Non-polluting heat<br>◆Breaks dependency on fossil fuels |

that reflects the average air temperature. For example, in a small greenhouse, the thermostat would be placed in the middle of the structure.

In large greenhouses and ridge-and-furrow greenhouses, the growing area is divided into small zones. Thermostats are placed in the middle of each zone that has its own heating equipment control (Figure 3.5). This so-called "zoned heating" results in accurate temperature control for large growing areas. It also allows for various temperature regimes within a large greenhouse. Zoned heating makes it possible to grow multiple crops with differing temperature requirements all in the same range.

For accurate measurement of air temperature, a thermostat should be placed just above or at the height of the crop being grown. If the thermostat were placed several feet above the plants, an inaccurate reading of the air temperature for that greenhouse crop would result. Air high above a crop, of course, will be considerably

**Figure 3.5**
Large greenhouse with zoned heating. A thermostat (T) is in the middle of each zone at or near crop level.

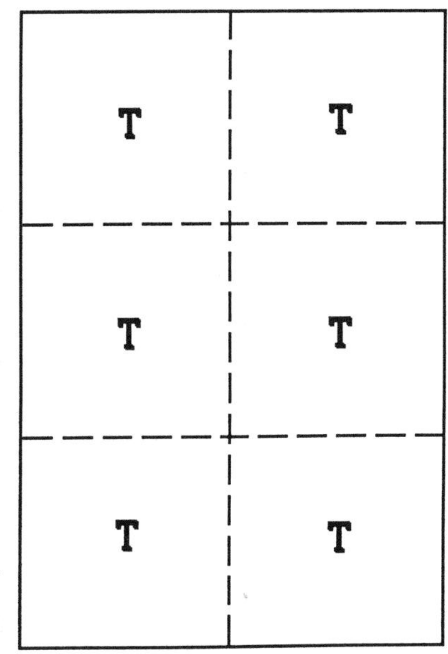

warmer because warm air rises. For example, a thermostat set at 70°F is placed four feet above a certain crop. The thermostat **where it is located** will maintain that air temperature at 70°F. But below it, at crop level, the air temperature will in fact be several degrees cooler. Inaccurate air temperature control will result if the thermostat is not installed at or near the height of the crop.

One further factor to ensure accuracy of a thermostat in measuring the heat level in a greenhouse is to shield it from sunlight. Direct sunlight striking a thermostat will result in elevated temperature measurements. A false measurement will keep the thermostat from operating the heating equipment even when the true greenhouse temperature is well below the desired set point.

The best way to shield a thermostat from the sun's rays is to place it in a box (Figure 3.6). This box should be painted white to reflect sunlight. It should also have a fan at one end and an opening at the other to pull air through the box. Such a box with a fan pulling air through is called an **aspirated box** (Figure 3.7). With this device, a thermostat will accurately measure the air temperature in a greenhouse and automatically set temperature controls correctly.

## Steam and Hot Water Heating Equipment

### Boilers

In any greenhouse, heat must be distributed so that uniform temperatures are achieved throughout. In many large greenhouse operations, a boiler system is used. A boiler is essentially a large furnace constructed of steel or cast iron that heats hot water or steam (Figure 3.8). The boiler is located in a room separate from the greenhouse, because humid greenhouse air can cause corrosion of the boiler. Boilers burn natural gas, fuel oil, or coal to heat the hot water or steam.

**Figure 3.6** Day and night thermostats housed with a fan in an aspirated box

**Figure 3.7** The aspirated box suspended in the middle of the greenhouse

**Figure 3.8** Boiler system used to heat a large greenhouse range

---

The hot water or steam from the boiler is circulated in pipes placed in the greenhouse and returned to the boiler for reheating. The pipes that distribute the hot water or steam heat may be mounted on the curtain wall (Figure 3.9A), under benches (Figure 3.9B), or above the crops (Figure 3.9C). The perimeter pipes on curtain walls are often finned to increase the heat output per linear foot of pipe (Figure 3.9A). Square metal fins in a series are attached to the pipe to increase its surface area for heating.

Steam heating systems require installation of a steam trap in the heating pipes. This device traps steam in the pipes, but allows condensed steam (water) to flow out and return to the boiler to be reheated into steam.

**Figure 3.9** Location of boiler heating pipes in greenhouses

**A.** Fin piping mounted on a curtain wall

**B.** Piping underneath a bench

**C.** Heat pipes installed over the crop, running the length of the greenhouse

In order to keep boilers operating and burning fuel efficiently, regular maintenance must be done. Every year (usually during the summer when heating is not required), the boilers should be thoroughly cleaned and inspected by qualified personnel. Throughout the year on a daily basis, boilers should also be checked for proper operation. Any irregularities should be corrected immediately. Following a routine maintenance schedule should result in a safe, efficient boiler. It should also help keep fuel costs down.

## Unit Heaters

Unit heaters fueled by gas or oil are commonly used in small greenhouses. They are sometimes used in combination with perimeter hot water or steam piping from boilers. Unit heaters either operate by circulating hot water or steam within, or by burning fuel to warm the air. Unlike boilers, unit heaters are located in the greenhouse they heat. Boilers are usually located in the headhouse or some other location. The two basic types of unit heaters are horizontal and vertical.

### *Horizontal*

Horizontal unit heaters are suspended from the roof (Figure 3.10), usually in pairs. In each heater is a fan that blows the warm air out horizontally; hence its name. The warm air is directed into a fan jet which in turn blows the warm air into a polyethylene air distribution tube for distribution throughout the greenhouse (Figure 3.11).

**Figure 3.10**
Front and back views of a gas-fired horizontal unit

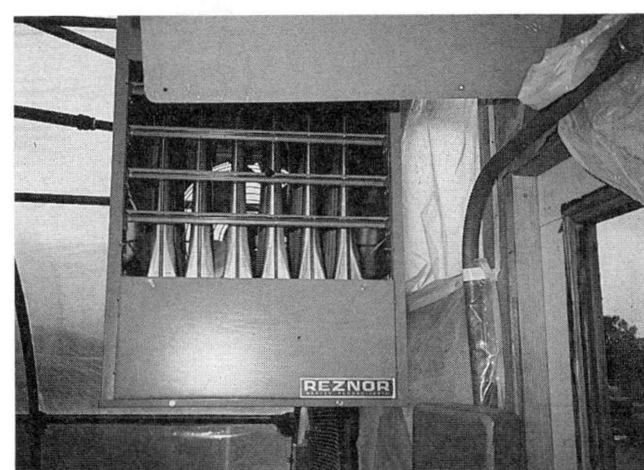

**Figure 3.11**
Two horizontal steam unit heaters equipped with fan jets blow air into polyethylene tubes for distribution throughout the greenhouse.

*Vertical*

Vertical unit heaters are also suspended from the roof (Figure 3.12). They blow the warm air vertically toward the ground. This warm air blowing on the crops below sometimes creates problems. There may be dry areas in the greenhouse and stress on the plants directly below the heater. To minimize such stress, fins (shown in Figure 3.12) can be installed directly beneath the fan to deflect the warm air and spread it more evenly in the greenhouse.

**Figure 3.12**

A vertical unit steam heater. Fins below the fan spread warm air out into the greenhouse.

Compared to boilers, unit heaters are more economical to install and operate. They usually require less maintenance than other heating systems. However, in colder climates, unit heaters may maintain less uniform greenhouse temperatures. Cold spots may occur along greenhouse walls. However, over all, well-designed unit heaters perform very well and are popular in the floriculture industry.

## Hot Water Biotherm Heating

A relatively new heating system, heating the crop from underneath, is called biotherm heating. Flexible plastic tubing through which hot water (typically at 120°F) is circulated, is installed on a bench (Figure 3.13). Potted flowering plants and bedding plants are placed directly on the biotherm. This heating system is also excellent for propagation benches, since bottom heat speeds rooting of cuttings and germination of seeds.

Temperature sensors are placed into pots or flats to monitor soil temperature. The desired soil temperature is set on a thermostat, which controls the flow of hot water into the biotherm. With heat supplied at plant level, the air temperature overhead can be several degrees cooler than in conventional perimeter pipe-heated greenhouses. Cooler air means less heat loss and lower heating fuel bills. However, in severe winter weather, a back-up system should be present with biotherm heating, because supplemental heating may be needed.

## Floor Heating

Floor heating is similar to biotherm heating except that the plastic tubing is buried in the greenhouse floor (Figure 3.14). Like biotherm heating on a bench, the plastic tubing is arranged in a series of loops extending the full length of the greenhouse. The result is constant heat across the greenhouse floor. Floor heating is excellent for crops like bedding plants and poinsettias that are commonly grown on the floor. Here, too, heating costs are frequently

**Figure 3.13** Biotherm hot water heating system

**A.** A bench with a biotherm hot water heating system

**B.** Supply and return pipes are at the end of the bench.

**Figure 3.14**

Floor heating system showing supply and return pipes at one end of the greenhouse

lower than in conventionally heated greenhouses since the air overhead can be several degrees cooler.

### Infrared Heaters

Infrared heaters are installed directly over the crop they are to heat. An infrared heater consists of a metal tube in which fuel (natural gas) is burned. Over the top of the tube is a metal reflector (Figure 3.15). The pipe is heated to several hundred degrees F. The infrared heat generated is directed down to the crop by the reflector.

Infrared heaters warm only the plants and other objects beneath them; the plants, in turn, warm the air. Once again, this heating system keeps plants warm while the surrounding air temperature can be significantly cooler than in a conventionally heated greenhouse. However, plants must be directly under the heater to be warmed. Plants at the edge of the greenhouse, out of the range of the heater, may get too cold.

**Figure 3.15** Infrared heater with reflector

As mentioned previously, sometimes a crop of large plants keeps the soil from being warmed enough. Cold, damp soils that favor root diseases may result. However, infrared heating maintains a foliage temperature that is warmer in the evening than air temperature. The warmer foliage has fewer problems with condensation and, therefore, greatly reduced outbreaks of foliar diseases.

### Solar Heating

Solar heating, discussed earlier on page 52, heats a greenhouse by collecting solar energy during the day and using it to heat the greenhouse at night. Reliance on fossil fuels is thus greatly reduced. Pollution is no longer a problem. Solar collectors are installed near greenhouses. Usually solar energy is collected and stored in the water or air that is circulated through the collector. Solar collectors require up to one square foot of area to heat one square foot of greenhouse floor area. Take a four-acre greenhouse range as an example. Up to four acres of land must be set aside for the collectors, land that could have been used for greenhouse space. This adds to the already costly collectors.

Present technology has not yet developed an efficient solar collector for heating greenhouses. Research will no doubt continue in the quest for an affordable, efficient solar collector. The fossil fuel supply we are now using for heating greenhouses and in our day-to-day energy consumption will not last forever!

## GREENHOUSE ENERGY CONSERVATION

With rising fuel prices and the inflation present in the world today, people in the greenhouse industry are continually challenged to keep their production practices as efficient as possible and their prices to the floral consumer as stable as possible. A major way to save on production costs is to conserve energy in the greenhouse by reducing heat loss. Reduction of heat loss means that less fuel is required to heat the greenhouse; lower heating bills result. Some conservation methods are very simple; others are more advanced. All have the same goal of lowering fuel consumption.

### Greenhouse Location

The location of a greenhouse itself can save on heating costs. Locating a greenhouse to the south of a hill or tree line will reduce the amount of heat lost to a prevailing wind. Windbreaks can save 5 to 10 percent in fuel usage.

### Interior Ceilings/Thermal Screens

The majority of heat loss from a greenhouse occurs through the roof, given its large surface area. Interior ceilings that close off the roof at eave height greatly reduce the area that has to be heated (Figure 3.16). An interior ceiling can be made out of polyethylene, cloth, or thin metallic strips. Depending on the material, an interior ceiling can also serve to reduce light intensity in the greenhouse (which will be discussed later). Interior ceilings typically are drawn at night and folded up by day. Such practices can reduce energy requirements by as much as 30 percent.

Thermal screens are similar to interior ceilings except that black polyethylene or heavy cloth is drawn not only across the crop overhead, but also surrounding the crop. Thermal screens, therefore, reduced heat loss through the roof and the side walls of the greenhouse. The total area that has to be

**Figure 3.16** Interior ceiling at eave height

heated is greatly reduced and therefore fuel consumption is also greatly reduced by as much as 60 percent. Since thermal screens block out light, they can be used for photoperiodically timed crops (which will be discussed in a later section).

A heavy snow storm is an unusual occurrence during which thermal screens and interior ceilings may be best left folded up, out of use. These systems then would not interfere with the process of snow melting by heat conduction through the glazing. Dangerous snow loads are thus less likely to build up on the roof.

## Glazing

The type of glazing affects the rate of heat loss from a greenhouse. A greenhouse covered with double-layer inflated polyethylene will use 35 to 40 percent less fuel than a comparable glass greenhouse. Double-layer inflated polyethylene can also be placed ***over*** an existing glass roof, since its insulating properties will reduce heat loss through the glass roof. Energy savings using this method can be over 40 percent. A single layer of polyethylene can also be attached to sash bars ***inside*** the greenhouse to create a dead air space between the polyethylene and the glass. This method will also significantly reduce heat loss.

But there is one drawback. Using polyethylene on an existing roof results in reduction of light intensity. So this "double-glazed" method should be used only when growing low light-intensity crops like African violets or if the greenhouse has a north-facing roof. The polyethylene would not significantly reduce light transmission since sunlight would be entering through the south-facing roof.

Like double-layer polyethylene, double-layer rigid plastics also significantly reduce heat loss from a greenhouse. Double-layer acrylics and polycarbonates have an insulating dead air space that greatly reduces heat loss by conduction. These glazings have been shown to reduce heating costs 50 to 60 percent compared to single-layer glazing materials. However, acrylic and polycarbonate glazings are very expensive and require a considerable initial investment by the greenhouse owner.

## Select-A-Shade Greenhouse

A new type of greenhouse has been developed by scientists from the Agricultural Engineering Department at the Ohio Agricultural Research and Development Center (OARDC) in Wooster. This small experimental or "prototype" greenhouse is called a "Select-A-Shade" greenhouse. It is totally computer-controlled. The greenhouse is constructed of double-layer acrylic sheets into which polystyrene pellets are drawn by a vacuum pump. The ribs of the acrylic sheets form tubes in which the pellets accumulate. When all the tubes are filled, the night time energy savings is an incredible 80 to 90 percent. The computer which controls the vacuum pump can be programmed to fill up every fourth tube (resulting in 25 percent shade), every other tube (for 50 percent shade), and so on - for 75 percent shade and nearly 100 percent shade (Figure 3.17). This system of selecting shade virtually eliminates both the cost and time involved in the conventional shading of greenhouses by applying whitewash.

Commercial application of this exciting new technology is not far off. Greenhouses that use this technology will be highly energy-efficient while at the same time offering advanced, precise environmental control for production of high quality crops. Figure 3.18 depicts an artist's rendition of a one-acre commercial select-a-shade greenhouse.

## Solar Heating

Another way to conserve energy is to **supplement** the existing greenhouse heating system with a partial conversion to solar heating. A heat exchanger would be needed to extract heat from the solar collectors and pump it into

**Figure 3.17**

Select-A-Shade greenhouse at OARDC with its developer, Dr. Ted Short, at the computer controls. Note the 25% shading by polystyrene pellets.
*(Photo courtesy of Ted Short, Agricultural Engineering, OARDC, Wooster)*

**Figure 3.18**

Artist's sketch of a one-acre, commercial Select-A-Shade greenhouse. The storage tank in front holds polystyrene pellets.
*(Photo courtesy of Ted Short, Agricultural Engineering, OARDC, Wooster)*

the circulation lines. Such a system would not totally eliminate fuel consumption, but could significantly reduce it in areas of the country with enough sun in winter. Considerable space, however, and a large investment are required for solar collectors. This system is therefore not feasible for many greenhouse producers.

### Waste Heat from Power Plants

Greenhouses that are located near nuclear power plants that use water for cooling purposes in the generation of electricity can use the waste water for heating. In nuclear power plants, water drawn from rivers or lakes is circulated through generating equipment to keep it cool. The resulting waste water has been heated by this process to well over 100°F.

This hot waste water, piped to nearby greenhouses, can be used for heating purposes instead of being returned as is to rivers and streams. Dumping of hot waste water into waterways creates many problems for the aquatic life, raising the water temperature significantly and disrupting the whole ecosystem. For the greenhouse manager, minimal heating of the waste water is necessary, since it is already hot when received from the power plant. Heating fuel bills thus are very low compared to those involved in heating cold water from a well or a city water supply.

---

Greenhouse energy conservation measures should be practiced by ***all*** producers of floriculture crops. Gone are the days of inexpensive fuels and unlimited fuel reserves. We know now that the world supply of fossil fuels will not last forever. It is imperative for each person to do his/her part to use this precious resource wisely while alternate methods of heating greenhouses are being developed. Reducing energy costs also means lower prices for greenhouse customers to pay. Energy conservation benefits **everyone** involved in the floriculture industry.

## GREENHOUSE VENTILATION AND COOLING EQUIPMENT

### Introduction

Just as the cold season requires heating of a greenhouse, warm seasons demand cooling of a greenhouse. Greenhouse ventilation and cooling serve three functions. They

- ☆ reduce excessive levels of heat,
- ☆ maintain the optimum carbon dioxide concentrations for photosynthesis, and
- ☆ reduce relative humidity, achieving better disease control.

While ventilation and cooling systems can be manually operated, most greenhouses today have automated systems with thermostats controlling the equipment. Like heating thermostats, cooling thermostats should be placed at crop level for accurate temperature control. Following is a discussion of the ventilation and cooling systems commonly used in greenhouses.

## In A-frame Greenhouses

Providing air to an A-frame greenhouse involves basically two types of ventilators: ridge and sidewall ventilators. Ridge ventilators are hinged at the peak or ridge of the greenhouse (Figure 3.19). Sidewall ventilators are usually hinged at the eave (Figure 3.20). Both run parallel to the ridge of the greenhouse. These ventilators can be operated manually with hand cranks (Figure 3.21A) or automatically by using motors and thermostats (Figure 3.21B).

**Figure 3.19** Open ridge vents in a greenhouse. Note white shading compound sprayed on the end wall.

**Figure 3.20** Open sidewall vent in a greenhouse, hinged at the eave

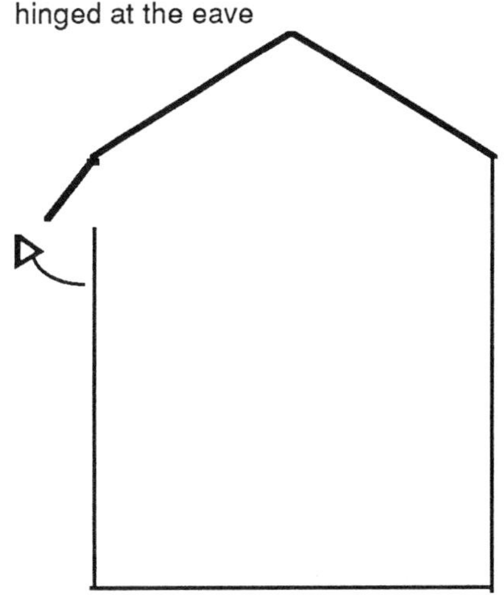

**Figure 3.21** Two kinds of ventilators

**A.** Hand-operated side ventilator

**B.** Automated ridge ventilator

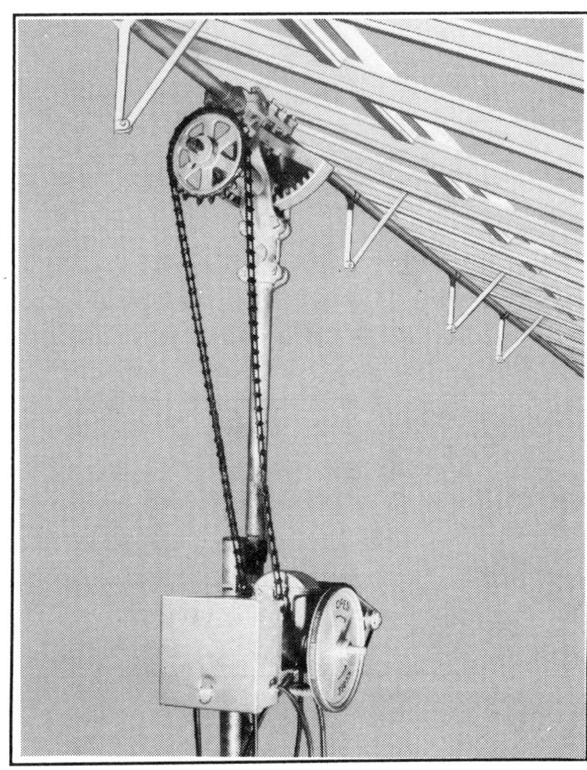

These ventilators operate on the "chimney effect" principle. As Figure 3.22 shows, hot air rising in a greenhouse needs to escape through opened ridge ventilators. In windy weather, the ridge ventilator ***opposite*** the prevailing wind direction should be opened to prevent damage to the ventilator system. The powerful suction created through the ridge ventilator helps pull hot air to the outside. Opening sidewall ventilators enhances the chimney effect by drawing in cool air to replace the hot air escaping through the ridge ventilators.

**Figure 3.22** Chimney-effect air flow through ridge and sidewall ventilators

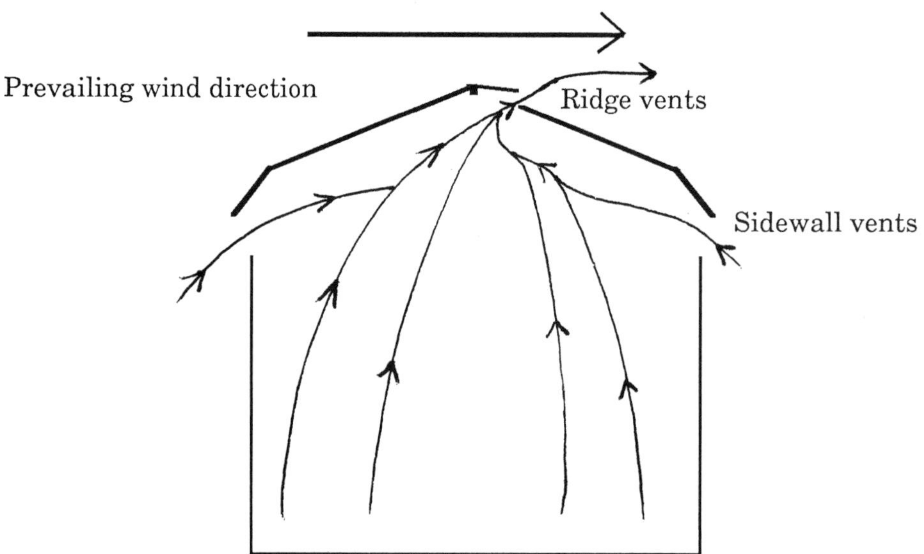


## In Quonset Greenhouses

In certain types of greenhouses, ridge and sidewall ventilators can not be used. Instead, greenhouses like quonset film plastic houses use forced air or fan ventilation. (This forced air ventilation can, of course, be used in A-frame greenhouses, too.) Exhaust fans are typically installed on one end or side wall of the greenhouse (Figure 3.23A). In the opposite wall are the louvers through which air enters the greenhouse (Figure 3.23B). Cool outside air is pulled into the greenhouse through the louvers by the exhaust fans at the same time as the fans exhaust and remove the hot air (Figure 3.24). Both fans and louvers should be installed at crop height so that the air at plant level is cooled to the right temperature.

A more recent, energy-efficient form of cooling used in quonset greenhouses is ***side vent cooling.*** Inflatable polyethylene tubes are rolled up or down by a crank over side vents. This method eliminates use of fans.

**Figure 3.23** **A**) Exhaust fans and **B**) louvers are both part of a fan ventilation system. When the fans are off, the louvers are closed to keep out rain and cold air.

A

B

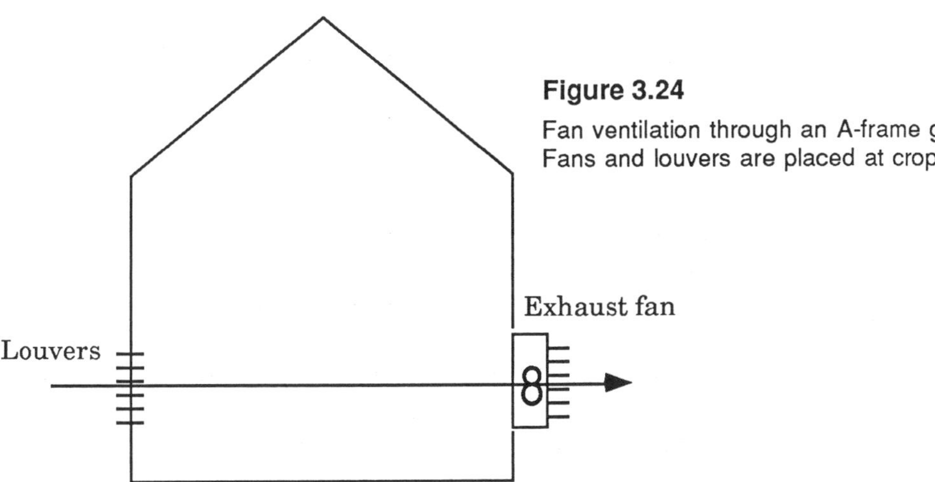


**Figure 3.24**

Fan ventilation through an A-frame greenhouse. Fans and louvers are placed at crop height.

## For Winter Cooling

Another form of fan ventilation is used for winter cooling. Greenhouses occasionally get overheated on sunny winter days. The same fan jets and polyethylene air distribution tubes that are used in the heating system can also distribute cold outside air through the greenhouse. When the thermostat indicates a need for cooling, inlet louvers open behind the fan jet and allow cold outside air to be drawn into the tube (Figure 3.25). The cold air is then forced into the greenhouse through holes in the tube and becomes mixed with the overheated greenhouse air. The greenhouse is thus cooled without the shock to plants of an abrupt temperature change.

**Figure 3.25**

Fan jet in front of open inlet louvers draws outside air into the convection tube for winter cooling.

# AIR COOLING METHODS

## Fan and Pad Cooling

In summer, often ventilation alone is not sufficient to prevent excessive heat build-up inside a greenhouse. On sunny hot days, it is not unusual for the greenhouse air temperature to be 20 or 30 degrees warmer than the outside air temperature, even with ventilators open. Thus, other methods must be used to cool greenhouses during hot weather. Fan and pad cooling is a commonly used "air conditioning" system that works on the principle of **evaporative cooling**. Water evaporation removes heat from the air and cools it. You have felt this on a windy day when you climbed out of the swimming pool. As soon as your body was exposed to the wind, you felt cold. The water on your skin, through rapid evaporation, was removing heat from your body.

The basic parts of a fan and pad cooling system are the following (Figure 3.26):

- ☆ exhaust fans
- ☆ cooling pad made out of excelsior or cross-fluted cellulose
- ☆ water reservoir or sump
- ☆ pump
- ☆ water distribution pipe and overhead baffle

The pad is installed just inside the end or sidewall that has vents or louvers in it to allow air in. Cross-fluted cellulose or formed paper pads last about ten years, while excelsior pads last only a few years.

Exhaust fans are installed in the opposite wall (Figure 3.27). As the fans pull the warm outside air through the pad, some of the trickling water evaporates. This evaporation removes heat from the air, reducing the temperature

**Figure 3.26** Cooling pad components. A baffle installed over the water distribution pipe distributes water evenly over the top of the pad.

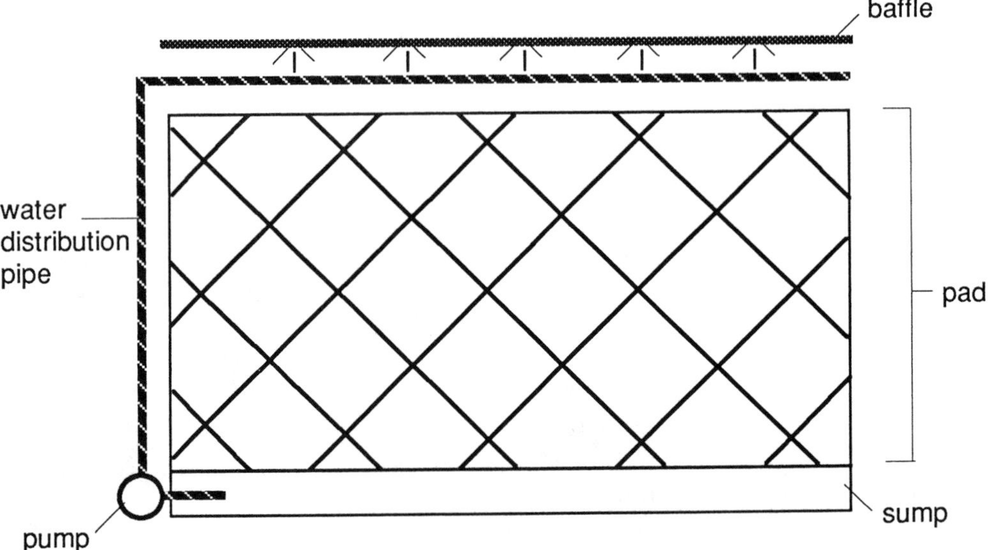

**Figure 3.27** Example of a fan and pad cooling system. Outside air (at 85°) is drawn through the pad by the exhaust fan, cooling it to 70°. As the air travels through the greenhouse, it absorbs heat and warms to 77° before it is exhausted.

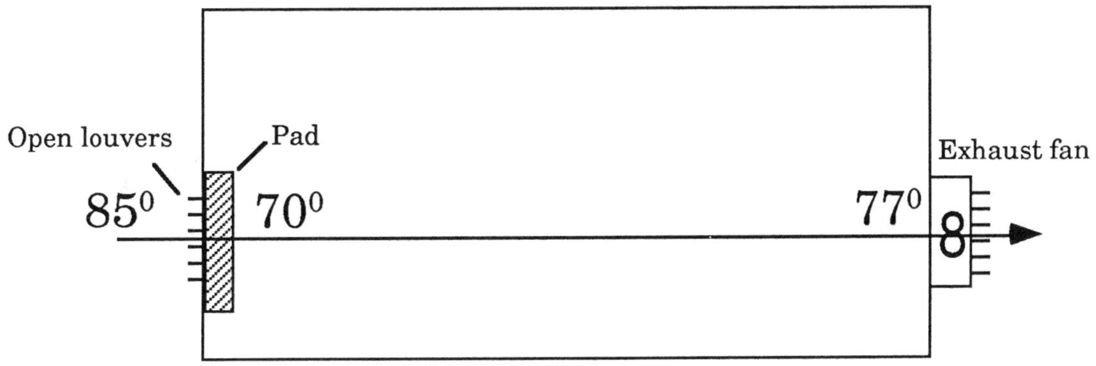


as much as 15-20 F degrees. The cooled air passes through the greenhouse, replacing the hot air, which is exhausted through the fans at the other end. The cooled air gets warmer as it removes heat - a recommended 7-degree temperature rise from pad to fan.

To ensure proper cooling of crops, the cooling pad should be installed across the entire length or width of the greenhouse at crop level. Fans also should be installed at the same height as the pad to ensure uniform air flow over the crop. All ridge ventilators should be closed so that air can pass only through the cooling pad.

## Evaporative Package Cooling

Evaporative package coolers or swamp coolers are another type of fan and pad cooling system. The swamp cooler, in metal housing, is usually installed inside and partially outside of a small greenhouse (Figure 3.28A). The three sides of the cooler on the outside are louvered with excelsior pads immediately inside (Figure 3.28B). Water pumped to the top of the pads trickles down through them. A squirrel cage fan pulls in air through the pads and blows the cooled air into the greenhouse.

In any evaporative cooling system, outside air with low relative humidity does the best job of cooling. This air is drier and so can absorb more moisture than can air that is high in relative humidity. Therefore, on very hot, humid days, evaporative coolers do not cool a greenhouse as efficiently as on days with low humidity.

Figure 3.28 An evaporative package cooler outside the greenhouse

A. Exterior view

B. Interior view of an evaporative package cooler with its squirrel cage fan, pumping equipment, and excelsior pad

## High Pressure Fog Cooling

Another cooling system that uses water evaporation to cool the greenhouse is high pressure fog. Nozzles mounted either overhead in the greenhouse or by sidewall vents produce fog from water forced through them at high pressure (Figure 3.29). Exhaust fans and open vents then circulate the fog throughout the greenhouse, where it quickly evaporates, cooling the air.

**Figure 3.29**

High pressure fog cooling. Fogging nozzles are located next to the sidewall vents.

It is very important that this fog consists of water droplets that are extremely small and that there is good air circulation. The fog should evaporate without leaving water on the plants. Fog that leaves foliage wet creates an ideal environment for the development of plant diseases.

## GREENHOUSE SHADING

As the intensity of solar energy increases from late spring on, heat builds up very quickly in greenhouses. Even with cooling and ventilating systems in full operation, a greenhouse can quickly become overheated. Ways must be found to reduce the amount of solar energy entering a greenhouse and thus to decrease the heat level.

A common way to keep some of this sunlight out of the greenhouse is to apply a whitewash to the outside surface in the spring. A white latex paint solution sprayed on the glazing reflects some of the sunlight striking the surface (Figure 3.30). The result is cooler greenhouse temperatures and less scorching or "sunburn" of foliage and flowers. However, light intensity must still be maintained at sufficient levels for quality growth of greenhouse crops. Whitewash gradually wears off during the summer. If it is not totally gone by October, it should be removed at that time, since light intensity in the fall is in rapid decline.

As previously mentioned in the discussion of conserving heat, interior ceilings can also be used to reduce light intensity. An interior ceiling that is popular for light reduction is made out of aluminized strips that reflect sunlight (Figure 3.31). This ceiling is drawn over the crops, usually at eave height, on sunny days to reduce the heat level in the greenhouse. With this ceiling in place, fan and pad and other cooling systems will have a better chance of cooling the greenhouse.

Saran is sometimes used for newly planted crops. It is effective in reducing light intensity over small areas like a single bench (Figure 3.32). Saran is a synthetic woven fabric that lets through only a portion of the light striking it. Saran is available in many percentages of light transmission: 25, 30, 35, 50, 75, and so on. If you want only 50 percent of the available light transmitted to a particular bench, hang 50 percent saran shading over that bench. The main benefit of saran is that it decreases the light intensity striking the plant itself, thereby reducing water stress.

**Figure 3.30**

Whitewash applied to the outside of a greenhouse

**Figure 3.31**

Interior ceiling made out of aluminized strips and used for light reduction

**Figure 3.32**
Saran placed over a bench of recently-planted mums to reduce light intensity

# CARBON DIOXIDE GENERATORS

## Necessity for $CO_2$

The use of supplemental carbon dioxide ($CO_2$) is common in the production of many greenhouse crops. Plants use carbon dioxide to make food (sugar) by the process of photosynthesis (Figure 3.33). Carbon dioxide is present in the atmosphere in very low amounts (350 parts per million). It enters the plant through pores in the leaf called stomata.

During the winter months, when ventilators are closed, the level of $CO_2$ on a sunny day can fall low enough to limit growth and affect the quality of the greenhouse crop. Therefore, $CO_2$ is often added to the air in a greenhouse. When $CO_2$ is added at a concentration higher than 350 parts per million, it enhances growth and helps produce a better quality crop. The usual practice is to add enough $CO_2$ to the greenhouse to maintain a concentration of 1,000 to 1,500 parts per million.

## Sources of $CO_2$

Carbon dioxide for greenhouse crops is obtained from several sources. Sometimes compressed gas or dry ice (solid, frozen $CO_2$) is used; it is kept in special storage containers. Carbon dioxide is then metered out as needed. It is introduced through tubes and distributed by fans throughout the greenhouse. Natural gas burned in an open flame is another source of carbon dioxide. It is mixed into the air by circulating fans.

## Dangers of Faulty Equipment

When carbon dioxide is generated by burning fuels such as natural gas, the equipment used is designed specifically for this purpose (Figure 3.34). Substitutes can be dangerous. Use of improperly designed equipment or impure fuel can, by incomplete combustion, result in the formation of such gases as ethylene and carbon monoxide. These toxic gases will ruin crops and can harm the health of people working in the greenhouse.

**Figure 3.33** A schematic of photosynthesis

**Figure 3.34**
A carbon dioxide generator suspended overhead in a greenhouse

## Time of Day for Adding $CO_2$

Carbon dioxide is required by plants only during the daylight hours when photosynthesis is actively taking place. Higher levels of carbon dioxide should be added to the greenhouse on bright days than on cloudy days. For rates of photosynthesis increase as the light intensity increases.

## Control of $CO_2$ Generators

Some carbon dioxide generators have manual controls, and others have automatic controls. Manual control tends to result in wide variations of $CO_2$ levels. Automated controls use either time clocks or computers. Computers offer the best control of $CO_2$ levels. They usually include monitors that constantly measure $CO_2$ concentration in the greenhouse and activate the generators when needed.

---

***In conclusion:***

In Chapter 3, we discussed how heat is lost from a greenhouse by conduction, air leakage, and radiation. Heating a greenhouse can be done with steam and hot water boilers, unit heaters, infrared radiant heating, or solar heating. Several fuel sources are available for heating equipment. There are several ways to reduce heat loss in a greenhouse. Cooling a greenhouse can be done simply by opening ventilators for natural air circulation. But often, other methods using evaporative cooling must be used. There are fan and pad cooling, high pressure fog, and swamp coolers. Carbon dioxide generators are often used during cold months to elevate carbon dioxide levels. More vigorous plant growth and better quality crops result.

# CHAPTER 3 REVIEW

This review is to help you check yourself on what you have learned about controlling the greenhouse environment. If you need to refresh your mind on any of the following questions, refer to the page number given in parentheses.

1. What are the three ways that heat is lost from a greenhouse? *(page 47)*
2. Define "Btu." At what rate should heat be added to a greenhouse? *(page 47)*
3. Which heating fuel is the most desirable? least desirable? Why? *(pages 48-49)*
4. What type of heating system is most commonly used for heating a large greenhouse range? a small greenhouse? *(page 50)*
5. Why should boilers **not** be located in the greenhouse? *(page 54)*
6. How do horizontal and vertical unit heaters differ? *(pages 57-58)*
7. Discuss the proper placement of thermostats in a greenhouse. *(pages 52-54)*
8. What are two ways to reduce heat loss from a greenhouse? *(page 48)*
9. Which glazings significantly reduce heat loss from a greenhouse? How is this possible? *(page 62)*
10. What are the three purposes of ventilating a greenhouse? *(page 64)*
11. What are the differences between ventilating an even-span, glass greenhouse and a quonset greenhouse? *(pages 65-66)*
12. What principle is illustrated by a fan and pad system of cooling the greenhouse? *(page 68)*
13. Draw and label the major parts of a fan and pad cooling system. *(page 68)*
14. Why are fan and pad cooling systems more effective in cooling a greenhouse in Ohio during the summer than in Florida? *(page 69)*
15. What are two other evaporative cooling systems used in greenhouses? *(pages 69-70)*
16. What is the purpose of applying whitewash to the glazing of a greenhouse? *(page 71)*
17. Discuss the use of saran in a greenhouse. *(page 71)*
18. Why is carbon dioxide important for greenhouse crops? *(page 72)*
19. At what time of year are carbon dioxide generators usually used? Why? *(page 72)*

*(continued)*

## Chapter 3 Review *(continued)*

20. What are three sources of carbon dioxide for greenhouse use? Discuss the most commonly used method. *(page 72)*

21. What level of carbon dioxide should be provided in the greenhouse by $CO_2$ generators? *(page 72)*

# CHAPTER 4

# GREENHOUSE EQUIPMENT AND LIGHTING

## Competencies for Chapter 4

As a result of studying this chapter, you should be able to do the following:

1. Identify major types of greenhouse benching.
2. Describe the major systems of supplemental lighting and the uses of each.
3. Describe the two major photoperiodic lighting techniques.
4. Set time clocks to regulate lighting.

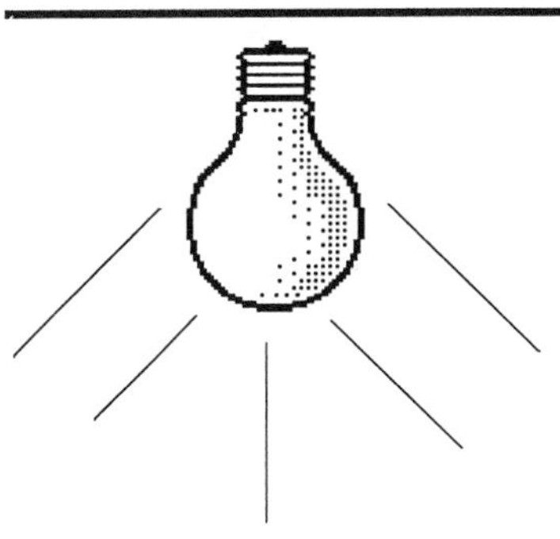

## Related Science Concept

1. Determine plant light needs.

## Related Math Concepts

1. Apply measuring skills to calculate aisle space and usable growing area in square feet.
2. Apply measuring skills to calculate footcandles needed for adequate lighting.
3. Apply basic operations to whole numbers, decimals, and fractions.
4. Apply basic operations to ratios and percents.
5. Read, interpret, and construct charts, graphs, and tables.

## Terms to Know

cyclic
fluorescent lamp
footcandle
ground bench
headhouse
High-Intensity Discharge (HID) lighting
high-pressure sodium lamp
incandescent lamp
leach
long-night plant
peninsula
photoperiod
porous
supplemental lighting
vegetative

## INTRODUCTION

In this chapter we will discuss the equipment commonly used in modern greenhouses. Knowing how to use this equipment efficiently is essential for producing quality floriculture crops. As you will see, equipment used in greenhouses can range from very simple in design and concept to very complex, at the cutting edge of technology. Both are needed and can be used successfully together to produce fine greenhouse crops.

## GREENHOUSE BENCHES

Greenhouse benches provide basic convenience in the production of crops. They permit better control of pests, watering, fertilization, and heating and cooling. The position of greenhouse benches is basically either 1) at ground level, or 2) raised.

The raised greenhouse benches can be constructed of

- ✰ snow fence,
- ✰ expanded metal, or
- ✰ wire mesh.

### Ground Benches

Most cut flower crops are grown in ground benches (Figure 4.1). Maintaining and harvesting cut flower crops is more easily done in ground benches because the plants usually attain heights of several feet with maturity (Figure 4.2). Ideally, ground benches should have a V-shaped concrete bottom to isolate the greenhouse soil from the field soil beneath the greenhouse. Such a bottom prevents harmful field soil organisms from invading the greenhouse soil. Usually drainage tile is installed at the bottom of the V. The tile should fall a minimum of 1 inch per 100 feet of bench length in order to drain off the water.

**Figure 4.1**

Ground bench for a cut-flower crop, ready for planting. The bed is slightly raised with 2" x 4" wooden boards.

Ground benches should be at least 6 inches deep and, for ease of handling crops, no more than 4 feet wide. (Some cut flower crops like roses grow best in benches where the soil is 12 inches deep.) Some ground benches have a short, raised edge to contain the soil or mulch better and to serve as an attachment for watering equipment.

## Raised Benches

Raised benches are the most common type of bench used for pot and bedding plant production. These benches can be made out of wood or metal, with or without side boards. Most raised benches are without side boards; thus there is better air circulation among the plants.

The maximum width for raised benches that can be worked from both sides is 6 feet. For benches that are against a side wall, the width should be no more than 3 feet. Raised benches are typically 30 to 36 inches high for convenience in handling and maintaining the potted crops grown on them.

**Figure 4.2**

Crops of most cut flowers are raised in ground benches for easy accessibility.

### Snow Fence

The snow fence bench is one of the most simply constructed benches available (Figure 4.3). Snow fencing is made from thin redwood slats or strips woven together by wire. A strip of snow fence can be laid out on a wooden frame of 2" x 4" boards and fastened to it. Supports for snow fencing can be metal post, concrete blocks, or other similar weighted material.

### Expanded Metal

Expanded metal benches are composed of a metal or wooden frame onto which an expanded metal "matrix" is attached (Figure 4.4). The metal should be rust resistant for longevity. Expanded metal benches can hold considerable weight and remain durable longer than snow fencing.

**Figure 4.3**

Snow fence bench composed of a wooden frame supported by concrete blocks

**Figure 4.4**
Expanded metal bench

### Wire Mesh

Wire mesh benches are similar to expanded metal benches. The heavy gauge wire that is used is "woven" into a 1- or 2-inch-square mesh pattern (Figure 4.5). Like expanded metal, wire mesh is easy to install on wooden or metal frames. However, it is not as strong as expanded metal.

## Bench Arrangement

Bench arrangement is an important consideration when planning a greenhouse. The greenhouse grower's goal is to use as much greenhouse floor space as possible for crop production. After all, no profit can be made on empty floor space! Aisle width must be kept to a minimum. Center aisles only are

**Figure 4.5**
Wire mesh bench

typically 3 to 4 feet wide to accommodate service carts and other large pieces of equipment. Side aisles, however, are typically 18 inches wide, allowing only for people access to the crop. Frugal use of space means more profit for the wise grower.

### Retail Benching

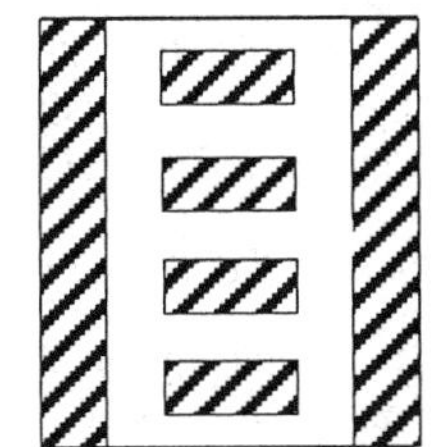

Retail benching is typically raised benches that are used for displaying plants for sale. Aisles are wide- 3 feet or more- to facilitate the flow of customer traffic (Figure 4.6). This benching arrangement makes use of 50 to 60 percent of the greenhouse floor area. Such benching would be found in a retail grower's customer greenhouse, attached to the retail building.

### Standard Benching

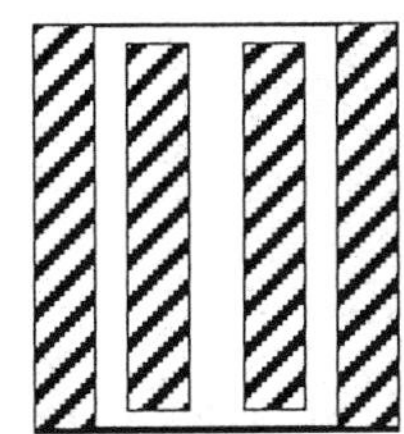

Standard benching, typically used for cut flower crops, makes use of about 70 percent of the greenhouse floor area. The benches run parallel to the length of the greenhouse (Figure 4.6). These long benches make maintenance of cut flower crops more convenient. Also, support wires and photoperiodic equipment can be more efficiently used.

### Peninsular Benching

Peninsular benching, used for potted plant production, features raised benches running along the sidewalls the full length of the greenhouse. From these benches, shorter benches project out toward the middle aisle like a series of peninsulas (Figure 4.6). The aisles between the peninsular benches are typically 18 inches wide. The usable production area in a peninsula bench greenhouse is 75 to 80 percent.

### Rolling Benches

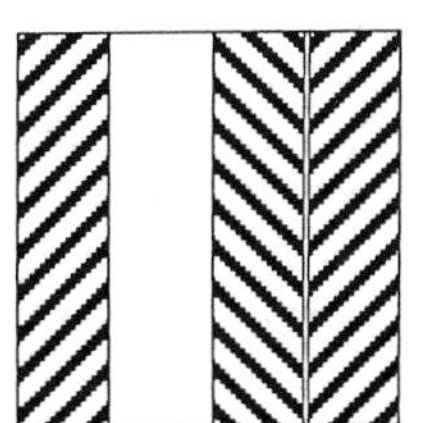

Rolling benches are a recent innovation in the greenhouse industry (Figure 4.7). They are typically used for potted plant production. The benches, in series, are typically oriented along the length or axis of the greenhouse (Figure 4.6), usually with one aisle separating. Eliminating aisle space greatly increases the usable growing area. The "floating aisle" can be created anywhere the grower chooses by simply moving apart two benches at the desired place (Figure 4.7B). This arrangement gives the grower 90 to 95 percent of the greenhouse floor area for crop production.

Some greenhouses with a rolling bench system have gone one step further. They also have a system for transporting the benches of finished plants from the greenhouse to the headhouse. Figure 4.8 shows a rolling bench being moved out of a row of benches and onto such a roller device. This is an efficient, easy way to move plants within a greenhouse using rolling bench technology.

**Figure 4.6**

Benching arrangements commonly used in floriculture greenhouses

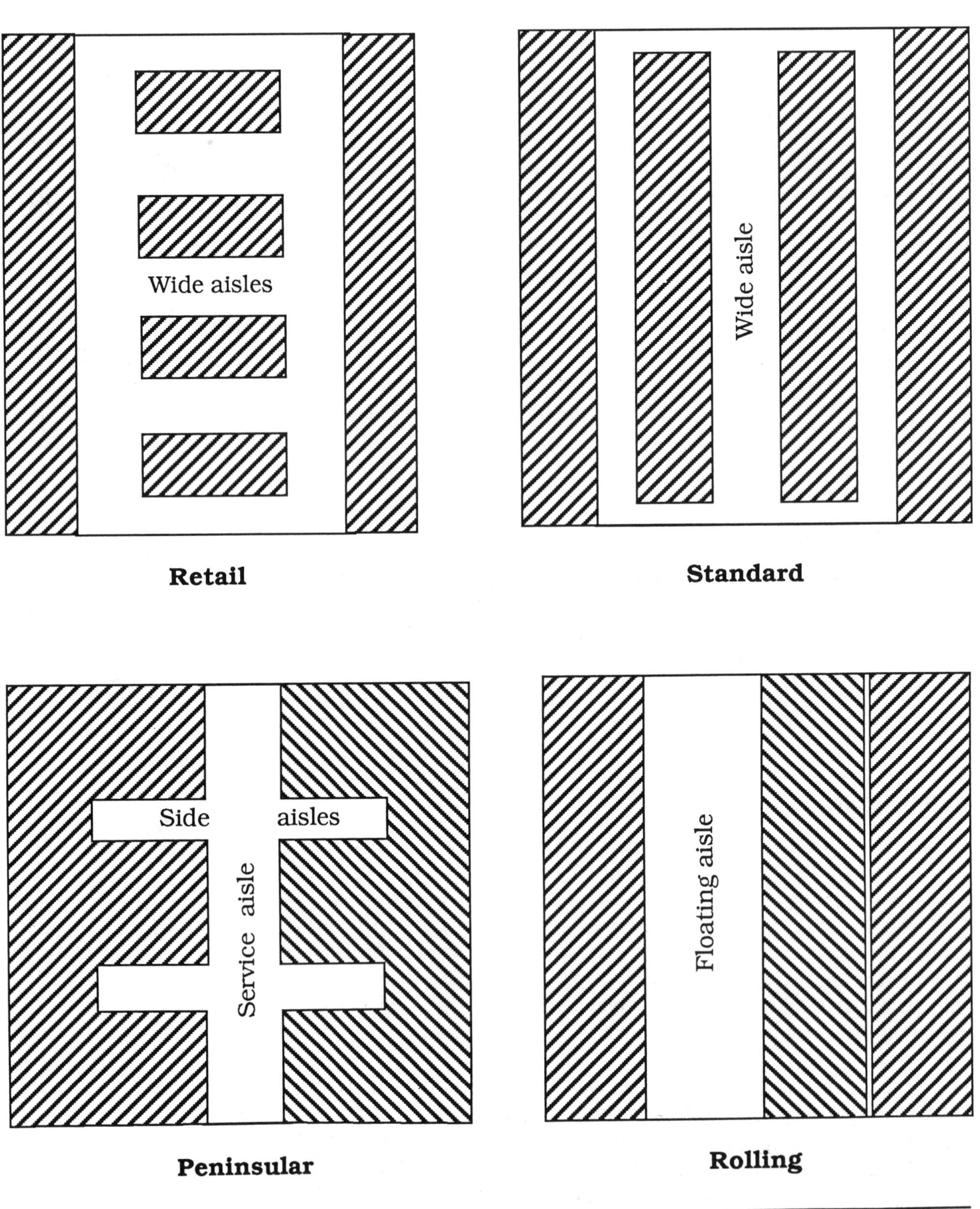

Figure 4.7 A rolling bench system showing **A)** the benches pushed together, and **B)** an aisle between the benches. Note the slots in the bench on the left that permit it to move past the equipment supports.

A

B

**Figure 4.8**

A rolling bench is being moved onto another roller device for transporting to the headhouse.

## Double-tiered Benches

Double-tiered benches make up the most technologically advanced benching system. Also, this bench arrangement uses the most area of any benching system - up to 180 percent of the production area - for potted plants. The high-tech equipment needed, however, requires considerable investment and demands careful maintenance after installation.

Use of the double-tiered benching system in the United States is very rare. Only large-scale, well-established greenhouse growers have such a system (Figure 4.9). Double-tiered benching has two requirements: 1) rolling benches, and 2) a source of light for the bottom tier of benches. The light, of course, must be provided, because the upper tier blocks direct light from reaching the crop on the lower tier. High Intensity Discharge (HID) lamps installed beneath the upper tier are the light source for the lower tier (Figure 4.10).

The double-tiered benches are rotated daily so that each tier receives one day of natural light alternating with one day of HID light. Machines at each end of the double-tiered row of benches coordinate the rotation.

Figure 4.9 shows the following progression.

1. A bench is moved onto a waiting machine by a second machine at the other end (Figure 4.9A & B).
2. The waiting machine raises the bench (Figure 4.9C).
3. The machine moves the bench onto the upper tier (Figure 4.9D).
4. At the same time, the second machine on the opposite end accepts the end bench pushed onto it from the upper tier, lowers it, and moves the bench onto the bottom tier.

This cycle is repeated until all the benches in a given row have been rotated. This system is fully automated. No workers need be present during the rotation.

## Ebb and Flow Bench Inserts

In certain bench systems, an irrigation system is built in and is an important part of the bench system. Ebb and flow bench irrigation is such a system.

---

**Figure 4.9** A double-tiered benching system showing the sequence of moving a rolling bench from the bottom tier to the top tier. The bottom tier is illuminated by HID lamps.

A

B

C

D

**Figure 4.10**

HID lamps installed beneath the upper tier provide light for the crop growing below.

(For more information on this system, see page 100.) Water is pumped onto the bench for a period of time. The potted plants take up the water through drainage holes. The unused water is drained into a reservoir and reused.

**Floor "Benching"** (without benches)

Many crops, including bedding plants, poinsettias, and Easter lilies, can be grown directly on the greenhouse floor. No benching equipment is required. The grower places bedding flats on the floor in rows with flats touching. Narrow aisles at appropriate intervals permit access to all the flats. Spacing of potted plants on the floor is done to ensure the best growth possible. At the same time, the grower wants to obtain maximum dollar value for each square foot of greenhouse space. Floor benching affords up to 90 percent use of the greenhouse floor area for growing crops.

For optimum growing conditions, the floor must be clean, well drained, and free of weeds. These conditions can be accomplished in several ways:

1. laying a synthetic weed barrier over greenhouse soil,
2. applying a layer of coarse gravel to the floor, or
3. installing a concrete floor.

Regular concrete floors should have a slope or "hump" to drain off irrigation water for recycling (Figure 4.11). Another form of concrete floor that can be used for floor benching is porous concrete (Figure 4.12). This special type of rough-looking, "unfinished" concrete allows water to pass through it; no sloping of the floor is required. However, experience has shown that porous concrete has its problems. It easily becomes clogged with soil and is difficult to clean. Also, weeds readily grow on its rough surface. Unlike solid concrete floors, porous concrete floors contribute to ground water contamination since they permit fertilizers and pesticides to leach through.

**Figure 4.11**

Bedding plants grown on humped concrete floors kept very clean. The floor gutter drains off excess irrigation water.

**Figure 4.12**
Porous concrete floor

---

## Summary

Table 4.1 summarizes the benching arrangements in use today. Usable space ranges from a low of about 50 percent for retail benching to 180 percent for double-tiered benching. The choice for the grower depends on the expense of the benching system involved, what type of crop is to be grown, and the profitability of the benching arrangement (percent usable space).

---

**Table 4.1** Commonly used greenhouse benching arrangements

| Benching Arrangement | Crops Grown | % Usable Production Area |
|---|---|---|
| Retail | Bedding plants, potted plants; display for sale | 50-60 |
| Standard | Mainly cut flowers; some potted and bedding plants | 70 |
| Peninsular | Potted plants | 75-80 |
| Rolling | Potted plants | 90-95 |
| Floor (no-bench) | Bedding plants; potted plants | Up to 90 |
| Double-tiered | Potted plants | Up to 180 |

# SUPPLEMENTAL LIGHTING

Light is one of the most important factors influencing plant growth. Photosynthesis can not take place in the absence of light. The intensity of light, especially at lower levels, is a major concern for growers, since it directly affects the rate of photosynthesis.

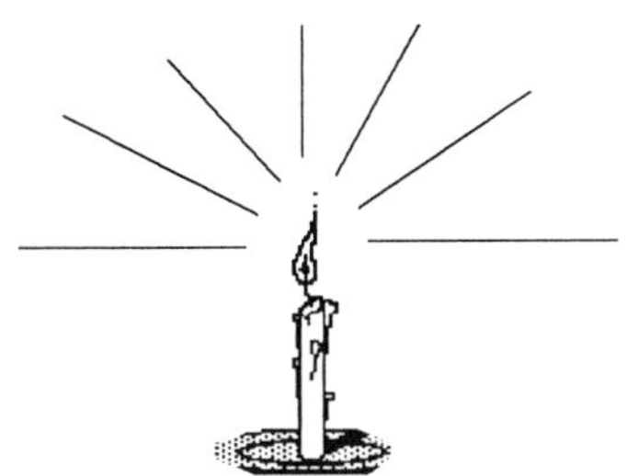

## Light Intensity

Light intensity varies through the year from summer levels at midday that exceed 10,000 footcandles to the darkest winter days with less than 500 footcandles. (One footcandle is the measure of the intensity of light one foot from a candle.) During the summer months, maximum photosynthetic rates are easily achieved due to high light intensity. Vigorous, stocky growth occurs. However, during the winter months, long periods of dark, cloudy weather greatly limit plant growth since rates of photosynthesis are significantly reduced. Plant quality will also decline, since the plant does not make enough food for vigorous growth. To offset this decline, supplemental lighting can be installed overhead in the greenhouse to raise light intensity and thereby improve the growth and quality of the crops beneath.

## HID Lighting

Several supplemental lighting systems are available. The most commonly used are High Intensity Discharge (HID) lamps of many different types. The most popular HID lamp in the floriculture industry is the high-pressure sodium lamp, which comes in 400 and 1000 watt sizes. (The 400-watt lamp is most frequently used.) These lamps are suspended several feet over the crop and have a reflector above them to direct light onto the crop below (Figure 4.13).

**Figure 4.13**

High Intensity Discharge (HID) lamps in operation. These are 400-watt, high-pressure sodium lamps in metal reflectors.

High-pressure sodium lamps emit good quality light and are very efficient. They convert 25 percent of the electricity used into usable light. (By contrast, incandescent lamps convert only 7 percent of the electricity used into usable light.) The life expectancy of the high-pressure sodium lamp is about 24,000 hours.

Other HID lamps that are used include high pressure mercury discharge and high pressure metal halide lamps (both more commonly used in Europe than in the U.S.) and low pressure sodium lamps.

### Fluorescent Lighting

Fluorescent lamps are commonly used in small germination rooms or other limited areas because of their low light intensity. They can be placed close to plants without burning them. They emit good quality light, however.

The use of fluorescent lighting in a large greenhouse operation would cast a lot of shade on the crop because of the number of fixtures required. In a large operation, fluorescent lighting would do more harm than good. So, it is limited to use in growth and germination chambers where supplemental light is the only light.

## Photoperiod Lighting and Shading

### Introduction

"Photoperiod" may be defined as the length of time experienced in light and in darkness by an organism in a 24-hour period. Photoperiod is very important in floriculture production because it affects the flowering and/or vegetative growth of several greenhouse crops. The photoperiod of these crops can be regulated so that they flower at a specific time.

By regulating photoperiod, growers can make plants flower at times of the year they would not naturally bloom. Mums (chrysanthemums) are one of the most important commercial crops that requires photoperiodic manipulation for year-round production. Mums normally flower in the fall when nights are long. (The length of night, **not** daylight, is actually what determines photoperiodic response in plants.) To bring mums into flower in late spring or summer, growers must artificially lengthen the night period. Some other photoperiodic greenhouse crops are poinsettias, kalanchoes, azaleas, and certain species of orchids. Most of these crops are "long night" plants; that is, they require long duration of darkness in order to bloom.

### Photoperiod Equipment

To lengthen the night, plants are covered with a light-proof cloth supported by wire framing (Figure 4.14). The wire keeps the cloth from damaging the plants as it is pulled past them. Shade cloth is applied in the late afternoon and removed in the morning. A tight-mesh, black sateen cloth or synthetic cloth is most commonly used for shading.

**Figure 4.14**

A light-proof shade cloth drawn over a bench of mums

One kind of shade cloth is white on one side and black on the other (Figure 4.15). On sunny, hot summer days, the white side of the shade cloth should be exposed when pulled. It will help reflect the late afternoon sun and thus greatly reduce heat build-up under the cloth. Many crops are delayed in blooming if exposed to high temperatures during bud and flower development.

Light penetration through the covering should be less than 2 footcandles in order to prevent delay of blooming and/or disfigured flowers. Shade cloth must be checked as it ages, as it may start to let light leak through. As it wears out, shade cloth can first be applied in double layers; then it should be discarded.

**Figure 4.15**

A light-proof shade cloth that is white on one side and black on the other

When growers want to keep long-night plants like mums from flowering (in late fall, winter, and early spring), they shorten the nights with supplemental light. One common practice is to split each long night into two short nights with supplemental light to prevent flowering and keep plants vegetative. Ten footcandles of light at crop level from incandescent lamps installed 2 to 3 feet above will prevent flower formation. This simulates plant growth conditions during the short nights of summer. It is commonly referred to as **standard mum lighting** (Figure 4.16).

If the light intensity of incandescent lamps is questionable, reflectors can be installed above them to increase the amount of light cast on the plants. Light meter readings should be taken periodically to make certain that the crop is receiving at least 10 footcandles of light.

A couple of lighting techniques in use are controlled by timers or computers.

- ✩ ***Continuous interrupted night lighting***, typically from 10 p.m to 2 a.m., has the same effect as extending the day. Both result in shortening of the night.
- ✩ ***Cyclic lighting*** is a method that supplies light at short intervals (typically 6 minutes per half hour) throughout the lighting period of 10 p.m. to 2 a.m. The results are the same as with the other two methods: shortened nights and vegetative growth. Growers save on their electric bills, since cyclic lighting uses significantly less electricity than does continuous lighting.

---

**Figure 4.16**

Poinsettia stock plants kept vegetative by the use of incandescent lamps above them (standard mum lighting)

### *In conclusion:*

Chapter 4 covered the two basic types of benches used in the greenhouse industry: ground benches for cut flowers and raised benches for bedding and flowering potted plants. The benching arrangements make use of from 50 percent to nearly 200 percent of usable production area. We discussed supplemental and photoperiodic lighting systems. Lighting systems such as HID lighting and fluorescent lighting are used primarily in winter when light intensities are low. By manipulating length of night, greenhouse crops that are photoperiodic can be forced into bloom on a year-round basis. Photoperiodic shade cloth and standard mum lighting are used to change the length of night.

## CHAPTER 4 REVIEW

This review is to help you check yourself on what you have learned about greenhouse equipment and lighting. If you need to refresh your mind on any of the following questions, refer to the page number given in parentheses.

1. What type of benches are used for cut flower production? for flowering potted plant production? *(pages 78-80)*
2. Draw the benching arrangements commonly used in the greenhouse industry. Which arrangements use more than 75% of the usable production area? *(pages 82-86)*
3. When is supplemental lighting needed in greenhouses? *(page 87)*
4. How does light intensity affect plant growth? *(page 87)*
5. What type of supplemental lighting is most commonly used in the greenhouse industry? *(page 87)*
6. What are the disadvantages of using fluorescent lighting for supplemental lighting? *(page 88)*
7. Define "photoperiod." *(page 88)*
8. How is photoperiod important to the greenhouse industry? *(page 88)*
9. Name three greenhouse crops that are photoperiodic with regard to flowering. *(page 88)*
10. What equipment is used to regulate the length of night, either delaying or promoting flowering of photoperiodic crops? *(pages 88-90)*

# CHAPTER 5

# GREENHOUSE IRRIGATION SYSTEMS

## Competencies for Chapter 5

As a result of studying this chapter, you should be able to do the following:

1. Determine plants' water needs.
2. Determine required quantity and quality of water.
3. Identify commonly used watering equipment.
4. Set and adjust irrigation system.
5. Maintain an automatic watering system.
6. Hand irrigate plants.
7. Discuss the use of intermittent mist systems.
8. Identify water quality monitoring devices.
9. Describe methods used to prevent ground water contamination.
10. Scout the crop for overwatering or underwatering problems.
11. Give the advantages of greenhouse environment control computers.
12. Control watering schedule by computer.

## Related Science Concepts

1. Define the measurement and use of the pH scale.
2. Follow steps to minimize spread of pathogens by watering system.
3. Time watering for most efficient use by plants.
4. Describe the physical and chemical properties of water.
5. Analyze water quality.
6. Interpret weather data from roof-mounted weather station.

## Related Math Concepts

1. Apply measuring skills to calculate amount of fertilizer to add to watering system.
2. Apply basic operations to whole numbers, decimals, and fractions.
3. Apply basic operations to ratios and percents.
4. Read, interpret, and construct charts, graphs, and tables.

## Terms to Know

acidity
aeroponics
alkalinity
asexual
aspirated chamber
capillary action
capillary mat
drip gutter
ECHO
geometric design
germination
hydroponics
intermittent mist
perimeter
pH
relative humidity
rockwool
runoff
soluble salts
spaghetti tubes
turgid
water breaker
weighted leaf

# INTRODUCTION

Water is one of the most important parts of a plant cell. It keeps plants turgid or crisp. Furthermore, water is the lifeblood of a plant. It transports food, carbon dioxide, and oxygen to all parts of the plant. If a plant does not get enough water, it will wilt and may even die. So, watering is an essential activity in any greenhouse operation. Several types of watering systems are available for watering greenhouse crops. These systems will be discussed next.

# WATERING SYSTEMS

## Hand Watering

Hand (manual) watering of greenhouse crops is the most accurate way of delivering water if the person who performs this task is conscientious and reliable. Every plant on a bench must be watered, and watered thoroughly with minimal waste of water. Some kind of water breaker is used on the end of the hose when hand watering to "break" the water pressure from the hose (Figure 5.1). This produces a gentle stream of water that will not wash soil out of pots and flats.

Greenhouse personnel who have the job of hand watering should remember one important rule: **Never allow the hose to touch the floor!** A hose dragged across the floor is very likely to spread disease to the crop, as no floor is germ-free. Disease organisms are easily transferred to the tip of the hose. Many growers suspend their hoses above the floor by a series of pulleys that allow the hose to be moved through an area without ever touching the floor (Figure 5.2).

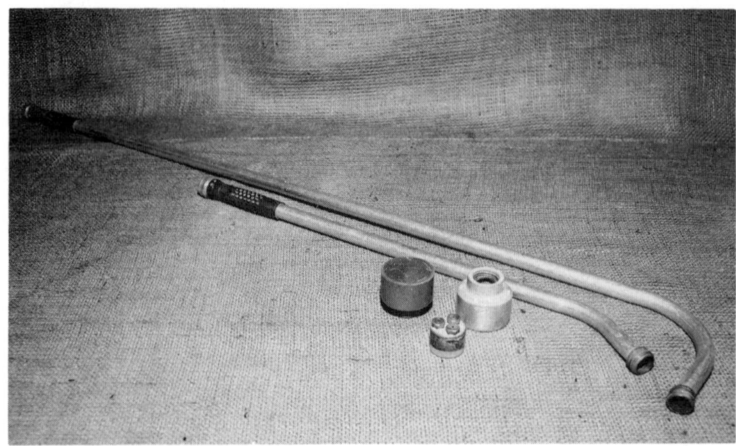

**Figure 5.1**

Breakers and extenders will be attached to hoses used in hand watering.

**Figure 5.2**
A hose used for watering is suspended above the greenhouse floor by pulleys.

## Automatic Watering

Though manual watering may be the "best" method of watering, it is very labor-intensive. Also, its effectiveness depends to a great degree on the person applying the water. There are several alternatives in watering systems that require a fraction of the labor of hose watering. These systems can be automated and are also very effective. They involve significantly lower production costs and can produce better quality crops.

### Spaghetti Tube Watering

#### *Chapin and Stuppy*

A spaghetti tube watering system for flowering potted crops consists of thin black tubes leading to individual pots from the water supply pipe, which is installed the length of the bench. At the end of each spaghetti tube is either a lead (Chapin) tube or yellow plastic (Stuppy) weight that holds the tube in the pot and disperses water into the pot (Figure 5.3). With this watering system, several hundred pots can be watered at the same time. Chapin and Stuppy tubes should be placed near the center of the pot for uniform wetting of the root medium.

#### *Water Loops*

Water loops are another form of spaghetti tube watering. With water loops, the spaghetti tube, in the shape of a ring at the end, has tiny holes through which water drips into the pot (Figure 5.4). Water loops distribute water more evenly through the pot. Particularly useful in large diameter pots, water loops are placed so that the plant is in the center of the loop.

### *Spray Tubes*

Spaghetti tubes can also be attached to spray tubes that consist of a plastic stake pushed into the soil. From a slanted surface at the top of the stake, water is dispersed into the pot (Figure 5.5). The stake makes a better anchor for this system than do the weights of the Chapin and Stuppy systems, which are easily dislodged.

---

**Figure 5.3** Two spaghetti tube watering systems. Note the larger black water supply line.

**A.** Chapin **B.** Stuppy

**Figure 5.4**

A water loop attached to the water supply pipe. Bottom view shows the tiny holes that allow the water to drop through.

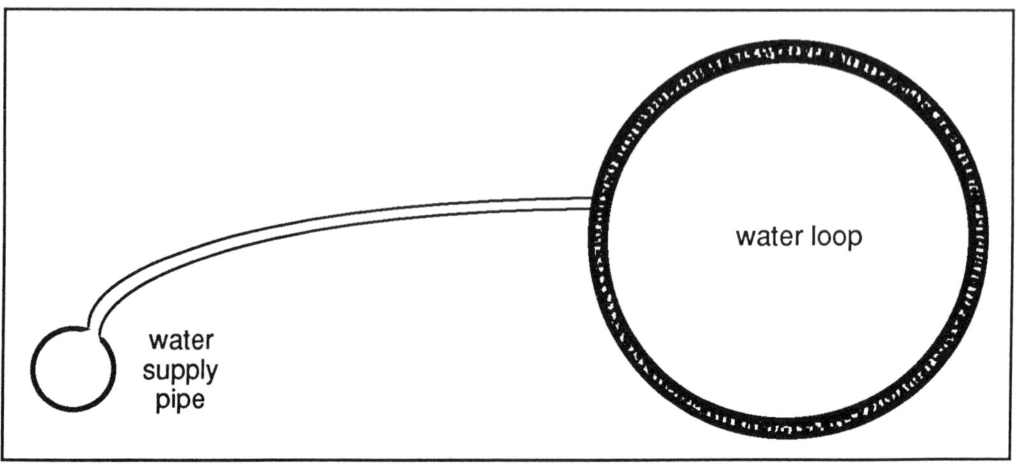

## Watering Systems for Hanging Baskets

### *Israeli Drip Watering*

This watering system was developed in Israel for use with hanging baskets. A plastic pipe is first installed above the hanging baskets. When the water supply is turned on, water drips into the hanging baskets from junctions evenly spaced in the supply pipe (Figure 5.6). Watering is uniform along the length of the water line. Since wet foliage results, watering should be done early in the day. Then by nightfall, with the plants dry again, there will be less chance for development of foliar disease.

### *ECHO Watering*

The ECHO system for hanging baskets enables growers to rotate and water hanging baskets without performing any labor. Several hundred hanging baskets are suspended from a moving cable (Figure 5.7). When they need watering, the cable rotates the hanging baskets slowly past a water breaker, which irrigates each plant as it passes underneath. As each basket clears the water breaker, the water shuts off until the next hanging basket is in place. The ECHO system can be totally automated as to time of watering and amount of water to be applied to each plant.

**Figure 5.5**
Spray tube showing spaghetti tube ending at slanted surface on stake for water dispersal

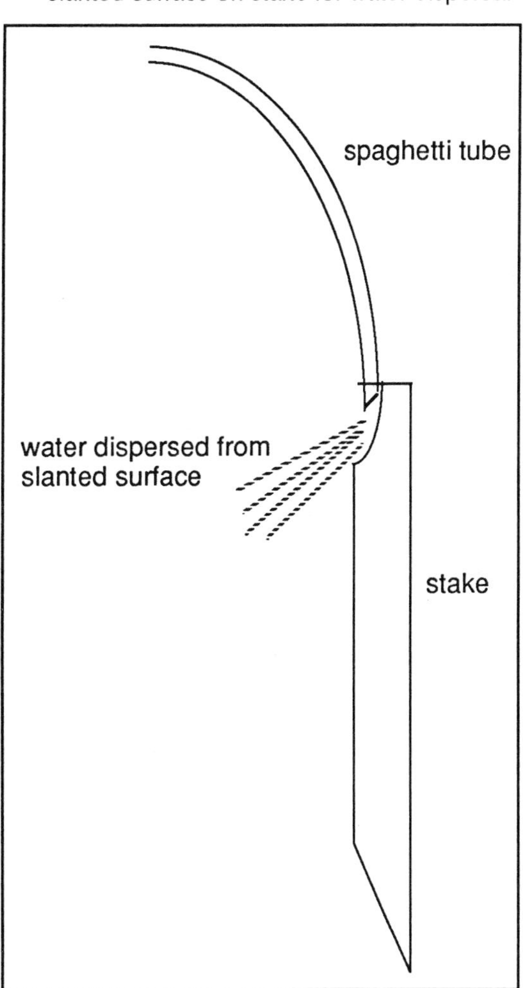


**Figure 5.6** An Israeli drip system, suspended by a support pipe, is used for irrigating hanging baskets.

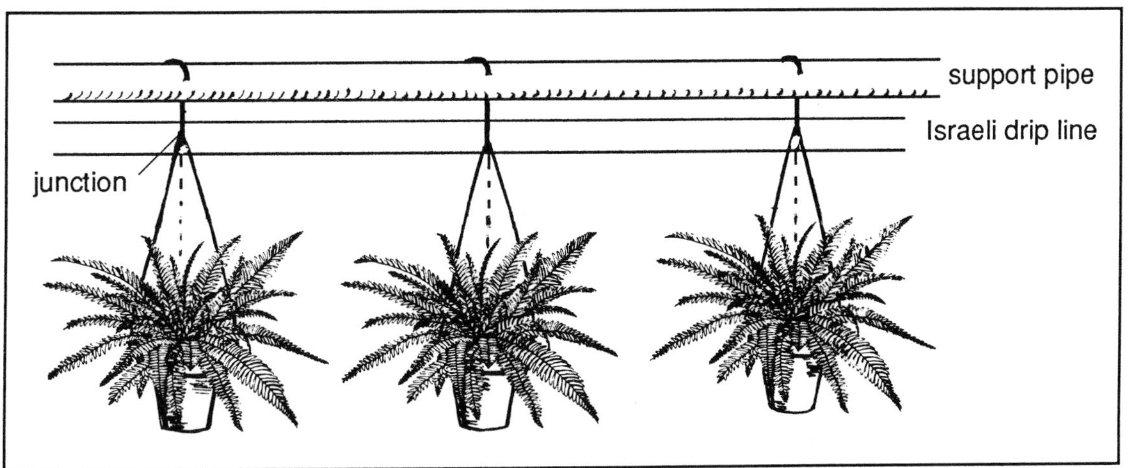

**Figure 5.7**
An ECHO watering system for hanging baskets

## Watering Systems for Cut Flower Crops

### *Ooze Tube Watering*

The ooze tube watering system is used for cut flower crops. Black plastic is sewn into tubes which run the length of the bench from a water supply line (Figure 5.8). Usually, ooze tubes are placed between every row in the bench to ensure uniform watering. When the water is turned on, water flows into the ooze tubes and inflates them. The pressure forces the seam apart somewhat and water oozes through to the soil. This slow, uniform method of irrigation does not wet the foliage of the cut flower crops.

### *Perimeter Watering*

A perimeter watering system is also used for cut flower crops. Plastic water supply pipe is anchored firmly around the outside edge (perimeter) of

**Figure 5.8** Ooze tube irrigation system with tubes between all the rows

Figure 5.9 A perimeter watering system used for cut flower crops

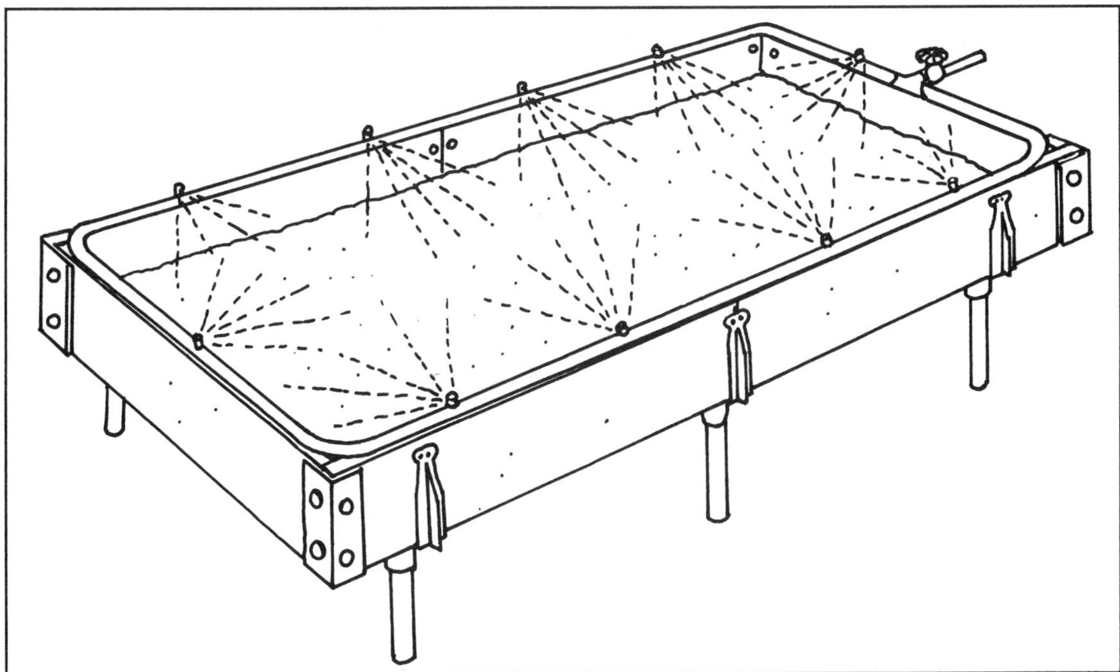

the bench (Figure 5.9). Nozzles, installed generally 20 to 30 inches apart in the pipe, apply water to the soil in a flat spray without wetting the foliage.

## Watering Systems for Potted Flowering Plants

### *Capillary Mat Watering*

Capillary mat watering is used for potted flowering plants. This is another method that does not wet the foliage, and thus is ideal for crops like African violets. Greenhouse producers who use this system must first level the benches and then lay a thin piece of plastic covering the bottom. A water-absorbent fiber mat is laid over the bottom layer of plastic. The mat is in turn covered by a second thin plastic sheet, perforated with thousands of tiny holes (Figure 5.10). This top layer of plastic is usually black for better control of algal growth. It also may be marked with a series of repeating geometric designs for spacing pots (Figure 5.11).

Figure 5.10 A capillary mat showing bottom plastic layer, water-absorbing fiber mat, and perforated plastic layer on top

The mat is kept moist usually by ooze tubes or spaghetti tubes installed on the bench. Potted flowering plants placed on the mat take up water by capillary action through the drainage holes in the bottom of the pot. The water in the mat travels through the holes or perforations in the top plastic layer and into the soil of the pot.

**Figure 5.11**

Geometric designs on the top layer of a capillary mat used for spacing a crop of African violets

With such a continually wet situation, however, algal growth on the mat can be a problem, even with the black plastic layer on top.

***Ebb and Flow Watering***

Ebb and flow watering is another irrigation system for potted flowering plants. It is like capillary mat watering in that 1) the foliage does not get wet, and 2) pots take up water through drainage holes by capillary action. Ebb and flow watering consists of level benches with plastic inserts to hold the water (Figure 5.12).

Water is pumped onto the bench until the bottoms of the pots are in water depths of between one-half and one inch. This usually takes 20 to 30 minutes. Water enters the pot through the drainage holes and moves up through the soil by capillary action. The water is then drained away into a reservoir to be reused (Figure 5.13).

**Figure 5.12**

Plastic insert in ebb and flow bench. Note grooves that rapidly drain off irrigation water.

Figure 5.13
An ebb and flow bench with a crop of poinsettias

Ebb and flow can also be used for floor-grown crops. Water is pumped onto concrete floors that have a very slight pitch to drain away the water.

Since this watering system reuses irrigation water, there is a danger of high soluble salts levels in the water becoming harmful for the plants. Therefore, the pH and salt levels in the water must be carefully monitored. (This topic will be discussed further under "Water Quality" on page103.) Often this is done automatically by computers. The computer can then direct any necessary corrective action. The computer can also be programmed as to frequency and timing of watering the benches (Figure 5.14).

## Overhead Nozzle Watering

Overhead nozzle watering is a method usually used only in the morning or early afternoon. Wet foliage needs time to dry by evening to avoid potential disease problems. Elevated nozzles are installed on a pipe that runs the length

**Figure 5.14** Computer used to control an ebb and flow system in a modern greenhouse

of the bench or greenhouse floor (Figure 5.15). On propagation benches, nozzles are commonly suspended overhead (Figure 5.16).

The nozzles used for watering crops produce a relatively coarse spray, while the nozzles used for rooting cuttings or germinating seeds produce a very fine mist. An overhead nozzle system can easily be automated for both crop and propagation applications.

---

**Figure 5.15**
An overhead watering system for bedding plants

**Figure 5.16** Mist system for plant propagation

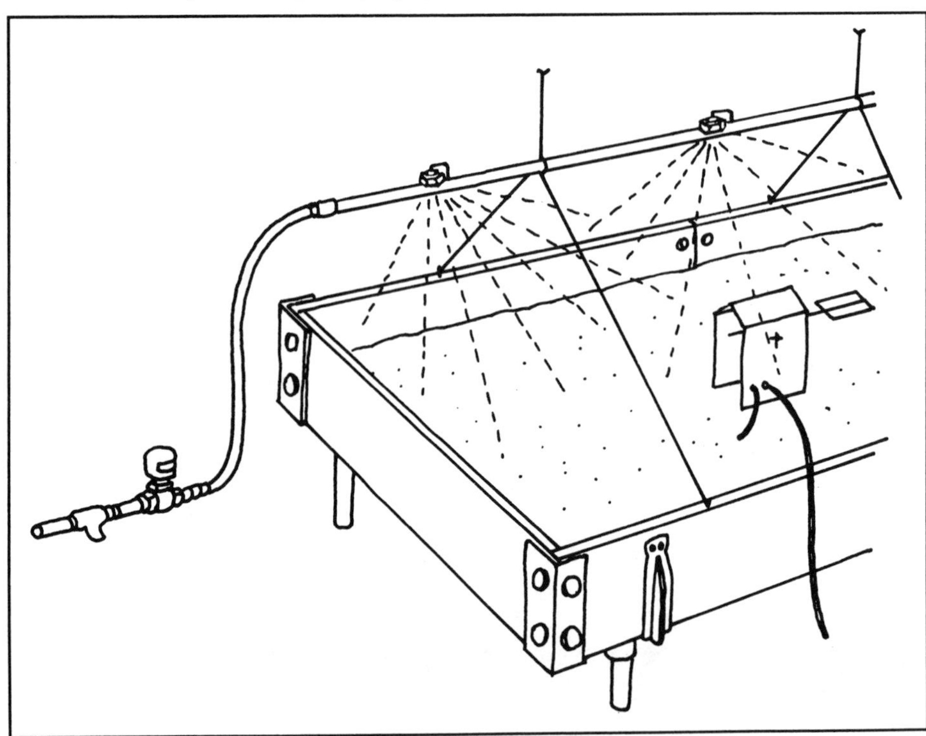

## WATER QUALITY

As mentioned in Chapter 2, good water quality is very important for any greenhouse business. All plants require water in large quantities. If water quality is poor, a poor crop will result no matter what else is done.

### pH

Two major factors of water quality are pH and the soluble salts level (a measure of alkalinity). The pH of a substance is a measure of its acidity or alkalinity using a scale of 0 to 14 (Figure 5.17). A pH of 7.0 is neutral, a pH reading less than 7.0 is acidic, and a pH reading greater than 7.0 is alkaline (basic). The pH scale is logarithmic. In other words, each one-unit increase in pH actually differs from the next by a factor of 10. For example, a pH of 5.0 is 10 times more acidic than a pH of 6.0. A pH of 9.0 is 100 times more basic than a pH of 7.0.

Why is the pH of water so important? The pH of water greatly influences the availability of nutrients in the water, as we will discuss later. Most greenhouses fertilize their crops by injecting concentrated liquid fertilizers in the water supply lines. If the pH is too acidic or too alkaline, the availability of some nutrients decreases and others will become toxic. For most greenhouse applications, water pH of 5.8 to 6.2 is satisfactory.

### Soluble Salts

Soluble salts are dissolved chemicals like fertilizer elements in the water. Ideally, irrigation water should be very low in soluble salts. Fertilizers can then be safely added to the water supply without ending up with a fertilizer solution that is too strong. A high soluble salt level plus fertilizer can result in a toxic water supply. High soluble salts levels in irrigation water will "burn" roots and ruin a crop. Soluble salts may also contain harmful pollutants.

Before ever building a greenhouse and starting a business, it is vital for you to have the water supply tested. Once in business, you also need to continue frequent checks of water quality. If you find that soluble salt levels rise fast in the water supply, you will have to install equipment (that is expensive) to remove soluble salts.

---

**Figure 5.17**
The pH scale. Numbers below 7.0 are acidic; 7.0 is neutral; numbers above 7.0 are alkaline (basic).

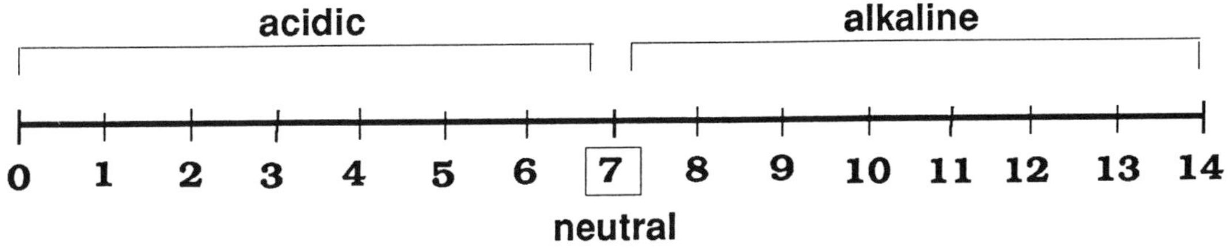

Alkalinity with regard to ***water quality*** is defined as the concentration of calcium carbonate and magnesium carbonate it contains. These two chemicals in the water, especially in high concentrations, make pH adjustment difficult. Adjustment of water pH must commonly be done for nutritional purposes. Research has also shown that water high in alkalinity may increase soil pH and thus harm the crop.

Thus, monitoring of water quality is a continuing task of prime importance. Equipment that monitors pH and soluble salt levels should be installed. Water tests should be frequently run. Good crops can not be raised using water of poor quality.

## Groundwater Contamination

Concern is mounting as to the status of our environmental well-being. Years of wasteful, careless practices by both the public sector and industry have resulted in damage to the earth's delicate ecosystems. The balance of nature can take only so much abuse before it is irreversibly upset. One of the major concerns involves groundwater. Approximately half of the population of the United States obtains drinking water from sources beneath the ground.

The agriculture industry has made a practice for years of applying chemicals to the soil for nutritional and pest control purposes. Now they are discovering that these chemicals are leaching into groundwater aquifers, polluting them. In many sites across the country, groundwater sources near chemical dumping areas and industrial sites are so polluted that the water is unfit to drink.

Like agronomic farming, the floriculture industry has contributed to groundwater contamination. Runoff water from greenhouses has often been shown to contain high levels of nitrates. Pesticide levels in greenhouse soil have frequently been tested high. Both nitrates and pesticides leach into the soil and contaminate groundwater. Soluble fertilizers and the whole fertilizer program used in the greenhouse industry contribute to this contamination problem. However, there are several options available to reduce or eliminate these problems.

### Responsible Measures to Take

1. **Use a closed irrigation system.**

   One method of reducing groundwater contamination is to use a closed irrigation system such as ebb and flow for benches and floors. Other systems that address the problem head-on are:

   * ***hydroponics*** - Plants are grown in a weak fertilizer solution that is recycled.
   * ***rockwool system*** - Nutrient solution is recycled through a synthetic, inert fiber.
   * ***aeroponics*** - Plants are suspended in air and their roots frequently misted by a nutrient solution.

In all these systems, there is no leaching of water into the soil. However, these systems, with their sophisticated equipment, are expensive to install.

**2. Water and fertilize only when necessary.**

Whether or not investing in a closed irrigation system is practical, there are simple ways to reduce groundwater contamination. Efficient fertilizer management is one of these. Water and fertilize only when needed by the plants. Base your schedule on environmental conditions, not on the clock or calendar. For example, do not water a moist root medium, but wait till the surface is dry. Learn how to recognize when the soil is dry by its appearance or by the weight of the pot. This practice saves time and water and reduces runoff.

**3. Limit leaching time.**

Leaching a crop involves continuing to water it after the soil has been saturated (i.e., when water has started to drip out of the pot's drainage holes). This practice is considered necessary to flush out excess soluble salts. But many growers allow water to leach from the pots for a long period of time after the soil has been saturated. Beneficial leaching actually takes less than one minute, usually. So leaching time during irrigation should be limited.

Leaching may not be required at all if a low volume of water is applied through a drip system like spaghetti tubes. The plants should be supplied just enough fertilizer that they use it all up, thus controlling salt levels in the soil.

**4. Select water-holding root media.**

Finally, select root media with good water-holding capacity. Soils that are too porous will not hold water very well; they dry out rapidly. Very porous soils require more frequent irrigation and offer greater potential for contamination. Root media with high water-holding capacity require significantly less irrigation and produce less runoff.

**5. Plan ahead for zero runoff.**

It is only a matter of time before legislation will be passed to prohibit water runoff from greenhouses. The time is already set by the government of the Netherlands. They have mandated a stop to all runoff from greenhouses in that country by the year 2000. Germany is about to follow the Netherlands' example. In the U.S., time is running out for our floriculture industry to curb groundwater contamination. **Now** is the time to severely limit or stop runoff before any more of our precious drinking water supplies are ruined. We have met and conquered many challenges before. With today's technology at our disposal and the will to meet those challenges, we can also solve this urgent problem of groundwater contamination.

# INTERMITTENT MIST SYSTEMS FOR PROPAGATION

## Introduction

Most of the crops used for potted flowering plants and some cut flower crops are propagated asexually by vegetative stem cuttings. Cuttings about 2 inches long are

- ☆ removed from stock plants,
- ☆ stuck in a rooting medium, and
- ☆ placed under an intermittent mist system so that roots will develop near the cut ends.

Intermittent mist maintains a constant film of moisture on the cuttings to keep them cool and prevent them from drying out. Rooting should then proceed without delay caused by water stress.

## Equipment for Intermittent Mist Systems

An efficient mist system must be able to deliver a fine mist consisting of tiny water droplets. Mist frequency should be easy to control. A basic mist system is composed of a water supply pipe with mist nozzles and a device to regulate frequency and duration of mist. Nozzles spray the fine mist out in a circular (360°) pattern. To cover the entire bench with mist, these nozzles are placed in the middle of the bench with proper spacing between them. The water supply pipe may be suspended directly over the bench. Or nozzles may be supported by vertical pipes that rise above the cuttings on the bench (Figure 5.18). The vertical pipes are supplied by the main water pipe installed on the bench.

---

**Figure 5.18** Propagation bench with poinsettia cuttings. Note the black mist nozzle supported by the white vertical supply line.

**Figure 5.19**

A drip gutter is installed beneath the water supply line to catch and drain away water dripping from the nozzles after misting.

A potential problem exists when nozzles that are suspended overhead continue to drip after misting is completed. Diseases readily develop in these areas of the bench that remain too wet. To prevent this, a drip gutter can be installed beneath the water supply pipe. Dripping water can be drained off by these gutters (Figure 5.19).

There is a control device in every mist system that activates a solenoid valve. This valve, an electromagnetic valve, is installed at the end of the supply pipe. The valve allows water to flow into the pipe to produce mist. The following discussion focuses on three mist control devices.

## Time Clock System

Different types of devices are used to control mist frequency and duration. One of the most common is the time clock. Two clocks are usually involved:

- ☆ a 24-hour time clock that determines the ***time of day*** that the mist system will operate (during daylight hours), and
- ☆ a minute timer that controls the ***frequency*** (usually with a 6-minute cycle) and ***duration*** (in seconds) of the mist.

## Weighted Leaf System

Another device to control intermittent mist is the weighted leaf (Figure 5.20). This mechanism is composed of a fine wire mesh screen or "leaf" attached to a switch. When the leaf is dry, it will be horizontal, activating the switch that turns on the mist. When the leaf collects enough water, it is weighed down, turning off the switch. The mist stops, and the cycle starts over again. At the other end of the leaf is a counter-balance that is adjustable. It controls the duration and the frequency of mist application.

**Figure 5.20** Weighted leaf mechanism (in the *on* position) for controlling the frequency and duration of intermittent mist

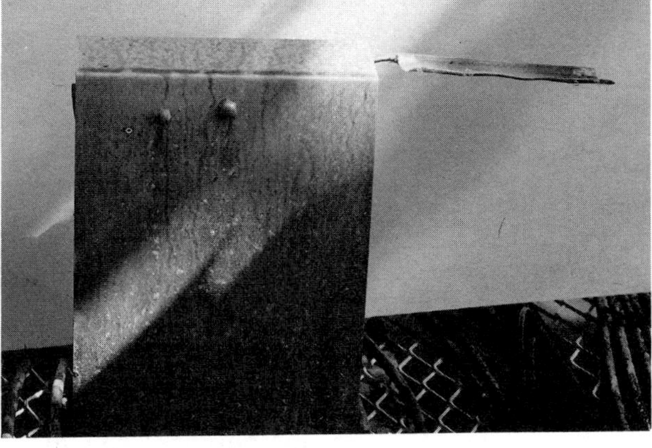

Unlike time clocks, the weighted leaf system of control reflects the current environmental conditions in the greenhouse. On sunny days, water evaporates faster from the leaf. Mist is automatically applied more frequently than on cloudy, cool days. Mist systems controlled by time clocks will not vary in frequency according to environmental changes. Time clock settings have to be changed. Otherwise, cuttings may become too wet for good disease prevention.

Use of the weighted leaf control system also results in water conservation, if operating properly. However, the weighted leaf system must be perfectly level and the leaf absolutely clean. If mineral deposits accumulate on the screen, the leaf will not operate properly. The screen must be cleaned periodically.

### Computer System

The other method of mist control is by computer. A computer can be programmed for mist frequency and duration. Some advanced models even take into account light intensity levels and temperature when determining misting cycles.

## GREENHOUSE ENVIRONMENT CONTROL COMPUTERS

### Introduction

Within the past ten years a revolutionary development has occurred in the greenhouse industry: the greenhouse environment control computer. This technology, already well established in Europe (especially the Netherlands), is now gaining momentum in the United States. Greenhouse environment control computers monitor many environmental factors and control them all precisely. The result of computer control is

- ✩ reduced labor costs,
- ✩ a more ideal production environment, and
- ✩ better quality crops.

The basic parts of a greenhouse environment control computer include the computer itself, sensors for monitoring indoor and outdoor conditions, and a personal computer used for programming and monitoring. There are also less expensive environment control computers called **zone maximizers**. These are similar to the larger computers except that they control fewer environmental factors. They are more affordable for the greenhouse grower who has a smaller operation.

### Monitored Environmental Factors

Greenhouse computers monitor many environmental factors:

- ✩ temperature
- ✩ light levels
- ✩ $CO_2$ concentration
- ✩ relative humidity
- ✩ (sometimes) soil moisture

Computers monitor these environmental factors by sensors installed in the greenhouse. These sensors are typically housed in aspirated chambers that are suspended close to the crop they are monitoring. The sensors can then get accurate readings of the immediate environmental conditions (Figure 5.21).

Conditions inside a greenhouse can be accurately controlled by a computer only if weather conditions outside the greenhouse are monitored. A weather station should be installed outside to measure wind direction and speed, temperature, and light intensity (Figure 5.22). The computer uses these factors for manipulating the inside environment.

---

**Figure 5.21**

Sensors for temperature, relative humidity, and $CO_2$ levels are housed in this aspirated chamber and monitored by a greenhouse environment control computer.

**Figure 5.22**

Weather station installed on the roof of a greenhouse monitors weather conditions for the greenhouse control computer.

## Controlled Environmental Factors

Greenhouse environment control computers monitor and control many environmental conditions in the greenhouse. These computers practically eliminate human error and the need for routine labor, which can then be used more efficiently in other areas.

### Temperature

The computer uses temperature sensors to measure heat levels in the greenhouse. It directs heating or cooling accordingly. All equipment controlled by the computer is directly wired into it or communicates over existing electric lines. Boilers, unit heaters, vents, and cooling systems are all activated by the computer according to programmed temperature limits.

### Light

Light intensity in the greenhouse is controlled by drawing a shade cloth across the greenhouse at eave height (Figure 5.23). (This shade cloth is different from the photoperiodic black-out cloth mentioned earlier.) The computer is programmed to pull the shade cloth when light intensity reaches a certain level. The drawn cloth reduces light intensity in the greenhouse and prevents burning of the crop. Cooling the whole greenhouse can be done more efficiently.

### Carbon Dioxide

The carbon dioxide ($CO_2$) level in the greenhouse is monitored by sensors. When it drops below a programmed set point, the computer activates a $CO_2$ generator (Figure 5.24). Sensors can be quite expensive, but they offer precise control of $CO_2$ levels. For efficient distribution of $CO_2$ throughout the greenhouse, the generator should be equipped with a fan or located near a fan.

---

**Figure 5.23**
A shade cloth drawn across the greenhouse lowers light intensity.

**Figure 5.24** Computer-controlled carbon dioxide generator disperses the gas with a fan.

## Relative Humidity

Relative humidity in a greenhouse is basically controlled in two ways:

1. by opening ventilators to reduce humidity, or
2. by adding a fine mist or fog to increase humidity.

Like the other factors, the limits for relative humidity are programmed into the computer. When the limits are exceeded, the computer takes corrective action.

## Watering

Greenhouse environment control computers can also control irrigation. Programming can include one or more of the following:

- ☆ set time periods
- ☆ soil moisture levels
- ☆ light intensity level
- ☆ weight of the pots

Probably the best control would be a combination of more than one of these items plus visual monitoring. Computer control of watering equipment requires the installation of solenoid valves in the water lines.

## Fertilizing

The level of fertilizers used in irrigation lines is frequently controlled by computers. Devices that measure the concentration and pH of the fertilizer solution are installed in the irrigation line. These devices continuously monitor the irrigation system and take corrective action instantly to maintain programmed set points.

## Alarm System

Most greenhouse environment control computers have built-in alarms that activate when environmental conditions exceed the set limits. The computer can activate alarms and even call responsible personnel by phone to alert them of the problem. An alarm system, whether it is computer-controlled or not, is an important part of any greenhouse operation.

## Disadvantages of Computer Control

While computers offer many advantages for controlling greenhouse environments, there are some disadvantages to consider.

1. Computers with a wide range of capabilities can be very expensive. Not all growers can afford such a large investment.
2. In the event of a power failure or computer malfunction during very hot or cold weather, the entire crop could be ruined. The safest practice is to have a procedure for disengaging the equipment from computer control so that the equipment can be operated manually.
3. Computers maintain set environmental factors; they do not have the capability of judging quality. A computer alone should never be relied on for long periods of time without the presence of greenhouse personnel. For example, it takes an experienced grower to detect a pest or disease problem in the early stages. Only such a qualified person can diagnose the start of nutrient deficiency symptoms and treat them.

In other words, the computer was never meant to replace the grower or manager. The computer can take over many routine tasks such as temperature control. Only ***people*** can judge the condition and quality of the crop. The computer is simply a complex tool that can help achieve ideal production conditions.

---

## *In conclusion:*

The watering systems discussed in Chapter 5 ranged from hose watering to such advanced systems as ebb and flow. Water quality should be constantly monitored in order to maintain pH and soluble salts at desired levels. Ground water contamination by the greenhouse industry must be stopped. Use of an alternate irrigation practice such as a closed, recirculating irrigation system is a possible solution. Mist systems apply mist through nozzles mounted overhead. This constant film of moisture is ideal for germinating seeds and rooting cuttings. Mist systems are controlled by timers, weighted leaf devices, and computers. Technological advances in the greenhouse industry include the greenhouse environment control computer. Such a computer is capable of monitoring many greenhouse environmental factors and maintaining them at pre-set levels. However, computers will never replace people (growers and others) who must make careful judgments on how to grow the crop.

## CHAPTER 5 REVIEW

This review is to help you check yourself on what you have learned about greenhouse irrigation systems. If you need to refresh your mind on any of the following questions, refer to the page number given in parentheses.

1. Why is hand watering not recommended for irrigating crops? *(page 95)*
2. What is the difference between Stuppy and Chapin spaghetti tubes? *(page 95)*
3. Name two irrigation systems that are used for hanging basket crops. *(page 97)*
4. How do capillary mat irrigation systems supply water to potted crops? *(page 99)*
5. What is an ebb and flow irrigation system? How does it work? *(page 100)*
6. Why is water quality so important for any greenhouse operation? *(pages 103-104)*
7. What aspects of water quality should be monitored? *(pages 103-104)*
8. Why is groundwater contamination such a concern? *(page 104)*
9. How does the greenhouse industry contribute to the groundwater contamination problem? *(page 104)*
10. How can present irrigation systems in the greenhouse industry be changed to stop groundwater contamination? *(page 104)*
11. What other cultural practices can growers change to lessen groundwater contamination? *(page 105)*
12. What is the main purpose of intermittent mist systems? *(page 106)*
13. Describe how mist is made and spread over the bench. *(pages 106-107)*
14. How are intermittent mist systems controlled? *(pages 107-108)*
15. What environmental factors are monitored or controlled by a greenhouse environment control computer? *(pages 108-111)*
16. Why do these computers have a weather station outside to monitor weather conditions? *(page 109)*
17. Why should the equipment controlled by an environment control computer also function when disconnected from the computer? *(page 112)*
18. As a greenhouse manager, how would you feel about leaving a greenhouse environment control computer growing your crops with no personnel present? Why? *(page 112)*

# CHAPTER 6

# ROOT MEDIA AND CONTAINERS

## Competencies for Chapter 6

As a result of studying this chapter, you should be able to do the following:

1. Give the four functions of a root medium.
2. Take a sample of root medium.
3. Identify the soil particles in soil.
4. Identify organic and inorganic components of soil.
5. Evaluate a soil sample for water-holding capacity, aeration, and compaction.
6. Define the difference between soil-based and soilless root media.
7. Identify amendments commonly added to root media and discuss their purpose.
8. Mix media materials.
9. Describe the process of and need for pasteurization of root media.
10. Use a pH meter and a solubridge.
11. Interpret results of root media tests as to pH, soluble salts, and nutrient levels.
12. Adjust root media pH with necessary chemicals.
13. Adjust soluble salts in root media.
14. Water and leach soil media as needed.
15. Identify containers commonly used for floriculture crops by name, size, and use.
16. Describe the commonly used propagation materials and the advantages of each.

## Related Science Concepts

1. Describe basic principles of cation exchange capacity (CEC).
2. Compare chemical properties of acids and bases.
3. Analyze soil structure.
4. Contrast the effects of pasteurization and of sterilization of soil.

## Related Math Concepts

1. Use percentages and ratios to formulate mix-your-own root media.
2. Apply basic operations to whole numbers, decimals, and fractions.
3. Apply basic operations to ratios and percents.
4. Read, interpret, and construct charts, graphs, and tables.

### Terms to Know

aeration
amendment
azalea pot
bulb pan
capillary pore
cation exchange capacity (CEC)
compaction
composted
decomposition
herbicide
inorganic
nematode
non-capillary pore
organic
pasteurization (soil)
peat pellet
plug tray
pore space
root medium
soilless media
standard pot
sterile
sterilization
water-holding capacity

---

## INTRODUCTION TO SOILS

All greenhouse crops are grown in some sort of root medium. This crop-growing substance greatly affects the functioning of the roots and hence the growth of the plant. Selection of the root medium is, therefore, one of the most important factors in producing quality plants in the greenhouse. While environmental factors like light intensity, temperature, and relative humidity can be easily changed, a root medium, once amended and used, can be quite difficult and costly to change.

Soil is a mixture of weathered particles of rock and decayed or decaying organic matter. These particles are separated by (usually) small pore spaces which contain water and air (Figure 6.1). Ideally, a soil should be composed of 50 percent solid matter, 25 percent air, and 25 percent water (Figure 6.2). As we shall see, pore spaces are very important.

---

**Figure 6.1** Soil particles and pore spaces

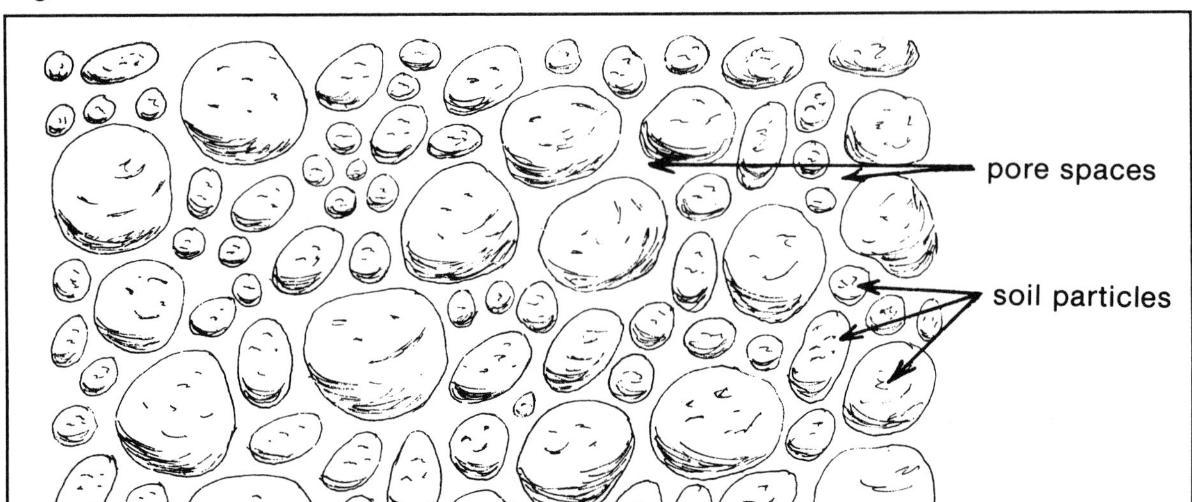

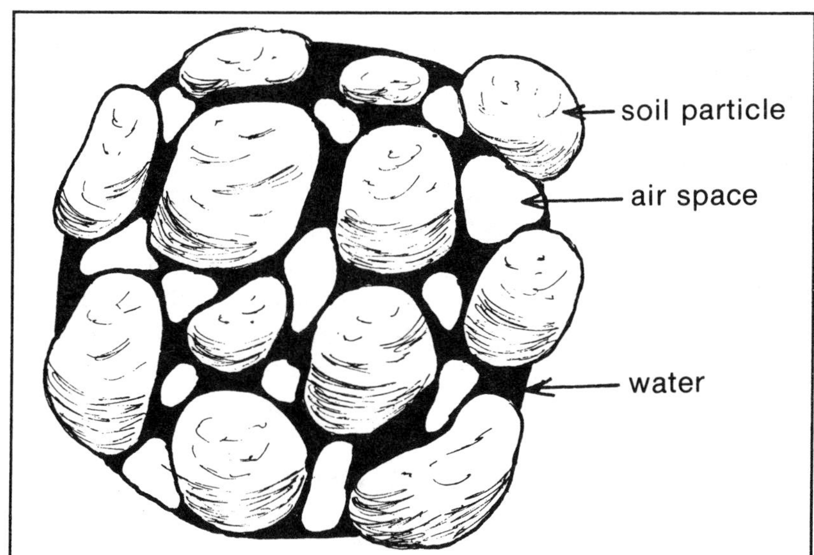


**Figure 6.2**

Ideal relationship of soil particles, air space, and water

Sand, silt and clay are the mineral particles found in soil. The size and relative amounts of these particles in a soil determine its texture (Figure 6.3). Texture is important in determining the water-holding capacity of a soil.

Clay particles are the smallest in diameter. Therefore, clay soils, with very small pore spaces, trap and hold more nutrients and water than do other soils. Clay soils can be slippery and heavy when wet. As they dry, the hard clumps that form are difficult to break up.

Sandy soils are composed of the most coarse-textured particles of the three sizes of minerals. These gritty soils have the lowest water-holding capacity of all the soils. Their relatively large pore spaces allow water to drain through very easily.

**Figure 6.3**

Soil texture refers to the size of the soil particles (sand, silt, and clay) and the relative amounts of each in the soil.

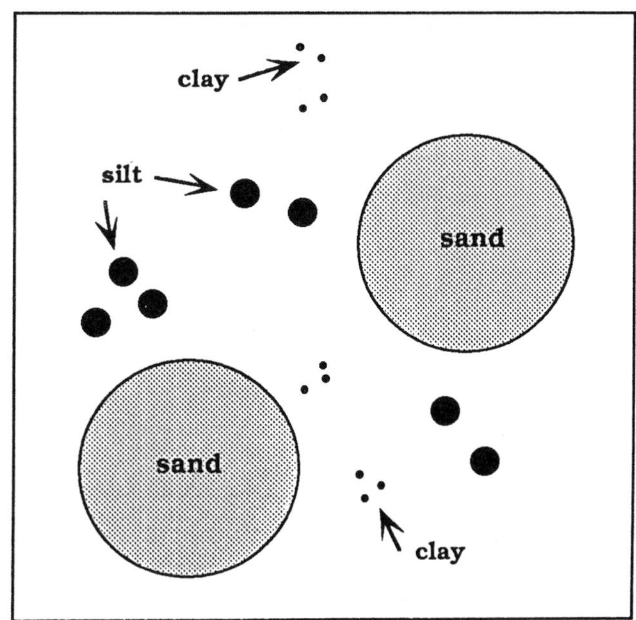


Particles of silt come in sizes that are between those of clay and sand particles (Figure 6.3). Therefore, silty soils are intermediate between clay and sandy soils in water-holding capacity. Various mixtures of sand, silt, and clay are referred to as **loam soils**. For example, a sandy loam soil is dominated by sand particles; a clay loam soil, which is a heavy soil, is dominated by clay.

One of the most important features of a soil is the pore spaces, which contain both water and air. There are two types of pore spaces: capillary and non-capillary. **Capillary** pore spaces are extremely small and therefore hold water. An example of capillary action is provided by an ordinary window screen. The spaces in the wire screen grid are the pore spaces. Dip the screen briefly into water. When you remove the screen, notice how much water is trapped in the screen. Most of the little spaces ("pores") are still filled with water that does not easily drain away. This is capillary action. Clay soils have the most capillary pore space of any soil.

**Non-capillary** pores can be compared to the large spaces in chicken wire. Dip a piece of chicken wire in water; remove it and examine it. You will find that the spaces do not retain water because they are too large. The water has run right through. Non-capillary spaces permit air movement, a desirable feature in aerating soils. Aeration is the flow of oxygen through the soil, an essential characteristic of a good root medium. For roots require oxygen just as the rest of the plant does. Sandy soils have the most non-capillary pore space of any soil (and the least capillary pore space).

# ROOT MEDIA

## Four Functions of Root Media

There are four main functions expected of all root media regardless of the crop being grown. These functions are:

1. to serve as a source of nutrients,
2. to supply a source of water,
3. to provide adequate aeration and drainage, and
4. to support the plant in its container.

These four functions of a root medium usually are characteristic of undisturbed field soils. But when soil from an undisturbed field is placed in a pot or flat, it often loses some of these properties (such as adequate capillary pore space). As a result, the soil no longer fulfills the four functions. It becomes a poor root medium for use with greenhouse crops. Our aim is to produce good greenhouse crops. So we will discuss next the types of root media that are used in the greenhouse industry, the components that are used, and proper media handling techniques.

## Types of Root Media

### Soil-based

Soil-based root media are used for cut flower crops grown in ground benches and for less than half of the potted flowering crops produced in the United States. Field soil is amended so that it is relatively lightweight. It has good water-holding capacity but also adequate pore space for good aeration and drainage. The soil used must be free of harmful insects, disease organisms, and weed seeds (all of which can be eliminated by pasteurization). The soil must also be free of herbicides. A common recipe for a soil-based root medium (by volume) is: one part loam soil, one part sphagnum peat moss, and one part perlite or sand. There is no single, ideal recipe, however, that can be used for all crops.

### Soilless

Soilless or artificial root media have become very popular for potted plant production in the past ten years. A soilless medium is a mixture of organic and inorganic ingredients, but contains no field soil (or very little of it). It can be mixed on site or purchased in bags already mixed. Soilless mixes are lightweight and easy to handle. They do not need to be pasteurized. The components of soilless root media are sphagnum peat moss, vermiculite, perlite, styrofoam, and bark or other organic ingredients.

Table 6.1 shows many of the advantages of soilless root media over soil-based mixes. Good, reliable, herbicide-free topsoil can be expensive and difficult to find. Growers must also consider the cost of labor, equipment, and facilities required to mix, sterilize, and store the soil.

## Sources of Root Media

### Commercial

All kinds of root media are readily available from commercial sources. The soilless root media are usually shipped in 4- or 6-cubic-foot bags from a wholesale greenhouse supply company. Commercially-produced root media commonly contain a "starter nutrient charge." In other words, the medium contains a small amount of fertilizer - just enough to boost the growth of a newly planted crop for a short time. There are available a lot of mixes that grow high quality crops. The grower must determine which mix is best for his/her particular situation.

The main reason for using commercially-produced mixes is ***convenience***. The time and cost of mixing your own root media is eliminated. Just make a quick phone call to order more root media. However, you lose control over how the mix is formulated. You have to assume that the mix was properly prepared. Also, the cost of commercially prepared mixes is considerably higher than for mixes made on site. You pay for the convenience of using mixes that are already prepared.

---

**Table 6.1** Advantages of soilless root media

1. A soilless root medium is prepared from a recipe and has the same characteristics from one batch to the next.
2. The components are easy to obtain.
3. Soilless root media can be mixed easily by mechanical methods.
4. Pasteurization usually is not needed, so preparation costs are reduced and energy is conserved.
5. Soilless root media are lightweight and easy to handle and use.
6. The four necessary functions of a root medium are easily achieved.

## Mix-Your-Own

Root media that are just as good in quality as commercially prepared media can also be prepared on site. The mix-your-own method offers the grower complete control of how the mix is prepared and what ingredients are added. The grower can "fine tune" the root medium to suit the particular needs of each greenhouse crop.

Mix-your-own root media do require labor and equipment, though with automated equipment, labor costs can be reduced. A soil-mixing machine is a necessity. In small greenhouses, some growers use portable cement mixers. In large greenhouse operations, the grower must invest in large equipment (Figure 6.4). Components of root media, such as sphagnum peat moss and perlite, must be obtained from supply companies and stockpiled to ensure a continuous supply. The needed chemical amendments, determined from soil tests, must also be added during mixing. Above all, various batches of the same root medium must be uniform over time. The grower must make sure that 1) the exact proportion of each ingredient is added (according to the recipe), and 2) thorough mixing of the root medium occurs.

So, mix-your-own root media do not have the convenience of commercial mixes. Mixing on site also requires an investment of labor and equipment. But the advantages are better quality control and usually lower-cost root media, when all factors are considered. The individual grower must weigh the advantages and disadvantages of commercially prepared mixes and compare them with those of mixes made on-site. The decision of which method to use (or whether to use both) is up to the grower.

---

**Figure 6.4**

A conveyor belt at the top feeds root media ingredients into a soil-mixing machine.

## Root Media Ingredients

All root media, both soil-based and soilless, must contain all the ingredients necessary for the four functions of a good root medium that we discussed. A single ingredient may partially meet the four requirements, but it takes a combination of two or more ingredients to get the job done. Root media ingredients are classified as either organic or inorganic.

***Organic*** root media ingredients, like tree bark, come from sources that were once alive. These ingredients make the following contributions to a root medium. They:

- ☆ improve water-holding capacity, drainage, and aeration.
- ☆ improve cation exchange capacity (which is the ability of a root medium to hold and make available nutrients for absorption by roots).
- ☆ reduce compacting of a root medium. (The improved structure or clumping of soil particles is especially important for soil-based root media.)
- ☆ decompose ***slowly*** enough that they do not tie up nitrogen. Fast decomposition will decrease the amount of available nitrogen for the roots and result in stunted plant growth.

***Inorganic*** ingredients come from non-living sources such as rock or clay. They do not decay like organic matter. Inorganic ingredients:

- ☆ improve aeration and drainage (like sand and perlite),
- ☆ improve cation exchange capacity (like clay and vermiculite),
- ☆ and provide support (like sand).

As we shall see, some of these ingredients are sterile, and others are not. With ingredients that are not sterile, the root medium must be pasteurized.

### Organic Ingredients

***Sphagnum peat moss*** is one of the most common organic ingredients used in root media. It is slightly decomposed sphagnum moss which grows in bogs. Sphagnum peat moss is light brown in color (dark brown when wet), and the sphagnum plant structure is still visible. It is very acidic. Root media containing peat moss may have to be amended with limestone to raise the pH to an acceptable level. Sphagnum peat moss has the highest water-holding capacity of any root medium ingredient. At the same time, it can be very difficult to wet. Root media high in peat moss should not be allowed to dry out completely. Sphagnum peat moss is shipped in 4- or 6-cubic-foot bales. The horticulture-grade material should be used.

Other types of peat are available, such as reed-sedge and peat humus. But these are not commonly used because they are much more decomposed and they become compacted easily. Also, they do not have the water-holding capacity of sphagnum peat moss.

***Composted bark*** is the other commonly used organic ingredient. The pieces of bark should be smaller than 1/4 inch in diameter for root media uniformity. Bark improves aeration and drainage and contributes to the cation exchange capacity. Certain types, such as pine bark, have been shown to inhibit root rot organisms.

***Composted yard waste***, a "new" root medium ingredient, is a mixture of composted leaves, grass clippings, and brush. Composting breaks down yard wastes into a rich, black root medium that is free of weed seeds, insects, and disease organisms. Root media that contain composted yard waste are still in the research stage. However, preliminary test results show that such media can grow fine-quality greenhouse crops.

There is increased interest in Ohio in using yard waste in the greenhouse industry because yard waste will soon be banned from Ohio landfills (in 1993). Landfills are rapidly filling up. Yard waste typically accounts for 20 percent of the volume of solid waste in landfills. Using composted yard waste in root media would be an environmentally suitable way to recycle some of the yard waste. It would also provide greenhouse growers with a high-quality root medium component.

## Inorganic Ingredients

***Perlite*** is volcanic rock that is heated to 1800°F. The heat "pops" the rock like popcorn and produces the familiar porous, white material known as perlite. Horticultural grade or coarse perlite is best for use in root media. It contributes drainage and aeration to the soil. But it has a low water-holding capacity and has no cation exchange capacity. The pH of perlite is slightly above pH 7.0.

***Vermiculite*** is a mica-type mineral that is heated at 1400°F. Instead of popping, the mineral expands and forms thin, parallel plates. The appearance of vermiculite is similar to the folds in an accordion. Vermiculite contains potassium, magnesium, and calcium for plant use. It also has good water-holding and cation exchange capacity. Vermiculite is somewhat alkaline, with a pH sometimes as high as 9.0. Horticultural grades 2, 3 and 4 are most commonly used in root media. When handled roughly, vermiculite can crumble and become compacted, losing its effectiveness.

***Calcined clay*** is a special type of clay heated to 1300°F. It is sold as 'Turface' in 50-pound bags. This clay is porous and has both good water-holding capacity and an excellent cation exchange capacity. It also provides good support. As an amendment, calcined clay usually makes up 10 to 15 percent of a root medium by volume.

The three inorganic ingredients just mentioned are all heated to high temperatures during their preparation. Therefore, they are sterile, free of weed seeds, disease organisms, and insects. No pasteurization is required when working with these root media ingredients.

***Rockwool pieces*** are a synthetic material that looks similar to fiberglass insulation. Small pieces of rockwool can be mixed into a root medium to improve its water-holding capacity.

***Coarse silica sand*** can be used to improve drainage and aeration of a root medium. It adds considerable weight and thus contributes support for plants. Sand does not have cation exchange capacity nor an appreciable water-holding capacity. Root media containing sand must be pasteurized since sand is not sterile.

***Water-holding compounds*** can also be mixed into the root medium to improve its water-holding capacity. These substances absorb many times their weight in water. Thus, they help extend the time between irrigations, reducing labor costs. Plant quality can be improved, since plants are less likely to wilt in such root media.

## Pasteurization of Root Media

Pasteurization of root media is sometimes done to kill harmful organisms (weeds, weed seeds, disease organisms, nematodes) without killing beneficial organisms (mainly fungi and bacteria) that maintain proper conditions in the soil. By contrast, sterilization of root media kills all organisms, both harmful and beneficial. In sterilized soil, the danger is that harmful organisms may recolonize the root medium first, while beneficial organisms lose out. With pasteurization, the beneficial organisms remain in the root medium and, hopefully, compete successfully with any harmful organisms that are trying to get established. In this way, beneficial organisms resist the establishment or spread of disease organisms in root media.

The most common pasteurizing agent for root media is steam. **Chemical pasteurization** is, however, used at times, especially in outdoor areas. Chemical root media pasteurization in greenhouses is very rare because:

1. the chemicals used are ***very*** toxic,
2. plants can not be planted in treated root media for seven to ten days after pasteurization,
3. workers must take extreme care while applying the chemicals, and
4. plants usually have to be removed during treatment.

**Steam-treated** root media, on the other hand, can be planted as soon as they cool. Steam is not toxic and is much easier to work with and apply. Care must be taken in the use of steam, however, as it easily burns skin and plants.

Ground beds in which cut flower crops are grown should be pasteurized after every crop. To prepare the bench for steaming, the soil is thoroughly tilled (broken up) and then mounded for better steam penetration. A steam distribution pipe is placed in the middle of the bench and extends the entire length. A tarp is placed over the bench and secured in place. Now the bench is ready for steam pasteurization (Figure 6.5).

While steam is applied, the heat level in the soil is monitored with a soil thermometer. The aim is to keep soil temperatures between 140° and 160°F, well below 212°F (the boiling point of water and the temperature of steam), when sterilization of the soil would take place. For these slightly lower temperatures, aerated steam is used. This mixture of steam and air lowers the temperature enough to complete pasteurization of the medium.

**Figure 6.5** Ground bed (for cut flowers) ready for steam pasteurization

**Figure 6.6**

A Lindig soil cart steaming a batch of root media for potted flowering plants

The process of pasteurization requires aerated steam to penetrate into the root medium under the tarp. From the time that the **coldest** part of the root medium has reached a temperature of 140°F to 160°F, steaming is done for 30 minutes. After the medium cools, it is ready for planting.

As previously mentioned, soilless root media do not usually require steaming because the ingredients do not harbor disease organisms. However, if soil-mixing equipment is exposed to dust and debris, or soilless media ingredients become contaminated (bags torn open and contents exposed), it is a good idea to pasteurize even soilless root media. Soil-based root media for potted and bedding plants should **always** be pasteurized.

One method of pasteurizing root media for potted and bedding plants is to use a Lindig soil cart with a perforated false bottom (Figure 6.6). Steam is injected into the area beneath the false bottom and is driven up into the soil through perforations. A tarp tied on to the top of the cart contains the steam. As with pasteurization of ground beds, the root medium in the cart is steamed for 30 minutes after the coldest portion of the medium reaches 140° to 160°F.

## Root Media Analysis

Nutritional requirements of plants vary among crops and according to season of the year, stage of crop growth, and environmental conditions. Excess fertilizer can injure plants; insufficient amounts can result in stunted growth and poor quality plants. For these reasons, it is very important for growers to monitor their fertilizer program by conducting root medium analyses. These can be done at the greenhouse using testing equipment and kits from manufacturers. Also, the grower can send root medium samples for analysis to the local Cooperative Extension Service. In Ohio, analysis of the sample is then done at the Research–Extension Analytical Laboratory (REAL) in Wooster.

## Sample Collection Procedure

Whether the root medium is analyzed in the greenhouse or at a lab some distance away, samples must first be obtained. Following are the steps recommended for taking samples from a ground bench or crop container (such as pots, flats, hanging baskets).

1. Obtain a clean container, preferably glass or plastic.
2. Randomly select sites for sampling ***throughout*** the ground bed or raised bench so that the root medium sample will be representative of the ***entire*** bench.
3. Remove any surface mulch and the top half-inch of root medium to obtain an accurate analysis.
4. With a trowel or soil sampling probe (which is similar to an oversized cork borer), remove samples of the root medium from the depth of the root zone in the randomly selected sites. Place samples into the clean container.
5. Mix the samples together and label.

Then, if sample testing is done in the greenhouse,

6. Take the samples to the testing area in the headhouse. A well-equipped greenhouse will have tables available for interpreting results (Table 6.2).

OR

If the sample is to be sent to a laboratory for analysis,

6. Place container with samples in a shipping container. Complete the information sheet supplied by the laboratory or Extension Service and submit it with the sample (Figure 6.7). This sheet provides pertinent information that is used by the laboratory to interpret the results correctly. Growers receive a detailed report that shows nutrient, soluble salt, and pH levels (Figure 6.8A, page 127). The report also includes recommendations for correcting any nutritional aspects that are not at optimum levels (Figure 6.8B, page 128).

---

**Table 6.2** Interpreting soil test results

| Soil Ingredient | Low | Slightly Low | Optimum | Slightly High | High | Excessively High |
|---|---|---|---|---|---|---|
| **Major Elements** | | | | | | |
| ppm nitrate (nitrogen) | below 60 | 60-100 | 100-175 | 175-200 | 200-275 | over 275 |
| ppm phosphorus | below 6 | 6-8 | 8-14 | 14-16 | 16-20 | over 20 |
| ppm potassium | below 150 | 150-175 | 175-225 | 225-250 | 250-350 | over 350 |
| ppm calcium | below 200 | 200-250 | 250-325 | 325-350 | 350-500 | over 500 |
| ppm magnesium | below 70 | 70-80 | 80-125 | 125-135 | 135-175 | over 175 |
| **pH** | | | | | | |
| soil mix [1] | 5.9 & below | 6-6.4 | 6.5-6.8 | 6.9-7.2 | 7.3-7.6 | 7.7 & over |
| soilless mix [2] | 5.2 & below | 5.3-5.5 | 5.6-6 | 6.1-6.5 | 6.6-7.3 | 7.4 & over |
| **Soluble Salts** | | | | | | |
| not planted | below 1.25 | 1.25-2 | 2-3 | 3-3.5 | 3.5-4.25 | over 4.25 |
| planted | below 1.5 | 1.5-2 | 2-3.5 | 3.5-3.75 | 3.75-5 | over 5 |

[1] more than 20% soil [2] less than 20% soil

**Figure 6.7** Information sheet submitted with root medium sample for testing at the Research–Extension Analytical Laboratory.

THE RESEARCH - EXTENSION ANALYTICAL LABORATORY
OHIO AGRICULTURAL RESEARCH AND DEVELOPMENT CENTER
THE OHIO STATE UNIVERSITY
WOOSTER, OHIO 44691 TELEPHONE (216) 263-3760

# FLORAL CROP GROWING MEDIUM ANALYSIS

(SOILLESS MIX -- FOR COMMERCIAL GROWERS ONLY)

PLEASE PRINT

CHECK ONE: ☐ STANDARD TEST - $10.00 ☐ STANDARD PLUS MICRONUTRIENTS - $20.00 (minimum 600cc/sample required)

☐☐☐☐☐☐☐ Copy No. from Sample Bag

DATE MAILED ________

GROWER NAME ________

STREET ROUTE ________

CITY/STATE/ZIP ________

YOUR TELEPHONE NUMBER (INCLUDING AREA CODE) ________

Accuracy of Recommendations depend on the completion of this form

**SAMPLE INFORMATION - WRITE APPROPRIATE NUMBERS IN BOXES AT LEFT AND FILL IN BLANKS**

**STANDARD TEST DISCOUNT INFORMATION:**

| | |
|---|---|
| 5 - 10 PREPAID SAMPLE BAGS | $9.00 / SAMPLE |
| 11 OR MORE PREPAID SAMPLE BAGS | $8.00 / SAMPLE |

one digit per box

☐☐☐☐☐ YOUR SAMPLE IDENTIFICATION

☐ CROP (check only one box)

| | | |
|---|---|---|
| 01 Azalea | 06 Easter Lily | 11 Kalanchoe |
| 02 Bedding plant (specify) ________ | 07 Foliage Plant (specify) ________ | 12 Poinsettia |
| 03 Bulb (specify) ________ | 08 Geranium | 13 Rose |
| 04 Chrysanthemum | 09 Gloxinia | 14 Other (specify) ________ |
| 05 Cyclamen | 10 Hydrangea | |

☐ CROP STATUS: 1. Not planted 2. Planted (number of weeks) ________ 3. Seedlings

☐ TYPE OF PLANTING: 1. Potted Plant 2. Ground bed 3. Raised bench 4. Paks or flats 5. Interior Plantscape (if so, light intensity measurement at sampling site was ______ foot candles.)

**GROWING MEDIUM SPECIFICS**

☐ STEAM STERILIZED? 1. Yes 2. No

☐ FUMIGATED? 1. Yes 2. No

Component Ratio (or Percentages) of Medium?

Soil ________ Sand ________ Sphagnum ________ Muck Peat ________ Perlite ________

Vermiculite ________ Styrofoam ________ Bark (type) ________ Other (specify) ________

(If components not known, then estimate percentage of field soil in growing medium)

☐ Was Lime applied? 1. Yes 2. No

☐ If so, what type? 1. Agricultural 2. Dolomitic 3 Hydrated, Rate ________

☐ How have or will plants be fertilized? 1 Dry Fertilizer 2. Slow Release 3. Injector 4. Hozon

☐ If Injector or Hozon, indicate frequency of application. 1. Constant 2. Once-weekly 3. Other (specify) ________

Type of fertilizer used or to be used.
Analysis or Components ________

Rate ________

**PROBLEM SITUATION**

☐ Are you now having a serious problem with this crop which may be related to nutrition?
1. Yes 2. No.

**Figure 6.8A** Example of a growing medium analysis report showing levels of pH, soluble salts, and selected nutrients. Note that pH is very high, and nitrate nitrogen, calcium, and magnesium are at optimum levels.

OHIO FLORAL CROP GROWING MEDIUM ANALYSIS REPORT

OHIO COOPERATIVE EXTENSION SERVICE, THE OHIO STATE UNIVERSITY, AND THE OHIO AGRICULTURAL RESEARCH AND DEVELOPMENT CENTER, COOPERATING
WED, JUL 10, 1991

LAB NUMBER 906

SAMPLE BAG # FT21932
YOUR ID # 10
DATE SUBMITTED / / WOOSTER OH 44691
RECEIVED 07/09/91

CROP INFORMATION:
CROP:
N GUINEA I
PLANTED
12 WEEKS
POTTED PLANT

MIXTURE INFORMATION:

| | | | | | |
|---|---|---|---|---|---|
| * SOIL | 0 | SPHAGNUM PEAT | 20 | *FERTILIZED | |
| * SAND | 0 | VERMICULITE | 0 | * N | 0 |
| * PERLITE | 35 | STYROFOAM | 0 | * P | 0 |
| * MUCK PEAT | 0 | BARK( ) | 0 | * K | 0 |
| * | | COMPO | 45 | * | |

STEAM STERILIZED? NO PLANNED FERTILIZATION:
FUMIGATED? NO NOT GIVEN 0: 0: 0
LIME? 1

ANALYTICAL RESULTS

| | PH | SOLUBLE SALTS (MMHO) | NITRATE NITROGEN (PPM) | PHOSPHORUS (PPM) | POTASSIUM (PPM) | CALCIUM (PPM) | MAGNESIUM (PPM) |
|---|---|---|---|---|---|---|---|
| TOXIC | | | | | | | |
| EXCESSIVE | | | | | | | |
| VERY HIGH | XXX | | | | | | |
| | XXX | | | | | | |
| HIGH | XXX | | | XXX | | | |
| | XXX | | | XXX | | | |
| SLIGHTLY HIGH | XXX | XXX | | XXX | XXX | | |
| | XXX | XXX | | XXX | XXX | | |
| OPTIMUM | XXX | XXX | XXX | XXX | XXX | XXX | XXX |
| | XXX | XXX | XXX | XXX | XXX | XXX | XXX |
| SLIGHTLY LOW | XXX | XXX | XXX | XXX | XXX | XXX | XXX |
| | XXX | XXX | XXX | XXX | XXX | XXX | XXX |
| LOW | XXX | XXX | XXX | XXX | XXX | XXX | XXX |
| | XXX | XXX | XXX | XXX | XXX | XXX | XXX |
| VERY LOW | XXX | XXX | XXX | XXX | XXX | XXX | XXX |
| | XXX | XXX | XXX | XXX | XXX | XXX | XXX |
| | XXX | XXX | XXX | XXX | XXX | XXX | XXX |
| EXTREMELY LOW | XXX | XXX | XXX | XXX | XXX | XXX | XXX |
| LABORATORY VALUE | 7.1 | 3.60 | 120 | 19 | 247 | 279 | 111 |
| PERCENT OF TOTAL SALTS | | | 5 | 1 | 10 | 11 | 4 |

*(over)*

**Figure 6.8B** Part of the same growing medium analysis report that gives recommendations.

**RECOMMENDATIONS**

PH:

APPLY 2 OUNCES OF IRON SULFATE IN 5 GALLONS OF WATER OR AS AN ALTERNATIVE, MIX 6.5 OUNCES IN OLNE GALLON OF WATER AND APPLY THIS SOLUTION USING A 1:15 PROPORTIONER (HOZON). REPEAT APPLICATIONS ONCE WEEKLY 2 TO 3 TIMES.

LOWERING PH

SULFUR- INCORPORATION OF SULFUR RESULTS IN A GRADUAL LOWERING OF PH. IT IS NOT WATER SOLUBLE SO IT SHOULD BY USED ONLY FOR PRE-PLANT PH ADJUSTMENT. MIX RECOMMENDED AMOUNT THOROUGHLY INTO MEDIUM.

IRON SULFATE- IRON SULFATE (FERROUS) QUICKLY LOWERS PH. AS A FINE POWDER IT CAN BE THOROUGHLY MIXED INTO GROWING MEDIUM PRIOR TO PLANTING OR THE RECOMMENDED AMOUNT CAN BE DISSOLVED IN WATER AND THE SOLUTION SPRINKLED ON DURING MIXING.

ALUMINUM SULFATE- ALUMINUM SULFATE IS RECOMMENDED FOR LOWERING GROWING PH FOR HYDRANGEA CROPS ONLY SO AS TO AVOID POTENTIAL ALUMINUM TOXICITY WITH OTHER CROPS. METHOD OF APPLICATION IS THE SAME FOR IRON SULFATE.

SOLUBLE SALTS:

BE CERTAIN YOU ARE APPLYING ENOUGH IRRIGATION SOLUTION SO THAT SOME DRAINS FROM POTS, PAKS, FLATS AND BENCHES OR SEEPS DEEPLY INTO GROUND BEDS TO LEACH OUT OLD SALTS. CALIBRATE YOUR FERTILIZER INJECTOR AND CHECK YOUR CALCULATIONS AND MIXING PROCEDURES. 200-300 PPM NITROGEN AND POTASSIUM IS RECOMMMENDED FOR A CONSTANT FEED PROGRAM.

PHOSPHORUS:

HIGH PHOSPHORUS LEVELS ARE GENERALLY NOT A PROBLEM. WITH A HIGH LEVEL OF PHOSPHORUS ONLY NITROGEN AND POTASSIUM NEED TO BE SUPPLIED WHEN USING A CONSTANT FEED PROGRAM.

## Importance of Root Medium pH

Measurement of root medium pH is important because pH governs the availability of fertilizer elements. (See page 103 for a discussion of pH.) The pH of a soil-based root medium should be in the range of 6.2 to 6.8. The pH of a soilless root medium should be between 5.4 and 6.0. In these pH ranges, the 17 essential nutritional elements are at their maximum availability ***when taken as a whole.*** In these pH ranges the best growth of most greenhouse crops occurs (Figure 6.9).

**Figure 6.9** Media pH for most plants should be in the 6.3 to 7.4 range.

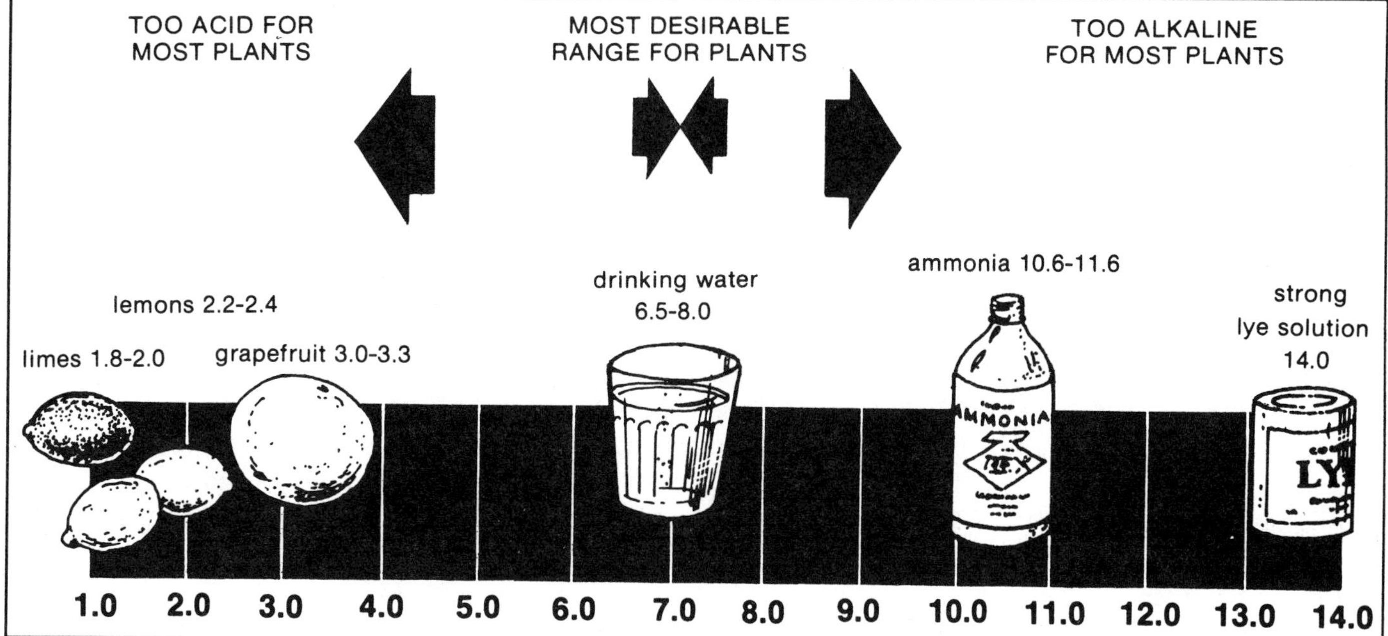


Some crops, however, have different root medium requirements. Azaleas and gardenias, for example, grow best in a very acidic root medium because of their high iron requirement. Iron is more readily available at low pH levels. Optimum pH ranges for specific greenhouse crops will be discussed later in the production chapters.

## Adjusting pH of Root Media

### Raising pH

There are several materials that can be used to adjust the pH of root media. The first group we will discuss includes amendments that can be mixed with the root medium to **raise** pH.

***Calcium hydroxide***, also known as hydrated lime, is used at a rate of one to four pounds per cubic yard of root medium. One pound of calcium hydroxide can also be mixed in five gallons of water and applied to 20 square feet of ground bench. The amount applied depends upon the starting pH and the type of root medium. A rapid (though rather short-lived) pH change and an increase in the soluble salts level are the results. But this amendment should be used with caution. Calcium hydroxide is much more reactive than agricultural limestone. Calcium hydroxide can damage roots and injure foliage.

***Calcium carbonate***, also known as agricultural limestone, is slower in action, but safer to use on plants than is hydrated lime. ***Dolomitic limestone*** is preferred over agricultural limestone because it is a combination of calcium and magnesium carbonate. It supplies both calcium and magnesium. Both agricultural and dolomitic limestone are applied at rates of 2 to 4 pounds per cubic yard, depending on the type and pH of the root medium.

### Lowering pH

In several instances, pH of the root medium has to be lowered. In the following section, we will discuss root medium amendments that **lower** the pH.

***Sulfur*** is slow-acting but relatively long-lasting. One-quarter to two pounds of sulfur per cubic yard will usually begin to lower pH of the root medium in six to eight weeks. Sulfur must be mixed into the root medium during preparation because it is not water soluble. Thus, sulfur can not be used to adjust the root medium pH of planted crops.

***Iron sulfate*** is faster-acting at lowering pH of the root medium than is sulfur. The rate of application in powder form is one-half to four pounds per cubic yard. In liquid applications, the rate is two ounces of iron sulfate per five gallons of water. Iron sulfate serves the dual purpose of lowering pH and supplying iron to plants. After application, any residue should be washed off plants to prevent injury.

## Adjusting Soluble Salts Levels

Excess soluble salts levels in the root medium can be lowered by leaching. (Leaching is the application of a small amount of excess water to wash away or reduce soluble salts levels.) This practice does contribute to ground water contamination, however, in any greenhouse that does not have a closed, recirculating irrigation system.

One leaching routine is to water the crop normally, wait for 1/4 to 1/2 hour to let the water soak through the root medium, water again normally, and repeat this procedure the next day. Conduct a soil test to see if this corrected the problem.

If the soluble salts level is only slightly high, stop fertilizing for a day or two. Then conduct a soil test to determine whether the problem has been corrected. **High** soluble salts levels in root media mean one of two things (and sometimes both):

1. fertilization is done too often, or
2. the concentration of fertilizer is too high.

Thus, along with leaching, an adjustment of the fertilizer program may be needed.

When levels of soluble salts are **low**, either frequency or concentration of fertilizer (and sometimes both) is at fault. Gradual increase of the concentration of fertilizer should solve the problem. If that fails, frequency of fertilization may also be increased. When you have to alter the fertilizer program, be sure to conduct frequent soil analyses to monitor changes in soluble salts levels.

## Adjusting Nutrient Elements

A report on nutrient element levels in a particular root medium can be obtained from soil testing laboratories such as the Research-Extension

Analytical Laboratory. Recommendations are given in the report for altering levels of individual elements in the root medium ***as needed.***

When root medium tests are conducted in the greenhouse, two pieces of equipment are needed: a pH meter, for measuring pH, and a solubridge (to be discussed in Chapter 7), an instrument for measuring the soluble salts content in the soil. The procedure is easy. Instructions are available from the county Extension Service and in other references.

# CONTAINERS FOR FLORICULTURE CROPS

Greenhouse crops are grown in ground benches, pots, flats, and hanging baskets. Most of them are propagated by cuttings or seed. The selection of containers to be used in production of potted flowering plants, bedding plants, and hanging baskets, and for propagation purposes is very important. The size and type of container affects quality, efficiency, and cost of production. The main factor to be considered in selection of containers is the type of crop being produced (for example, potted flowering crops or bedding plants).

## Pots

### Materials

#### *Clay*

For many years, right through the first half of the twentieth century, nearly all pots were made of clay. Clay is porous; that is, it allows air to pass through it. Root media in pots, therefore, are well aerated and are less likely to develop root rot diseases. Also, clay pots often last a long time. They can be used and reused many times, provided they have been steam-sterilized.

However, the cost of clay pots has increased considerably, adding to the costs of production. Also, clay pots are quite heavy. This can be an advantage in that clay potted plants are less likely to tip over. But these pots are also heavier to lift, a factor which adds strain to workers handling the pots. Also, shipping costs are increased. Because clay pots are porous, the root medium tends to dry out more quickly, and thus may require more frequent watering and fertilizing. Over time, an unsightly white crust builds up on the outside of clay pots. This build-up is actually fertilizer salts that will have to be removed by scrubbing. Finally, clay pots are subject to breakage.

#### *Plastic*

Most growers today use plastic pots. Plastic pots are much less expensive than clay pots. Plastic pots are lightweight, a characteristic which means lower production costs and easier handling of crops. Since plastic pots are ***not*** porous, fertilizer salts can not pass through the walls of the pot. There is no unsightly build-up on the outside of a plastic pot. Any residues that do accumulate on the plastic pot are easily removed. These thin-walled pots are available in many sizes and colors. Also, the root media in plastic pots require less frequent watering, since air can not pass through the walls of the pot.

The main disadvantage of plastic pots is that overwatering can occur very easily. The root medium in a plastic pot stays moist for longer periods of time than in a clay pot, and aeration is reduced. It is very important to let the surface of the soil dry out before watering crops grown in plastic pots. This will allow for aeration of the soil and prevent root rot organisms from getting established. If this "drying-out" procedure is not followed, overwatering and root rot will probably occur.

Plastic pots that are being reused should be stored in closed containers to prevent them from being contaminated. New plastic pots are sterile and can be used directly out of the box. In addition, plastic pots should be stored out of direct light, as light makes pots brittle and more readily breakable.

**Pot Types**

Regardless of the material used in making pots - clay or plastic - there are three basic types of pots that are commonly used in the greenhouse industry (Figure 6.10):

- ☆ standard pot
- ☆ azalea pot
- ☆ bulb pot or pan

**Figure 6.10** Three types of pots used in greenhouses (left to right): standard, azalea, and bulb pots. All have a top diameter of six inches.

***Standard pots***

These pots are as tall as they are wide at the top. (In diameter measurements of a pot, the top diameter is used.). For example, a six-inch-wide standard pot is six inches high. Standard pots require the most soil. They are used for crops requiring a deep root medium (like Easter lilies). Since these pots are not as stable as the next two types, top-heavy crops should not be grown in standard pots.

### *Azalea pots*

The height of an azalea pot is three-quarters of the top diameter. For example, an eight-inch azalea pot would be six inches tall. Because azalea pots are not as tall as standard pots, they are more stable. They are used for crops with a large canopy like poinsettias and mums. Azalea pots also hold less soil than do standard pots. Azalea pots are probably the most commonly used type of pot in the greenhouse industry.

### *Bulb pot or pan*

The height of a bulb pot is half of the top diameter. Thus, a six-inch bulb pan would be three inches tall. Bulb pots are used for shallow-rooted crops like spring bulbs. These pots are the least commonly used of the three types of pots.

## Flats

Flats are very common equipment in the greenhouse. Their uses are many:

- ✰ production of bedding plants (including seed germination)
- ✰ transportation of plants
- ✰ production of some flowering potted plants

Flats were originally made from wood, but now nearly all flats are made from thin, durable plastic. The size of flat most commonly used in the industry is 11 inches wide by 22 inches long (Figure 6.11). Shorter versions are also used sometimes - flats about 15 inches in length.

Most flats have a basic flat bottom with or without ribs running the length of the flat to secure containers (cell packs and pots). Some flats are "pocketed" on the bottom to hold pot plants more securely. Other flats are "webbed" on the bottom and are used to hold potted crops. Air circulation and drainage are assured in these webbed flats.

Bedding plants are finished in flats. Each flat is filled with small fused-plastic inserts or cell packs which in turn are filled with root media. Seedlings of bedding plants are then transplanted into these cell packs. When the bedding plants are ready for planting outside by the customer, the plants are easily pushed out of the cell pack and transplanted without any damage to the root system. The bedding plants thus get established quickly without any loss in quality.

Cell packs come in a variety of sizes. They are named for the number of cells and packs they contain. For example,

**Figure 6.11**

Three types of flats of standard size, each 11" x 22" (left to right): flat with solid ribbed bottom; flat pocketed to hold pots securely; and flat with webbed bottom.

- ☆ an 806 cell pack: 8 packs with 6 cells per pack for a total of 48 plants
- ☆ a 1204 cell pack: 12 packs with 4 cells per pack for a total of 48 plants (Figure 6.12)

The first number or two denote the number of packs and the last two numbers denote the number of cells per pack.

**Figure 6.12**
A 1204 cell pack insert in an 11" x 22" flat. The 12 packs with 4 cells each can hold a total of 48 plants.

## Hanging Baskets

Hanging baskets are also made from plastic, but of a heavier grade than that used for flats. Hanging baskets come in a variety of colors and styles. The most commonly used sizes are 8- and 10-inch diameters, with and without saucers on the bottom to collect runoff water. A wide variety of crops are grown in hanging baskets. Examples are impatiens, ivy geraniums, fuchsia, ferns, and poinsettias. Any plant that can be trained to cascade down over the edge is also a good candidate for a hanging basket.

# PROPAGATION MATERIALS

A good variety of propagation materials is available for rooting cuttings and germinating seeds. We will next discuss organic materials like Jiffy 7 peat pellets and synthetic materials like rockwool cubes.

### Jiffy 7's and Peat Pots

Spring bedding plants and cuttings of various crops are often started in compressed peat disks called Jiffy 7's. These peat disks expand to seven times their original size or volume when thoroughly wet. The cutting or seed is then placed into the Jiffy 7 for rooting or germination (Figure 6.13). No additional root medium is required.

**Figure 6.13**
(Left) Jiffy 7 before moisture is added. (Right) Cutting stuck in an expanded Jiffy 7.

Peat pots are square or round pots made out of compressed peat. They are typically two to three inches across at the top. The pot, when filled with a root medium, is ready to use for rooting cuttings or germinating seeds (Figure 6.14).

All these organic-material containers allow plant roots to grow through them. Container and plant are planted together in the garden when the plants are ready. There is no root damage during transplanting and no transplant shock. But it is most important during propagation to see that these peat containers do not dry out. Once they are dry, they are very difficult to moisten.

## Synthetic Cubes and Wedges

The use of synthetic cubes and wedges for rooting cuttings has increased greatly in the past ten years. Lightweight synthetic foam is molded into wedges and cubes of various sizes (Figure 6.15). These sterile cubes and wedges are very easy to use. Cuttings stuck in them have no disease organisms

**Figure 6.14**
(Left to right) Square peat pot, round peat pot, and peat pot with cutting ready for transplanting

**Figure 6.15**
Synthetic foam propagation cubes, wedges, and strips used for rooting cuttings

to contend with. Cubes typically are partially joined together. These rooting strips are then contained by a styrofoam collar which surrounds them on the sides and bottom. Wedges are placed into plastic flat inserts that contain wedge-shaped cells. Before use, these foam propagation materials must be ***thoroughly*** moistened.

## Rockwool

Rockwool is a synthetic wool-like material that is used for propagating seeds and cuttings and for growing greenhouse crops. It is available in cubes for propagation and in slabs for production purposes (Figure 6.16). The greenhouse vegetable industry has been using rockwool slabs for a number of years, while the greenhouse floriculture industry is just beginning to use them.

Cubes and slabs come in many sizes. Each cube is covered by plastic on four sides with the top and bottom open. A preformed hole in the top of the cube will range in size from a fraction of an inch for inserting cuttings to two or three inches in diameter. The hole should be filled with a root medium for germinating seeds. When the roots of the cutting or seedling have grown through the bottom of the rockwool cube, it is ready for transplanting.

Slabs of rockwool are completely covered with plastic. Usually, crops grown in slabs were started in rockwool cubes. The cubes are then "transplanted" onto the slabs. A hole is cut in the plastic on top of the slab to match the perimeter size of the cube. The cube is then placed directly onto the exposed portion of the rockwool slab. Roots from the plant in the cube then grow into the slab.

Crops grown in rockwool slabs are usually irrigated by a spaghetti tube system with one tube placed by each plant (Figure 6.17). Since rockwool is inert, a weak nutrient solution is also applied with each irrigation. As long as the nutrient levels are carefully monitored, the irrigation water used on rockwool slabs can be recycled.

**Figure 6.16**
Rockwool propagation cubes in a variety of sizes and a rockwool slab on the right

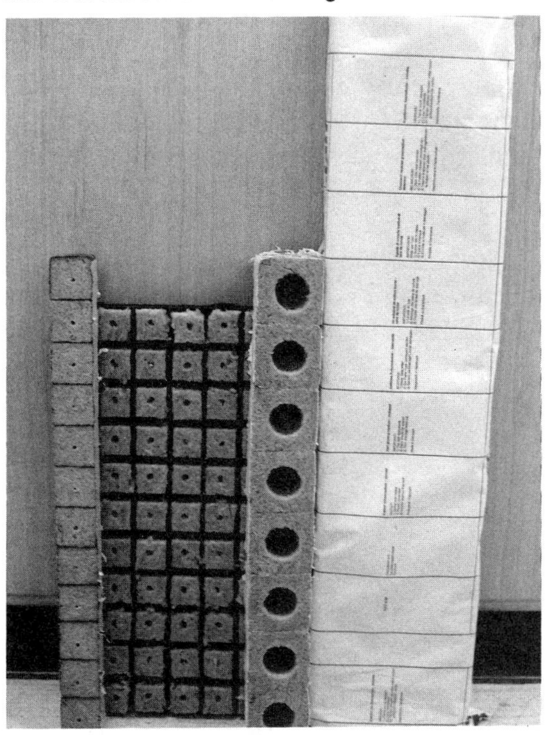

**Figure 6.17**
Tomato plants grown in rockwool slabs, irrigated by a spaghetti tube system

## Plug Trays

Plug trays are a fairly recent innovation in the greenhouse industry. They have revolutionized seed germination and transplanting for bedding plant production. Plug trays are typically the same size as the standard flat (11 by 22 inches). A plug tray is made up of tiny pots or cells fused together (Figure 6.18). The number of cells per tray ranges from 88 to over 800. As the ***number*** of cells per tray ***increases***, the ***size*** of each cell ***decreases.***

**Figure 6.18**
Three commonly used plug trays (left to right): 288, 392, and 512 cells per tray. Notice the decrease in cell size, left to right.

Plug trays with larger cells (e.g. 128, 200, or 288 cells per tray) are suitable for bedding plants requiring more space and root media like seed geraniums. Plug trays with small cells are suitable for crops like petunias and begonias that do not require as much space or germination medium.

The cells of plug trays are either square or round. Square cells are usually deeper and so hold more germination medium. They allow for better drainage than do round cells. Square cells also distribute moisture and nutrients more uniformly.

In the bottom of each cell is a large drainage hole. The seedlings or plugs are "popped out" through this hole when they are ready for transplanting. No root damage or transplant shock occurs with the use of plugs. A better quality bedding plant crop can be produced faster when plugs are used for germination instead of flats with seed sown in them. (See Chapter 10 on bedding plant production.)

---

***In conclusion:***

The different types of root media used in the greenhouse industry were discussed in Chapter 6. There are basically two types: soil-based and soilless. All root media must fulfill four functions in order to grow good quality floriculture crops. Growers may purchase root media or mix them themselves. Soil-based root media must be steam-pasteurized before use. The nutritional status of the root medium should be monitored frequently to assure proper growth of the crop growing in it. Containers for growing floriculture crops include pots, flats, and hanging baskets. Propagation containers include Jiffy 7's, synthetic foam cubes and wedges, rockwool cubes, and plug trays.

---

## CHAPTER 6 REVIEW

This review is to help you check yourself on what you have learned about root media and containers. If you need to refresh your mind on any of the following questions, refer to the page number given in parentheses.

1. Define "root medium." *(page 116)*
2. What is the composition of soil? *(pages 116-117)*
3. What are the four functions of a root medium? *(page 118)*
4. What are the characteristics of a soil-based root medium? of a soilless root medium? *(pages 118-119)*
5. What are the advantages of each type of root medium? *(pages 118-119)*
6. List three organic and three inorganic components of a root medium. *(pages 121-122)*
7. What is involved in the process of pasteurization? How does it differ from sterilization? *(pages 123-124)*
8. What type of root medium must be pasteurized before use? *(page 124)*
9. What factors should be measured when monitoring the nutritional status of a root medium? *(page 125)*
10. What is included on a soil test report from the REAL laboratory? *(pages 127-128)*
11. How can excess soluble salts levels be reduced in root media without leaching the soil? *(page 130)*
12. Why are clay pots no longer commonly used in the greenhouse industry? *(page 131)*
13. Name the defining characteristics of standard, azalea, and bulb pots. *(pages 132-133)*
14. What are flats used for in the greenhouse? *(page 133)*
15. What two sizes of hanging baskets are most commonly used for crops like ivy geraniums and fuchsia? *(page 134)*
16. How many plants will a 1204 flat hold (assuming one plant per cell)? *(page 134)*
17. What propagation materials are used for rooting cuttings? *(pages 134-136)*
18. What are plug trays used for? *(pages 137-138)*
19. Which plug tray has larger cells—one with 273 cells or one with 512 cells? *(page 137)*

# CHAPTER 7

# NUTRITION

## Competencies for Chapter 7

As a result of studying this chapter, you should be able to do the following:

1. Identify the 17 essential elements for plant growth and categorize them as micro-elements or macro-elements.
2. List the characteristics of micro-elements and macro-elements.
3. Discuss the effect of pH on the availability to plants of the essential elements.
4. Describe the forms in which fertilizers are commonly applied to greenhouse crops.
5. Describe the function of fertilizer injectors.
6. Identify nutrient deficiency symptoms in plants.
7. Describe the procedure for controlling soluble salts levels in root media.
8. Interpret fertilizer bag labels.
9. Mix fertilizer solutions.
10. Apply liquid fertilizers.
11. Apply dry fertilizers.
12. Use fertilizer injectors.
13. Calibrate fertilizer application equipment.
14. Take soluble salts readings with a solubridge.

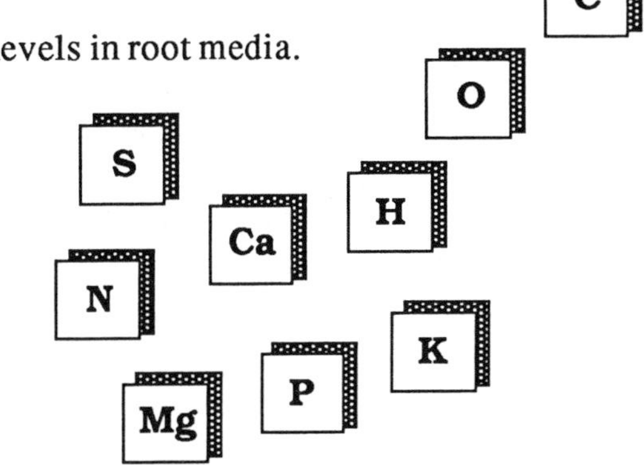


## Related Science Concepts

1. Give the one- or two-letter chemical symbol of each essential element.
2. Compare chemical properties of acids and bases.

## Related Math Concepts

1. Use formulas for fertilizer calculations; adjust the concentration using ratios, percents, conversion factor, and ppm.
2. Apply basic operations to ratios and percents to calibrate an injector.
3. Apply basic operations to whole numbers, decimals, and fractions.
4. Read, interpret, and construct charts, graphs, and tables.

## Terms to Know

calibration
chlorosis
complete fertilizer
constant feed
fertilizer analysis
Hozon®
injector
interveinal
macro-elements
micro-elements
ppm
proportioner
slow-release fertilizer
solubridge
stock tank
target ratio

# INTRODUCTION

Besides sunlight and water, plants need nutrients in order to grow properly. Therefore, applying fertilizers is an important activity in any greenhouse operation, since they will directly affect the quality of the crop. Knowing what types of fertilizers are available and how and when to apply them is equally important. Failure to apply fertilizers correctly will result in nutrient imbalances in the plant and subsequent poor growth.

# THE SEVENTEEN ESSENTIAL ELEMENTS

There are 17 nutrient elements that every plant requires in order to complete its life cycle, hence the name "**essential**" elements (Table 7.1). These elements are divided into two classes based on the amount used. Those that are used in relatively large quantities are the **macro-elements**: nitrogen (N), potassium (K), phosphorus (P), calcium (Ca), magnesium (Mg), sulfur (S), hydrogen (H), oxygen (O), and carbon (C). All but the last three can be supplied to greenhouse crops in a fertilizer program. Carbon, oxygen, and hydrogen are referred to as **non-fertilizer** elements since plants obtain them from carbon dioxide and water. Nitrogen, phosphorus, and potassium, all **fertilizer** elements, are also referred to as **primary nutrients** since they are required by the plant in the largest amounts. The rest of the macro-elements are called **secondary nutrients**, as they are required in smaller amounts than the primary nutrients.

**Micro-elements** are the elements used by plants in very small quantities: iron (Fe), manganese (Mn), boron (B), copper (Cu), zinc (Zn), molybdenum (Mo), sodium (Na), and chlorine (Cl).

**Table 7.1** The seventeen essential elements and their chemical symbols

| Macro-elements | | Micro-elements | |
|---|---|---|---|
| *Non-fertilizer nutrients* | | iron | **Fe** |
| hydrogen | **H** | copper | **Cu** |
| oxygen | **O** | zinc | **Zn** |
| carbon | **C** | manganese | **Mn** |
| *Primary nutrients* | | boron | **B** |
| nitrogen | **N** | molybdenum | **Mo** |
| phosphorus | **P** | chlorine | **Cl** |
| potassium | **K** | sodium | **Na** |
| *Secondary nutrients* | | | |
| magnesium | **Mg** | | |
| sulfur | **S** | | |
| calcium | **Ca** | | |

Keep in mind that the relative quantities of the essential elements are in no way a measure of their importance to the plant. Micro-elements are ***just as important*** to plant growth as macro-elements. For example, molybdenum, a micro-element, is a strict requirement for poinsettia growth. Failure to include it in a fertilizer program for poinsettias will mean the appearance of deficiency symptoms in mid October followed by ruin of the whole crop.

## EFFECT OF PH ON NUTRIENT AVAILABILITY

As we mentioned in Chapter 6, root media pH is very important to monitor and maintain at recommended ranges. ***Taken as a whole,*** the essential elements in soilless root media are at their maximum availability in the pH range of 5.5 to 6.5 (Figure 7.1). Note that iron and manganese are at their maximum

**Figure 7.1** Effect of soilless root medium pH on availability of selected essential elements. The widest portion of the bar indicates maximum availability.

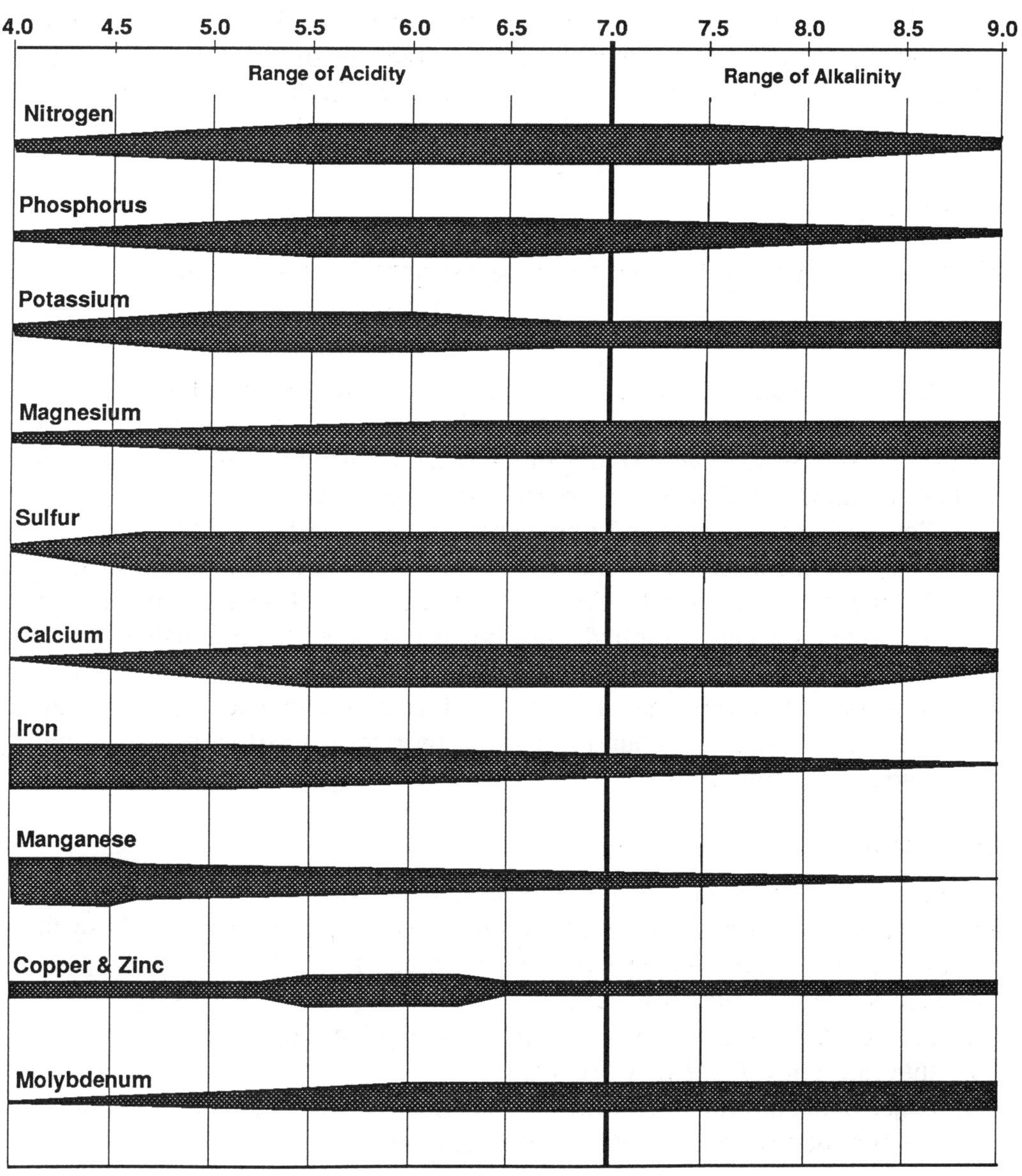

availability in soilless root media below pH 6.0 and that every element has its own pH range for maximum availability.

In general, micro-elements are more readily available at lower pH ranges, while macro-elements are more readily available at pH 6.0 and higher. Learning how pH affects nutrient availability will enable you to predict what elements will become deficient or build up to toxic levels if root medium pH is allowed to drift from its optimum range. You will have a good start in diagnosing and correcting nutrient imbalance.

# FERTILIZERS

## Introduction

Fertilizers are substances that supply required nutrient elements to the root medium. Use of fertilizers on greenhouse crops dates back to the beginning of greenhouse culture. The first fertilizers were animal manure and bone meal. Today chemical compounds are the most common fertilizers used. Concern for nutrition of plants no longer involves hit-or-miss practices. Plant nutrition has become a precise science in today's high-technology world.

## Classes of Fertilizers

Fertilizers can be divided into two classes: organic and inorganic.

### Organic

Common organic fertilizers are of plant or animal origin. Examples are manure, cottonseed meal, dried blood, bone meal, and sludge (material recovered from sewage waste). Organic fertilizers currently are not used often in the greenhouse industry for the following reasons.

1. They can be difficult and unpleasant to work with.
2. They do not dissolve in water for convenient application to crops.
3. Their analysis is variable. Thus, the exact amount of nitrogen, potassium, and other elements applied may be in doubt with organic fertilizers. However, organic fertilizers may make a comeback if they can be processed in forms that are easy and accurate to use. For there are mounting concerns about the use of inorganic fertilizers and ground water contamination.

### Inorganic

Inorganic fertilizers are minerals obtained from the earth's crust like sodium nitrate, and manufactured materials like superphosphate. These inorganic fertilizers are and were non-living. Inorganic fertilizers are the most commonly used fertilizers because

1. they dissolve readily in water for easy application,
2. they are convenient to work with, and
3. ***exact*** concentrations of nutrient elements can be applied. (See the calculations on pages 149-152 in this chapter.)

Table 7.2 lists rates of application for some of the common inorganic and organic fertilizers. ***Note:*** Recommendations given in this table are only generalizations. Root media can vary widely in their nutritional content. The exact quantity to be applied in a given situation should be determined from soil test results.

---

**Table 7.2** Common fertilizer ingredients for greenhouse use

| Material | Analysis | Rate of Application | | Effect on pH |
|---|---|---|---|---|
| | | Dry | Liquid | |
| Ammonium sulfate | 20-0-0 | ½ - 1 lb. per 100 sq. ft. | 2 - 3 lb. per 100 gal | Acid |
| Sodium nitrate | 15-0-0 | ¾ - 1¼ lb. per 100 sq. ft. | 2 oz. per 2 gal | Alkaline |
| Calcium nitrate | 15-0-0 | ¾ - 1½ lb. per 100 sq. ft. | 3 oz. per 2 gal | Alkaline |
| Potassium nitrate | 13-0-44 | ½ - 1 lb. per 100 sq. ft. | 2 oz. per 3 gal | Neutral |
| Ammonium nitrate | 33-0-0 | ¼ - ½ lb. per 100 sq. ft. | 1½ oz. per 5 gal | Acid |
| Di-ammonium phosphate | 21-53-0 | ½ - ¾ lb. per 100 sq. ft. | 1¼ - 1½ oz. per 4-5 gal | Acid |
| Treble super-phosphate | 0-40-0 | 1 - 2½ lb. per 100 sq. ft. | Insoluble | Neutral |
| Superphosphate | 0-20-0 | As recommended by soil test | Insoluble | Neutral |
| Potassium chloride | 0-0-60 | ½ - ¾ lb. per 100 sq. ft. | 1¼ - 1½ oz. per 4-5 gal | Neutral |
| Potassium sulfate | 0-0-50 | ½ - 1 lb. per 100 sq. ft. | Not advisable | Neutral |
| Urea formaldehyde | 38-0-0 | 3 - 5 lb. per 100 sq. ft. | Insoluble | Acid |
| Activated sludge | Usually 5-4-0 | 3 - 5 lb. per 100 sq. ft. | Insoluble | Acid |
| Animal tankage | Usually 7-9-0 | 3 - 4 lb. per 100 sq. ft. | Insoluble | Acid |
| Cottonseed meal | 7-2-2 | 3 - 4 lb. per 100 sq. ft. | Insoluble | Acid |
| Dried blood | 12-0-0 | 2 - 3 lb. per 100 sq. ft. | Insoluble | Acid |
| Steamed bone meal | Usually 3-20-0 | 5 lb. per 100 sq. ft. | Insoluble | Alkaline |
| Dolomitic limestone | None | As recommended by soil test | Insoluble | Alkaline |
| Gypsum (calcium sulfate) | None | 2 - 5 lb. per 100 sq. ft. | Insoluble | Neutral |
| Sulfur | None | 1 - 2 lb. per 100 sq. ft. | Insoluble | Acid |
| Magnesium sulfate - epsom salts | None | 8 - 12 oz. per 100 sq. ft. | 1¼ lb. per 100 gal | Neutral |
| Aluminum sulfate | None | Not advisable | 20 lb. per 100 gal | Acid |

## Forms of Fertilizers for Application

### Dry Fertilizers

Dry fertilizers, as the name implies, are applied as dry granules to the root medium, not dissolved in water. Examples of dry fertilizers are dolomitic limestone (to raise root medium pH), gypsum or calcium sulfate (to add sulfur and calcium), and superphosphate (to add phosphorus). In general, dry fertilizers can not be applied in liquid solutions because they are insoluble in water. Thus, dry fertilizers are mixed uniformly into the root medium before planting is done. Once in the medium, they readily release nutrients directly into the root zone of the crop.

### Slow-Release Fertilizers

Several of the dry fertilizers that are incorporated into root media are slow-release fertilizers; that is, they release their nutrients to the root medium over a period of several months. These fertilizer granules are usually coated with a layer of porous plastic. When the granules become moistened, the fertilizer inside is released slowly into the root medium. Slow-release fertilizers can be mixed in the root medium before planting or applied to the surface after planting. But plastic-coated slow-release fertilizers should ***never*** be added to the root media before steaming. Steam pasteurization will melt the plastic coating and release ***all*** the fertilizer into the root medium at once. The result will be a ruined crop.

Slow-release fertilizers are a convenient way of supplying nutrients to a crop gradually, since the only labor involved is the initial application. However, once these fertilizers are mixed into the root medium, control of crop nutrition is lost. If a mistake is made, such as too much slow-release fertilizer mixed into the root medium, little can be done to correct the situation once the crop is planted. Therefore, always follow label directions carefully when applying slow-release fertilizers.

### Liquid Fertilizers

Liquid fertilizer programs are the most common means of fertilizing crops. Fertilizers such as calcium nitrate and potassium nitrate are dissolved in warm water and applied as a liquid to the greenhouse crop. Another type of water-soluble fertilizer used as a liquid is known as a "complete" fertilizer. It supplies nitrogen, phosphorus, and potassium, the three primary macro-elements. However, a complete fertilizer does ***not*** necessarily supply any other macro- or micro-element.

### Methods of Application

There are two methods of applying liquid fertilizers to greenhouse crops: intermittent and constant-feed. With intermittent applications, liquid fertilizer is applied at regular intervals such as weekly, bi-weekly or even monthly. The problem with such applications is that there are wide fluctuations in the amount of fertilizer available in the root medium. At the time of application, relatively high concentrations of fertilizer are available, and the plant immediately starts absorbing it. By the time the next application is made, fertilizer levels may be very low or non-existent. This fluctuation can result in uneven plant growth rates and even stress, producing a poor-quality crop.

Low concentrations of fertilizer applied at every irrigation are much better for the greenhouse crop. Such applications keep a constant level of nutrients available to the plants for steady growth without stressful fluctuations. This is the **constant feed** method of liquid fertilizer application. It is the most commonly used method in the greenhouse industry. It affords the grower the greatest control over the nutrition of a greenhouse crop.

## Fertilizer Injectors

When liquid fertilizers are used, the needed solution can be mixed up for each application. However, this is inefficient and time-consuming. Most growers use a device known as a fertilizer injector. This device injects small amounts of concentrated liquid fertilizer directly into the water lines so that greenhouse crops are fertilized with each watering (**constant feed**). The fertilizer injector makes the job easy and fast and eliminates the labor involved in repeated preparation and application of fertilizer solution.

### Types of Fertilizer Injectors

There are many types of fertilizer injectors in use today. They range from a simple siphon mechanism ("Hozon®") to multiple injectors each of which injects a single element into the water line (Figure 7.2). Some injectors are controlled by a computer which is programmed to maintain fertilizer concentrations at desired set points.

Most fertilizer injectors are proportioners that inject precise amounts of concentrated fertilizer into the water line either by a pump or by pressure (Figure 7.2A-C). These proportioners are used in large irrigation systems because they have a large water-flow capacity. Siphon injectors, such as a Hozon®, draw concentrated fertilizer solution up a siphon hose and into the water line (Figure 7.2D). Since their water flow capacity is small, siphon injectors are suitable only for hose watering and for small irrigation systems limited to one or two benches (e.g. spaghetti tubes).

### Injector Ratios

Injectors have either fixed or variable dilution ratios. They range from 1:15 for Hozon® injectors to 1:1,000 and greater. Commonly used ratios are 1:100, 1:128, and 1:200. For example, an injector with a 1:100 dilution ratio has one gallon of concentrated fertilizer injected into the water line per 99 gallons of water flowing through the injector. In other words, 100 gallons of this fertilizer solution collected from the 1:100 ratio injector would be comprised of one gallon of concentrated fertilizer diluted in 99 gallons of water.

**Figure 7.2** Most fertilizer injectors (**A, B, C**) are proportioners. The hozon injector (**D**) can be used for hose watering and small spaghetti tube irrigation systems. Note the concentrated fertilizer stock tanks in A, C, and D.

**A**

**B**

**C**

**D**

---

### Stock Tanks

Stock tanks containing concentrated fertilizer are located near the injector. The siphon or fertilizer intake tube should be suspended just above the bottom of the tank. Otherwise it may become clogged with sediments that settle out of the solution. If more than one stock tank is in use, each tank should be labeled as to the fertilizer it contains so that the correct fertilizer is used. The tanks should be covered so that no debris or harmful organisms can fall into the tank. To control algal growth, stock tanks and covers should not permit light to pass through. Siphon tube openings in the cover should be as small as possible.

# FERTILIZER CALCULATIONS

## Introduction

A good grower, who must know exactly how much fertilizer is to be applied to a given crop, will learn just how fertilizer concentrations are measured. He or she must learn how to calculate the amounts of fertilizer to dissolve in water to achieve the desired concentrations. In this section we will learn about fertilizer calculations with some examples.

## Fertilizer Analysis

Before you start working with fertilizer calculations, you must know what the three numbers separated by dashes represent on the fertilizer label. These numbers, called the analysis, are also found on bags of complete fertilizer. The first number is the percentage of nitrogen in the fertilizer, the second number the percentage of phosphorus compound ($P_2O_5$), and the third number the percentage of potassium compound ($K_2O$). Take the commonly used complete fertilizer analysis of 20-20-20. ***By weight***, this fertilizer contains 20 percent nitrogen, 20 percent $P_2O_5$ and 20 percent $K_2O$.

But both $P_2O_5$ and $K_2O$ have correction factors to apply. To convert from percent $P_2O_5$ to percent phosphorus, multiply $P_2O_5$ by the correction factor 0.44. To convert percent $K_2O$ to percent potassium, multiply $K_2O$ by the correction factor 0.83. Therefore, a 20-20-20 fertilizer analysis would include 20 percent nitrogen, 8.8 percent phosphorus (20 x 0.44 = 8.8), and 16.6 percent potassium (20 x 0.83 = 16.6), or **20-8.8-16.6** percent nitrogen, phosphorus, and potassium, respectively. Other fertilizer analysis combinations and their rate of application are given in Table 7.2 (page 145).

## Parts Per Million Measurements

Fertilizer concentrations are measured in parts per million or **ppm**. This is a very accurate way of measuring fertilizer concentration because it represents the **actual amount** of the nutrient elements in the fertilizer solution. Fertilizer recommendations and formulas are all based on ppm. Unfortunately, many growers still prepare their fertilizer solutions by adding "so many" six-inch azalea pots of one fertilizer and "so many" pots of another fertilizer because "It's always been done that way." These growers have no idea how much fertilizer is actually applied to the crop. That is not good greenhouse practice. A grower who knows how to apply ppm formulas will always know the concentration of fertilizer applied to the crop. He or she can make adjustments accordingly.

There are charts that give quantities of fertilizers to dissolve in injector stock tanks for different injection ratios for various fertilizer concentrations (Table 7.3). However, only selected ppm solutions and ratios are given. Knowing how to calculate fertilizer amounts yourself will give you the ability to handle your particular situation. You will not be limited to the specifications of these reference charts.

**Table 7.3** Commonly used formulas, injection ratios, and fertilizer concentrations for constant feeding.

| Injection Ratio | Per Gallon of Concentrate | | |
|---|---|---|---|
| | 100 ppm Nitrogen | 150 ppm Nitrogen | 200 ppm Nitrogen |
| **30% NITROGEN FORMULAS** (30-10-10, etc.) | | | |
| 1:200 | 9.00 oz. | 13.50 oz. | 18.00 oz. |
| 1:150 | 6.75 oz. | 10.125 oz. | 13.50 oz. |
| 1:128 | 5.76 oz. | 8.64 oz. | 11.52 oz. |
| 1:100 | 4.50 oz. | 6.75 oz. | 9.00 oz. |
| 1:24 | 1.08 oz. | 1.62 oz. | 2.16 oz. |
| 1:15 | 0.675 oz. | 1.012 oz. | 1.35 oz. |
| **25% NITROGEN FORMULAS** (25-5-20, 25-0-25, etc.) | | | |
| 1:200 | 11.00 oz. | 16.50 oz. | 22.00 oz. |
| 1:150 | 8.25 oz. | 12.375 oz. | 16.50 oz. |
| 1:128 | 7.04 oz. | 10.56 oz. | 14.08 oz. |
| 1:100 | 5.50 oz. | 8.25 oz. | 11.00 oz. |
| 1:24 | 1.32 oz. | 1.98 oz. | 2.64 oz. |
| 1:15 | 0.825 oz. | 1.237 oz. | 1.65 oz. |
| **20% NITROGEN FORMULAS** (20-20-20, 20-7-7, etc.) | | | |
| 1:200 | 13.50 oz. | 20.25 oz. | 27.00 oz. |
| 1:150 | 10.125 oz. | 15.187 oz. | 20.25 oz. |
| 1:128 | 8.64 oz. | 12.96 oz. | 17.28 oz. |
| 1:100 | 6.75 oz. | 10.125 oz. | 13.50 oz. |
| 1:24 | 1.62 oz. | 2.43 oz. | 3.24 oz. |
| 1:15 | 1.012 oz. | 1.518 oz. | 2.025 oz. |

## Formulas for Calculating Fertilizer Amounts

Two formulas will be used in calculating fertilizer amounts:

**Formula #1**

$$\text{ounces in 100 gallons of water} = \frac{\text{ppm desired}}{\text{\% element} \times \text{correction factor*} \times 0.75}$$

**Formula #2**

$$\text{pounds to add to stock tank} = \frac{\text{ounces per 100 gallons} \times \text{second number of injector ratio} \times \text{volume of stock tank in gal.}}{100 \times 16}$$

* Correction factors:
% $P_2O_5$ X 0.44 = % P
% $K_2O$ X 0.83 = % K

☆ Formula #1 is used to calculate how many ounces of fertilizer to dissolve in 100 gallons of water to achieve the desired ppm.

☆ Formula #2 is used to calculate how many pounds of fertilizer are needed to dissolve in the stock tank to obtain the desired ppm in a constant feed program.

Formula #1 ***must*** be used first in order to apply Formula #2. Note the correction factor in Formula #1, which we mentioned earlier as applying to $P_2O_5$ and $K_2O$. (Nitrogen does not require a correction factor.) With ppm, conversion factors, and formulas in mind, let's look at an example of fertilizer calculation.

## Example of Fertilizer Calculation

A grower with a 1:128 ratio injector and a 30-gallon stock tank wants to apply 250 ppm of nitrogen to a crop of mums. The available fertilizer has a 20-10-20 analysis, so it contains 20 percent nitrogen by weight. How many pounds of this fertilizer should the grower dissolve in the stock tank?

### *Step 1*

Calculate how many ounces of the fertilizer will be needed to dissolve in 100 gallons of water to produce a solution containing 250 ppm of nitrogen. Use ***Formula #1***.

$$\text{ounces/100 gallons} = \frac{250}{20 \times 0.75} = \frac{250}{15} = 16.7$$

16.7 ounces of 20-10-20 fertilizer dissolved in 100 gallons of water will result in a fertilizer solution of 250 ppm of nitrogen. Note that with nitrogen, there is no correction factor in the denominator.

*Step 2*

Take the answer from Formula #1 and plug it into ***Formula #2***. This will tell you how many pounds of the 20-10-20 fertilizer will be needed in the stock tank to produce a 250 ppm fertilizer solution from the 1:128 ratio injector.

$$\text{pounds to add to stock tank} = 16.7 \times 128 \times 30/100 \times 16$$
$$= 16.7 \times 128 \times 30/1600$$
$$= \frac{64{,}128}{1600} = 40.1$$

If the grower dissolves 40.1 pounds of the 20-10-20 fertilizer in the 30-gallon fertilizer stock tank, the 1:128 ratio injector will produce a fertilizer solution of 250 ppm of nitrogen in the water lines.

## Calibrating Fertilizer Injectors

To ensure that a fertilizer injector is working properly, it must be calibrated periodically; that is, the dilution ratio must be calculated. Calibrations that show a discrepancy from the target ratio indicate that the injector is not operating correctly. It must be repaired immediately. Otherwise, the greenhouse crops will continue to receive the wrong amount of fertilizer; an entire crop could be ruined.

### Calibration Procedure

A simple way to calibrate an injector is to collect a known amount of fertilizer solution from the injector. Then measure the quantity of concentrated fertilizer that was taken up by the injector. Determine the ratio by dividing the amount of fertilizer solution collected from the injector by the amount of concentrated fertilizer taken up by the injector.

*Example*

The equipment to be calibrated is a 1:100 ratio injector. The injector intake hose is placed in a known amount of fertilizer stock solution, and twenty liters (20,000 milliliters) of fertilizer solution is collected. The stock solution volume is measured before and after collecting the fertilizer solution. The difference is 195 ml of stock solution - the amount injected by the proportioner.

The ratio can now be calculated. It is 195:20,000 according to the original measurements. Divide both sides of the ratio by 195 (the volume of stock solution used by the injector) and the true ratio is 1:103. This is very close to the target ratio of 1:100. No adjustment is needed. Injectors with ratios that are more than 5 percent off the target ratio should be adjusted, if possible, or replaced.

## NUTRITIONAL PROBLEMS

Nutritional problems can result from a number of factors. Some common causes are over- or under-fertilizing, overwatering, and poor drainage and aeration in the root medium. Diagnosing nutrient deficiency can be very difficult because a number of environmental factors and diseases can cause similar symptoms. Figure 7.3 (pages 156-157) shows some of the many possibilities. In addition, an **excess** of a nutrient element or elements in a root medium can tie up other nutrients and result in deficiency symptoms of the latter nutrients. To confirm nutrient deficiency symptoms, samples of the affected foliage should be sent to a laboratory for analysis.

### Nutrient Deficiency Symptoms

Watch for the following **deficiency symptoms** associated with each of these nutrients.

***Nitrogen*** There is general chlorosis (yellowing) of the plant. As time progresses, the lower leaves turn brown and fall off. Growth of the plant is stunted.

***Phosphorus*** There is stunting of the plant and poor bud formation. Dark green foliage turns chlorotic with a purplish cast, especially on lower part of the plant.

***Potassium*** Leaf margins first develop chlorosis and then turn brown in color. Leaf tissue eventually dies. Besides on the margins, discolored areas may be scattered across the leaf. These symptoms begin in the lowest part of the plant and progress upward.

***Calcium*** Young leaves are prominently malformed and often chlorotic. Development of the stem's growing point is arrested; root growth is poor.

***Magnesium*** Interveinal chlorosis (yellowing of the leaf between the veins) occurs in *lower* or *older* leaves and eventually progresses toward the top of the plant.

***Iron*** *Young* leaves develop interveinal chlorosis (in contrast to the older leaves for magnesium deficiency). Damage is confined to upper portions of the plant.

***Boron*** Symptoms vary according to the affected plant species: death of the growing point followed by growth of many side shoots below it (called a "witch's broom"); young leaves becoming thick and leathery and often chlorotic; and young leaves becoming very wrinkled. Damage is confined to upper portions of the plant.

***Molybdenum*** Symptoms, usually found only in poinsettias, develop in October. First, margins of the middle leaves turn chlorotic and then curl inward. As the chlorosis spreads inward, the curled leaf margins turn brown.

## Nutrient Toxicity Problems

Excess fertilizer can also cause poor growth. Roots can be easily damaged by the resulting high soluble salts levels in the root medium. With the reduction of water and nutrient uptake, nutrient deficiency symptoms of some essential elements will develop. Sometimes, due to an improper fertilizer program, these essential elements accumulate in the plant to toxic levels. The result is reduced growth, chlorosis, and other visual clues that plants are not healthy. Regardless of the cause, deficiency or toxicity of nutrients, always have your diagnosis confirmed by a soil and/or foliar analysis before taking corrective action.

## Soluble Salts

Whether you run your own soil test or have a sample tested in a laboratory, a conductivity reading or measure of the soluble salts level should be part of the procedure. As mentioned previously, "soluble salts" refers to the salts contributed to the root medium by fertilizers (both organic and inorganic).

Excess soluble salts tend to accumulate in the root medium when fertilizer is applied either too much at one time (concentration is excessive) or too frequently. Other causes are insufficient watering and poor drainage, or a combination of these. The result is insufficient leaching of the root medium.

An instrument called a solubridge is used to measure soluble salts levels in the root medium (Figure 7.4). A solubridge is easy to use. Every greenhouse should have one to monitor the soluble salts levels in the root media being used.

---

**Figure 7.4**
A solubridge used for measuring soluble salts levels in root media

### *Using a Solubridge*

Following are the steps in using a solubridge.

1. Take a sample of the root medium and allow it to dry.
2. Moisten the root medium sample with distilled water, using twice as much water as root medium. Let it soak for 24 hours.
3. Insert the probe of the solubridge into the root medium-water mixture.
4. Take a reading. Then consult a chart to help interpret the results.

In Chapter 6 we discussed control of soluble salts levels in root media. Remember that the best way to control soluble salts levels in root media is to use a sound fertilizer program which supplies nutrients in known amounts at recommended rates.

When you are implementing a constant feed program, include a plain water application every third or fourth irrigation. Plain water will leach away excess soluble salts from the root medium. Also, when applying the dilute fertilizer solution, allow for a small amount of leaching to control soluble salts levels further.

---

### *In conclusion:*

Chapter 7 dealt with the topic of nutrition of greenhouse crops. Seventeen essential elements, both macro-elements and micro-elements, are known to be vital to plants in the greenhouse. To supply these essential elements, growers use fertilizers in dry, liquid, or slow-release form. The most common method of application is constant feed, which uses fertilizer injectors to supply fertilizer directly in the water lines. If nutrients are in short supply in the plant, deficiency symptoms develop that can usually be identified. Excess soluble salts in the root medium will damage roots and eventually ruin the crop. Soil samples taken periodically should be analyzed for soluble salts either in the greenhouse using a solubridge or at a soil testing lab. High soluble salts levels in the root medium can be avoided by implementing a wise fertilizer management program.

---

**Figure 7.3** Key for diagnosing plant problems

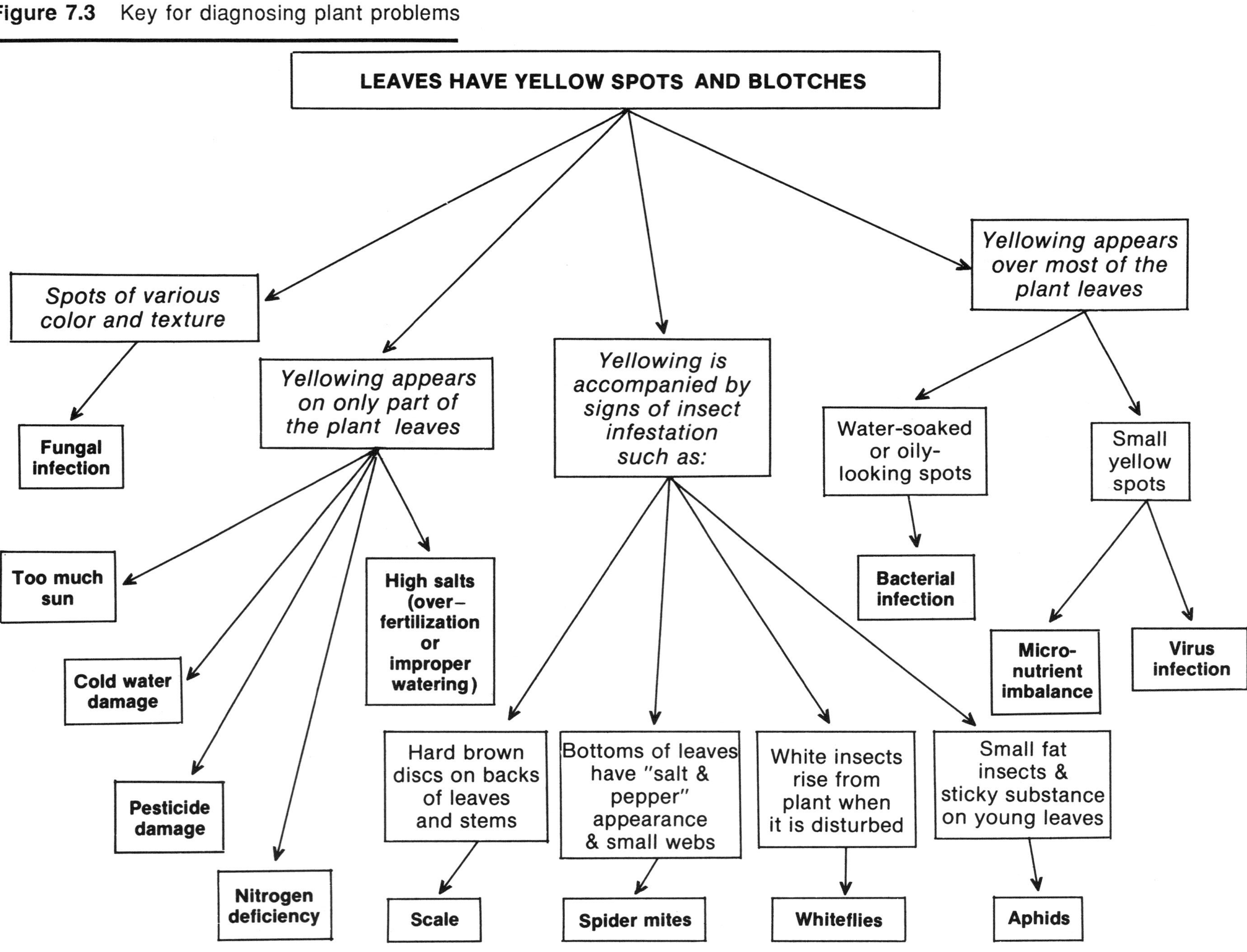

Figure 7.3 *(continued)*

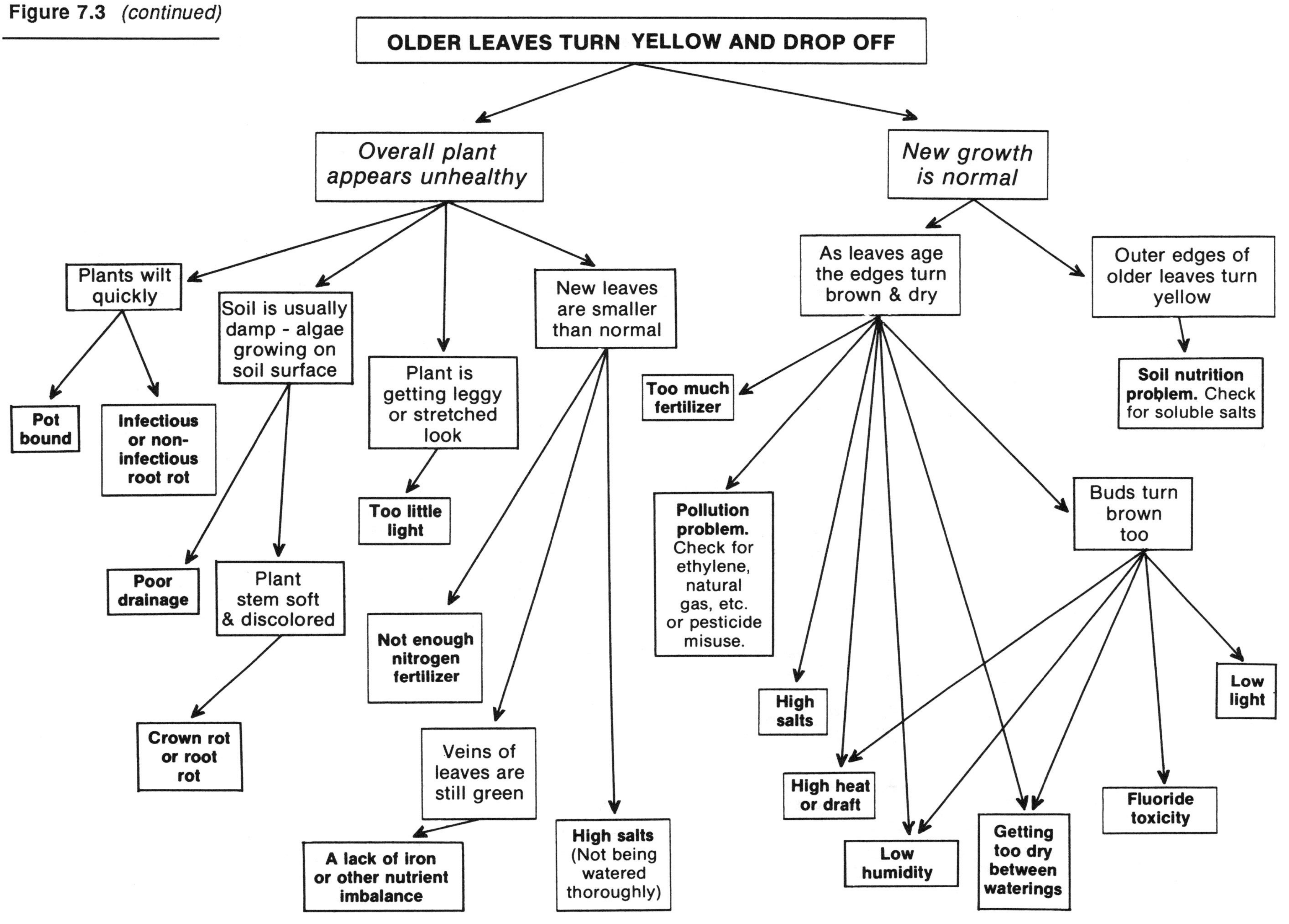

## CHAPTER 7 REVIEW

This review is to help you check yourself on what you have learned about nutrition. If you need to refresh your mind on any of the following questions, refer to the page number given in parentheses.

1. Name the essential macro-elements. Which three are not supplied by a fertilizer program? *(page 142)*
2. What differentiates a macro-element from a micro-element? *(page 142)*
3. Name the essential micro-elements. How does their importance compare with that of macro-elements? *(pages 142-143)*
4. In what root medium pH range are the essential elements at their maximum availability for uptake by plants? *(page 143)*
5. Why are inorganic fertilizers more widely used in the greenhouse industry than organic fertilizers? *(page 144)*
6. In what form are fertilizers most commonly applied to greenhouse crops? Why? *(page 146)*
7. Define "constant feed" with regard to a fertilizer application program. *(page 147)*
8. Discuss how a fertilizer injector works. *(pages 147-148)*
9. On a fertilizer label, what does "15-16-17" mean? *(page 149)*
10. How many pounds of a 20-10-20 fertilizer should be dissolved in a 20 gallon stock tank using a 1:100 ratio injector to supply 225 ppm of nitrogen to a mum crop? *(pages 151-152)*
11. Describe briefly how to calibrate a fertilizer injector. *(page 152)*
12. What factors can cause nutrients to become deficient in a greenhouse floriculture crop? *(page 153)*
13. How do magnesium deficiency symptoms differ from those of iron? *(page 153)*
14. If a poinsettia crop is short on nitrogen, what will the crop look like? *(page 153)*
15. Why should soluble salts levels in root media be measured frequently during the production of a greenhouse crop? *(page 154)*
16. What factors contribute to high soluble salts levels in root media? *(page 154)*
17. What instrument is used to measure soluble salts levels in a root medium? *(page 155)*

# CHAPTER 8

# INTEGRATED PEST MANAGEMENT

## Competencies for Chapter 8

As a result of studying this chapter, you should be able to do the following:

1. Describe the four main parts of an integrated pest management program.
2. Use sanitary measures to prevent pest infestations.
3. Use weed barriers on ground benches.
4. Eradicate weeds inside and outside the greenhouse.
5. Follow proper cleaning and sterilization procedures to maintain a healthy environment.
6. Monitor pest populations with sticky traps.
7. Estimate pest population numbers.
8. Evaluate chemical/cultural/biological control options.
9. Maintain records of pest populations and chemical applications.

## Related Science Concepts

1. Discuss the implications of pesticide resistance to horticulture.
2. Explain the serious nature of pesticide hazards to people.

## Related Math Concepts

1. Read, interpret, and construct charts, graphs, and tables to monitor pest populations.
2. Apply basic operations to ratios and percents.
3. Apply basic operations to whole numbers, decimals, and fractions.

## Terms to Know

biological control
*Encarsia formosa*
EPA
fumigant
infestation
**IPM**
life cycle
microbe
parasite
predator
"soft" pesticide
target pest

## INTRODUCTION

In the recent past, pests of greenhouse crops were controlled almost entirely by chemical pesticides. The objective of the grower was to control insect pests by completely eradicating them. (Some growers still follow this pattern.) Chemical pesticides are chemicals that are specifically formulated to kill target (selected) pests. There are several problems with intensive use of chemical pesticides, however.

Every time a pesticide is applied, there are a few insects that resist the damaging effects and survive. These resistant insects then reproduce and populate the area with offspring that are also resistant to that pesticide. Each time the same or a similar pesticide is applied, it will kill fewer and fewer of the target pests. It will no longer be effective. This **pesticide resistance** occurs all too frequently in the greenhouse industry.

Another serious problem with pesticides is the severe hazard they pose to the environment and to plants and people when the proper precautions are not taken. Because of this hazard, the EPA (Environmental Protection Agency) removes many pesticide registrations every year, limiting the number of chemical pesticides that are available for pest control.

A new, more realistic goal of pest control is now set by increasing numbers of greenhouse growers: to keep pest populations low enough that damage is negligible. It is no longer realistic to strive for zero populations of pests.

## DEFINITION OF IPM

Instead of relying almost entirely on chemical pesticides, the grower will have to change strategies and use a combination of methods to control pests safely and effectively. This combination or ***system*** of methods is known as **integrated pest management (IPM).**

While the ***principles*** of integrated pest management remain the same, each individual greenhouse requires its own unique IPM ***program*** to suit its needs. Greenhouses vary in physical layout and number and type of crops produced each year.

## PRINCIPLES OF IPM

The four basic areas that are addressed in any IPM program are:

1. Greenhouse sanitation
2. Physical control
3. Biological control
4. Pesticides

Each of these areas will be discussed in detail and examples given of applications for IPM programs.

# Greenhouse Sanitation

## Weed Control

To control pests in a greenhouse effectively, weeds (oxalis, chickweed, and many others) must be removed from ***all locations*** both inside and immediately outside the structure. Not only are weeds unsightly, giving a most unprofessional appearance, but they are also a source of pests. Pesticide applications are directed toward greenhouse crops, not at the weeds.

Infested weeds growing directly outside a greenhouse serve as a source of pests. For they can freely enter the greenhouse through ventilators and louvers. Weed populations can be eliminated by

- ☆ using weed barriers on cut flower ground benches and beneath raised benches (Figure 8.1),
- ☆ using concrete or gravel for flooring materials, and/or
- ☆ conducting regular weed eradication "patrols" inside and outside the greenhouse.

## Removal of Debris

Sanitary measures for pest control include prompt disposal of plant debris (fallen leaves, old flowers, etc.) from floors and benches. Debris often harbors disease organisms and insect pests. Do not keep any "pet" plants in the greenhouse. They are likely to become infested and serve as a source of pests for the entire greenhouse.

When these simple preventive measures are taken, major sources of pest infestation will be eliminated. Even the appearance of the greenhouse and the surrounding area will be greatly improved.

---

**Figure 8.1**

Weed barrier of black synthetic cloth in a cut mum bench. Water and air pass through it, but weeds can not grow beneath it. Mum cuttings were planted through openings cut in the weed barrier.

## Physical Control

The second area of IPM is the use of physical manipulation to prevent pest infestation. Several methods can be implemented.

### Screens

The first method is installation of fine mesh screens over greenhouse openings like ventilators and louvers. These screens prevent the entry of common flying insect pests like aphids, thrips, whiteflies, and others through openings in the greenhouse.

### Yellow Sticky Traps

Yellow sticky traps are another physical control method (Figure 8.2). They come in either strips or squares (commonly, 2 x 2 inches). The yellow color attracts winged pests like whiteflies, thrips, and winged aphids. Once they land on the sticky surface of the trap, they are stuck and soon die. Traps should be placed at plant level either suspended from overhead supports by wire or string, or placed on a stake.

The main purpose of yellow sticky traps is to ***monitor*** pest populations, though traps do help to reduce populations as well. For monitoring purposes, one trap per 1,000 square feet is recommended. It is important to record the types and numbers of pests caught on the trap and to graph the results over time. When pest populations start to increase, greenhouse growers can take immediate corrective action.

---

**Figure 8.2**

A 2"x 2" yellow sticky trap mounted at the canopy height of a poinsettia stock plant

### Regulating Greenhouse Environment

The last, and most important, physical control method is manipulation of the greenhouse environment. Basically, this means providing as ideal an environment as possible for healthy plant growth. Just like people, plants that are healthy and vigorous are less likely to contract diseases or become infested with insect pests. However, if plants are stressed by being overwatered, grown in extreme temperatures, underfertilized, etc., they will have lower resistance to disease and insect pests. Growing greenhouse crops according to recommended cultural guidelines will greatly reduce, if not totally prevent, pest infestations. Also, crop quality will be significantly improved.

## Biological Control

"Biological control" is using one organism to control another. Several groups of organisms can be used to control greenhouse insect pests.

### Microbial Organisms

Certain species of bacteria and fungi have been shown to control pests like aphids and whiteflies. These microbial organisms invade the body tissues of the pest and kill it. These organisms are environmentally safe to use. The problem is that some of them, like fungi, require high humidity or other special conditions that are difficult or impossible for growers to provide in the greenhouse.

### Parasites

A parasite is an organism that lives off the nutrients obtained from another living organism. The latter is known as the host. Several parasitic insects show promise for use in the greenhouse industry. One of these is a parasitic wasp that appears to be well suited for controlling whiteflies that infest poinsettia crops. This tiny wasp, *Encarsia formosa,* lays eggs on the immature stages of the whitefly (Figure 8.3). When the eggs hatch, the larval wasp consumes the immature whitefly. The wasp develops into an adult inside the shell of the parasitized, immature whitefly, and then emerges to continue the process.

**Figure 8.3**

*Encarsia formosa,* a parasitic wasp that provides excellent biological control on whiteflies infesting poinsettias *(Photo by Richard Lindquist)*

It is vital that no pesticides be used prior to or during the use of parasites for biological control, as they will be killed. Also, parasites can not be used to control a heavy pest infestation. Rather, they should be released into the greenhouse at the first signs of a pest infestation (as indicated by trapping). Once again, this is an environmentally safe method of pest control.

### Predators

Predators are organisms that prey upon or eat other organisms. There are several predators that may be used for controlling greenhouse pests. One is a beetle that in both its immature and adult stages voraciously devours immature whiteflies and adults. There is a predatory mite that is used against thrips (Figure 8.4). These mites are packaged in a bottle containing a carrier substance with food for the mites in it. The material containing the mites is simply poured out into a measuring spoon and sprinkled over the crop.

Like parasites, predators should be released only when pest infestations are small so that effective control can be achieved. Keep in mind that any use of pesticides on crops containing predators will wipe out both predator and pest.

The use of biological control in the greenhouse industry is very promising. Research is still being conducted to determine such factors as appropriate release rates for a given organism, optimum release times in the crop cycle, and many others. Biological control will not totally eradicate a pest population; it is only one of the methods used in an IPM program for control of pest populations.

**Figure 8.4** **A.** A predatory mite used for biological control of thrips is packaged in a bottle. **B.** The mites in a nutrient carrier substance are simply sprinkled by spoonfuls over a rose crop.

## Pesticides

### "Soft" Pesticides

As the EPA removes pesticides that are very harmful to the environment, new pesticides have appeared on the market that are "softer" towards the environment, plants, and people. These less toxic pesticides should be incorporated into the IPM program. Some of these "soft" pesticides are the following:

1. Special lightweight, horticultural oils. When sprayed on plants, they kill pests by suffocation and do no harm to the plant.

2. A class of insecticidal soaps that are effective against many insect pests.
3. Natural-product insecticides derived from plants and other living organisms.
4. Insect growth regulators. These usually do not kill adults. They interfere with the pest's life cycle and prevent the young from developing into adults.

### Using Pesticides Sparingly

When you must use pesticides, apply them only when necessary. Avoid the "spray and pray" method which includes pesticide applications whether needed or not. Use yellow sticky trap data to determine pesticide applications. Be sure to rotate the classes of pesticides used so that no pesticide resistance occurs. Apply the pesticide wisely; that is, apply it to the part of the plant where the pest is located. For example, if the pest is located on the underside of the leaf, direct the pesticide spray from below the leaf up to its underside rather than from above onto the top of the leaf.

Wise pesticide management as outlined above will result in reduced pesticide usage and costs, increased greenhouse personnel safety, and reduced pesticide contamination of the environment. Everyone benefits from this badly needed change in pesticide management.

## SETTING UP AN IPM PROGRAM

As we mentioned previously, each greenhouse should have an IPM program unique to its situation. Factors to consider are

1. how many different crops will be planted,
2. what types of crops will be planted,
3. whether crops will be physically separated, and
4. whether the greenhouse will be in continuous production.

The number and types of crops will determine how complicated the IPM will be. Smaller numbers and fewer types of crops will make it simpler to implement IPM, since there will be fewer types of pests to control.

If the growing area is separated into sections by walls, a different crop can be grown in each separate area. This makes IPM easier because pests unique to that crop will be isolated from other crops and pests. A pest control method can then be formulated just for that pest, and control will be more effective.

If there can be a short period of time between crops when there are no plants in the greenhouse, the greenhouse can be given a thorough treatment to eliminate pests and disease organisms. Fumigants can be released without fear of killing beneficial predatory or parasitic insects. Benches, aisles, and other surfaces can be scrubbed down to sanitize the greenhouse. The result will be a good start for the next crop – a clean greenhouse that is free of insect pests and disease organisms. This is difficult to accomplish when greenhouses are in continuous production.

These are some of the main factors to consider in implementing an IPM program for a greenhouse. Careful planning and a lot of time go into such a program, but the results will be more than worth the investment. Also, you will have a pest control program that is much safer for the environment.

---

***In conclusion:***

Chapter 8 dealt with the principles of integrated pest management (IPM). IPM is actually a number of pest control methods used together to control greenhouse crop pests. Each greenhouse should have its own unique IPM program. Four principles of IPM are used together not only to control pest infestations, but also to prevent them in the first place.

---

## CHAPTER 8 REVIEW

This review is to help you check yourself on what you have learned about Integrated Pest Management. If you need to refresh your mind on any of the following questions, refer to the page number given in parentheses.

1. Define "IPM." *(page 160)*
2. Why has IPM become the focus of attention for the greenhouse industry? *(page 160)*
3. What are the four principles of IPM that are used in an IPM program? *(page 160)*
4. Why should all weeds be eliminated from inside and outside a greenhouse? *(page 161)*
5. Discuss greenhouse sanitation and how it reduces pest populations. *(page 161)*
6. How are yellow sticky traps used in an IPM program? What types of pests are caught on these traps? *(page 162)*
7. Explain how providing an ideal greenhouse environment for your crop will help to prevent pest infestations. *(page 163)*
8. Define "biological control" of greenhouse pests. *(page 163)*
9. What are the three classes of biological control organisms used in greenhouses to control pests? *(pages 163-164)*
10. What is *Encarsia formosa*? How does this organism control whitefly, a major greenhouse pest? *(page 163)*
11. What types of pesticides in use today are not as harmful to the environment as those used previously? *(pages 164-165)*
12. What are the four primary factors to consider when setting up an IPM program for your greenhouse? *(page 165)*

# CHAPTER 9

# PLANT HEIGHT CONTROL BY DIF

## Competencies for Chapter 9

As a result of studying this chapter, you should be able to do the following:

1. Discuss the effects of DIF on plant growth.
2. Implement DIF on greenhouse crops to control plant height.
3. Describe circumstances which limit the application of DIF.
4. List greenhouse crops that can be height-limited by DIF.
5. Describe the advantages of the use of DIF.

## Related Science Concepts

1. Examine plant development.
2. Explain role of light in internode elongation.

## Related Math Concepts

1. Apply mathematical concepts and operations to solve problems relevant to plant height control by DIF.
2. Apply measuring skills to obtain data necessary to solve problems relevant to plant height control by DIF.
3. Read, interpret, and construct charts, graphs, and tables that are relevant to plant height control by DIF.

## Terms to Know

chlorophyll
DIF
growth regulator
internode
leaf orientation
node
temperature regime

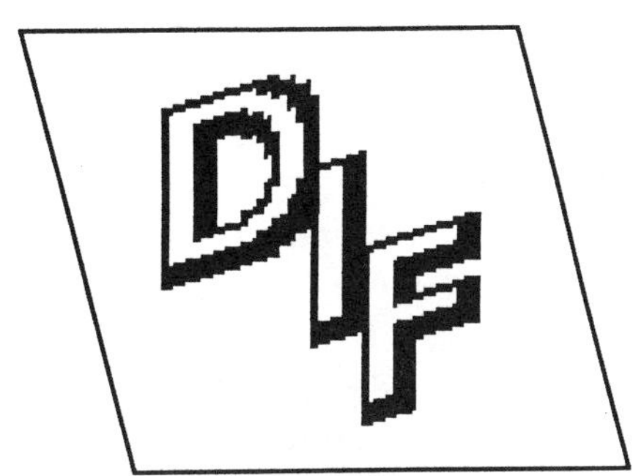

# INTRODUCTION

A common concern in the greenhouse industry is bedding plants and potted flowering crops that grow too tall. To prevent this, chemical growth retardants are frequently used. These chemicals do an excellent job of controlling height. However, growth retardants can be very expensive. Also, if they are not properly applied, they may harm the plants by burning the foliage. Some of the newest growth regulators are very powerful; they do not leave much room for error. Even a very small amount of excess chemical applied can cause a dwarfed crop.

Another method that has been used to control the height of selected crops like impatiens is controlled withholding of water. Plants grown on the dry side tend to be more compact. This method requires considerable skill and constant monitoring. If plants are allowed to dry out too much, they will suffer loss of quality.

Research at Michigan State University has shown that certain day-night temperature regimes also control plant height. This new concept, called DIF, has proved to be just as effective as chemical growth regulators. This day-night temperature regulation will be the focus of this chapter.

# DEFINITION OF *DIF*

"DIF" is simply an abbreviation for the mathematical DIFference between the day temperature (**DT**) and the night temperature (**NT**). In other words,

**DIF = DT – NT.** Therefore,

- ✩ A **positive** DIF occurs when DT is ***greater*** than NT.
  *Example:* greenhouse with DT of 75°F and NT of 65°F
  75–65 = +10 DIF
- ✩ A **negative** DIF occurs when DT is ***less*** than NT.
  *Example:* greenhouse with DT of 68°F and NT of 72°F
  68–72 = –4 DIF
- ✩ A **zero** DIF occurs when DT and NT are ***equal*** in a greenhouse.
  *Example:* greenhouse with DT of 70°F and NT of 70°F
  70–70 = 0 DIF

# EFFECTS OF DIF ON PLANT GROWTH

## Internode Length

Plant height is determined by the number and length of internodes on the stem. An internode is the portion of the stem between two nodes (Figure 9.1). A node is the point from which leaves and buds arise on a stem. DIF affects the length of the internode and thus also affects the height of the plant. Research has shown that as DIF decreases from positive values into negative values, stem internode length also decreases. As DIF increases, stem internode length also increases (Figure 9.2).

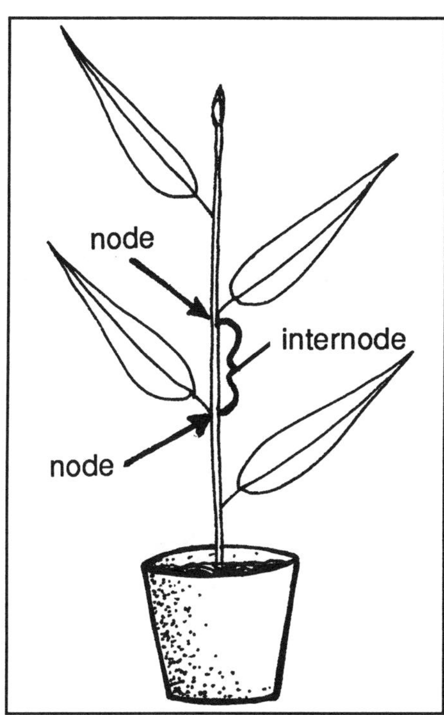


**Figure 9.1**
A plant showing an internode and two nodes

Suppose three plants as identical as possible are placed in three greenhouses that are identical in all respects except for DIF (Figure 9.3). All three greenhouses have a DT of 68°F. However, greenhouse A has an NT of 64°F, greenhouse B has an NT of 68°F, and greenhouse C has an NT of 72°F. How will the height of these three plants compare after they have grown for several weeks in the respective greenhouses? To answer this, DIF must be calculated.

| | |
|---|---|
| Greenhouse A DIF | 68–64 = +4 |
| Greenhouse B DIF | 68–68 = 0 |
| Greenhouse C DIF | 68–72 = –4 |

Greenhouse A has the largest (positive) DIF; so the plant in that greenhouse will be the tallest. The plant in greenhouse B will be shorter than the first because its DIF is smaller in value. The plant in greenhouse C will be the shortest of the three because the DIF for that greenhouse is the smallest in value (Figure 9.3). The internode length of each plant is affected by the higher or lower DIF value.

**Figure 9.2** Effects of changes in DIF on stem internode length

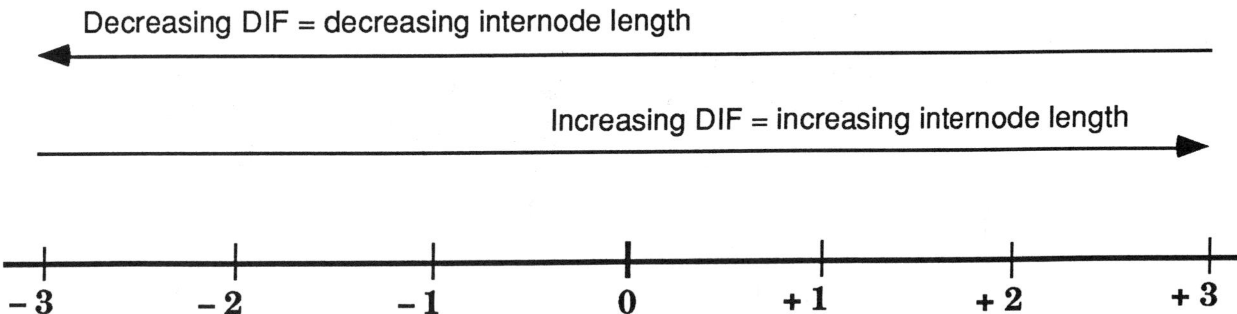

**Figure 9.3** Effect of three different DIF values on three similar plants

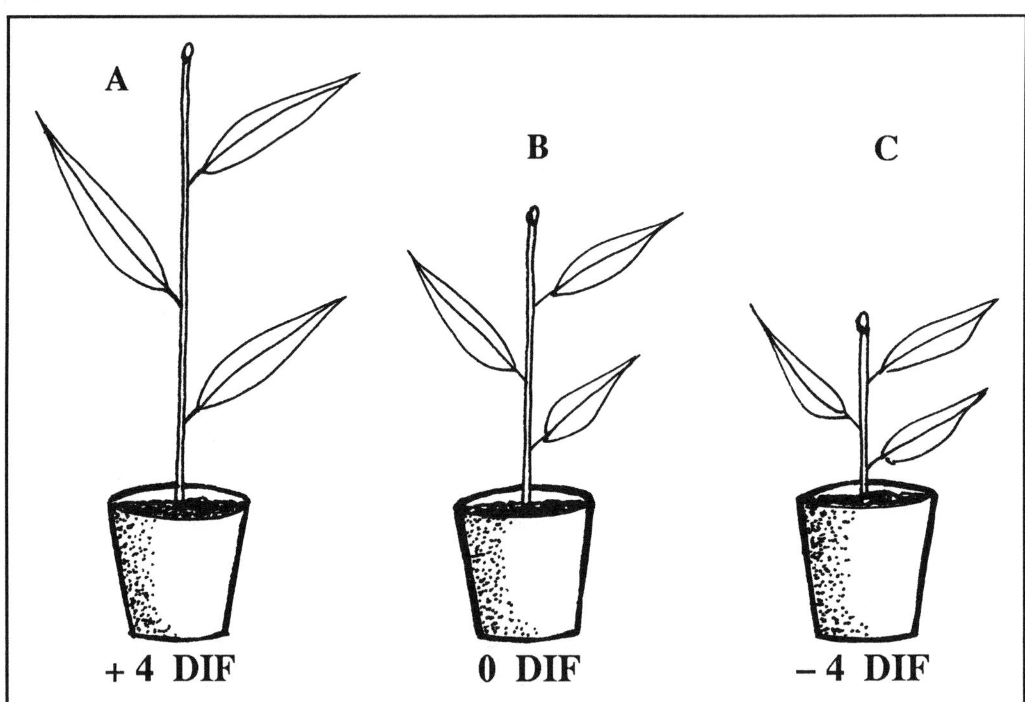


## Leaf Orientation

Leaf orientation is also affected by DIF. An example of a plant that is greatly affected by DIF is the Easter lily (Figure 9.4). With positive values of DIF, the leaf orientation of the lily is upright. As DIF decreases, leaf orientation changes to a downward-pointing position. At 0 DIF, the leaves are nearly horizontal. The leaves droop more and more as DIF gets into negative values. A DIF smaller than −4 for Easter lilies should be avoided, as their droopy appearance is not attractive.

**Figure 9.4**
Effect of DIF on Easter lily leaf orientation

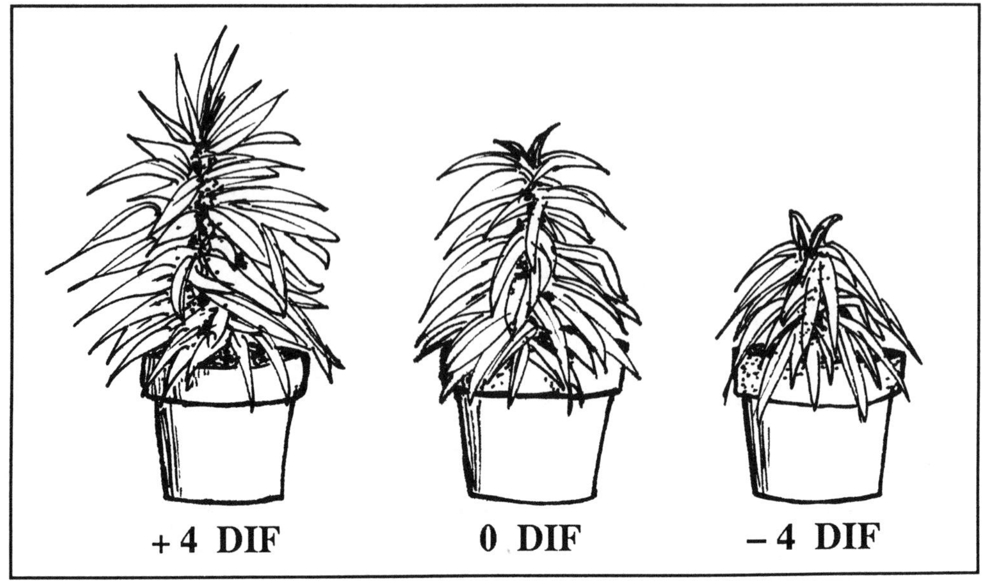

## Chlorophyll Content

The chlorophyll content of leaves can be affected by DIF. The young leaves of many greenhouse crops lose some of their chlorophyll and thus turn lighter green as DIF decreases into negative values. Seedlings like those of salvia (especially) are the most sensitive to this. They become very chlorotic if DIF is –5 or less. Thus, DIF should not be allowed to drop below -4 in order to avoid yellow or chlorotic upper leaves. Chlorotic leaves will reduce rates of photosynthesis and result in slowed growth and poorer plant quality.

# APPLICATIONS OF DIF

DIF is used to control the height of poinsettias, mums, Easter lilies, and many bedding plant species. In order to apply DIF, heating and cooling systems must be automated for efficient temperature control. A DIF of 0 or slightly negative (e.g. –1 to –4) will reduce crop height significantly compared to crops grown at a positive DIF.

There are several distinct advantages in using DIF to control crop height.

1. DIF either reduces or eliminates the use of chemical retardants. This can mean significant savings.
2. DIF does not damage plants like chemicals do.
3. Production costs are lower because labor costs are largely replaced.
4. The environment, rather than toxic chemicals, controls plant height.

## Timing

To use DIF, the greenhouse manager selects times for changing the greenhouse temperature to day and night settings (for example, at 6:00 a.m. and 8:00 p.m.). Since it takes time for greenhouse temperatures to reach desired levels, a ***lag time*** must be allowed. The manager should program temperature settings to be changed 15 minutes before 6:00 a.m. and 8:00 p.m. for unit heaters, and up to one hour before the selected times for hot water heating systems.

Because relatively warm nights are required for 0 DIF or –DIF, greenhouses should have an interior ceiling or thermal blanket to conserve heat during cold weather. It is actually possible to have a ***lower*** heating bill using 0 or –DIF than the conventional +DIF temperature regimes when heat conservation devices are in use.

Applications of DIF are up to the individual grower for implementation. Whether to use a 0 or –DIF depends on the crop being grown and the degree of height control desired.

## Limitations of Applying DIF

The primary limitation of using a 0 or –DIF for height control is the climatic effects on the greenhouse environment of typical summer weather. During hot weather, it is very difficult, if not impossible, to maintain greenhouse temperatures during the day that are cool enough to implement a 0 or –DIF. For example, if the DT is 92°F, then the NT would have to be at least that same temperature to achieve height control (in this case, 0 DIF). Such a night temperature would be excessively hot and could cause serious damage to the plants. In general, night temperatures above 75°F should be avoided because many crops are adversely affected by them.

Therefore, during hot weather, chemical growth regulators often have to be used. When cooler temperatures return, DIF can be reinstated for height control.

## Crops Responding to DIF

There are many potted flowering plants and bedding plant species that respond to DIF height control. Some of these are:

| **Bedding Plants** | **Potted Flowering Plants** |
|---|---|
| Celosia | Asiatic hybrid lilies |
| Geraniums | Chrysanthemums |
| Fuchsia | Easter lilies |
| Salvia | Gerbera daisies |
| Impatiens | Poinsettias |

***In conclusion:***

Controlling plant height by temperature regulation was the topic of Chapter 9. This height control method, called DIF, is the mathematical difference between day and night temperatures. A positive DIF results in tall plants, and a 0 or slightly negative DIF results in shorter plants. DIF saves a grower considerably on the cost of chemical growth regulators. However, DIF can not be used routinely for height control in summer when night temperatures in the greenhouse are relatively high.

## CHAPTER 9 REVIEW

This review is to help you check yourself on what you have learned about plant height control by DIF. If you need to refresh your mind on any of the following questions, refer to the page number given in parentheses.

1. What is the definition of DIF? *(page 170)*
2. Write the mathematical equation for DIF. *(page 170)*
3. In order to achieve a DIF of −4 when the greenhouse night temperature is 68°F, what should the day temperature be? *(page 170)*
4. How is plant growth affected by a 0 or negative DIF? by a positive DIF? *(pages 170-171)*
5. Besides height control, state two other aspects of plant growth that are affected by DIF. *(pages 172-173)*
6. Name four advantages of using DIF to control plant height, compared to using chemicals. *(page 173)*
7. When setting times for changing temperatures in a greenhouse to implement DIF, why is a lag time factored in? *(page 173)*
8. Explain why DIF can not be implemented during hot weather for height control of floriculture crops. *(page 174)*
9. List three floriculture crops whose height can be controlled by DIF. *(page 174)*

# CHAPTER 10

# BEDDING PLANT PRODUCTION (including GERANIUMS)

## Competencies for Chapter 10

As a result of studying this chapter, you should be able to do the following:

1. Give the scientific name of geranium.
2. Categorize the different areas of bedding plant production as to wholesale value in the U.S.
3. Categorize the different areas of bedding plant production as to wholesale value in your state.
4. List major bedding plant species.
5. Provide favorable conditions for seed germination.
6. Sow bedding plant seed in flats and in plug trays.
7. Contrast advantages with disadvantages of sowing seed in flats.
8. Contrast advantages with disadvantages of sowing seed in plug trays.
9. Define plug stages one through four.
10. Transplant seedlings from flats.
11. Transplant seedlings from plug trays.
12. Use a constant feed program on bedding plants.
13. Apply water as needed.
14. Monitor root medium moisture, porosity, and nutrient content.
15. Read thermometer.
16. Calculate DIF.
17. Finish a crop of bedding plants for sale using commercially up-to-date methods.
18. Interpret and follow production schedules.
19. Carry out cultural practices designed to avoid disease and pest occurrence.
20. List the four strategies of IPHM.
21. Recognize pests by their appearance on a host plant.
22. Recognize pests by the damage they do to bedding plant crops.
23. Recognize disease symptoms on bedding plants.
24. Market finished bedding plant crops.
25. Discuss the following items in connection with **geranium** production:
    - ☆ production statistics
    - ☆ varieties
    - ☆ propagation (including root media)
    - ☆ general culture (temperature, watering, nutrition, lighting, etc.)
    - ☆ pinching and height control
    - ☆ scheduling guidelines
    - ☆ pest and disease problems
    - ☆ marketing

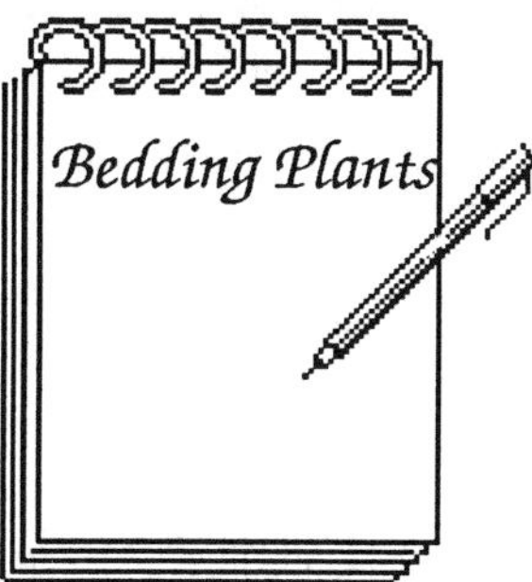

**Related Science Concepts**

1. Examine plant development.
2. Determine the cultural needs of bedding plants.
3. Describe stages of seedling development.
4. Describe disease transmission by soil organisms.

**Related Math Concepts**

1. Apply basic operations to whole numbers, decimals, and fractions as they relate to bedding plant production.
2. Apply basic operations to ratios and percents as they relate to bedding plant production.
3. Apply mathematical concepts and operations to bedding plant production.
4. Read, interpret, and construct charts, graphs, and tables related to bedding plant production.

**Terms to Know**

B-Nine®
bacterial blight
**bedding plants**
blackleg
Bonzi®
*Botrytis* blight
broadcasting seed
buffering
cotyledon
culture-indexed cuttings
Cycocel®
damping-off
dibble
disinfectant
DNA
finishing plants
foliar
fungicide
genetic
honeydew
IPHM
oedema
petiole
plant hardening
plug growth stages
primed seed
*Pythium*
refined seed
saran
seeders
seedling
soft pinch
water boom

# BEDDING PLANTS

## OVERVIEW OF THE BEDDING PLANT INDUSTRY

### Introduction

Bedding plants are greenhouse crops that are primarily annuals. These plants are usually started from seed in the greenhouse during the winter. They are sold in the spring as blooming plants, ready to be transplanted directly into the garden. As we noted earlier, the bedding plant industry is the largest segment of the floriculture industry. The 1990 wholesale value of bedding plants in the United States was nearly $1 billion.

Bedding plants are very popular because they add a lot of beauty to our surroundings. Nearly every house has at least a small flower garden containing colorful bedding plants. Many people also have vegetable gardens. Growing their own vegetables saves on food costs and provides high quality vegetables that may be hard to find in supermarkets.

Bedding plants are used extensively in parks, around commercial buildings, and even in interior landscapes. Bedding plants are essential to gardening, America's number one hobby.

## Production Statistics

### At the National Level

Bedding plants sold in flats (including geraniums and vegetables) totaled nearly $496 million, well over half the total wholesale value of $971 million in 1990, according to the USDA's *Floriculture Crops 1990 Summary* (Table 10.1). Flowering and foliar bedding plants sold in pots (other than geraniums) were worth $363 million in 1990, the second largest bedding plant category. Flowering hanging baskets, at $112 million, accounted for almost 12 percent of the total bedding plant wholesale value in 1990. They comprised the third largest bedding plant category. (See Figure 10.1.) (Statistics for geraniums are given on page 205.)

**Figure 10.1**
Wholesale value of the top three bedding plant categories in the U.S. in 1990

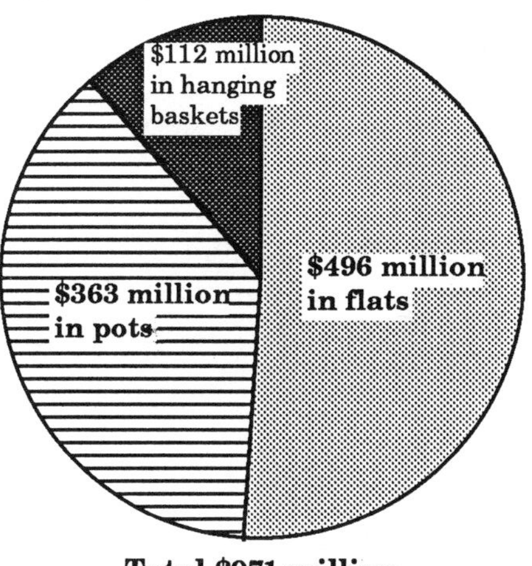


**Total $971 million**

**Table 10.1** U.S. bedding plant production statistics in 1990

| Bedding Plant Category | Wholesale Value ($ million) |
|---|---|
| Crops in flats | |
| Geraniums | 30.0 |
| Other flowering/foliar plants | 402.4 |
| Vegetables | 63.5 |
| TOTAL flats | 495.9 |
| Potted crops | |
| Garden mums | 46.9 |
| Cutting geraniums | 86.5 |
| Seed geraniums | 43.5 |
| Other flowering/foliar plants | 175.2 |
| Vegetables | 11.0 |
| TOTAL potted crops | 363.1 |
| Flowering hanging baskets | 112.1 |
| TOTAL flats, potted crops, hanging baskets | 971.1 |

Source: *Floriculture Crops 1990 Summary.* United States Department of Agriculture, National Agricultural Statistics Service, Agricultural Statistics Board, Washington, DC, April 1991

## In Ohio

Ohio placed fifth nationally in 1990 in bedding plant production (Table 10.2). Her total wholesale production value was $71 million. The category with the highest production in Ohio (the same as nationally) was bedding plants sold in flats. Their wholesale value was $38.8 million or nearly 55 percent of the total bedding plant wholesale value. Bedding plants sold in pots were second at $22.1 million, or 30 percent of the total wholesale value. Flowering hanging baskets came in third in Ohio for wholesale value at $10.1 million or 14 percent of the total wholesale value. (See Figure 10.2.)

**Figure 10.2**

Wholesale value of the top three bedding plant categories in Ohio in 1990

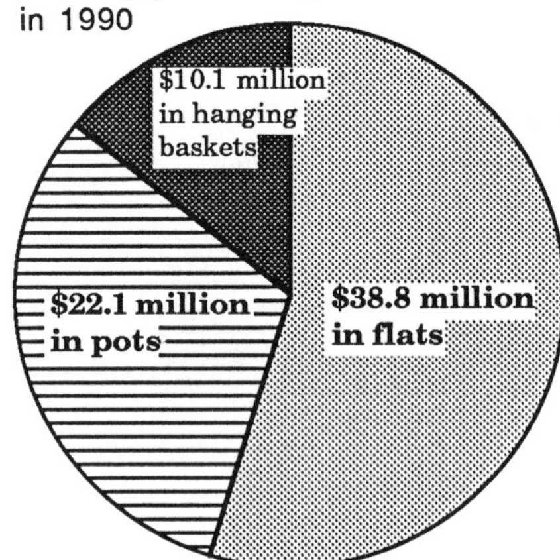


In the different categories, Ohio ranked very impressively on the national level (Table 10.2):

- ☆ ***first*** in flowering hanging baskets and in potted garden mums
- ☆ ***second*** in geraniums in flats
- ☆ ***third*** in **all** bedding plants sold in flats
- ☆ ***third*** in potted cutting geraniums and potted seed geraniums
- ☆ ***fourth*** in flowering/foliar bedding plants (excluding geraniums) sold in flats
- ☆ ***fifth*** in vegetable bedding plants sold in flats
- ☆ ***fifth*** in total bedding plant production

You can clearly see from these figures that Ohio is a major bedding plant producer. You will soon be part of this exciting industry!

**Table 10.2**

Ohio bedding plant production statistics in 1990

| Bedding Plant Category | Wholesale Value ($ million) | National Rank |
|---|---|---|
| Crops in flats | | |
| Geraniums | 3.0 | 2 |
| Other flowering/foliar plants | 31.0 | 4 |
| Vegetables | 4.8 | 5 |
| TOTAL flats | 38.8 | 3 |
| Potted crops | | |
| Garden mums | 4.1 | 1 |
| Cutting geraniums | 6.4 | 3 |
| Seed geraniums | 3.3 | 3 |
| Other flowering/foliar plants | 7.9 | 6 |
| Vegetables | 0.4 | 6 |
| TOTAL potted crops | 22.1 | 5 |
| Flowering hanging baskets | 10.1 | 1 |
| TOTAL flats, potted crops, hanging baskets | 71.0 | 5 |

Source: *Floriculture Crops 1990 Summary.* United States Department of Agriculture, National Agricultural Statistics Service, Agricultural Statistics Board, Washington, DC, April 1991

# SEED GERMINATION IN FLATS AND PLUG TRAYS

There are two primary methods of producing bedding plants from seed: germinating seed in flats and germinating seed in plug trays. (Refer back to Figure 6.18, page 137, for a picture of plug trays.) There are advantages to each method. But, increasingly, growers are using plug trays for reasons we will discuss next.

## Flats

The use of flats for seed germination has its ***advantages***.

1. Little equipment is required. Seed is usually sown by hand, though there are simple seeding machines that speed up the process.
2. Good use is made of available germination area. Several thousand tiny seeds of plants like tomato and marigold can be sown in a single flat.

However, there are several ***disadvantages*** of sowing seed in flats.

1. Diseases in the soil are readily spread from seedling to seedling through adjacent root systems. When damping off, root rots, and other diseases get started, they can wipe out whole flats of seedlings.
2. Seedlings that are left in a flat for several weeks will compete for nutrients and sunlight. As a result, seedlings can become stretched (leggy) and chlorotic (pale green) from lack of light and nutrients.
3. Transplanting seedlings from flats to cell packs or pots for growing on probably presents the worst problem. Considerable root damage can occur when roots of seedlings that are close together are separated from each other and from the germination medium. Adjacent seedlings may be snapped off by fingers or tools that are being used to lift seedlings out of the flat.
4. Transplanting seedlings from flats takes considerable labor. It is very tedious and time-consuming.

## Plug Trays

Plug trays are made up of many cells that function as tiny pots (as we discussed in Chapter 6). Eighty-five percent of the bedding plants produced in the United States are started in plug trays. The use of plug trays for germinating bedding plant seed offers many ***advantages***.

1. Seeding machines (seeders) can sow hundreds of plug trays per hour; therefore, labor costs are reduced.
2. Each seedling is grown in its own container (cell); it does not have to compete with other plants for nutrients.
3. Seedlings produced in plug trays are spaced further apart and thus receive more light.
4. If a soil-borne disease attacks a seedling or seedlings, the disease will be confined to that particular cell(s). There is no intermingling of roots of adjacent seedlings.

*(continued)*

5. There is virtually no transplant shock. Seedlings are "popped out" of the plug tray with the root ball intact. Therefore, seedlings quickly become established in the new container. Production time can be decreased by one or two weeks.
6. Transplanting from plug trays is much faster and so labor costs are reduced.
7. Plugs can be purchased to replace crops that failed or to grow crops that were not compatible with the majority of the other bedding plant species in the greenhouse.

Many aspects of plug production can be automated to make it so fast and efficient that sowing in flats seems almost primitive. When properly done, plug culture results in vigorous, healthy seedlings that establish rapidly after transplanting. Overall production of crops grown from plugs can be faster and of higher quality than those grown from flats. Because of automation, production costs that involve labor and time can be significantly reduced with bedding plant crops grown from plugs.

There are some ***disadvantages***, however, in the use of plug trays.

1. Bedding plant production in plug trays requires a large investment in specialized equipment like seeders, plug trays, etc.
2. Skilled personnel are needed to maintain the growing seedlings. With the very small volume of root medium that supports each seedling, watering and fertilizing must be precisely timed. Especially in the plug trays that contain several hundred cells (e.g. 512's, 800's, etc.), each cell dries out very quickly.
3. Considerably more germination area (up to four times as much) is needed for seedlings to germinate in plug trays as compared to flats. As many as 1,000 seedlings can be produced in a flat. With plug trays, the largest ones contain 800 cells, but most growers use 288's, 392's and 512's.

## Seed Quality

Because nearly all bedding plants are produced from seed, the use of **high quality seed is extremely important**. The grower who tries to save on production costs by purchasing cheap, low quality seed may end up losing everything. Low quality seed often germinates poorly and slowly and produces weak seedlings. The result is a delayed, smaller-than-planned crop of low quality that will find no interested customers. Since good quality seed accounts for no more than five percent of total production costs, the extra money spent to start a good crop will save a lot of money later.

### *Good Germination Percentages*

Good quality seed has a high germination percentage (well over 90 percent). This germination percentage should be printed on the seed packet. Only seed that is packaged for the current production year should be purchased. Seed carried over from the previous year will probably have reduced germination percentages and lower vigor. High quality seed germinates rapidly and shows subsequent vigorous seedling growth.

### *Refined and Primed Seed*

Two types of seed to look for are 1) refined seed, which is sorted by physical characteristics, and 2) primed seed, which is already partially germinated. Both types germinate faster and have improved germination percentages and greater uniformity. These types of seed, however, are more expensive than the conventional seed used for bedding plants.

## GERMINATING SEED IN FLATS

### Germination Media

Many different kinds of germination media for flats are available - both soil-based and soilless. Excellent germination results can be obtained from either kind. A good germination medium should have good water-holding capacity, yet allow for good drainage and aeration. The pH of the mix should be between 5.5 and 6.0. Growers can choose commercial, soilless mixes for raising their crops with excellent results. Or growers can mix their own soilless or soil-based mixes.

A common soilless germination medium is a mix (by volume) of 1:1 sphagnum peat moss and vermiculite or perlite. A soil-based mix often used is (by volume) 1:1:1 loamy field soil, sphagnum peat moss, and coarse perlite. Any soil-based germination medium must be steam pasteurized before use.

### Flats

Flats that are used for seed germination are shallow, usually 2 3/4 inches deep. A small volume of rooting medium in a shallow flat is all that seedlings need at the start, since most species are transplanted within two weeks, upon emergence. In the first short period of time, they will not develop an extensive root system. Shallow flats with small volumes of soil are lightweight and easier to handle than deep flats. Also, they mean reduced production costs.

Whereas wooden flats were once the only available kind of flat, nearly all flats used today are plastic. Wooden flats had to be sterilized by steaming; plastic flats are more easily sterilized by soaking in a disinfectant. Wooden flats were quite heavy and bulky, whereas plastic flats are lightweight and more economical.

### Sowing the Seed

Seed is sown in flats by one of two ways - broadcasting or sowing in rows. Either way gives good results. The germination medium must be firmed into place and thoroughly moistened before seed is sown.

#### *Broadcasting*

The goal of broadcasting seed is to distribute seed uniformly over the entire area of the flat. One method to accomplish this is to divide the seed to be sown into equal halves. Sow one half of the seed along the length of the flat (covering the entire surface), and sow the other half of the seed along the width of the flat (at right angles to the length) (Figure 10.3). Use a salt or pepper shaker or similar device to distribute the seed. Broadcasting is a quick method of sowing seed, but most growers sow seed in rows when using flats.

**Figure 10.3**
Broadcasting seed the length and width of the flat

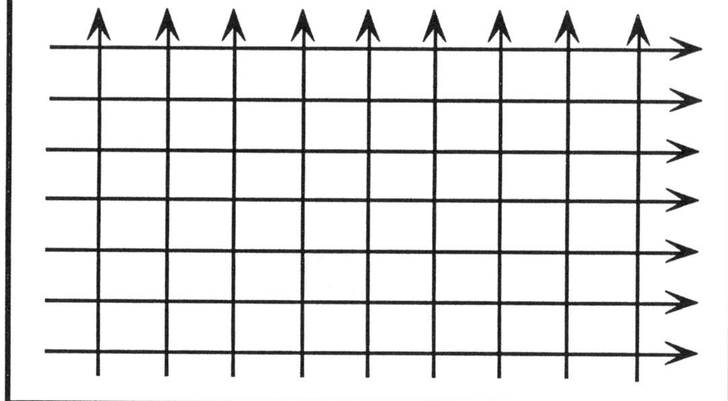

***In Rows***

Before seed can be sown in rows, small depressions or rows must be pressed into the medium. These rows usually extend the ***width*** of the flat. Seed packets are tapped and moved along the rows, dropping seeds into the rows (Figure 10.4). Compared to broadcast seedlings, seedlings growing in rows are easier to transplant without damaging adjacent seedlings. Also, if a root rot disease strikes, it is more likely to be confined to a row; with the broadcast method, it is more likely to spread throughout the flat.

Fine seed like petunia should be sown on the surface so that it receives enough oxygen to germinate. Larger seed should be covered with a thin layer of germination medium. Seed should not be sown too thickly, or overcrowding will result and seedlings will be spindly. They also may be nutrient-deficient and more susceptible to disease. Experience has shown that a standard flat can satisfactorily accommodate up to 1,000 seedlings without overcrowding.

## Germination Conditions

In order to germinate, seeds need warmth, moisture, light (for many species), and oxygen. The grower must supply these requirements to the

**Figure 10.4**
Hand seeding by tapping the seed envelope

germinating seed. Seeds should be kept moist, but not soaked, or they will be deprived of oxygen and will rot. A good way to provide moisture is placing the flats under an intermittent mist system. It should be set to keep a fine layer of moisture on the seeds (like petunia) or on the germination medium over the larger, covered seeds.

Early in winter, germination flats can be placed in direct sun. As the season progresses and light intensity increases, however, saran should be installed over the germination flats to reduce light intensity. Saran will prevent sunburn or scorch of the seedlings and keep the germination medium from drying out so quickly.

For most bedding plant species, a germination temperature of 70° to 80°F in the medium will result in rapid, uniform emergence of seedlings. Temperature of the medium can be monitored by a soil thermometer to make sure it is at the desired germination temperature. Heating systems like biotherms are excellent for germinating seed, since they supply heat directly to the germination medium.

## Germination Problems

The amount of water applied to germination media plays a major role in nearly all problems related to seed germination. If the medium is allowed to dry out completely shortly after sowing, germination will be greatly reduced. Newly-emerged, tender seedlings may die from lack of water or be severely stressed in such dry conditions. They also may become "hardened," not growing well after transplanting.

On the other hand, if the germination medium is kept too wet, there will be little or no oxygen available for the seed or seedling. The seed would be deprived of oxygen, reducing its germination potential. Or seedling roots, deprived of oxygen, would die, killing the plant. Another problem caused by overwatering is **damping off**, a disease caused by fungi that are present in germination media. These fungi damage the seedling stems at soil level, causing them to weaken until the entire seedling falls over and dies (Figure 10.5). The best way to control this disease is to allow the ***surface*** of the germination medium to become ***just*** dry before it is moistened again. Damping-off fungi do not grow very well in a dry medium surface.

**Figure 10.5**

A flat of seedlings affected by damping off. The fungus is killing seedlings in three rows.

## When to Transplant Seedlings

Seedlings are ready for transplanting when their first **true leaves** have developed. The first (lowest) set of leaves typically seen on a seedling are the **seed leaves** or cotyledons (Figure 10.6). They are usually a different shape from the true leaves. They serve as a source of food for the young seedling. True leaves develop after the seed leaves and have the shape of the mature plant's leaves.

**Figure 10.6**

A seedling ready for transplanting–with a fully developed first set of true leaves

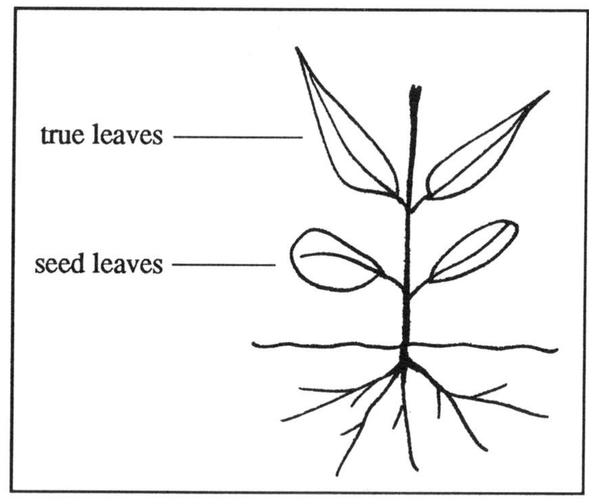


Seedlings should be transplanted as soon as they reach the first true leaf stage for several reasons.

1. At this stage, the seedling root system is sufficiently developed so that the seedling can become established after transplanting.
2. The seedling root system is still small enough that root damage will not likely be extensive enough to kill the seedling when it is lifted out of the flat.
3. The seedlings will not have begun to stretch or experience nutrient deficiency. Seedlings that are left in the flat beyond the first true leaf stage do stretch and harden, lowering the quality of the finished crop.

# GERMINATING SEED IN PLUG TRAYS

## Plug Tray Sizes

A wide variety of plug trays is available for use in germinating bedding plant seed. Plug trays with 512 or more small cells are used to produce small "plugs" (or started plants). Trays with fewer than 512 cells are used for producing large plugs. Small plugs finish well in flats. The larger plugs are used for finishing plants that are suitable for hanging baskets and pots.

Since larger-celled plug trays hold more root media, they should be used for crops that are grown for a longer period of time before transplanting, like impatiens and begonia. The larger volume of root medium in each cell supplies more nutrients to the seedling and will not dry out as fast. Thus, with reduced stress levels, the seedlings will finish faster and produce a better quality crop than in a small-celled plug tray.

## Germination Media

The germination media requirements for plug trays are quite different from those for flats. Flats hold a relatively large volume of germination medium that supplies water and nutrients for a relatively long time period. By contrast, cells in plug trays hold very small volumes of germination medium (especially the 512 and smaller plug trays). Research has shown that in just a few hours, these small volumes of germination media experience wide fluctuations of pH, nutrient level, and water content.

To prevent such harmful fluctuations, germination media used in plug trays should be formulated

1. to resist changes in pH (referred to as "buffering capacity"),
2. with good water-holding capacity, and
3. to allow for good drainage and aeration.

Nearly all germination mixes for plugs are soilless. There are many germination media mixes on the market that are specifically blended for plug trays. Some growers formulate their own. However they are prepared, all germination media should be tested to verify that they meet the above conditions. The following test can be very helpful to the grower who is just starting to use plug trays. He or she can plant seeds in a number of different germination mixes and then compare the results. Mixes that do not afford good germination can be eliminated. Remember that the success of germination depends on three factors: optimum conditions for germination, seed quality, and characteristics of the germination medium.

## Seeders

When plug trays are used for bedding plant seed germination, it is possible to sow the plug trays by hand. However, this is a very tedious, exacting, time-consuming job. The smaller the seed (like petunia) the more difficult it is to place **one** seed in each cell. Labor costs and the time involved make hand-sowing seeds in plug trays impractical.

Because of this problem, sowing seed in plug trays is now almost totally automated by the use of seeders. There are several types of seeders in use. Some can be used only for a certain-sized plug tray, while others can accommodate many sizes. Most seeders work with a vacuum that picks up the seed and releases it onto the plug tray. The seeder deposits one seed in each cell quickly and accurately. The working of some of the seeders is as follows:

1. One kind of seeder that uses the vacuum principle has a revolving drum (Figure 10.7A). The drum has rows of perforations across it. Each perforation picks up one seed by the vacuum inside the drum and then rotates and expels the seed by water pressure.

**Figure 10.7** Types of seeders

**A.** Drum seeder

**B.** Computerized electronic-eye seeder

**C.** Vacuum 'turbo' seeder
*(Photo courtesy of Blackmore Co., Inc., 10800 Blackmore Ave., Belleville, Michigan)*

2. Another type of seeder has a computerized electronic eye that counts seeds, lines them up in a trough, and drops them by gravity onto the plug tray (Figure 10.7B).
3. A third kind of seeder uses a perforated metal bar that oscillates between the seed hopper and the chutes. As one seed is picked up through each hole (again by vacuum), the bar with the seed rotates 180 degrees and drops the seed down the individual chute to the plug tray below (Figure 10.7C). This process is repeated for every row of the plug tray.

Automated seeders do the job of sowing seed many times faster than can be done by hand. In fact, there are seeders capable of sowing several hundred flats per hour. A conveyer belt moves plug trays continuously through the seeder at a constant speed. After sowing, a hopper dispenses a thin layer of the germination medium (like vermiculite) onto the plug tray to cover the seed (Figure 10.8). Some seeding set-ups have a watering device at the end of the line to water the sown plug trays very gently.

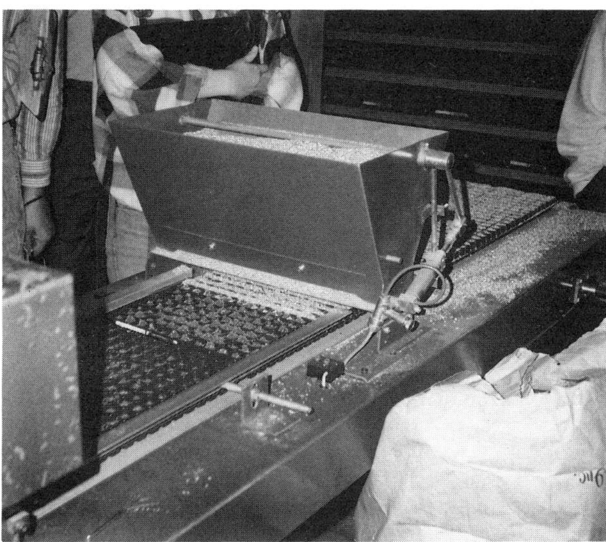

**Figure 10.8**
Vermiculite from a hopper is used to cover seeds in plug trays.

# SEEDLING GROWTH STAGES

## Four Stages of Plug Growth

In our discussion of plug trays used for seed germination, we need to become familiar with the four stages of plug growth (as shown in Figure 10.9).

**Stage 1** - emergence of the seedling root from the seed. This is the definition of germination.
**Stage 2** - development of the seed leaves and root system.
**Stage 3** - emergence of the first set of true leaves.
**Stage 4** - the plant is ready for transplanting.

Keep these stages in mind as we discuss the different environmental conditions for plug seedlings in each stage.

**Figure 10.9** The four growth stages of a plug seedling

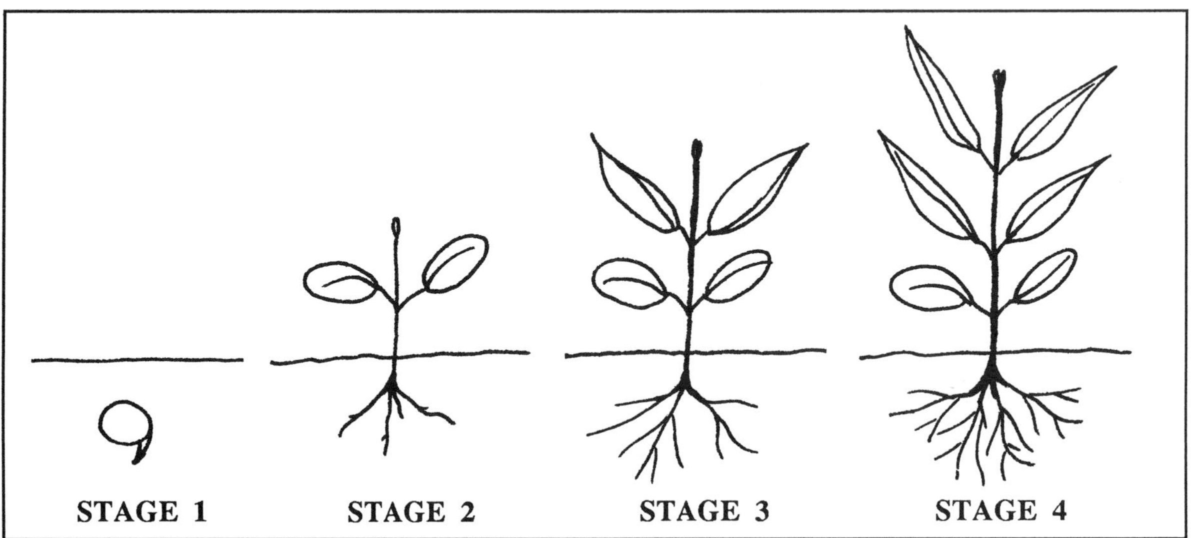


### *Stage 1 Conditions*

For uniform germination, the temperature of the germination medium must be kept constant throughout Stage 1. Like seeds sown in flats, seeds sown in plug trays vary in their optimum germination temperature requirements depending on the species. However, most bedding plant seed will readily germinate if the temperature of the germination medium is between 75° and 80°F. Bottom heating is excellent for maintaining constant germination media temperature.

Moisture levels are critical during Stage 1. The seed must receive enough water and oxygen for germination, but it should not be soaked with too much water. Applying a ***fine*** mist to keep germination medium moist (***not*** wet) is the preferred way of supplying water to plug trays. Plug trays should never be inundated with large volumes of water which will "drown" or displace the seed. A porous material known as "Agricloth" provides ideal germination conditions for Stage 1 (Figure 10.10). Placed over plug trays before watering, this cloth prevents large water droplets from striking the plug cells. When the seedling enters Stage 2, the Agricloth is removed.

**Figure 10.10** Agricloth placed over plug trays

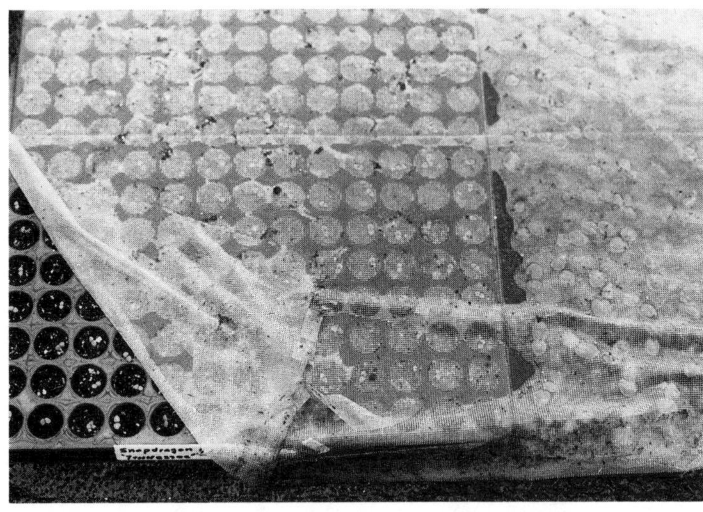

Many species of bedding plants benefit from periodic applications of 25 to 50 ppm of nitrogen starting a few days after the seed is sown. Growth is faster and more vigorous, especially with petunias and begonias.

Supplemental lighting from HID lights during Stage 1 is also known to improve the growth of seedlings, especially those of impatiens, begonia, and geranium. The HID lights should supply at least 450 footcandles of light at plug tray level for 16 to 18 hours a day.

### *Stages 2-4 Conditions*

As seedlings progress through stages 2 through 4, their requirements change. Each species has its unique environmental conditions for optimum growth. A **general** observation is that seedlings in Stage 2 have environmental requirements similar to those of Stage 1 except that in Stage 2 the moisture level of the germination medium should be somewhat drier. Allow it to dry out slightly between irrigations. In some species, such as petunia, the temperature is reduced slightly.

During Stage 3, the seedlings make a significant increase in size. Watering should be done daily. Fertilizer application with watering is recommended every other day.

Temperature of the growing medium is reduced in Stage 3 to between 72° and 75°F. Many bedding plant species still benefit from supplemental HID lighting during this stage.

Seedlings in Stage 4 are ready for transplanting. They should be somewhat "hardened" to make this transition from the plug cell to the finishing container. Hardening can be achieved by decreasing fertilizer applications and avoiding those that contain ammonia. Temperatures can be lowered into the low to mid-60°'s to hold seedlings until they can be transplanted. Decreasing water can also help harden seedlings for transplanting.

## FINISHING THE CROP

### Transplanting from Flats

When seedlings have developed their first set of true leaves, they are transplanted into a finishing container (cell packs in flats, pots, etc.). Transplanting is one of the most time-consuming and tedious tasks of bedding plant production. The basic steps of the process are as follows.

1. Prepare the finishing container by filling it with moist root medium.
2. Use a clean dibble board, pencil, or other small, cylindrical object to make holes in the root medium (Figure 10.11).
3. Using a spoon, plastic label for flats, or similar tool, lift the seedlings out of the germination flat carefully so that root damage is minimal.
4. Grasp the seedling by one of its seed leaves, ***never*** by its stem. You can easily damage the tender stem and will likely kill the plant.
5. Gently pry apart the roots of seedlings that have become entangled.

*(continued)*

**Figure 10.11**

A flat containing cell packs filled with a root medium. The dibble was used to make the holes for the seedlings.

6. Plant the seedlings in the holes in the finishing container (Figure 10.12A).
7. Push the root medium gently against the roots (Figure 10.12B). The water and nutrients in the medium will help get the plant established quickly.
8. Gently water the transplanted seedlings in the finishing container.
9. Place the containers under saran until the plants are established and actively growing.

**Figure 10.12**

**A.** A seedling handled by its seed leaves, ready to be inserted into a hole in the cell pack.
**B.** The root medium is gently pushed against the roots of the newly-transplanted seedling.

A

B

# Transplanting From Plug Trays

Transplanting seedlings (plugs) from plug trays to finishing containers is fast and easy. Very little, if any, transplant shock occurs, and the seedling establishes itself rapidly. The steps of this process are as follows.

1. Prepare the cell packs, pots, and other finishing containers by filling them with moist root medium.
2. With a dibble, make holes in the root medium, ready for the seedlings.
3. Water plug trays several hours before transplanting. The seedlings, then, will not be experiencing water stress. Also, moist plugs are removed more easily than dry ones.
4. Remove plugs from the trays by simply "popping" (pushing) them out of the cell through the drainage hole.
   a. Manually - Use a narrow object (like a piece of bamboo stake) with a blunt end to push through the drainage hole until the plug pops out (a slow, inefficient process).
   b. Mechanically - Use a plug popper, a machine equipped with blunt projections that line up with the cells of the plug tray (Figure 10.13). Position the plug tray over the projections and push a lever. All the plugs in the tray are "popped" at once, but only partially. The plugs are now loosened and easy to move out.
5. Grasp the seedling by a seed leaf and transplant it manually into the finishing container. Or simply place the plug into a hole in the medium in the finishing container.
6. Gently firm up the root medium against the root ball of the plug.

## Transplanting Assembly Line

This plug transplanting process is often mechanized on an assembly line format. People are spaced along a conveyor belt that moves flats, pots, or other finishing containers past them. Each worker is responsible for a certain portion of the flat or a certain number of pots. The workers transplant plugs from plug cell trays just above the conveyor belt into the containers as they are moved along (Figure 10.14). At the end of the transplanting line there is frequently a watering station where water is applied to the newly transplanted

**Figure 10.13**
A plug popper machine that loosens plug seedlings in their cells

**Figure 10.14**
A plug transplanting assembly line. Workers transplant plugs into flats as the conveyor moves them along.

plugs. The finishing containers are then loaded onto carts and moved into place in the greenhouse. With this method, several hundred flats can be transplanted per hour.

## Root Media

Root media for bedding plants started in flats or plug trays must supply the four functions of a root medium listed in Chapter 6. To get a finished crop of high quality, the root medium must have good water-holding capacity, yet allow for good drainage and aeration. It must supply the 17 essential nutrients for absorption by the roots. And it must provide anchorage for the plant. There are many commercial mixes that growers use and homemade mixes as well. Both soil-based and soilless mixes can produce crops of excellent quality. The majority of growers use various soilless Peat-Lite mixes.

For best results with soilless mixes, the pH of the root medium should be around 5.5 to 6.0; with soil-based mixes it should be around 6.5. If soil-based mixes are used, they must be steamed to eliminate weeds, weed seeds, disease organisms, and insects.

Lists of suitable root media for growing bedding plants can be found in publications that are available through your local county Extension office.

## Watering

In Chapter 5 we discussed the importance of the watering procedure in influencing the quality of the finished crop. Conditions that are too dry will stunt growth, lower resistance of the crop to pest infestations (both insect and disease), and significantly reduce the quality of the finished crop. Therefore, bedding plants should not be stressed from lack of water.

Growers must carefully monitor the levels of root medium moisture and apply water when needed. To control root rot diseases, the surface of the root medium should be allowed to dry between irrigations. When water is applied (either plain or as a constant feed program), allowance should be made for some leaching to control soluble salts levels.

To prevent foliar diseases, water should be applied in the morning or early afternoon so that the foliage will be dry before evening. The various methods of water application are

1. hose watering using a water breaker,
2. nozzles spaced throughout the greenhouse to apply a flat spray of water to the flats below, and
3. automated, overhead water booms that apply water to the bedding plants below by nozzles attached to the boom (Figure 10.15).

The water used should be tested for pH, alkalinity, and soluble salts levels on a regular basis. If any of these factors becomes excessive, corrective action must be taken immediately. High pH readings and high alkalinity are both common water quality problems. To lower the pH and reduce alkalinity, phosphoric acid is often injected directly into the water line.

## Nutrients

Bedding plants should be given fertilizer nutrients on a regular basis to obtain rapid, vigorous growth. Most growers use a **constant feed program**; fertilizer injectors supply nutrients to the bedding plant crop. Bedding plants grown in soilless root media should be supplied with 250 to 300 ppm of nitrogen, while soil-based crops require 200 to 250 ppm of nitrogen on a constant feed basis.

As plants grow, their water and nutrient requirements increase. More frequent irrigations of fertilizer solution must be done. Leaching must also be planned for during irrigation to reduce excess soluble salts levels. Irrigation with plain water occasionally will accomplish this.

Slow-release fertilizers can be ***uniformly*** mixed into the root medium to supply nutrients to the bedding plant crop. Slow-release fertilizers can be used

**Figure 10.15**
An automated overhead water boom applying water through nozzles to the crop below

by themselves or in combination with liquid constant-feed programs. When slow-release fertilizers supply ***all*** the nutrients, plain water can be used for irrigation. For combined slow-release and liquid fertilizer programs, slow-release fertilizers are mixed into the root medium at ***half*** the recommended rate. Remember that when you use slow-release fertilizers, you lose control over the nutrition of the crop. You must take extreme care when determining the quantity of slow-release fertilizer to mix into the root medium.

## Height Control

Chemical growth retardants are applied to certain bedding plant crops to keep them from stretching and becoming leggy and unsightly. The most commonly used growth retardant is B-Nine®, a chemical that inhibits elongation of the plant stem. (The plant will have shorter internodes.) B-Nine® is applied as a spray to coat the foliage uniformly with a thin film of solution. Plants should be turgid with dry leaves. The chemical should be applied early in the morning or during cloudy weather for maximum uptake by the plant and to prevent foliar burn. **Always follow directions** on the label when using chemical growth retardants.

Watering practices also affect the height of bedding plants. If the root medium is kept on the dry side (watered thoroughly but infrequently), the plants will be shorter than if the root medium is kept moist much of the time. Skill and experience are required to keep plants at just the desired moisture level - not so dry that they wilt and suffer from visible damage such as brown leaf edges, or even die. Even without significant wilting, flowering can be delayed.

Before hot weather sets in, a 0 or slightly negative DIF can be applied to bedding plant crops for height control. Remember to avoid a large negative DIF or one smaller than –4, or chlorosis of young leaves will occur. As outside night temperatures become progressively warmer in the spring, DIF height control will be impossible to implement (as we discussed in Chapter 9). Thus, chemical growth retardants may have to be used if height control is needed as the sale date of the crop approaches.

## Temperature

The recommended temperatures for growing most bedding plants are 70° to 75°F during the day and approximately 10 degrees cooler during the night. Two weeks before the sale date, the temperature should be lowered (usually about 5°) to harden the plants for transplanting into the customer's garden. This hardening helps the plant adjust to outdoor conditions and reduces transplant shock.

## Light

Most bedding plants should be grown in full light intensity for rapid, vigorous development. However, bedding plants grown in hanging baskets need reduced light intensity to prevent sunburn of foliage and flowers. Since transplanting occurs for many bedding plants during the mid- to late winter, they experience very low light intensity for long periods of time. This greatly slows the establishment and growth of transplanted seedlings. HID lighting applied to seedlings during the first month after transplanting is very helpful in promoting rapid establishment and vigorous growth.

## Diseases (Damping off)

Damping off is the most common disease of bedding plants. As mentioned earlier, it is a problem particularly during germination, though it can also strike older plants. *Pythium* and *Rhizoctonia* are the two fungi that cause most of the damping off observed in bedding plants. These fungi, living in the soil, invade the stems of seedlings in cool, moist conditions. When the support tissue of the stem is destroyed, the seedling falls over and dies. (See Figure 10.5, page 185.) Damping off can quickly destroy a flat of seedlings, especially if the seed was broadcast in the germination flat.

Several steps that can be taken to prevent or control damping off are:

1. Keep the ***surface*** of the germination medium dry between irrigations.
2. In flats, sow seed thinly so that there is air circulation after germination. The surface of the germination medium will then be able to dry out.
3. Use steam pasteurization on the germination medium if it is soil-based or if the soilless germination medium was contaminated.
4. Use fungicide only as needed and directed.

## Disease Control

There are four widely-used strategies for disease control on bedding plants in the greenhouse. Used interactively, they are known as **Integrated Plant Health Management (IPHM)** (a program very similar to IPM for insect pests). These four strategies are:

1. good greenhouse sanitation
2. ideal cultural environment for vigorous plant growth
3. use of disease-resistant varieties
4. use of fungicides when necessary

Keeping the greenhouse as clean as possible is the first strategy of the greenhouse manager. Walkways, benches, and other structural aspects of the greenhouse should be disinfected several times a year with an approved disinfectant. All recycled containers should also be disinfected.

Secondly, seedlings should be kept healthy and growing vigorously by means of ideal environmental conditions for plants. (Disease organisms usually find such an environment less favorable.) Like people, healthy plants are more resistant to disease.

Another important strategy is to purchase seed of bedding plant cultivars that are **resistant** to disease (especially damping off). This is a genetic characteristic bred into the plant's DNA. A resistant cultivar is able to "fight off" disease organisms better than is a non-resistant cultivar.

Finally, fungicides are used when necessary to control diseases caused by fungi. Fungicides may be applied as a drench or mixed with the root medium. Regardless of application method, **always follow label directions** for use of fungicides. Application of fungicides (or any pesticide) at excessive rates or to crops not listed on the label is **illegal**.

IPHM is mainly a preventive strategy that is cost effective and "soft" on the environment. What's more, it really works!

## Pests

The most common pests of bedding plants are aphids, spider mites, thrips, and whiteflies. These pests feed on the plant, distorting growth. In severe infestations, they even kill the plant. Sometimes in warm weather, populations of these pests can "explode", literally covering a crop in a matter of days.

### Aphids (Figure 10.16 A,B)

Aphids are typically plump green or brown insects that feed on various plant parts, including stems and flower buds (Figure 10.16A). Most aphids do not have wings, though sometimes winged individuals are present (Figure 10.16B). Aphids have piercing/sucking mouthparts. As these mouthparts are used to withdraw plant sap from the plant, new growth becomes distorted. Aphids also excrete a sticky substance known as honeydew. If populations are large enough, honeydew will cover large areas of the plant. A type of fungus known as black mold or sooty mold grows on the honeydew. It ruins the appearance of the infested bedding plant crop. One other symptom of aphid infestation is the presence of white flecks on the foliage. These are the old skins of the aphids, cast off as they molt.

### Spider Mites (Figure 10.16C)

Two-spotted spider mites are the most common mites to infest bedding plant crops. They look like small moving dots, barely visible to the naked eye. With their rasping-scraping mouthparts, two-spotted spider mites obtain nutrients from the plant, usually from the undersides of the leaves. As a result, the upper surfaces of leaves become mottled or take on a "salt and pepper" appearance. Tiny webbing is visible on the undersides of leaves and on the flowers.

### Thrips (Figure 10.16D)

Thrips are very small, cylindrical insects that are commonly found in flower buds and flowers and on leaves. Like spider mites, thrips damage the plant with their scraping mouthparts. Symptoms of thrips damage are streaking and distorting of flower petals and deformed leaves. The winged adults can spread rapidly over large areas. They enter greenhouses through ventilators, doors, and other openings.

The most damaging thrips species is the western flower thrips *(Frankliniella occidentalis)*. It reproduces rapidly. Its resistance to many pesticides makes any infestation very difficult to control. Western flower thrips also transmit viral diseases from plant to plant.

**Figure 10.16**
Common bedding plant pests
*(greatly magnified)*
(courtesy of Richard Lindquist, Department of Entomology, OARDC, Wooster, Ohio)

**A.** Adult aphid with two young aphids

**B.** Winged adult aphid

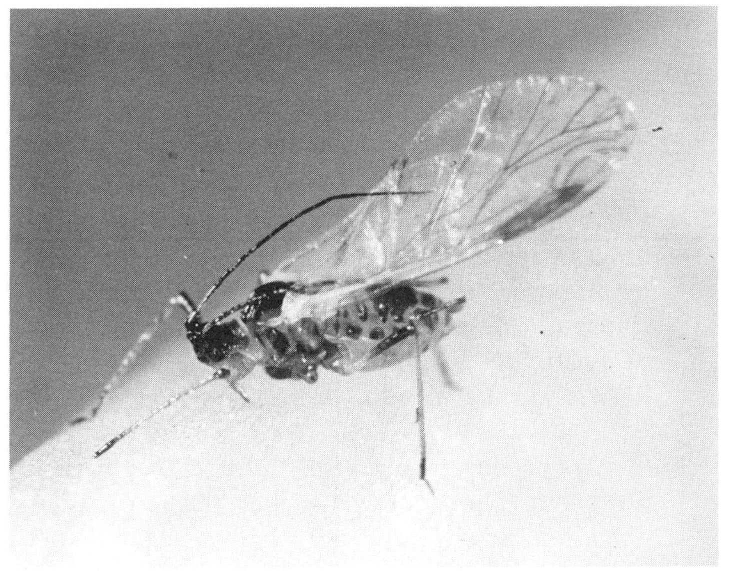

**C.** Two-spotted spider mite

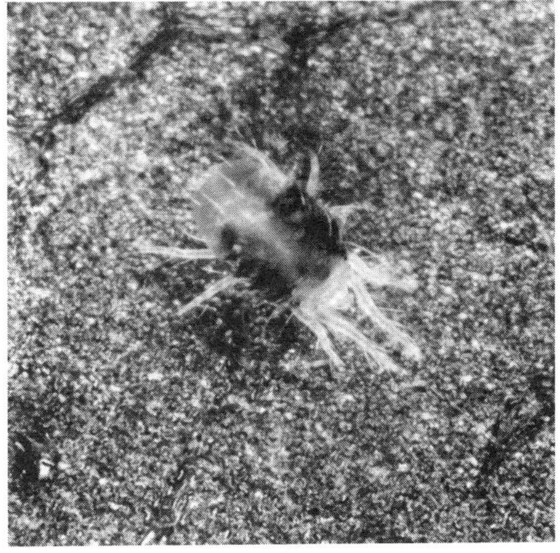

**D.** Adult thrips

**E.** Adult greenhouse whitefly

### Whiteflies (Figure 10.16E)

Whiteflies are oval-shaped white insects that feed primarily on the undersides of leaves. They reproduce rapidly, quickly achieving huge populations. Whiteflies have piercing mouthparts that damage foliage as they feed. Black sooty mold often appears on foliage beneath large infestations.

To control pests on bedding plant crops, implement the IPM strategies we discussed in Chapter 8. Remember, the best control is **prevention**.

1. Keep the greenhouse free of weeds, debris, and old plants from previous crops.
2. Screen vents to prevent entry of these winged pests.
3. Monitor winged pest populations using yellow sticky traps.
4. Use the data gathered to apply environmentally "soft" pesticides.

## Pesticide Application

When a pesticide is called for in the greenhouse, use the "best" one for the job. Direct the pesticide spray to where the pest is located (e.g. the leaf undersides for whiteflies and spider mites). Use a fine spray because it will penetrate the foliage better and kill the target pests more effectively.

**Figure 10.17**

Licensed greenhouse foreman in protective gear: a spray suit with a sealed helmet equipped with its own filtered air supply

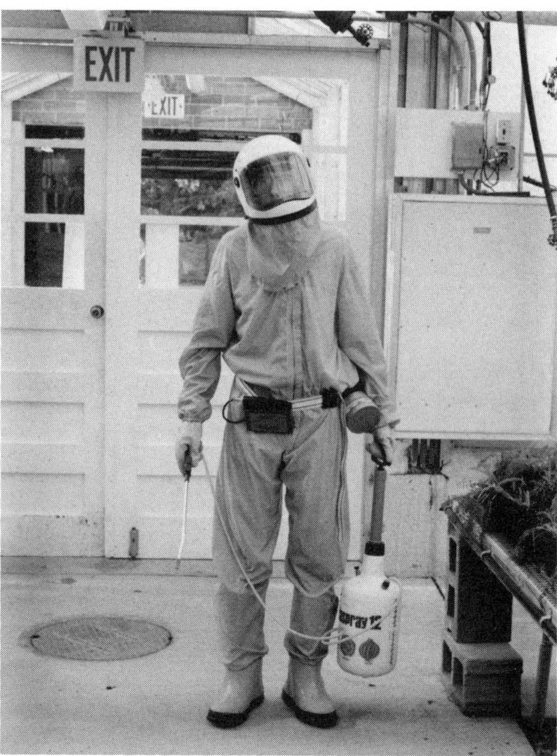


A person who is to apply pesticides must have an applicator's license. Obtaining a license requires much study and passing a comprehensive test. The aim is safe and proper application of pesticides. Applying pesticides without a license is not only **dangerous**, but **illegal**.

Once you are licensed, **follow label directions** and apply only pesticides that are registered for the pest and crop being treated. You **must** wear protective clothing and use the prescribed equipment:

- ☆ rubber boots, gloves, and coat that do not allow pesticides to penetrate
- ☆ goggles
- ☆ respirator mask that filters out any pesticide particles in the air

A type of one-piece spray suit comes with an airtight helmet equipped with its own supply of filtered air (Figure 10.17). With this suit, only rubber boots and gloves need to be supplied.

## SCHEDULES FOR BEDDING PLANT CROPS

Scheduling bedding plants for sale in the spring can be quite complicated, especially if many bedding plant species are produced. However, specific schedules for many species are published in various greenhouse industry publications. Check with your local Cooperative Extension Service office for current recommendations. An example of schedules for a number of common bedding plants is given on the next page in Table 10.3. These production schedules should be used only as a guide. The environment of each greenhouse will be different from others due to variations in weather conditions, cultural practices, etc. that affect growth rates. Therefore, a grower will not always follow the exact dates on published schedules. Instead, he/she is free to modify the schedule slightly based on crop growth in that particular greenhouse.

Growers should always keep careful, accurate records for scheduling purposes. Records should be kept of seed sowing dates, transplanting dates, environmental conditions throughout the crop, growth retardant applications, the date the crop was judged ready for sale, and other events and conditions. These records will be a very valuable reference when scheduling future bedding plant crops.

### Popularity of Major Bedding Plant Species

There are hundreds of bedding plant species and cultivars grown today in the U.S. According to a survey conducted by the Professional Plant Growers' Association, impatiens in 1988 was the best-selling bedding plant crop in the United States. It has remained number 1 since that time. Cutting geraniums are the second most popular bedding plant crop. Until 1979, petunias were the most popular bedding plant; they are now a distant third. Seed geraniums are in fourth place. Tomatoes are the most popular vegetable bedding plant.

Table 10.4 lists the most popular bedding plants grown today. Illustrations or photographs of many of these crops are available in various industry

**Table 10.4**

Common bedding plants grown in the United States

| | |
|---|---|
| Ageratum | Marigolds |
| Alyssum | Pansies |
| Asters | Peppers |
| Begonia | Petunias |
| Browallia | Phlox |
| Cabbage | Portulaca |
| Celosia | Salvia |
| Coleus | Snapdragons |
| Dahlias | Tomatoes |
| Dusty miller | Verbena |
| Geranium (seed & cutting) | Vinca |
| Impatiens | Zinnia |
| Lobelia | |

**Table 10.3** Sample of schedules for various commonly grown ornamental plants

| Plant | Seeding Date | Germination (emergence) | | Growing-on | | Hardening | | Transplanting | | Selling Period |
|---|---|---|---|---|---|---|---|---|---|---|
| | | Days | Temp.°F | Days | Temp.°F | Days | Temp.°F | Date | Temp.°F | |
| Ageratum | 1/7 | 6 | 75 to 80 | 10 | 60 to 65 | 10 | 50 to 55 | 2/2 | 60 | April 10 to 20 |
| | 3/31 | 5 | 75 to 80 | 8 | 65+ | 8 | 65+ | 4/21 | 65+ | May 10 to 20 |
| Alyssum | 1/26 | 4 | 75 | 10 | 60 to 65 | 5 | 50 to 55 | 2/18 | 60 to 65 | April 10 to 20 |
| | 3/31 | 4 | 75 | 5 | 65 | 10 | 50 to 55 | 4/19 | 60 | May 10 to 20 |
| Aster | 2/22 | 4 | 75 | 10 | 60 to 65 | — | — — | 3/7 | 60 to 65 | April 15 to 20 |
| | 4/1 | 4 | 75 | 10 | 60 to 65 | | | 4/15 | 65 | May 10 to 20 |
| Begonia | 12/12 | 21 | 75 to 80 | 21 | 60 | — | — — | 1/23 | 60 | April 12 to May 1 |
| Coleus | 1/5 | 8 | 75 to 80 | 20 | 60 to 65 | 7 | 55 to 60 | 2/11 | 62 to 65 | April 10 to 20 |
| | 3/31 | 5 | 75 to 80 | 12 | 65 | — | — — | 4/20 | 62+ | May 10 to 20 |
| Dusty Miller | 12/15 | 18 | 75 to 80 | 21 | 60 | — | — — | 1/28 | 60 | April 10 to 20 |
| Geranium (seed) | 1/2 | 6 | 75 to 80 | 21 | 60 | — | — — | 2/4 | 60 | April 12 to 30 |
| Impatiens | 1/3 | 6 | 80 | 21 | 60 | — | — — | 2/4 | 62 | April 12 to 30 |
| Marigold —Dwarfs | 1/5 | 8 | 70 to 75 | 10 | 60 | 12 | 50 to 55 | 2/8 | 60 | April 10 to 20 |
| —Large flowered | 1/5 | 8 | 70 to 75 | 10 | 60 | 12 | 50 to 55 | 2/8 | 60 | April 10 to 20 |
| —Dwarfs | 4/1 | 6 | 70 to 75 | 6 | 60 to 65 | 10 | 60 | 4/23 | 60 | May 10 to 20 |
| Pansy | 10/16 | 10 | 75 | 15 | 55 to 60 | 12 | 45 to 50 | 11/23 | 50 to 55 | March 20 to April 20 |
| | 11/6 | 10 | 75 | 15 | 55 to 60 | 12 | 45 to 50 | 12/15 | 50 to 55 | March 30 to April 25 |
| | 1/14 | 7 | 75 to 78 | 7 | 55 to 60 | 12 to 20 | 50 to 55 | 2/15 to 20 | 58 | April 15 to May 1 |
| Petunia and Snapdragon | 11/20 | 6 | 75 | 10 | 60 | 16 | 45 to 50 | 12/22 | 60 | March 25 to April 5 |
| | 12/3 | 5 | 75 | 7 | 55 to 60 | 16 | 45 to 50 | 1/4 | 60 | April 10 to 20 |
| | 12/12 | 5 | 55 | 7 | 55 to 60 | 16 | 45 to 50 | 1/9 | 60 | April 20 |
| | 1/7 | 5 | 75 | 5 | 55 to 60 | 12 | 45 to 50 | 1/30 | 60 | April 30 to May 5 |
| | 2/25 | 5 | 75 | 5 | 55 to 60 | 12 | 55 to 60 | 3/18 | 60 | May 5 to 12 |
| | 3/15 | 5 | 75 | 5 | 55 to 60 | 12 | 55 to 60 | 4/6 | 60 | May 15 to 18 |
| | 4/1 | 5 | 75 | 5 | 55 to 60 | 12 | 60 | 4/21 | 60 | May 25 |
| | 4/7 | 5 | 75 | 5 | 55 to 60 | 12 | 60 | 4/29 | 60 | May 27 to June 3 |
| Phlox | 12/21 | 12 | 65 | 21 | 55 to 60 | — | — — | 2/1 | 55 | April 15 to May 5 |
| Portulaca | 1/24 | 4 | 75 | 14 | 60 to 65 | 12 | 55 to 55 | 2/25 | 60 | April 20 to 30 |
| | 3/31 | 4 | 75 | 8 | — — | — | — — | 4/14 | 65 | May 10 to 20 |
| Salvia | 1/24 | 6 | 75 to 80 | 6 | 55 to 60 | 6 | 50 to 55 | 2/12 | 60 | April 10 |
| | 3/31 | 6 | 75 to 80 | 8 | 60 to 65 | — | — — | 4/14 | 65 | May 10 to 20 |
| Verbena | 12/29 | 7 | 75 | 21 | 55 to 60 | 14 | 55 | 2/1 | 55 to 58 | April 15 to May 1 |
| Vinca | 12/15 | 12 | 75 to 80 | 3 | 55 to 60 | 14 | 55 to 60 | 2/15 | 60+ | May 1 to June 1 |

(Source: *Tips on Growing Bedding Plants,* second edition, Ohio Cooperative Extension Service, The Ohio State University, 1989)

publications.[1] Various professional florist associations[2] also have descriptions of and information about many bedding plant species.

## MARKETING BEDDING PLANTS

As we saw at the beginning of this chapter, bedding plant production is the largest segment of the floriculture industry. The wholesale value of bedding plants nationally ($971 million) accounted for 35 percent of the ***total*** floriculture wholesale value in 1990. Flowering/foliar bedding plants accounted for 92 percent of the total bedding plants produced in 1990; the other 8 percent were vegetables.

Bedding plants sold in flats are the most popular marketing method, making up 52 percent of the total (Figure 10.18). Potted bedding plants were second at 37 percent. Flowering hanging baskets came in third at 11 percent (Figure 10.19).

There are many different retail outlets for bedding plants: garden centers, roadside markets, mass market discount stores, retail greenhouses, and grocery stores. Growers supplying these outlets must know what their customers want - the quality the customer expects, the varieties, and even the containers the plants should be sold in. The smart grower will produce what the customer wants. No matter how bedding plants are marketed, all containers should have culture tags with the name, picture of the flower, mature height, and a brief cultural description of the species (Figure 10.20).

---

1 Examples are "Greenhouse Grower", "Grower Talks", and "Greenhouse Manager."

2 Examples are Ohio Florists' Association and Professional Plant Growers' Association.

---

**Figure 10.18**

A bedding plant wholesale grower with a large crop of bedding plants in flats near the time of sale.

**Figure 10.19**

Bedding plants in hanging baskets make colorful additions to any porch or enclosed patio.

Some growers even hold a workshop for their retail customers to inform them about important aspects of bedding plant culture **while the plants are on display**. Informed retailers will then care for the bedding plants properly so that they will retain greenhouse quality while on display in the retail store.

Most customers want instant color when they buy bedding plants. So most growers sell bedding plants in flower or at least with buds showing color. Vegetable bedding plants should be of good size with flower buds showing in crops like tomatoes or peppers.

When bedding plants are marketed at either the wholesale or retail level, they should be displayed in an orderly fashion in arrangements that allow easy access for the customer. Wholesale growers display their bedding plant crops in their production greenhouses; retail outlets usually display the bedding plants on raised benches and counters. Retail areas sometimes have plants grouped by similar cultural requirements to help customers decide what plants will grow well in their gardens. Other display strategies include grouping plants by flower color or mature size.

---

**Figure 10.20**

Bedding plant flats with labels in each section describing the particular plant and its culture

# GERANIUMS

## INTRODUCTION

The geranium (*Pelargonium* x *hortorum*) is a flowering plant that becomes more popular every year for several reasons.

1. Geraniums flower continuously throughout the summer.
2. They are available in a wide variety of colors and shades.
3. They adapt readily to a wide range of climatic conditions.

Because of the many new hybrid varieties available (those produced from seed), geraniums, both cutting and seed grown, are now generally considered **bedding plants** rather than flowering potted plants. Their total wholesale value in the U.S. in 1990 was $160 million, and the potted plants alone were worth $130 million. In Ohio, the wholesale value of the potted plants was $9.7 million, $6.4 million for the geraniums grown from cuttings and $3.3 million for those grown from seed. As **flowering potted plants**, geraniums in 1990 ranked second only to poinsettias in economic importance.

A recently-introduced geranium known as Martha Washington or Regal geranium is becoming especially popular. These geraniums require cool conditions in order to grow well and bloom profusely. When grown correctly, they are very large, showy plants. They are sold mostly in spring because of their requirement for cool temperatures. Easter and Mother's Day account for the largest number of sales of these geraniums. See Table 10.5 for a list of the cultivars of several forms of geraniums that are currently grown.

Ivy geraniums are also showy. Due to their vining growth habit, they are grown mostly for hanging baskets. Ivy geraniums perform well outside, like zonal geraniums. They will last all summer when properly cared for by the homeowner.

Novelty geraniums include those with scented or variegated foliage. The earlier varieties, with small, inconspicuous flowers, were grown mainly for their foliage and/or scent. More recent introductions, however, have large, beautiful blooms as well. Figure 10.21 (page 207) illustrates the major types of geraniums grown in Ohio greenhouses.

The more exotic geranium forms have their place, but the "bread-and-butter" of geranium production is cutting or zonal geraniums. The most popular color is red, followed by pink and white.

## PROPAGATION

### Seed

Zonal geraniums started from seed in late December and early January are usually ready for sale by Memorial Day, if proper germination requirements are provided. Bottom heat should be applied to keep the germination medium temperature around 75°F. The germination medium should have good

**Table 10.5** Geranium cultivars

**VEGETATIVE GERANIUMS**

***Propagated by cuttings***

| Red* | Pink and Salmon* | White* |
|---|---|---|
| Red Perfection | Apple Blossom | Snowmass |
| Irene | Salmon Irene | Modesty |
| Yours Truly | Genie Irene | Snowhite |
| Fame | Cherry Blossom | |
| Mars | Capri | |
| Tango | | |
| Crimson Fire | | |

| Variegated/Novelty* | Ivy Geraniums | Regal Geraniums |
|---|---|---|
| Mrs. Cox | Pascal | Allure |
| Ben Franklin | Sugar Baby | Crystal |
| William Langguth | Cornell | Mary |
| Mrs. Parker | Butterfly | Shirley |
| | Lulu | Peggy |

**HYBRID GERANIUMS**

***Propagated by seed (varieties)***

| | |
|---|---|
| Sprinter | Mustang |
| Ringo | Flash |
| Sooner | Encounter |

* Zonal geraniums

water-holding capacity, yet allow for drainage and aeration. It should be kept moist, but not wet, so that oxygen will be available for the germinating seed. Applying intermittent mist is a good way to get the right amount of moisture to the germinating seed.

Geranium seed can be germinated in flats or plug trays. If plug trays are used, the best choice in size is trays with large cells; that is, plug trays that have fewer cells per tray (like 288's). Seed geraniums require a relatively large volume of germination medium and more space for growth. These can both be supplied in plug trays with large cells.

Approximately three weeks after the seed has been sown in flats, the geranium seedlings are ready for transplanting into cell packs or 4- or 4 1\2-inch pots. At this stage they have developed their first set of true leaves. When seed is sown in plug trays, the seedlings are transplanted about four to six weeks after sowing. At this time they have developed two or more sets of true leaves.

## Cuttings

Many growers prefer to produce vegetatively propagated zonal geraniums. They purchase disease-free cuttings ("culture-indexed" cuttings) from

Figure 10.21 Different types of geraniums

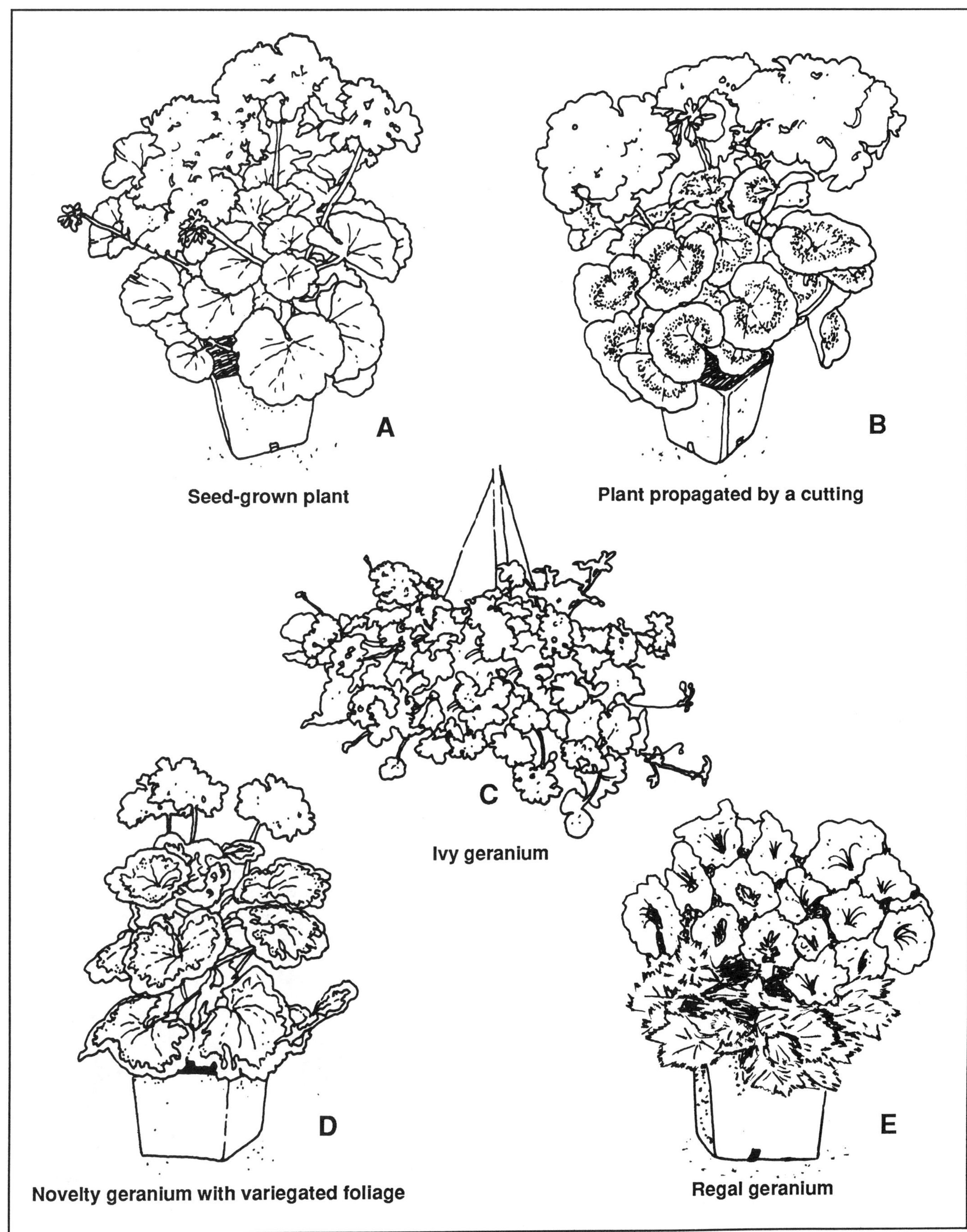

a specialist propagator. These cuttings are **initially** free of disease organisms. The grower must then keep the geranium crop free of disease by implementing IPHM principles.

Some growers produce their own cuttings from stock plants they raise in the greenhouse. These stock plants must be raised from culture-indexed cuttings that are purchased from a specialist propagator. The cuttings, purchased any time from May to August, are planted as soon as they arrive. All equipment and products, including root medium, containers, tools, and benches, **must be disinfected** before the stock plants are planted. This practice greatly reduces, if not eliminates, the risk of disease. Stock plants that are diseased will produce inferior cuttings, which may, in turn, mean ruin of the crop.

As the stock plants grow, they are pinched several times to encourage branching. This is continued all summer to establish plants that contain many branches (Figure 10.22). A single stock plant established in June can potentially yield between 30 and 40 cuttings the following spring.

Cuttings are usually removed by being **snapped off** by hand to prevent the spread of disease through contaminated knives or other tools. In preparation, everyone who handles the cuttings should wash his or her hands thoroughly with soap to prevent contamination. Terminal stem cuttings range from 1 1/2 to 3 inches in length (Figure 10.23). They should be taken in the morning when the stock plants are turgid, so that the snap-off is clean. All leaves at the base of the cutting should be removed so that the **petiole** (leaf stem) is not covered by rooting medium.

---

**Figure 10.22**
A well-branched geranium stock plant that has been pinched

To promote root growth on the cuttings, they are usually dusted with a rooting hormone before they are stuck in the rooting medium. The rooting medium may be a soilless mix or a series of foam rooting cubes (which are becoming very popular). Intermittent mist is applied to keep the cuttings turgid. Misting frequency is gradually reduced as rooting progresses. To prevent disease and provide air circulation, cuttings should be spaced in the bench so that the leaves of one cutting do not overlap those of adjacent cuttings. The rooting medium should be maintained around 70°F for rapid rooting.

Cuttings start to develop roots during the second week after sticking. At this time and periodically until the cuttings are potted, fertilizer must be applied. A 20-10-20 fertilizer at 200 to 300 ppm of nitrogen is recommended. Without fertilizer, the cuttings will become chlorotic.

When the cuttings have developed a vigorous root system with roots about one inch long, they are ready for transplanting (Figure 10.24). This is usually three to four weeks after sticking.

## Transplanting

To transplant the rooted cuttings and seedlings of geraniums into their finishing containers, follow these simple steps:

1. Get ready all the 4- or 4 1/2-inch pots (round or square) that you will need.
2. Fill each pot with moist root medium.
3. Plant the cuttings at the same depth as they were during rooting.
4. Press the medium against the roots, making good contact. This will ensure rapid establishment of the rooted cutting.

*(continued)*

**Figure 10.23**
A geranium cutting ready to be rooted

**Figure 10.24**
A rooted geranium plant ready for transplanting

5. Water in the cuttings.
6. Move them to their assigned place in the greenhouse.
7. Use saran over the crop if shading is needed.

### Root Media

Growers use both soil-based and soilless root media with equal success. The root media must have good water- and nutrient-holding capacity yet allow for drainage and aeration. Many recipes are available for both soil-based and soilless root media. The grower must decide which kind to use, based on availability of ingredients, cost factors, and other considerations. A typical soil-based root medium is composed of equal parts (by volume) of field soil, sphagnum peat moss, and perlite. Soil-based root media must be steam pasteurized before use.

Many commercial and homemade soilless root media are used by geranium growers. Soilless mixes are uniform from batch to batch. Common choices are the Peat-Lite mixes. Soilless mixes do not need steam pasteurization unless they were exposed to contaminating dust or debris.

However, the light weight of soilless mixes can be a problem. Large geraniums tend to dry out more quickly when grown in soilless mixes. Also, they are more prone to falling over. By contrast, soil-based mixes do not dry out as quickly. They are heavier and offer the plant more support. In addition, geraniums grown in soil-based mixes transplant more easily into gardens, especially those with heavy soils.

The pH of soil-based mixes should be maintained around 6.5 and the pH of soilless media held to 6.0. Before a crop is planted in a new root medium, the root medium should be analyzed in a soil testing laboratory for measurement of pH and determination of the levels of soluble salts and nutrients. The soil laboratory can then provide recommendations on correcting any factors that are not optimum.

## GROWING THE GERANIUM CROP

### Temperature

Geraniums grow and flower best if night temperatures are kept between 55° and 60°F. Day temperatures should be approximately 10 degrees higher. Plant quality will **decrease** if day temperatures are above 82°F. If night temperatures fall below 50°F, plant quality will suffer, plant development will be very slow, and reddening of the foliage will occur. Research has shown that the rate of flower bud development in cutting geraniums increases as the temperature increases from 50° to 72°F (Figure 10.25). Temperatures higher than 72°F result in reduced rates of flower bud development.

### Watering

Geraniums must have a uniform supply of water. The surface of the root medium should be allowed to dry between irrigations, but not to the point

**Figure 10.25** Rate of flower bud development increases as temperature rises to the optimum of 72°F.

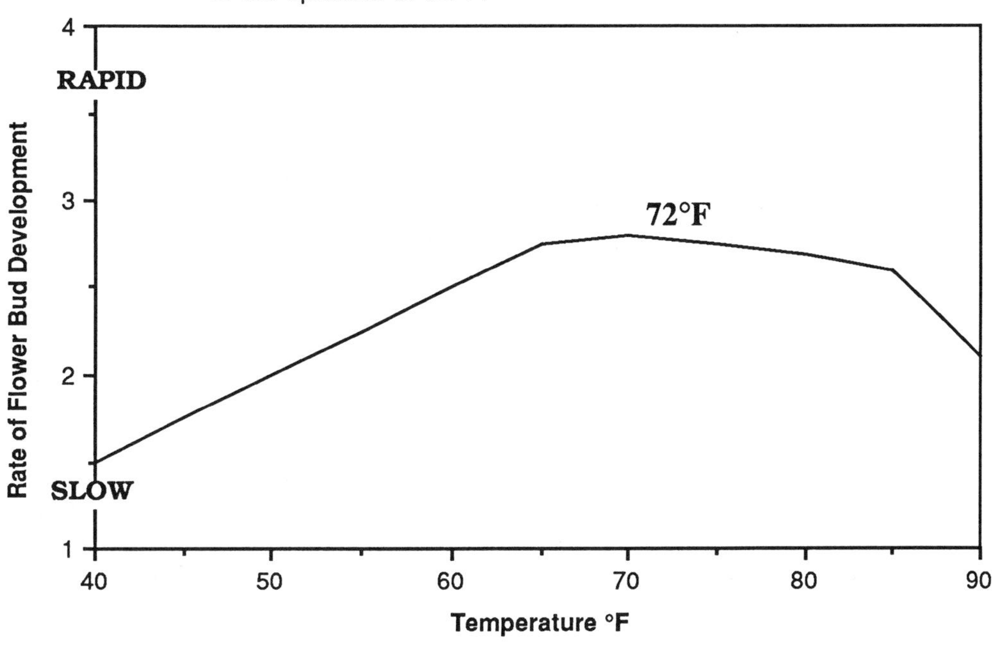


that plants start to wilt. The use of an overhead watering system should usually be avoided, especially when the crop begins to bloom. Wet foliage is an ideal growing environment for many foliar diseases such as *Botrytis*, which also affects flowers.

The irrigation systems that are preferred moisten only the root medium. These are spaghetti tubes, capillary mats, and ebb and flow benches. The frequency of irrigation will increase as the plants grow in size. Also, they will need more water when outside temperatures rise and light levels intensify from late winter to late spring.

## Nutrition

Geraniums respond very well to a constant feed program. Also, a constant feed program gives the grower the best control over the crop's nutrition compared to intermittent feed (weekly applications) or slow-release fertilizer programs. Geraniums on a constant feed program are supplied with low concentrations of fertilizer at each irrigation. The result is a constant low level of nutrients in the root medium without the stressful "peaks and valleys" that occur with other application methods.

Crops growing in soil-based root media should be supplied a constant feed program of 200 ppm of both nitrogen and potassium. Crops growing in soilless root media will need 250 ppm of both nitrogen and potassium.

Though a loss of control over the crop's nutrition occurs, many growers incorporate slow-release fertilizers into the root medium. These fertilizers must be **uniformly** mixed into the root medium before planting. Osmocote® 19-6-12 at the rate of 9 pounds per cubic yard or Osmocote® 14-14-14 at the rate of 12 pounds per cubic yard is mixed into the root medium. Osmocote® can also be applied to each pot as a top-dress.

## Light

Geraniums require high light intensity for rapid growth and profuse flowering. Shading may be required for some varieties because the flowers are susceptible to sunburn when exposed to full sun. High light intensities result in thicker-diameter stems, more branching, and more flowering. Geraniums grown under low light intensity show slowed growth rates, spindly stems, and less intense color in both flower and foliage.

## Pinching

Some growers pinch cutting geraniums to produce well-branched, compact plants with many flowers. For most modern varieties, pinching is not necessary, since well-branched, compact characteristics are bred into them. If pinching is done, a soft pinch is made three to four weeks after the rooted cutting is planted. This will allow enough time to insure that the plant is actively growing with an established root system. Geraniums at this stage of growth branch readily after pinching.

A pinch involves removing one-half to one inch of the terminal stem while leaving at least three nodes intact beneath the pinch. From these nodes new branches will develop. Geraniums grown in 4 1/2-inch pots can be pinched up to early or mid April for Memorial Day sales.

## Height Control

There are several things that growers can do to keep geraniums from becoming leggy.

1. Make sure that the geraniums are receiving full sun.
2. Space the plants so that sunlight can reach each individual plant without interference from adjacent plants.
3. Allow the root medium to dry somewhat between irrigations. Moist soils tend to promote succulent, stretched growth.

Height of geraniums can also be controlled chemically. Cycocel®, the most commonly used growth retardant, can be applied to geraniums as a 1,500 ppm spray. The first application is made to the newly potted plant when it has new growth approximately 1 1/2 inches long. Additional applications can be made every two weeks, if necessary, until two weeks before the sale date.

A new, much stronger growth retardant called Bonzi® is also available for geranium height control. It is applied as a spray, but at much lower concentrations than Cycocel®. The recommended rates are 6 to 16 ppm. The lower rates would apply early in the growing season and 16 ppm would be used in the second half of the season.

Finally, DIF can also be used to control the height of geraniums. Growers can often implement a 0 or slightly negative DIF to shorten stem internodes and produce a shorter plant. However, the use of DIF is feasible only while the daytime outside temperatures are moderately warm. When daytime temperatures get very high (in late spring), DIF must be discontinued, or the crop will be damaged.

## Spacing

Spacing geraniums is very important to the quality of the crop. Plants should be spaced so that adjacent plants are not touching. This will result in excellent light penetration into the crop and adequate air circulation through it. Good air circulation keeps the foliage dry and helps control relative humidity around the crop. In so doing, it helps prevent foliar diseases and aerates the root medium.

After potting, geraniums can be grown pot-to-pot to conserve space (if other crops are being grown at the same time), and to produce a larger crop. When the needed additional greenhouse space is available, the geraniums are then moved to their final spacing and the first application of growth retardant is made.

Geraniums in 4- or 4 1/2-inch pots can be spaced 6 x 6 inches, or four pots per square foot. This is somewhat crowded spacing, however, and quality of the crop may be reduced. Good quality crops can be produced when geraniums are spaced 7 x 7 inches, or three pots per square foot. The larger spacing increases the amount of light reaching the crop and allows for better air circulation. Each grower must decide on the actual spacing that is best in the given situation. More plants per square foot translates to a higher dollar return up to a certain point. But geraniums spaced closer together than 6 x 6 inches are likely to be stretched, more prone to disease, and overall lower in quality. They will bring a lower price, canceling any gains made by growing more plants per square foot.

## Scheduling

Published schedules for geraniums are readily available in greenhouse industry literature. In general, cuttings for non-pinched geranium crops (grown in 4- to 4 1/2-inch pots) are taken starting in early February for early to late May sales. Three to four weeks are needed for rooting and six to eight weeks for finishing the crop. Crops scheduled earlier than May require more production time because of usually cooler, more cloudy weather conditions.

Exact scheduling often differs from published guidelines because of environmental and cultural differences at that particular location. An important task for all growers is to make sure that **all activities and dates** are recorded for future reference when scheduling the next year's crop.

## Pests

Geraniums are not as susceptible to insect pests as many other greenhouse crops are. However, geraniums can be infested by aphids, whiteflies, thrips, and other insects and mites. Aphids and whiteflies feed on the foliage and excrete honeydew onto the leaves below. A black sooty mold then grows on the honeydew and ruins the appearance of the crop. Sometimes, the actual feeding of certain pests causes distortion of plant growth. Thrips damage the flower petals by their feeding habits. The petals appear streaked, and the flowers are ruined.

The best control of geranium pests is to implement IPM methods in the greenhouse; (see Chapter 8). Greenhouse sanitation, the use of physical and biological controls, and the use of appropriate pesticides will greatly reduce or eliminate present pest populations. IPM methods will also **prevent** new pests from becoming established on the geranium crop.

## Diseases

### *Bacterial*

A bacterial disease called **bacterial blight** is the most serious disease of geraniums in the United States. Once it affects a crop, it can rapidly wipe out the entire crop. There is no effective cure for this disease. Symptoms include wilting of leaf margins and leaf spotting and yellowing (Figure 10.26). Finally, the stem rots and the plant dies.

**Figure 10.26**
Bacterial blight of geranium

The best way to prevent this bacterial disease is to use culture-indexed cuttings that are free of disease. Implement all the good IPHM techniques that we have discussed.

1. Practice strict greenhouse sanitation.
2. Provide an optimum growing environment for the geranium crop.
   * Avoid high heat levels in the greenhouse.
   * Do not apply high levels of nitrogen to the crop.
   (High levels of heat or nitrogen encourage development of this disease.)
3. Remove any infected geraniums immediately from the greenhouse and discard them.

### *Fungal*

A serious fungal disease is ***Botrytis* blight**. Flowers, leaves, and stems of the geranium are affected. Flower petals turn dark, wilt, and fall off. Irregular brown, water-soaked spots appear on the leaves (Figure 10.27). In very humid conditions, the fungus will produce masses of gray spores that cover the water-soaked spots.

Spores of the *Botrytis* fungus germinate readily on moist plant surfaces and are often carried on plant debris. Therefore, the best control of *Botrytis* blight is to avoid wetting the foliage and to keep the greenhouse clean and free of plant debris. Be careful to provide enough air circulation to lower relative humidity levels and to prevent "wet spots" from occurring in the geranium crop. Apply appropriate fungicides on a regular schedule to help prevent *Botrytis* from becoming established.

**Blackleg** is a common stem rot of geraniums caused by the fungus ***Pythium***. It strikes during the propagation stage and early in production, because cuttings and young plants are most susceptible. The first symptom of blackleg is blackening of the base of the stem (Figure 10.28). Eventually, the foliage yellows and the cutting or young plant dies.

*Pythium* is commonly found in the root medium. Conditions in the root medium that favor blackleg are too much water and too high levels of soluble salts that damage the roots of the young plant. These conditions allow the fungus to invade the stem.

The following control measures are the most effective:

1. Steam pasteurize the soil.
2. Disinfect all containers and tools that are used during propagation and production.
3. Use a rooting medium that is porous enough to allow good drainage and aeration. Then developing roots are never deprived of oxygen.
4. Drench the root medium with an appropriate fungicide. It will prevent *Pythium* from becoming established in the soil.
5. Remove and discard all affected plants.

**Figure 10.27** *Botrytis* blight of geranium

**Figure 10.28** Blackleg of geranium

*(Figures 10.27-10.29 courtesy of Photo Science, Cornell University, Ithaca, New York)*

**Figure 10.29** Oedema on a geranium leaf

### *Oedema*

Oedema is a physiological disorder of geraniums caused by high moisture levels in the root medium. Ivy geraniums are especially susceptible. The symptom of oedema is raised, corky areas on the underside of the leaf (Figure 10.29). Preventive measures are:

1. Use only root media with good aeration and drainage.
2. Provide good air circulation.
3. Water only in the morning.

## MARKETING

Geraniums are sold typically with one or more flower clusters fully open (Figure 10.30). Most sales are made between Easter and Mother's Day; early May is the prime time. Potted zonal geraniums are sold in 3-, 4- or 4 1/2-inch and in the larger 6- or 6 1/2-inch pot sizes. Red is the most popular color (though this preference may vary by locality).

**Figure 10.30** A 4 1/2-inch geranium ready for marketing

As statistics showed early in this chapter, geraniums are a very profitable crop. The future appears bright for their continuing popularity. New varieties are introduced every year to satisfy the demand of the American gardener for variety and beauty. Geranium growers should recognize the importance of producing not only the varieties that are standards in the industry, but also some new varieties that will further attract the interest of the customer.

---

### *In conclusion:*

The topic of Chapter 10 was bedding plant production, including geraniums. Bedding plant seed is started in either germination flats or, more commonly, plug trays. The basics of transplanting bedding plant seedlings were covered, from germination flats and plug trays to the finishing container. Geraniums are commonly produced from cuttings, and the names of a number of cultivars were given. Finally, environmental/cultural procedures were given to help produce a healthy crop free of diseases and pests. Some helpful marketing procedures for geraniums were identified.

---

## CHAPTER 10 REVIEW

This review is to help you check yourself on what you have learned about production of geraniums and bedding plants in general. If you need to refresh your mind on any of the following questions, refer to the page number given in parentheses.

### **Bedding Plants** (in general)

1. Define "bedding plants." *(page 178)*
2. What was the wholesale value of bedding plants in the U.S. in 1990? *(page 178)*
3. What were the top four states in wholesale value of bedding plants in 1990? *(page 6)*
4. Describe the two procedures that are used for sowing bedding plant seed in flats. *(pages 183-184)*
5. How are seeds sown in plug trays? *(pages 187-189)*
6. Name three advantages of producing bedding plants in plug trays. *(pages 181-182)*
7. Why is it more expensive to sow seed in plug trays than in flats? *(page 182)*
8. Describe a plug seedling in Stage 3 of development. *(pages 189-191)*
9. When is a seedling started in a germination flat ready for transplanting? *(pages 186,191)* When is a seedling started in a plug tray ready? *(pages 189,191)*
10. How are seedlings removed from a germination flat during transplanting? *(pages 191-192)* from a plug tray? *(page 193)*
11. What is the recommended watering and fertilization schedule for newly transplanted bedding plants that are growing rapidly? *(pages 194-196)*
12. Describe two methods used to control the height of bedding plants other than by withholding water. *(page 196)*
13. How does damping off affect bedding plant seedlings? What conditions favor this disease? *(page 197)*
14. Discuss the four principles of IPHM in a disease control program for bedding plants. *(pages 197-198)*
15. What are three major pests of bedding plants? *(pages 198-200)*
16. How can bedding plant pest infestations be prevented? *(page 200)*
17. Where can a grower obtain scheduling guidelines for producing bedding plants? *(page 201)*
18. Name ten bedding plant species that are grown today. *(page 201)*
19. What is the most popular marketing method used for bedding plants? *(page 203)*

Chapter 10 Review *(continued)*

## Geraniums

1. What is the scientific name of geranium? *(page 205)*

2. Name other types of geraniums produced by growers besides the cutting or zonal geranium. *(page 205)*

3. How are zonal geraniums propagated by a grower? *(pages 206-209)*

4. What is a "culture-indexed" geranium cutting? *(pages 206, 208)*

5. Give the recommended night temperature range for producing geraniums. *(page 210)*

6. Besides the constant liquid feed program, what other method is commonly used for applying fertilizers to geranium crops? *(pages 211-212)*

7. Give three methods of height control of a geranium crop. How does each method work? *(page 212)*

8. What is the recommended spacing for geraniums grown in 4 1/2-inch pots? *(page 213)*

9. Name two pests that infest geranium crops. *(page 213)*

10. What is the most important thing a grower can do to prevent diseases from affecting his or her geranium crop? *(page 214)*

11. During which stage of production does the disease blackleg affect geranium crops? *(page 215)*

12. How does oedema affect a geranium crop? What can be done to prevent it? *(page 216)*

13. During what part of the year are most zonal geraniums marketed? *(page 216)*

# CHAPTER 11

# FLOWERING POTTED PLANT PRODUCTION

## Poinsettias, Chrysanthemums, and Easter Lilies

### Competencies for Chapter 11

As a result of studying this chapter, you should be able to do the following:

1. Give the scientific names of poinsettia, chrysanthemum, and Easter lily.
2. Compare the production value of poinsettias, chrysanthemums, and Easter lilies in the U.S.
3. List the commonly grown flowering potted crops in your state.
4. Discuss the following items in connection with production of poinsettias, chrysanthemums, and Easter lilies:
   - ☆ production statistics
   - ☆ varieties or cultivars
   - ☆ propagation (including root media)
   - ☆ general culture (temperature, watering, nutrition, lighting, etc.)
   - ☆ pinching (where applicable)
   - ☆ photoperiod
   - ☆ height control
   - ☆ pest and disease problems
   - ☆ scheduling guidelines
   - ☆ post-harvest care
   - ☆ marketing

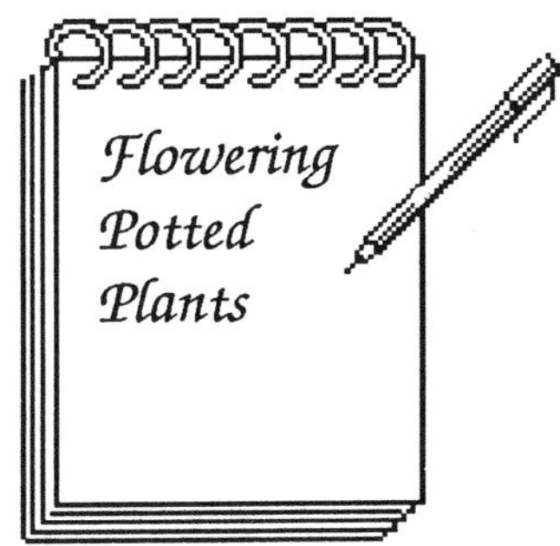


### Related Science Concepts

1. Implement IPM strategies.
2. Monitor root media for nutrient content.
3. Describe how photoperiodic manipulation works.
4. Contrast use of DIF with other methods of height control.
5. Relate pinching the growing tip to lateral branching (removing apical dominance).
6. Recognize disease and insect pest infestations.
7. Recognize dangers of pesticide use.
8. Describe how cooling Easter lily bulbs helps to schedule the bloom date.

### Related Math Concepts

1. Apply basic operations to whole numbers, decimals, and fractions as they relate to flowering potted plant production.
2. Apply basic operations to ratios and percents as they relate to flowering potted plant production.
3. Apply mathematical concepts and operations to flowering potted plant production.

*(continued)*

4. Read, interpret, and construct charts, graphs, and tables related to flowering potted plant production.
5. Read thermometers.
6. Calculate crop spacing.
7. Calculate DIF.
8. Read and interpret fertilizer labels.
9. Time watering.
10. Time crop for optimum marketability.

### Terms to Know

| | |
|---|---|
| A-Rest® | pistillate |
| apical dominance | pompons |
| bract | powdery mildew |
| buds breaking | ray florets |
| controlled temperature forcing (CTF) | rooting hormone |
| crown buds | scouting a crop |
| cultivar | sleeving |
| cyathia | splitting |
| disbud mum | spray mum |
| disk florets | staminate |
| foliar analysis | standard mum |
| non-tunicate bulb | tunicate bulb |

---

## INTRODUCTION - STATISTICS

### National Production Statistics

Potted flowering plants as a whole comprise the second largest segment of the floriculture industry behind bedding plants. According to the 1990 USDA Floriculture Crops Summary, the total wholesale value for potted flowering plants in the U.S. was $672.3 million, an impressive 25 percent increase from 1989. Poinsettias had by far the largest production value, $183.5 million or 27 percent of the total wholesale value (Table 11.1). Chrysanthemums were a distant second at $95.8 million or 14 percent of the total wholesale value. Finished florist azaleas were third at $55.1 million and Easter lilies were fourth at $36.9 million. These top four crops accounted for 55 percent of the total wholesale value.

Since 1989, the wholesale value of poinsettias has increased by 7 percent, azaleas by 21 percent, and Easter lilies by 11 percent. The value of chrysanthemums has remained essentially unchanged.

### Ohio Production Statistics

As with bedding plants, Ohio ranked very impressively for potted flowering plant production in 1990. Overall, Ohio ranked **fourth** in the country in potted flowering plant production with a wholesale value of $34.4 million (Table 11.2). Ohio's ranking for the different crops was:

* *first* in African violet production
* *second* in poinsettia production
* *fourth* in Easter lily production
* *fifth* in finished florist azaleas
* *ninth* in chrysanthemums

These top five crops accounted for 84 percent of Ohio's total production value of potted flowering plants.

Keep these production statistics in mind as we discuss three specific crops in this chapter: poinsettias, chrysanthemums, and Easter lilies. General recommendations will be made for propagation, culture, and marketing of crops of these three important potted flowering plants.

**Table 11.1** Production statistics of potted flowering plants in 1990 in the U.S. Given in order of production value.

U.S.A.

| | Crop | Wholesale Value ($ millions) |
|---|---|---|
| 1 | Poinsettias | 183.5 |
| 2 | Crysanthemums (excluding garden mums) | 95.8 |
| 3 | Finished florist azaleas | 55.1 |
| 4 | Easter lilies | 36.9 |
| 5 | African violets | 27.7 |
| 6 | Other lilies | 4.8 |
| 7 | Other flowering plants (excluding annuals) | 268.8 |
| ❋ | Total 1990 wholesale value | 672.3 |

Source: *Floriculture Crops 1990 Summary*. United States Department of Agriculture, National Agricultural Statistics Service, Agricultural Statistics Board, Washington, DC, April 1991

**Table 11.2** Production statistics of potted flowering plants in 1990 in Ohio. Given in order of production value.

OHIO

| | Crop | Wholesale Value ($ millions) | National Rank |
|---|---|---|---|
| 1 | Poinsettias | 12.9 | 2 |
| 2 | African violets | 5.5 | 1 |
| 3 | Finished florist azaleas | 4.9 | 5 |
| 4 | Crysanthemums (excluding garden mums) | 3.2 | 9 |
| 5 | Easter lilies | 2.4 | 4 |
| 6 | Other lilies | 0.2 | NA |
| 7 | Other flowering plants (excluding annuals) | 5.3 | 7 |
| ❋ | Total 1990 wholesale value | 34.4 | 4 |

Source: *Floriculture Crops 1990 Summary*. United States Department of Agriculture, National Agricultural Statistics Service, Agricultural Statistics Board, Washington, DC, April 1991

# Part One — POINSETTIA PRODUCTION

## INTRODUCTION

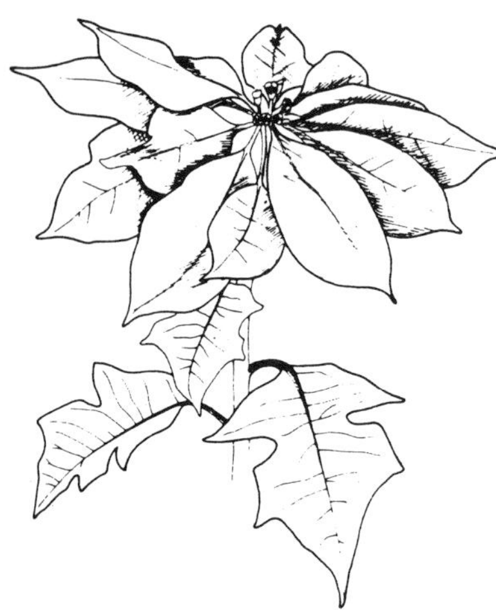

Poinsettia *(Euphorbia pulcherrima)* is a very popular flowering plant and a very profitable crop. It is the **number 1** crop in the United States and Ohio in terms of wholesale value. (Refer again to Tables 11.1 and 11.2.) Poinsettias grow naturally in Mexico. They are named for Joel Poinsett, who introduced them into the United States in the early 1800's when he was U.S. ambassador to Mexico.

Poinsettias were used primarily as cut flowers until the early 1900s, when the Ecke family started breeding them in California. The Eckes developed long-lasting varieties and made the poinsettia suitable for potted culture and marketing. They also bred many colors into the wide assortment of their poinsettias. Many of the poinsettia cultivars on the market today were developed by the Ecke family. (See page 236.)

The inconspicuous flowers of the poinsettia, known as **cyathia**, are yellow cup-like structures clustered at the end of the stem (Figure 11.1). The cyathia contain separate female (pistillate) and male (staminate) flower parts. Surrounding the cyathia are the colorful bracts that are commonly mistaken for the flowers of the plant.

Poinsettias are photoperiodic with respect to flowering and are classified as a long-night plant. To bloom properly, these plants require 12 hours or more of continuous darkness per day.

**Figure 11.1**

Colorful red poinsettia bracts surround the inconspicuous yellow flowers of poinsettia called cyathia. (Courtesy of Paul Ecke Poinsettia Ranch, Encinitas, California)

## PROPAGATION

### Stock Plants

Many poinsettia growers buy callused or rooted cuttings from a specialist propagator. Callused cuttings still have to be rooted under intermittent mist. Rooted cuttings typically arrive in a foam strip (Figure 11.2), ready for planting. However, a considerable number of growers choose to produce their own cuttings from stock plants. Growers order rooted cuttings for the spring (between March and May, depending on the number of cuttings to be produced). Cuttings grow into large, well-branched plants from which terminal stem cuttings are taken (Figure 11.3).

The culture of stock plants is much like that of the Christmas crop (which is covered later in this chapter). However, stock plants grown before May 15 **must** be lighted at night using mum lighting to prevent flower bud formation. Since stock plants can grow quite large, cuttings are typically potted in 8-inch or larger azalea pots.

## Cuttings from Stock Plants

Terminal stem cuttings 2 to 3 1/2 inches in length are taken from sturdy, vigorous growth (Figure 11.4). Excessively long stems should be avoided along with stems that are weak (those with a small diameter). The best time to take cuttings is in the morning when plants are turgid from being watered the previous afternoon. Also, heat levels in the greenhouse are usually lower in the morning. Cuttings are removed by hand - either snapping them off or using a sharp knife or similar tool. To prevent the spread of disease organisms, **hands and tools must be clean** before cuttings are taken. Cuttings are collected in a sterilized container and stuck into the rooting medium before they start to wilt.

**Figure 11.2**
Rooted poinsettia cuttings shipped in a foam strip and ready for planting

**Figure 11.3** Poinsettia stock plants

**Figure 11.4**
Poinsettia terminal stem cuttings taken from stock plants. (Courtesy of Paul Ecke Poinsettia Ranch, Encinitas, California)

Producing cuttings by stock plants takes more greenhouse space and involves extra work on the part of the grower. But overall cost of the cuttings can be reduced. Growers can also control the quality of their cuttings; quality control by the grower is not possible with purchased cuttings. In many cases, a cultivar is patented by the company which developed it. The grower must pay the royalty of a few cents per cutting to the owner of the plant patent.

## Rooting Cuttings

Cuttings taken from stock plants are **unrooted cuttings** that are purchased from a specialist propagator and rooted under intermittent mist. These cuttings may be stuck directly into the pot in which they will be finished. This method reduces production time by one week since no further adjustments (from transplanting) need to be made by the cutting after it has rooted. The size of cuttings should be as uniform as possible for best results.

While sticking cuttings directly in pots eliminates transplanting labor, it also significantly increases greenhouse space required for rooting the individual cuttings. The grower may not have the needed space available. Thus, in many greenhouses, poinsettia cuttings are rooted in flats containing a rooting medium. For good root development, the medium must have good water-holding capacity, yet allow for aeration. Many growers use synthetic foam cubes, wedges, or strips; (see Chapter 6). These are specially designed for rooting cuttings; they provide ideal conditions for root development and growth. The rooting medium must be free of disease organisms. Propagation benches and aisles should be thoroughly disinfected before cuttings arrive.

Intermittent mist is programmed to keep a constant film of moisture on the cuttings during the first week on the propagation bench (Figure 11.5). The mist prevents the cuttings from drying out and keeps them cool during the

**Figure 11.5**

Poinsettia cuttings rooting on a propagation bench under intermittent mist rooting process. During the second week, when roots start to form, the mist applications can be spaced further apart to gradually "wean" the cuttings off the mist. Less frequent misting also reduces the possibility of foliar diseases.

If cuttings take on a pale green appearance during propagation, they need a light application of a complete fertilizer, e.g. 100 ppm of a 20-20-20 fertilizer. The intermittent mist can leach nutrients out of the leaves, and the rooting medium by itself has few if any nutrients in it.

In about three to four weeks, the cuttings develop a good root system; i.e., roots that are 1 to 2 inches long. The plants are now ready for transplanting into their finishing containers.

### Transplanting Cuttings and the Root Medium

The root medium into which the cuttings are transplanted can be either a soil-based or a soilless mix. Excellent crops can be grown in either type. Most poinsettia growers use the Peat-Lite soilless mixes (as we discussed in Chapter 6). Root media pH is very important for poinsettia growth. Soilless root media should have a pH of 5.5 to 6.0, while soil-based root media should have a pH of 6.0 to 6.5. At these pH ranges, the 17 essential nutrients as a whole will be at their maximum availability.

#### *Steps for transplanting rooted cuttings*

1. Get azalea pots ready. They give stability to the substantial canopy of the finished plant.
2. Fill the pots with moistened root medium.
3. Plant each cutting **at the same depth** as it was in the propagation medium. If the cutting is planted deeper than this, the roots may suffocate and rot; cuttings planted too shallow will dry out too quickly.
4. Push the root medium gently around the roots to make good contact, eliminating air pockets.
5. Water the transplanted cuttings thoroughly.
6. Place the potted plants under saran in the greenhouse.

## CULTURE OF THE CHRISTMAS CROP

### Nutrition

When the transplanted cuttings have become established and are actively growing, it is time to start the regular nutritional program. Compared to other flowering potted crops, poinsettias require relatively high amounts of nitrogen and potassium. Therefore, most poinsettia growers use a constant liquid feed program because it is convenient and it gives them control over the crop's nutrition.

A variety of fertilizers can be used, such as complete fertilizers (15-16-17 and 20-10-20), potassium nitrate, ammonium nitrate, and calcium nitrate. For poinsettias growing in soil-based root media, 250 ppm of nitrogen and potassium should be applied. Poinsettias growing in soilless root media should receive at least 300 ppm of nitrogen and potassium. When bract development begins in mid to late October, the amount of nitrogen should be reduced to no more than 200 ppm. Two weeks before sale, fertilization is discontinued in order to harden the plants.

Another method of fertilization is application of slow-release fertilizer to the root medium. Osmocote® 14-14-14 or 19-6-12 can be uniformly mixed into the root medium during preparation or added to the surface of the root medium after the plants have been potted. The volume of water used and frequency of irrigation will affect the release of the fertilizer into the root medium. High temperatures also increase the rate of fertilizer release from Osmocote®. Slow-release fertilizers can help produce excellent quality crops if used correctly. However, the grower's control over the nutrition of the crop is considerably reduced.

Poinsettias also have a strict magnesium and molybdenum requirement. Magnesium can be applied as a separate epsom salt (magnesium sulfate) drench at 8 ounces/100 gallons of water every month. Or magnesium (as epsom salts) can be mixed into the soil before planting. Molybdenum is added at 0.1 ppm on a constant feed basis with the addition of ammonium molybdate to the fertilizer stock tank.

## Watering

Pot sizes and types (clay and plastic), root medium, stage of growth, and environmental conditions all affect the amount and frequency of watering. The surface of the root medium should be allowed to dry out between waterings. If the root medium stays too wet, root rot will occur; if it is kept too dry, there will be wilting and loss of quality in the plant. Therefore, the moisture level of the root medium should be checked frequently, especially during sunny, warm weather. The weight of the pot is one clue - heavy when moist and lighter when dry. The color of the root medium is another clue for moisture - dark brown for moist and light brown for dry.

Poinsettia crops are watered by a number of automated irrigation systems such as spaghetti tubes, capillary mat, and ebb and flow. These systems water the crop in a fraction of the time required for hose watering and therefore save considerable labor costs.

Some growers produce poinsettias by growing them on the floor. Pots are placed on square plastic water collectors (Figure 11.6). Overhead irrigation water that runs off the foliage is channeled to the bottom of the pot, where it is absorbed by the root medium. Water collectors not only cut down significantly on wasted water and water runoff, but also automatically space the crop.

Hose watering is sometimes still needed for those isolated groups of plants on a bench or floor that may have dried out because of environmental irregularities in the greenhouse.

**Figure 11.6**

Poinsettias growing on the floor in pots set on plastic water collectors

## Temperature

Poinsettias require warm temperatures for healthy growth and excellent quality. (With slight differences from one variety to another) night temperatures over all should be in the low to mid 60°'s and day temperatures around 70°F on cloudy days and 75° to 80°F on sunny days.

During bract development and expansion, night temperatures should be 65° to 67°F. These warmer night temperatures result in large bracts that completely cover the foliage. If they get above 70°F, however, flower bud formation and development will be delayed. The bracts are fully developed when pollen is visible in the cyathia. Greenhouse night temperatures can then be **gradually** lowered over a period of several days to about 60°F to intensify the bract color. This is called "finishing" the poinsettia crop.

### Single-Stem and Pinched, Branched Poinsettia Crops

Poinsettias may be grown as a single-stem or a pinched, branched crop. Single-stem plants are not pinched. Each plant produces one large flower. Pinched plants produce several flowers. The plants are much larger than single-stem plants. To compensate for the size differences and number of flowers per pot, more cuttings are planted per pot for single-stem crops than for pinched crops (Table 11.3).

**Table 11.3**

Recommended number of poinsettia cuttings to plant per pot for single-stem and pinched crops

| Pot Size (inches) | Cuttings per pot | Pinched or Single-stem |
|---|---|---|
| 4" | 1 | Pinched |
| 4" | 1 | Single-stem |
| 5" | 2 or 3 | Single-stem |
| 5" | 1 | Pinched |
| 6" | 3 or 4 | Single-stem |
| 6" | 1 or 2 | Pinched |
| 7" | 4-7 | Single-stem |
| 7" | 2-3 | Pinched |

*Source:* Ball Red Book, 15th edition. Geo. J. Ball Publishing, West Chicago, IL

Most poinsettias in Ohio are grown as pinched, branched plants. Fewer cuttings are needed to plant such a crop, and transplanting labor is reduced. Pinching involves **removal of the top 1/2 to 1 inch of the stem** (Figure 11.7). This so-called "soft pinch" removes the growing point and the expanding young leaves. Their removal allows the buds in the nodes below to "break" (sprout) and grow. The number of nodes below the pinch determine how many branches will be formed, as all buds below the pinch usually "break" (Figure 11.8). Breaking of the buds is inhibited by a plant hormone called an auxin that is produced by the growing point (apex) and the expanding leaves. Apical dominance is broken when this source of auxin is removed by pinching.

Pinching should be done about two to three weeks after transplanting, when the cutting is well established with a good root system. If cuttings are

**Figure 11.7**
Soft pinch of a poinsettia plant

**Figure 11.8**
Buds breaking on a poinsettia after a soft pinch

pinched earlier than this, the buds will break slowly and some not at all, resulting in a smaller plant with fewer blooms.

These critical pinching dates are available in various industry publications. The key factor is to allow enough time between the pinch and the start of long nights for sufficient vegetative growth to occur. Too short a time will result in a smaller-than-desired plant.

### Photoperiod

As we mentioned previously, poinsettias require 12 hours or more of continuous darkness per day in order to bloom. In northern Ohio, darkness reaches 12 hours per day around the first day of fall and increases thereafter. For many poinsettia cultivars, this natural onset of long nights coincides with their natural time for blooming: late November and early December. This, of course, is also the peak sales time for poinsettias. However, in greenhouses that are lighted at night (internally or by external sources), this extra light may prevent the plants from setting bud.

To ensure darkness over the crop, photoperiodic blackout shade cloth is pulled over the crop every night at 5:00 p.m. It is removed the next morning at 8:00 a.m. The poinsettias will thus be provided "night" that is 15 hours in length - more than enough to induce flower bud formation.

To delay flowering of early flowering cultivars, standard mum lighting is used from 10 p.m. to 2 a.m. beginning in mid-September. This breaks the night into two short periods of darkness and prevents flower bud formation. When the mum lighting is stopped, the poinsettias will set bud and flower at the date desired.

### Height Control

A common problem growers face is a crop of poinsettias that has grown too tall and become leggy with weak stems. Certain factors like periods of cloudy weather cause plants to stretch. Proper spacing (to be discussed next) helps counteract this. However, the most common height control measure is applying Cycocel®, a chemical growth retardant that shortens the length of the internodes. Spray applications of 1,500 ppm are made when lateral shoots are 1 to 1 1/2 inches long and repeated, if necessary, at weekly intervals until October 15. Application of Cycocel® or any other growth retardant after October 15 is likely to damage developing bracts.

There are several other chemical growth regulators that can be used to control poinsettia height. Whatever chemical you use, **always follow label directions.**

DIF can also be used to control the height of poinsettias. A 0 or slightly negative DIF can be implemented after pinching to keep the internodes short on new lateral branches. However, if night temperatures rise above 70°F in late September through mid October, heat delay of flowering will occur. Also, if day temperatures rise above 70°F, it will be difficult or impossible to implement a 0 or negative DIF. At such times, chemical growth regulators will be needed.

## Spacing

Poinsettias should be placed in their final spacing as soon as possible after transplanting. Proper spacing provides adequate light penetration and air circulation for the crop. Higher light intensity will mean less plant stretching. Good air movement will lessen the likelihood of foliar and root rot diseases developing because the leaf surface and root medium surface will be drier.

Some growers space their crop pot-to-pot when it is first planted and gradually move the pots to their final spacing as the crop grows. This requires a great deal more labor than placing the pots in their final spacing immediately after planting. But sometimes at the time of planting there is not enough space available for the wider spacing.

Spacing guides found in many industry publications for single-stem and pinched, branched crops can be very helpful. (See Table 11.4 for some examples for pinched, branched crops.)

**Table 11.4**
Spacing recommendations for pinched, branched poinsettias

| Pot Size | Plants per pot | Spacing (inches) |
|---|---|---|
| 4 | 1 | 9 x 9 |
| 5 | 1 | 12 x 12 |
| 6 | 1 | 13 x 14 |
| 7 | 2 | 17 x 17 |
| 8 | 3 | 19 x 19 |

*Source:* Ball Red Book, 15th edition. Geo. J. Ball Publishing, West Chicago, IL

## Insect Pests

The pests that affect poinsettias are primarily whiteflies; (refer back to Figure 10.16E). The two pest species are the greenhouse whitefly and (more recently) the sweet potato whitefly. They are very similar in appearance except that the sweet potato whitefly is a little smaller and usually yellowish in color.

Whiteflies feed and lay eggs on the underside of leaves. If unchecked, whitefly populations can reach explosive numbers in a matter of days, making control extremely difficult. The best control strategy is to implement IPM methods in the greenhouse (as we discussed in Chapter 8). It is very important to "scout the crop" and to monitor the whitefly population by setting out and reading yellow sticky traps.

Scouting a poinsettia crop involves walking through it, randomly turning over leaves and inspecting them (Figure 11.9). This will give additional data that yellow sticky traps will not provide. With the combined information, a well-planned pesticide program can be formulated and implemented. Only those pesticides that are labeled for control of whiteflies on poinsettias **must** be used. (Current industry literature and publications of the Cooperative Extension Service list pesticides which may be used.)

**Figure 11.9**

Scouting for a whitefly infestation involves turning leaves over and inspecting them. Note the whitefly in front of the "inspector's" thumb.

Research is currently under way to determine the effectiveness of *Encarsia formosa* in a biological control program for both greenhouse and sweet potato whiteflies infesting poinsettias. (See page 163 and Figure 8.3 for more information about this wasp.) Results so far seem promising when compared to chemical pesticide control methods.

## Diseases

As with insect control, poinsettia disease control strategies should be mainly preventive. Implement the principles of IPHM in your poinsettia production program. Keep the growing area clean and provide ideal cultural conditions for poinsettia growth, and you will certainly prevent many diseases from getting started in the crop. Sometimes, however, in spite of all the preventive measures you take, other factors enter in and diseases do become established. They must be dealt with immediately to prevent their spread throughout the crop.

### *Gray Mold*

Gray mold is a foliar disease that covers leaves and bracts with a gray fungal growth. It eventually kills the tissue, causing brown leaf and bract margins and, ultimately, ruin of the crop. The causative fungus is *Botrytis*. It can affect all stages of plant growth. Wet foliage, cool temperatures, and injured plant tissue all favor its development.

The best line of defense involves the following steps.

1. Keep foliage dry by using irrigation systems that do not wet the foliage or bracts.
2. Provide constant air circulation to control relative humidity levels.
3. Space plants so that air circulates throughout the crop.
4. Keep night temperatures above 60°F.

***Stem and Root Rots***

Stem and root rots of poinsettia are caused most often by two fungi, *Rhizoctonia* and *Pythium.* These are soil-borne organisms that invade stems and roots, rotting them and killing the plant (Figure 11.10). Healthy plant stems are free of black areas; the roots have a vigorous white growth (Figure 11.11). The best defense against stem and root rots is sanitation. Use only sterilized tools and containers. Pasteurize all soil-based root media and any soilless root media that may be contaminated.

**Figure 11.10** Rhizoctonia stem and root rot

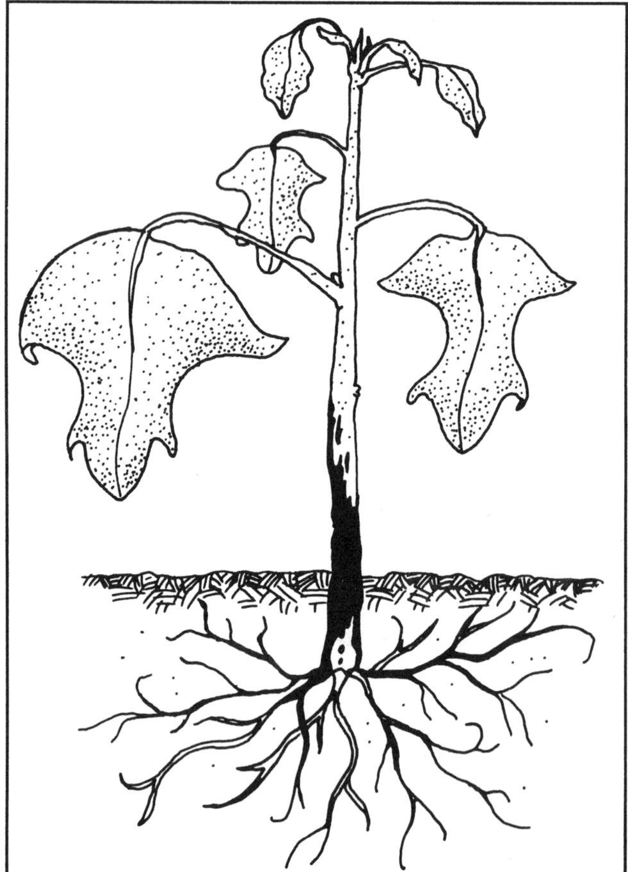

If you are using overhead watering for the poinsettias, avoid splashing water, as the two fungi can be transported to other plants in drops of water. Allow the root medium to dry somewhat to control these fungi, as they favor wet conditions.

Both *Rhizoctonia* and *Pythium* diseases can be treated with appropriate, labelled fungicides. Consult greenhouse industry publications for recommendations of fungicides and directions for their application.

**Figure 11.11**
Typical healthy poinsettia root development

## Physiological Disorders

There are two major types of physiological disorders that may impact a poinsettia crop: splitting and selected nutrient deficiencies.

### *Splitting*

Splitting is a disorder that causes the poinsettia plant to set flower buds prematurely and then typically to produce three vegetative by-pass shoots (Figure 11.12). This disorder occurs in plants that receive improper photoperiod treatment or in plants that were propagated as cuttings taken from long stems of stock plants. The result can be a misshapen plant. Flowers may also split. As the bracts separate more and spread out, the beauty of the plant is decreased.

To prevent splitting, make sure that nights are **at least** 12 hours in length (and preferably longer) during flower bud development. Keep stock plant stems from becoming excessively long by pinching them about every four weeks to encourage branching. Stop pinching four weeks before cuttings are to be taken.

### *Nutrient Deficiencies*

Improper nutritional programs will lead to a number of nutrient deficiencies (discussed in Chapter 7). Poinsettias have a higher requirement for magnesium and molybdenum than do most greenhouse crops. If poinsettias are not supplied with these two elements, deficiency symptoms will occur.

*Magnesium* deficiency causes lower leaves to become chlorotic along the edges while the leaf veins remain green. These symptoms will gradually progress up the plant if magnesium is not supplied.

*Molybdenum* deficiency causes the margins of leaves in the top half of the plant to turn brown and curl upward (Figure 11.13). Symptoms start to appear in October. If they affect the bracts too, the crop is ruined. It is vital to supply molybdenum in any poinsettia nutrition program.

---

**Figure 11.12**
Splitting in poinsettia with three branches rising from the end of the main stem

**Figure 11.13** Molybdenum deficiency in poinsettias

## PRODUCTION SCHEDULE GUIDELINES

Poinsettias are typically scheduled to bloom in late November to early December for Christmas sales. However, a significant number of poinsettias (25 percent for some growers) is being grown for Thanksgiving sales as well.

Major considerations in setting up a growing schedule for poinsettias are:

1. selection of cultivars to be used (see next section)
2. size of pot and finished plant desired
3. number of plants per pot and growth form (single-stem or pinched)
4. sale date of the crop

Many factors enter in to scheduling a poinsettia crop. The most critical is figuring out the date to start the crop so that it will bloom ***on time.*** (See Figure 11.14 for a sample growing schedule.). The total number of days necessary to accomplish all the steps of production must be counted ***backwards*** from the sale date to determine when the crop should be started. For a pinched crop, the major time periods involved are:

1. length of rooting time for cuttings produced by the grower (usually 3 to 4 weeks)
2. time from planting to the pinch (2 to 3 weeks in most cases)
3. time from pinching to the start of long nights (to obtain sufficient crop height, and this varies with pot size)
4. the start of long nights and up to bloom date (which varies according to the cultivar)

Specific schedule guidelines may be obtained from industry publications and from sales representatives of companies that sell poinsettia cuttings and plants.

## POINSETTIA CULTIVARS

Poinsettia cultivars are classified according to the **number of weeks** of long nights they require to bloom. (For example, a nine-week cultivar requires nine weeks of long nights in order to bloom.) Within each of these cultivar groupings, there are many colors - shades of red, pink, and white; pink/white, red/white, and red/pink novelty types; and even yellow cultivars (Table 11.5). Specific information on growing these cultivars is available from poinsettia sources and industry publications.

## POST-HARVEST CARE

When poinsettias are ready to be shipped to the customer, proper handling of the plants during shipment is very important to maintain their quality. Because they are of tropical origin, poinsettias must be protected from cold weather by sleeving of the plants. They must be transported in sealed boxes in a heated truck.

When the plants arrive at the store (or home), they should be removed from the box and unsleeved ***immediately.*** (If the poinsettias must be left sleeved for a while, they should be unsleeved within 24 hours.) Leaving the plants boxed up or sleeved will cause drooping leaves and bracts and possibly leaf and bract drop.

After carefully removing the sleeve by tearing it off, inspect the plant for damage. Water it if the medium feels dry. Place it in light bright enough to read by easily and in a room temperature between 65° and 75°F.

Home consumers need easy-to-read care tags included with the poinsettia so they will know how to care for it. The tag should state basic cultural requirements for growth in the home.

If the grower follows these procedures, the beautiful poinsettia that left the greenhouse will reach its destination without any loss of quality. Growers must educate their customers on the ***importance*** of post-harvest care and handling of the crop that they worked so hard to produce.

**Figure 11.14 SAMPLE GROWING SCHEDULE FOR POINSETTIAS**

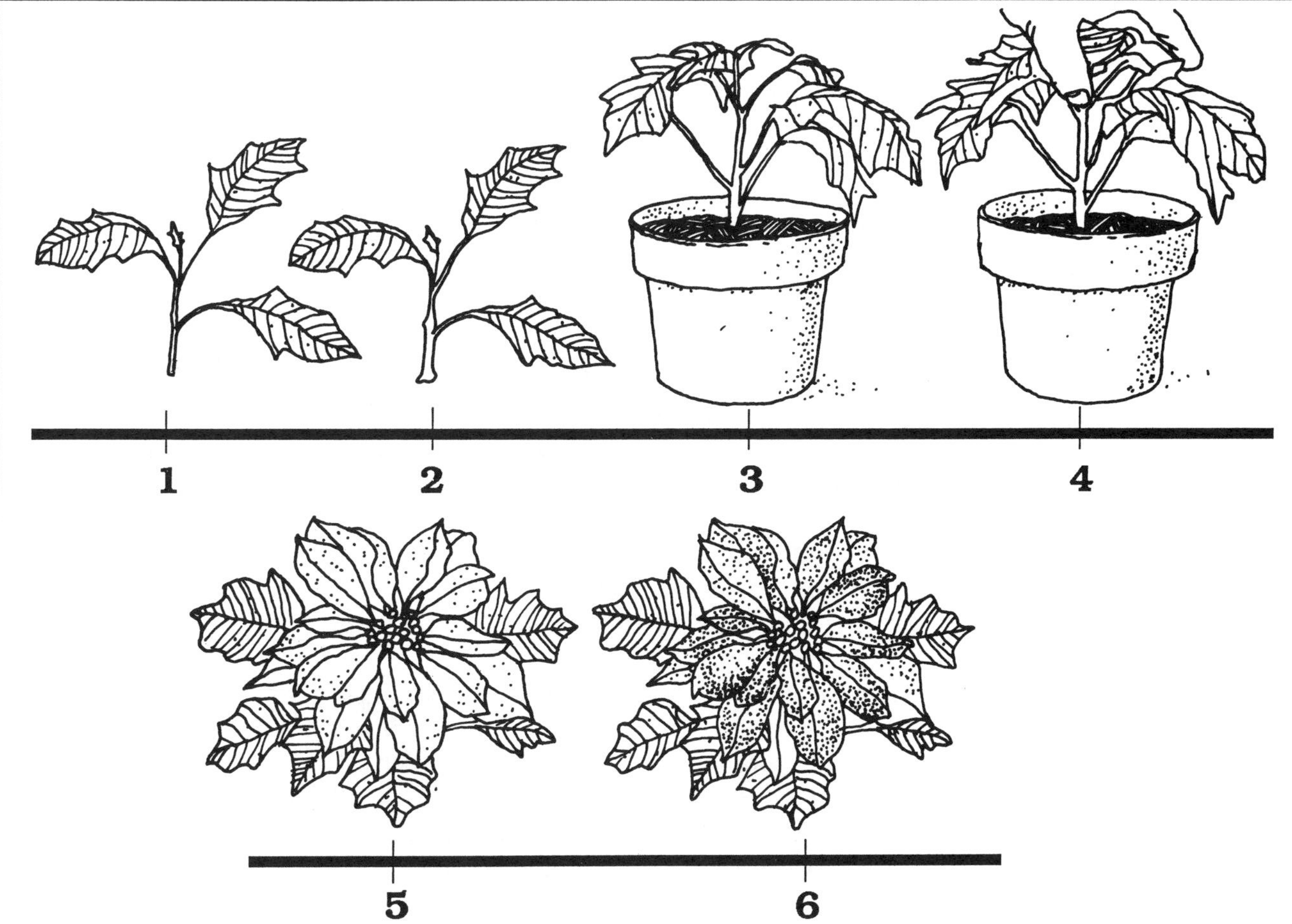


1. Cuttings are taken from disease-free stock plants.
2. After one week, cuttings are callused. Unrooted cuttings may be purchased at this stage.
3. After about 4 weeks, rooted cuttings are transferred to pots. Rooted cuttings may be purchased at this stage.
4. Plants are pinched to encourage branching. The pinch date varies with the cultivar and height desired.
5. Bracts should begin to show color in early November.
6. Plants ready for market in early December can be held at reduced temperatures.

**Table 11.5** Poinsettia cultivars commonly grown in Ohio greenhouses

| Red Cultivars | Pink Cultivars |
|---|---|
| Eckespoint® Lilo | Annette Hegg ™ Hot Pink |
| Eckespoint® Red Sails | Gutbier™ V-14 Pink |
| Annette Hegg ™ Brilliant Diamond | Eckespoint® Pink Peppermint |
| Gross™ Supjibi | Gutbier™ V-14 Hot Pink |
| Mikkel® Rochford | **White Cultivars** |
| Gutbier™ V-14 Glory | Annette Hegg™ Topwhite |
| | Gutbier™ V-14 White |
| **Novelty Types** | Mikkel® White Rochford |
| Eckespoint® Jingle Bells | |
| Gutbier™ V-14 Marble | **Yellow Cultivar** |
| Annette Hegg™ Marble | Eckespoint® Lemon Drop |

## MARKETING

As we stated earlier, poinsettias are the most popular potted plant crop grown in the United States. Poinsettias are a very profitable crop because they are so beautiful in any setting. Poinsettias are grown in a wide variety of containers - from a pot barely an inch in diameter (for mini-poinsettias) to 12-inch and larger azalea pots. Poinsettias are also grown in hanging baskets and even as trees! Both make spectacular splashes of color (Figure 11.15).

With continuing research in plant breeding, new cultivars are introduced on the market every year. New colors and color shades bred into poinsettias satisfy a wide variety of tastes among consumers.

There has been a definite trend to grow more poinsettias for Thanksgiving. Many growers are supplying retail outlets with poinsettias in early to mid-November as sales increase every year for Thanksgiving. There have even been discussions of the plausibility of introducing poinsettias into the market for other holidays such as Easter! For now, in the consumer's mind, poinsettias are still associated with the Christmas season (which, for retail stores, includes Thanksgiving). Convincing the American public to buy this plant at any other season of the year will likely be a major challenge.

**A.** Conventional-sized poinsettias, mini-poinsettias, and "personal" poinsettias in transparent plastic containers

**B.** Poinsettias grown in hanging baskets

**Figure 11.15**

Poinsettias are marketed in many forms.

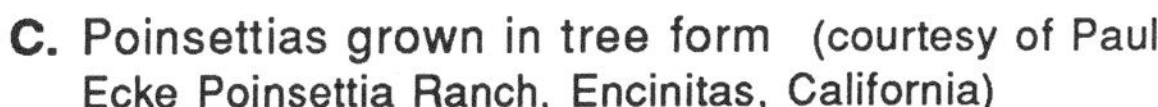

**C.** Poinsettias grown in tree form (courtesy of Paul Ecke Poinsettia Ranch, Encinitas, California)

## POINSETTIA REVIEW

This review is to help you check yourself on what you have learned about production of flowering potted plants and, specifically, poinsettias. If you need to refresh your mind on any of the following questions, refer to the page number given in parentheses.

1. According to the USDA, what was the 1990 wholesale value of potted flowering plants in the U.S.A.? *(pages 220-221)*
2. Which potted flowering crop had the largest wholesale value both nationally and in Ohio in 1990? *(pages 220-221)*
3. List the top four potted flowering crops in the U.S. in order of wholesale value. *(pages 220-221)*
4. What is the scientific name of poinsettia? *(page 222)*
5. Who introduced the poinsettia to the United States? *(page 222)*
6. Describe the true flowers of the poinsettia. *(page 222)*
7. Where are the bracts of a poinsettia located? *(page 222)*
8. What do poinsettia growers use poinsettia stock plants for? *(pages 222-223)*
9. What are two advantages of producing your own poinsettia cuttings? *(page 224)*
10. Name three types of rooting media used for rooting poinsettia cuttings. *(page 224)*
11. How many ppm of nitrogen and potassium should be applied to a poinsettia crop growing in a soilless root medium, before the plants start to show color? *(pages 225-226)*
12. Name a popular type of root medium used for poinsettia crops. *(page 225)*
13. Why should night temperatures be warm during bract development? *(page 227)*
14. What is the purpose of pinching poinsettias? *(page 227)*
15. Describe the procedure for pinching a poinsettia plant. *(page 228)*
16. How many hours of continuous darkness per day must a poinsettia crop receive in order to bloom? *(page 229)*
17. What is Cycocel® used for in poinsettia production? *(page 229)*
18. Name the two species of whiteflies that are major pests of poinsettias. *(page 230)*
19. What two fungi cause stem and root rots of poinsettia crops? *(page 232)*
20. Describe splitting of poinsettias. What steps can be taken to prevent splitting? *(page 233)*
21. On an average, how many weeks should be allowed for rooting poinsettia cuttings? *(pages 234-235)*
22. Where can growers get scheduling information for poinsettia crops? *(page 234)*
23. Name three types of containers that poinsettias are marketed in. *(pages 236-237)*

# POTTED CHRYSANTHEMUM PRODUCTION — Part Two

## INTRODUCTION

Potted chrysanthemums *(Chrysanthemum morifolium)* are the second most important crop in the United States. The 1990 wholesale value was reported at $95.8 million or 14 percent of the total wholesale value for potted plants. Ohio ranked ninth in the nation at $3.2 million; and 9 percent of the total wholesale value of potted crops in Ohio was from potted mums.

Mums come in a variety of colors. They are relatively easy to grow and they last a long time in the home. What appears to be a single mum flower is actually a composite of flowers called florets, quite complex in structure. The flat, outermost, petal-shaped florets are called ray florets; the short, innermost florets (which are totally hidden in some flower forms) are called disk florets (Figure 11.16).

The size and arrangement of these two types of florets make for a variety of flower forms. They generally fall into the following groups (shown in Figure 11.17):

- daisy
- anemone
- decorative
- pompon
- incurve
- fuji
- spider
- spoon tip

Chrysanthemums are also classified according to the number of weeks of long nights they need in order to bloom. Response groups vary from 6 to 15 weeks. The majority of pot mums require 7 to 10 weeks of long nights to bloom.

## PROPAGATION

Commercial propagation of mum cuttings is a highly specialized business. Special cultural techniques are used to develop vigorous stock plants and produce disease- and insect-free cuttings.

*(continued page 242)*

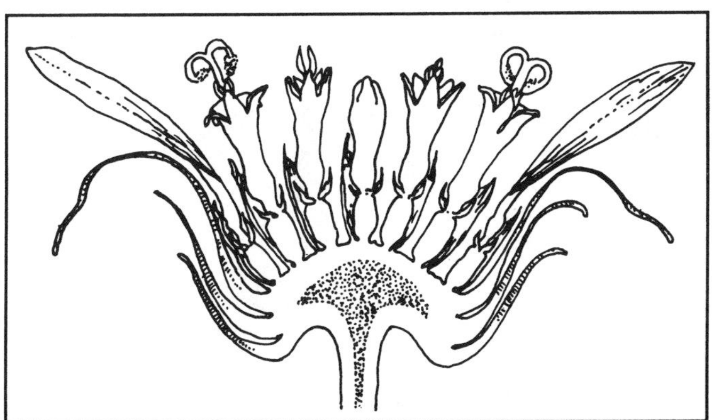

**Figure 11.16**
Cross section of a mum showing petal-like outer ray florets and short inner disk florets

**A.** Daisy mum

**Figure 11.17**

Mum flower classes are based on size and arrangement of ray and disk florets. *(courtesy of Yoder Brothers Inc., Barberton, Ohio)*

**B.** Anemone mum

**C.** Decorative mum

**D.** Pompon mum

E. Incurve mum

**Figure 11.17** *(continued)*

F. Fuji mum

G. Spider mum

H. Spoon tip mum

Most growers purchase cuttings from specialist propagators because the quality of the cutting is very important. Cuttings obtained from propagators are reliably uniform, vigorous, and free of insects and disease. Growers who try to produce their own cuttings have a very difficult time achieving such goals; their cuttings are almost always of inferior quality.

Cuttings may be purchased already rooted and ready to plant. While they are more expensive, rooted cuttings eliminate the labor, space, equipment, and time needed for unrooted cuttings. However, growers who have the time and equipment do purchase unrooted cuttings.

Unrooted cuttings are handled as follows:

1. Choose a pot that will serve for the finished mum plants.
2. Fill it with rooting medium and moisten it.
3. Take the mum cutting and dip the tip of it in a rooting hormone. (This will cause faster rooting and produce more roots.)
4. Stick the cutting 1 to 1 1/2 inches into the root medium.
5. Water it in.
6. Place the cutting under intermittent mist for about two weeks.
   * Keep a constant film of moisture for the first several days.
   * Gradually decrease misting frequency as cuttings root.
7. Place saran over misting bench if necessary on warm, sunny days.
8. When the cutting has a vigorous root system, it is ready to be placed in the greenhouse (Figure 11.18).

## Root Media

Growers use a variety of soil-based and soilless mixes for pot mums. Growing media must be loose and well drained, yet with good water- and nutrient-holding capacity. Soil-based media should be steam pasteurized before use. Most growers use soilless media composed of various amounts of peat moss, perlite, vermiculite, pine bark, and other ingredients.

## Potting

Pot mums are usually planted

- ✰ one cutting to a 4 or 4 1/2 inch pot,
- ✰ two or three cuttings per 5 or 5 1/2 inch pot, and
- ✰ four or five cuttings per 6 or 6 1/2 inch pot.

Azalea pots are typically used for pot mums. Rooted cuttings should be planted so that the root system is completely covered by **moist** root medium. In soilless root media, rooted cuttings can be planted an inch deeper than the level at which they were rooted. Planting this deep will firmly anchor the cutting in the root medium and promote better branching.

Cuttings should be graded by size, vigor, and extent of root system. Those with similar characteristics should be planted together in a pot. Cuttings should be planted at a 45° angle with the tops extending over the pot rim (Figure 11.19). This allows more room for growth for each cutting and results in a better shaped plant.

Immediately after potting, the crop should be maintained in an environment of high humidity and warm nights (usually 65° to 68°F) for rapid establishment. Short night conditions are also needed to keep plants vegetative. The crop should be lighted from 10 p.m. to 2 a.m. with incandescent lighting. If needed, saran can be used over the crop to reduce the water stress resulting from high light intensity.

**Figure 11.18**
Mum cutting which has taken root

**Figure 11.19**
Contrast of correct and incorrect potting of mum cuttings

## POT MUM CULTURE

### Temperature

Temperature control is important with mums because temperature can influence flower bud initiation and development. Most commercial mum varieties initiate flower buds and grow best at night temperatures of 62° to 65°F and day temperatures of 72° to 75°F. Night temperatures should not drop lower than 62°F until flower buds begin to show color.

When flower buds begin to show color, night temperatures should be lowered to 56° to 60°F and day temperatures to 66° to 70°F. These temperatures will help intensify flower color and strengthen the stems.

During the summer, growers often have problems maintaining proper temperatures. Temperatures that are too warm may cause **heat delay**. Daytime temperatures that stay above 90°F for a week or more, or night temperatures that are over 80°F will cause heat delay. This means that the pot mum crop blooms several days to weeks after its scheduled flowering date.

Careful selection of varieties that are resistant to heat delay should reduce or eliminate the problem. Reduce heat levels in the greenhouse as much as possible and pull photoperiodic shade cloth early in the evening when the greenhouse has started to cool. Heat can build up very rapidly under shade cloth and become a major cause of stress on summer pot mums.

### Watering

Mums have a relatively high water requirement. The plants will wilt quickly in sunny, warm conditions if the root medium dries out. The medium must be kept moist, but not wet. The medium surface should be allowed to dry out between irrigations to help control root rot diseases.

Most pot mums are watered by automated irrigation systems that do not wet the foliage. Many growers use spaghetti tubes with one tube per pot (Figure 11.20). Other systems used for pot mum irrigation are capillary mat and ebb and flow. As the crop nears the sale date, the frequency of watering should be lessened to help harden the plant to the home environment.

### Nutrition

Constant feeding is recommended for pot mum culture, since it gives the best control over the nutrition of the crop. Pot mums require large amounts of nitrogen and potassium, especially during the vegetative stage before flower development. To get rooted cuttings off to a rapid start, they should be watered in with a fertilizer solution containing 200 to 300 ppm of nitrogen. Once the crop is established, a constant feed program of 350 to 400 ppm of nitrogen and potassium should be implemented for a soilless root medium (200 to 300 ppm for a soil-based root medium).

To increase the longevity of pot mums in the home, fertilizer applications should be totally stopped three weeks before the sale date. This helps harden the plant and increase its post-harvest life in the home environment.

**Figure 11.20**
Close-up of a spaghetti tube being used to water a pot mum

Throughout production of the crop, soil and plant fertility levels should be monitored with soil tests and foliar analyses. Crop requirements for nutrients are affected by environmental conditions; (for example, dark, cloudy weather will lower nutritional requirements). Soil tests and foliar analyses will indicate whether there is a need for changing fertilizer applications. When a constant feed program is in use, a small amount of leaching should be figured in each time to control soluble salt levels.

## Light

Pot mums should be grown in full light intensity to obtain vigorous, rapid growth. Low light intensity results in leggy growth (stretching), fewer flowers, and smaller flowers. In the summer, when light intensity is very high, saran installation may be needed over the pot mums, or shading applied to the roof. Intensity of the light striking the pot mums must be lowered to prevent petal scorching (sunburn) and to reduce water stress in the plants.

## Photoperiod

When grown naturally, mums bloom in the fall. Through the use of photoperiodic equipment, however, pot mums can be brought into flower at any time of the year. They are long-night plants with respect to their photoperiodic requirement for flowering. They require a minimum night length (darkness) of 12 hours per day in order to bloom. The number of weeks of long nights required varies with the cultivar. This information can be obtained from chrysanthemum propagator companies.

Pot mums scheduled to bloom from May into early November must be supplied an artificial long night, since natural night length is not enough for these crops to initiate flower buds. Photoperiodic blackout shade cloth is drawn over the crop typically at 5 p.m. and removed the next morning at 8 a.m. (Figure 11.21). This results in a long night of 15 hours, more than enough to produce a blooming crop.

It is very important that the shade cloth does not leak any light through it. Pot mums exposed to even low levels of light during flower bud initiation

**Figure 11.21**

Photoperiodic blackout shade cloth pulled over a crop of pot mums

will be delayed. They may bloom unevenly or not bloom at all. Also, it is important to be consistent in use of the shade cloth. If certain nights of shading are missed during flower bud development, the crop will be delayed and flowers may be disfigured.

In the early stages of their growth, pot mums require a period of short nights to maintain vegetative growth. This will enable the plant to grow to a sufficient height once it is in bloom. If cuttings are planted during the fall or winter, the nights are long. The cuttings will develop flower buds right away, when the plants are too short and have very little vegetative growth.

To prevent the pot mums from forming flower buds too quickly, the crop should be lighted from 10 p.m. to 2 a.m., starting the night they were planted (Figure 11.22). This lighting schedule splits the long night into two short nights. Standard mum lighting can be used to accomplish this (as discussed in Chapter 4). The plants should be kept vegetative until the schedule indicates that long nights are needed.

**Figure 11.22**

Standard mum lighting used to keep pot mums vegetative

## Pinching

Pot mums are pinched to encourage branching. Multiple branched plants have a fuller, better-shaped appearance and produce more flowers. To pinch a pot mum, remove an inch or less of the tip of the stem (Figure 11.23). A pot mum is ready to be pinched about two weeks after the cutting is planted. In that time, the cutting should grow a well-established root system and approximately one inch of new stem growth. It is now ready to branch vigorously after pinching (Figure 11.24).

## Height Control

Growers of pot mums are concerned with controlling plant height because of its effect on the quality of the finished product. Certain cultivars with attractive flowers tend to grow too tall. The most common method of height control is to apply a growth retardant called B-Nine®.

When the lateral branches are 1 1/2 to 2 inches in length after pinching, it is time to apply B-Nine® to the crop. B-Nine® is applied as a spray at a rate of 2,500 to 5,000 ppm, depending on the cultivar and environmental conditions. This treatment may have to be repeated in two or three weeks. The need for such treatment should be carefully considered, however. Short- and medium-growing cultivars usually do not require any height control. Information on cultivar height is available in pot mum catalogs and manuals.

DIF can also be used to control mum height from late summer to the following spring whenever day temperatures are relatively low. Research has shown that a slightly negative DIF of –1 to –4 will control the height of pot mums.

**Figure 11.23** Pinching a mum

**Figure 11.24** Pot mums growing lateral branches after pinching

## Spacing

Spacing pot mums is very important. Proper spacing will allow sufficient light to strike the plants and prevent stretching. Also, air circulation must be adequate to prevent "wet spots" from occurring within the crop, causing disease. One method of pot mum production is to place the newly-potted plants in their final spacing. They do not need to be moved again until the crop is ready for shipping.

The other spacing method is to place newly planted pot mums pot-to-pot on the bench. Pot-to-pot spacing increases relative humidity around the crop and helps establish the cuttings. With less space used, less equipment and a smaller area are needed for short-night treatments. When the pot mums are established, they can then be moved to their final spacing (Table 11.6). The only problem with this method is that handling the pots twice increases labor costs.

**Table 11.6**
Final spacing recommendations for pot mums

| **Pot Size** (inches) | **Spacing** (inches) |
|---|---|
| 4 to 4 1/2 | 6 x 6 to 8 x 8 |
| 5 to 5 1/2 | 10 x 10 to 13 x 13 |
| 6 to 6 1/2 | 12 x 12 to 15 x 15 |
| 7 to 7 1/2 | 14 x 14 to 17 x 17 |

Source: *Yoder Pot Mums 1991 Catalog and Manual,* Yoder Brothers, Inc., Barberton, Ohio

**Figure 11.25**
Mum buds are removed at the arrows.

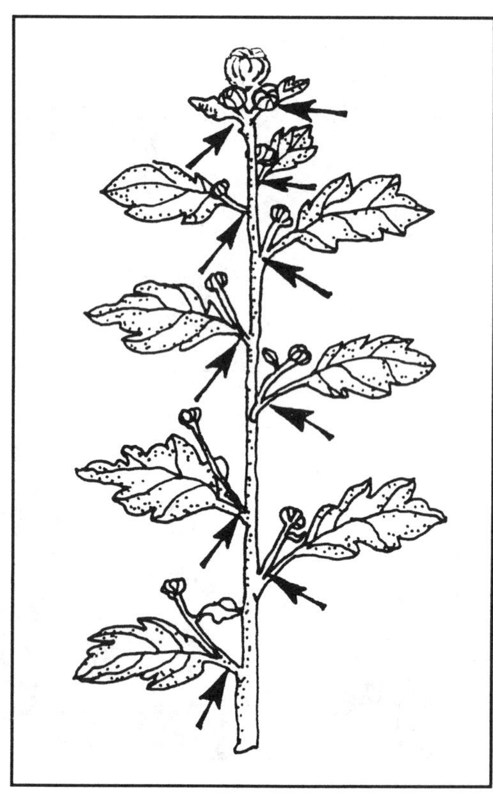

## Disbudding

One method of disbudding is removing all lateral flower buds below the main terminal flower bud (Figure 11.25). The result is a much larger, more showy flower. Pot mums grown this way are referred to as **standards**, with a single large flower per stem.

Another type of disbudding, used for spray mums, is center bud removal or CBR. The lateral buds are left on the stem and the terminal flower bud is removed (Figure 11.26). This is essentially the opposite of the method used for standard mums. It eliminates the terminal flower bud that would open first and start to fade before the lateral flowers. The result is a better-looking spray mum.

Disbudding is done as soon as the flower buds can be removed safely without damaging any part of the plant. If disbudding is done too late, blooming of the crop will be delayed and flower size and color intensity will be reduced.

**Figure 11.26**
Center bud removal (CBR) used on pot mums

## Scheduling

Though they bloom naturally only in the long-night months, pot mums are in demand year-round. The grower must manipulate photoperiod with all the other cultural conditions to obtain good-quality blooming pot mums all twelve months of the year.

Pot mums can be scheduled very precisely when all cultural considerations are optimum. Production schedules are based on cultivars selected, season of the year, and growing techniques. Using a continuous pot mum rotation, it is possible to produce up to four crops per bench each year.

To determine their crop schedules, commercial growers usually refer to chrysanthemum manuals published by suppliers. These manuals provide tables with suggested dates for planting, pinching, lighting, photoperiodic shading, and blooming. Growers using these publications may follow the printed schedules exactly. More likely, they will use them as guidelines to develop their own particular schedules. (You may want to do the same in scheduling your crop.)

## Pests

The major insect pests of pot mums are aphids, leaf miners, spider mites, thrips, and whiteflies. The larval stage of the leaf miner bores through leaf tissue. The primary symptom of leaf miner damage is white, meandering trails which disfigure the foliage. (See Chapter 8 for descriptions of damage caused by the other pests.) Figure 11.27 shows some of the common pests of pot mums (greatly enlarged) and in some cases the damage they caused.

The most effective pest control is achieved by implementing IPM strategies in the greenhouse.

1. Keep greenhouses inside and outside free of weeds and accumulated dead plant material.
2. Monitor pest populations with yellow sticky traps; scout the crop and graph pest populations over time.
3. Install screening material over vents to keep pests from entering the greenhouse.
4. Purchase disease- and insect-free cuttings from a mum specialist propagator.
5. Use only pesticides that are registered for control of the particular pest on pot mums; apply pesticides carefully, as directed.

**Figure 11.27**
Insects and other pests that attack mums

**A.** Aphids

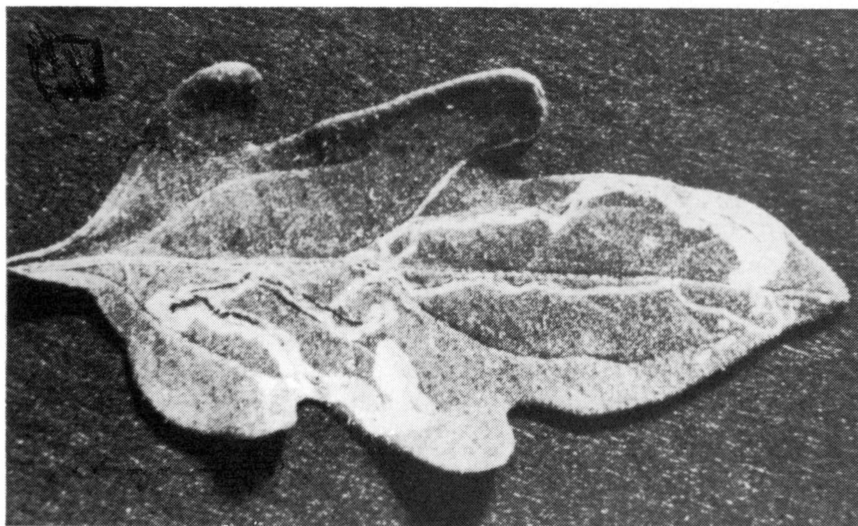

**B.** Leaf miners

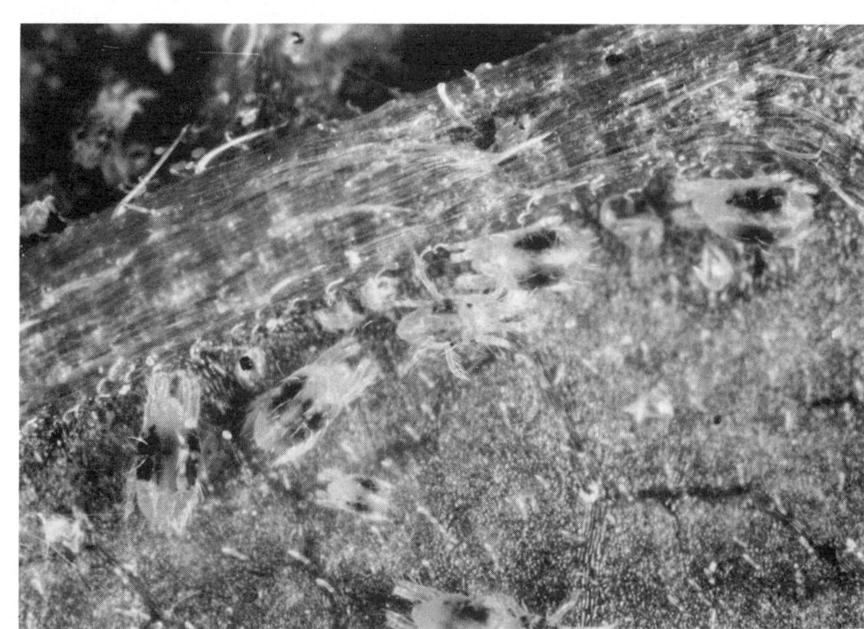

**C.** Spider mites

**Figure 11.27** *(continued)*

**D.** Whiteflies

## Diseases

There are a number of diseases that attack pot mums. The most common are caused by fungi. Most root and stem rots are caused by *Pythium* and *Rhizoctonia*; most foliar and flower diseases are caused by powdery mildew and *Botrytis* (Figure 11.28). There are also bacterial diseases such as bacterial blight and bacterial leaf spot, and viral diseases.

Remember that a healthy and vigorous plant will be more resistant to disease organisms. As with pest control, the best strategy against diseases is a preventive one. Implement IPHM (integrated plant health management) methods to minimize or completely eliminate disease threats.

1. Provide an ideal cultural environment.
   * Provide adequate nutrition.
   * Keep temperature levels optimum.
   * Provide adequate irrigation.
   * Avoid wetting the foliage and splashing water.
   * Keep relative humidity levels from becoming too high.
   * Provide adequate air circulation.
2. Observe strict greenhouse sanitation measures.
   * Disinfect all tools, equipment, etc.
   * Isolate or discard diseased plants.
3. Steam pasteurize soil-based root media and any type of medium that has been contaminated.
4. Use disease-resistant mum varieties.
5. Use fungicides when appropriate as a preventive/control measure.

A. Pythium root and stem rot

**Figure 11.28**
Diseases of mums

B. Rhizoctonia root and stem rot

C. Botrytis (gray mold)

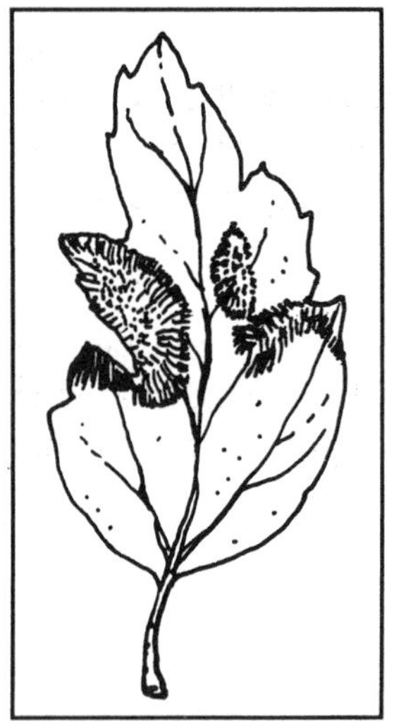

D. Powdery mildew

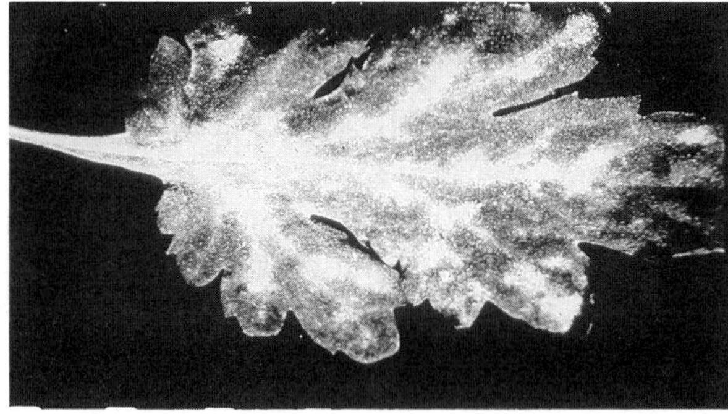

## Crown Bud Formation

Crown buds are small terminal flower buds on the mum plant that **never fully develop and open**. They form when the plants are exposed to improper photoperiod. Immediately below the crown bud are small strap-shaped leaves (Figure 11.29). Sometimes, vegetative by-pass shoots form below these leaves and grow up around the crown bud. Flowering is seriously delayed, and the shape of the flowering plant can be distorted. The formation of crown buds can ruin a crop.

**Figure 11.29**

Crown bud formation in pot mums. Note the strap-shaped leaves right below the crown bud.

Crown buds will form in response to even small amounts of light during flower bud development - light leaking through the shade cloth or light from nearby outside sources such as street lights. It is very important to keep the shade cloth in good condition. **No more than two footcandles of light should pass through it.** If the pot mum crop is exposed to extraneous light at night, it will have to be shaded even if the nights are naturally long enough for the crop to bloom.

Inconsistent shading of a crop can also result in crown bud formation. Growers must pull the shade cloth **every night** until the flower buds show color. Missing several nights may result in crown bud formation. Also, blooming of the crop will be delayed one day for every missed night.

Table 11.7 lists some of the common physiological disorders that pot mum growers encounter, along with the possible causes. Many of these problems can be avoided if proper cultural procedures are implemented.

## CUT MUM APPLICATIONS

### Introduction

The mum flower forms that are used for cut flower production are the same as those for pot mums. Many cultivars are available for cut mum culture. Some can be flowered on a year-round basis; others flower best only at certain times of the year. Refer to the manuals published by mum suppliers for help in choosing cultivars that will perform best in your situation.

Mums grown for cut flowers are classified into three categories (Figure 11.30):

1. **Standard mums** are large-flowered cultivars (with the flower more than 4 inches in diameter). They have all lateral or side buds removed. The remaining terminal flower bud produces a large flower, often called a "football" mum.
2. **Spray mums** are smaller-flowered cultivars with all flower buds allowed to develop except one. The center bud is removed to give the spray mum

**Figure 11.30**
Comparison of the three kinds of mums: (left to right) spray mum, disbud mum, standard mum

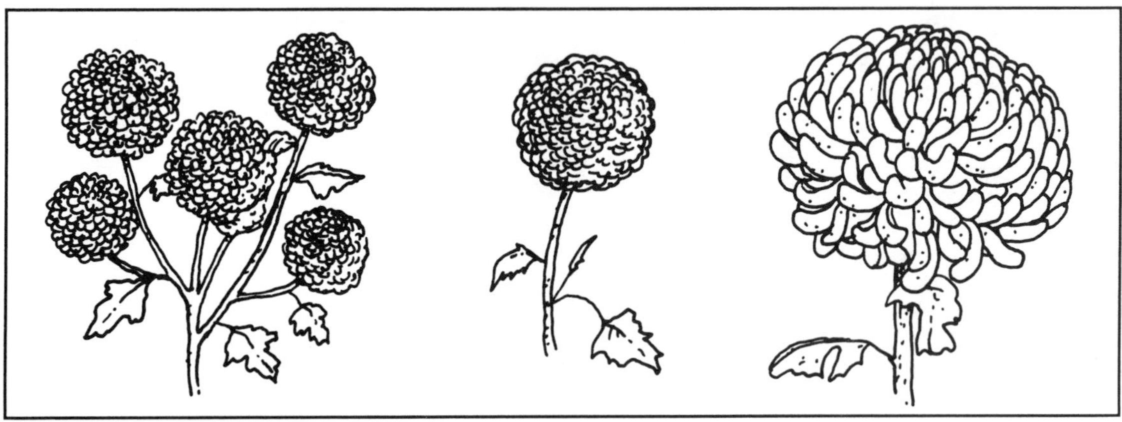

**Table 11.7** Possible causes of physiological disorders of pot mums

| PROBLEM | POSSIBLE CAUSE |
|---|---|
| Plants too short | Poor root system<br>Lack of fertilizer<br>Excess growth retardant<br>Not enough long days |
| Plants too tall | Too many long days<br>Spaced too closely<br>Temperature too high<br>Not enough light |
| Uneven flowering | Cool night temperatures<br>Failure to provide complete darkness at night |
| Malformed flowers | Insects<br>Improper day length control |
| Poor growth | Not enough light<br>Too much or too little fertilizer<br>Improper soil pH<br>Improper watering |
| Not enough shoots | Cool night temperatures<br>Lack of humidity<br>Improper pinch<br>Lack of fertilizer |

a better appearance. Spray mums are often pinched; two or more stems develop per plant. The terms "pompon" and "spray" are used interchangeably.

3. **Disbud mums** are grown in the same manner as standard mums. Only one flower is allowed to develop per stem. Disbud mum flowers are smaller than standard mums and the plants have shorter stems. The flowers are larger than those of spray mums. The major advantage of growing disbuds is that the plants can be spaced closer together than standards on the bench.

Many aspects of cut mum and pot mum culture are similar: propagation; scheduling (except that *cut mum* schedules should be consulted in mum manuals); light and photoperiod; temperature; disbudding procedures; and problems (insect pests, diseases, and crown bud formation). Refer to the pot mum section for details of these cultural requirements and concerns. The ways that cut mum requirements differ from those of pot mums will be discussed next.

## Root Media

Cut mums are grown in ground benches for convenience in handling the crop (Figure 11.31). Thus, the root media are almost always soil-based mixtures of field soil with organic and inorganic amendments. A loose, open texture for the medium is important. Organic matter like peat moss or inorganic materials like perlite can be incorporated to prevent compaction.

**Figure 11.31**

A cut mum ground bench with recently planted cuttings

Growers reuse the same growing medium in mum benches year after year. It is steam pasteurized **at least** annually (and preferably after every crop) to eliminate weeds, disease organisms, and insects.

## Planting and Spacing

Cuttings should be planted in the ground bench at the same depth at which they were propagated; that is, quite shallow (Figure 11.32). After being watered in, any cuttings that fall over slightly should be straightened immediately. Support is required to keep the stems straight. A series of welded wire grids is often used and gradually raised as the crop increases in height (Figure 11.33).

**Figure 11.32**
Rooted mum cutting properly planted

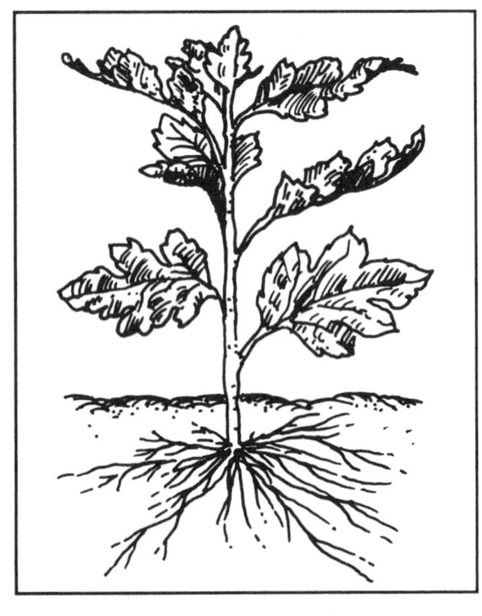

Cut mums are spaced 4 x 6 inches in the summer and 5 x 6 inches in the winter for single-stem plants. Recommended spacing for pinched crops is 6 x 8 inches in the summer and 7 x 8 inches in the winter. More space is needed per plant in the winter because light intensity in the greenhouse then is considerably lower than during the summer. Some growers leave out the center row of mums entirely during the winter to "open up" the bench so that more light will penetrate the crop.

## Watering

The principles concerning pot mum irrigation also apply to cut mum irrigation. However, as water is applied to a crop of cut mums, it should **never** wet the foliage. Mature crops take a longer time to dry; while they are drying, disease organisms have a chance to

**Figure 11.33**
As the crop grows, this welded wire grid is raised just enough to keep the upper part of each stem protruding through the openings in the fabric.

**Figure 11.34**
Ooze tube irrigation for cut mums growing in a ground bench

establish themselves. The most common "safe" way to irrigate a cut mum crop is by using ooze tubes (Figure 11.34) or a perimeter nozzle system that wets the root medium only.

## Nutrition

The principles of nutrition are the same for cut and pot mums. However, since cut mums are grown in soil-based root media, they should be provided with lower amounts of fertilizer than if they were growing in soilless root media. A constant feed program of 200 to 250 ppm of nitrogen should be used. During the winter, however, the root medium in the ground bench can become quite cool or even cold. At that time, avoid using ammonium nitrogen fertilizers, for their rate of utilization by the crop is greatly slowed in cold weather. Ammonium levels tend to build up in the root medium, becoming toxic to the plant.

## Harvesting

Cut mum flowers may be harvested in the bud stage or when the bud is about two-thirds fully open. Cut mums that are to be shipped long distances usually travel better if harvested in the bud stage (showing color). The retailer can then "open" the flower buds upon arrival before the flowers are sold. Cut mums that are sold locally, however, are usually harvested two-thirds fully open. Their short trip (shipping) to the customer is not likely to damage the tender petals.

Mum stems are cut about two inches above the soil line when the cut mum flowers are ready for harvesting. The lower quarter or third of the foliage is stripped from the stems and the flowers are placed in a warm floral preservative solution. (This warm solution is absorbed faster by the stems than a cold solution.) Buckets of cut mums are then placed in coolers for storage.

# MARKETING OF POT MUMS AND CUT MUMS

## Pot Mums

### Packaging and Shipping

Pot mums are ready to sell when flowers are at least half open. If plants are shipped at this stage, the flowers will continue to open normally and will be in top quality when they reach the consumers.

Pot mums (like most potted plants) should be sleeved and/or boxed for delivery. Different sizes of paper and plastic sleeves are available. A special stand with a wide base is used for sleeving. The sleeves are nested over a rod. A plate on top of the rod supports the pot (Figure 11.35). The pot mum is sleeved by pulling the sleeve up around the plant (Figure 11.36). Finally the sleeve is stapled shut at the top.

In cold weather, all packing should be done inside in a warm area. Loading of delivery trucks should also be done in the headhouse. Furthermore, the truck must be kept warm during transport using electric heaters that will not pollute the air with harmful gases.

### Statistics

Pot mums are second only to poinsettias in economic importance of flowering potted plants. The national wholesale value in 1990 was $95.8 million or 14 percent of the total flowering potted plant wholesale value.

**Figure 11.35**
A sleeving device composed of a wide base, rod, and plate on top

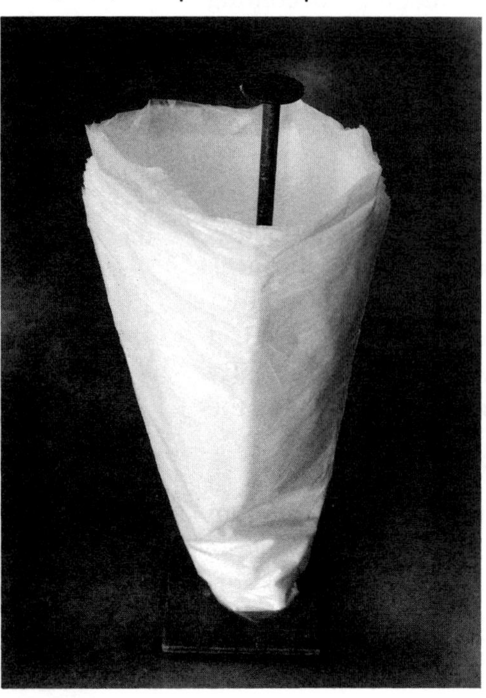

**Figure 11.36**
Sleeved pot mums before the sleeves are stapled shut

However, in Ohio, pot mum production was not as significant, ranking fourth in economic importance behind poinsettias, African violets, and azaleas. (Refer back to Table 11.2, page 221.) The wholesale value of pot mums produced in Ohio was $3.2 million or 9 percent of the state's total wholesale value of flowering potted plants.

## Cut Mums

### Packaging and Shipping

Cut mums, both standard and spray, are sleeved before shipping to prevent damage to the easily bruised flowers (Figure 11.37). When shipped long distances, the bunched mums are also boxed to further prevent damage to the flowers. Cut mums should be loaded into trucks inside in warm air surroundings. The delivery/shipping truck must be heated in the winter and air conditioned in the summer. This will prevent excessively high or low temperatures from damaging the flowers during transit.

**Figure 11.37**
A bunch of mums sleeved and ready for shipment

### Statistics

According to the USDA *1990 Floriculture Crops Summary,* the total wholesale value of cut mums in the United States was $38 million or 7 percent of the total cut flower wholesale value. Specifically, 26 percent of these cut mums were standards and 74 percent were pompons (spray mums).

Ohio's wholesale value for cut mums in 1990 was $583 thousand or 7 percent of the total cut flower wholesale value of $8.7 million. Forty-seven percent of Ohio's cut mums were standards and 53 percent were pompon mums.

## CHRYSANTHEMUM REVIEW

This review is to help you check yourself on what you have learned about production of potted chrysanthemums. If you need to refresh your mind on any of the following questions, refer to the page number given in parentheses.

1. What is the scientific name of chrysanthemum? *(page 239)*

2. Describe the following mum flower forms: daisy, anemone, decorative, pompon, incurve, fuji, spider, and spoon tip. *(pages 239-241)*

3. How are potted and cut chrysanthemums propagated? *(pages 239, 242)*

4. What are the three most common pot sizes for growing pot mums? *(page 242)*

5. Why are cuttings placed at a 45° angle when they are planted in a pot? *(pages 242-243)*

6. What is the recommended night temperature for pot mums during flower bud development? *(page 244)*

7. Why is the night temperature lowered when flower buds show color? *(page 244)*

8. For a constant feed program, how many ppm of nitrogen and potassium should be applied to a vigorously growing pot mum crop? to a cut mum crop? *(page 244)*

9. Since chrysanthemums are a long-night crop with respect to photoperiod, how do growers produce pot and cut mum crops during the short nights of summer? *(pages 245-246)*

10. What are two methods a grower can use to control the height of pot mum crops? *(page 247)*

11. What is a standard pot mum? *(page 248)*

12. Where can growers get scheduling information for pot and cut mum crops? *(page 249)*

13. Discuss IPM strategies for preventing pest infestations of pot and cut mum crops. *(pages 249-251)*

14. What is the best way to prevent pot and cut mum diseases? *(pages 251-252)*

15. Why do crown buds form in pot and cut mum crops? *(pages 252-253)*

16. What is the difference between a standard and a spray cut mum? *(pages 253-255)*

17. At what stages of development are cut mums ready for harvesting? *(page 257)*

18. Describe the procedure for harvesting cut mums. *(page 257)*

19. State the procedure for sleeving pot mums when they are ready for sale. *(page 258)*

20. Why should pot and cut mums be loaded into trucks **inside** the headhouse for shipping in winter? *(page 258)*

# EASTER LILY PRODUCTION — Part Three

## INTRODUCTION

The Easter lily *(Lilium longiflorum)* is grown primarily for Easter sales in the United States. It grows from a bulb and produces a cluster of beautiful, fragrant white flowers over a one- to two-week period (Figure 11.38). Most Easter lily bulbs produced in the United States come from the Pacific coastal states of Oregon and northern California. Bulbs are dug from the fields in the fall and shipped to growers in crates filled with damp sphagnum peat moss (Figure 11.39). The peat moss keeps the bulbs moist and prevents them from rubbing against each other and damaging the bulbs.

**Figure 11.38** A beautiful Easter lily

An Easter lily bulb is technically a **non-tunicate** bulb (Figure 11.40). That is, it lacks the tunic or outer paper-like, brown covering found on tulip and onion bulbs (tunicate bulbs). The Easter lily bulb is made up of separate scales, rather than continuous scales (like an onion's), that surround the central stem of the bulb. A tunic reduces water loss from a bulb and helps to protect it from damage. Thus, unprotected Easter lily bulbs must never be left exposed for long periods of time. They must be handled carefully.

The two main cultivars used for Easter lily production in the United States are Ace and Nellie White. Several other cultivars are used for cut flower production, such as Ari and Georgia from Florida.

The top five states in Easter lily production in 1990 were California, Michigan, Pennsylvania, Ohio, and New

**Figure 11.39**
Easter lily bulbs on sphagnum peat moss used to pack the bulbs in shipping crates

**Figure 11.40**
The Easter lily bulb is a non-tunicate bulb made up of separate fleshy scales.

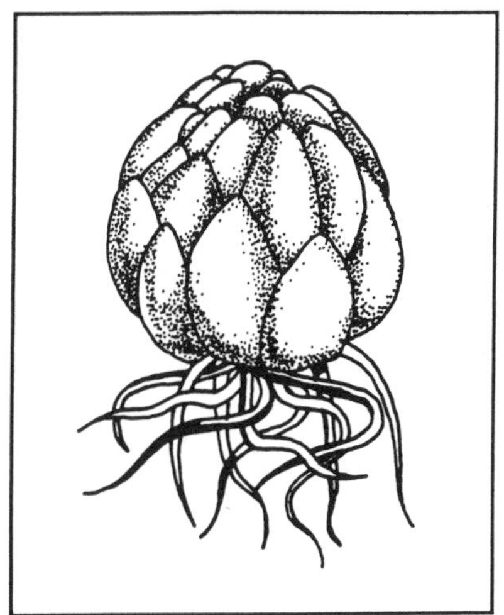

York (Table 11.8). Ohio's wholesale value for Easter lily production was $2.4 million, or 6.5 percent of the total Easter lily wholesale value. The total Easter lily wholesale value for the United States in 1990 was $36.9 million, or 5.5 percent of the total flowering potted plant wholesale value. Easter lilies rank in fourth place behind poinsettias, chrysanthemums, and azaleas in the flowering potted plant segment of the floriculture industry.

**Table 11.8** Top five states for Easter lily production in 1990

| State | Wholesale Value ($ million) | Percent Wholesale Value |
|---|---|---|
| 1 California | 7.88 | 21.3 |
| 2 Michigan | 3.71 | 10.0 |
| 3 Pennsylvania | 2.81 | 7.6 |
| **4 Ohio** | **2.41** | **6.5** |
| 5 New York | 2.16 | 5.8 |

Source: *Floriculture Crops 1990 Summary.* United States Department of Agriculture, National Agricultural Statistics Service, Agricultural Statistics Board, Washington, DC, April 1991

## COOLING EASTER LILY BULBS

To make Easter lilies bloom at the desired time and to achieve uniform flowering, the bulbs must be cooled for six weeks at a temperature of 40°F. This can be done using a variety of methods which we will discuss next.

### Commercial Case Cooling

Commercial case-cooled bulbs are bulbs that were cooled by the supplier. These bulbs were cooled in their shipping crate for six weeks and then shipped to the grower, ready to be potted. This practice is helpful for growers who do not have coolers or who do not have the time or space for cooling the bulbs.

A major disadvantage of commercial case-cooled bulbs is that the grower can not be certain that the bulbs received the entire six weeks of cooling. Reduced cooling time can cause the crop to bloom off-schedule and not in uniform fashion.

### Case Cooling by the Grower

This method is similar to commercial case cooling, except that the grower cools the bulbs in shipping crates in a cooler on the premises. The main advantage of this method is that the grower knows exactly how long the bulbs were cooled and at what temperature. To monitor the temperature of the packing material (usually damp sphagnum moss), a soil thermometer should be inserted into it. The thermometer can then be checked daily to be sure that the packing material stays at 40°F.

### Natural Cooling

Natural cooling is different from the previous two methods. The bulbs are removed from the shipping case and potted **before** cooling. As soon as bulbs are potted, they are placed in an outdoor location where the temperature is cool, but not freezing. With this method, some rooting of the bulb takes place before cooling is completed. The result is an increased number of flowers per plant.

However, weather conditions can be quite variable. The bulbs may not have received enough cooling when it is time to force them into bloom. Monitoring the root medium temperature is essential during this time. A lighting treatment may be required to complete the cooling effects on the bulb at the end of the cooling period (to be discussed under *lighting*).

### Controlled Temperature Forcing

Controlled temperature forcing (CTF) is the cooling method of choice for producing top quality Easter lilies. In this method, the bulbs are potted as soon as they arrive and are allowed to root for three weeks. The root medium is kept around 63°F for rapid root development. At the end of the three-week period, the bulbs are placed in a cooler at 40°F for six weeks.

Thus, CTF offers the grower the most control over the cooling phase of Easter lily production. CTF produces the highest quality crop because it

- ✰ produces more flowers per plant,
- ✰ produces longer lower leaves,
- ✰ makes the crop easier to force, and
- ✰ brings the whole crop into bloom at once (rather than over a period of a week or more).

## PLANTING EASTER LILY BULBS

### Root Media

Easter lilies are susceptible to root rot diseases. To prevent their development, selection of a root medium that has good aeration and drainage is important. With soil-based mixes, the field soil should be amended with perlite and sphagnum peat moss. One such mix that works well is 4 parts soil, 1 part perlite, and 1 part coarse sphagnum peat moss (by volume). The mix must be steam pasteurized before use. Many growers use Peat-Lite root media mixes, since they are light and well-drained and promote healthy root development.

The pH of the root medium should be between 6.5 and 6.7. Superphosphate should not be used to amend the root medium. Leafscorch will result from pH levels that are too low or the presence of superphosphate in the root medium.

### Pots

Easter lilies are usually planted in 6-inch standard pots because they are deeper than azalea pots (Figure 11.41). The bulb is placed in the pot with its tip at least two inches below the surface to allow for stem root development (Figure 11.42). Then the pot is filled with root medium and watered in thoroughly. As it develops, the lily plant forms roots on the stem beneath the root medium surface (Figure 11.43). These roots help support the plant.

**Figure 11.41**
Easter lilies are potted in standard pots *(left)* instead of azalea pots to give the plants more support.

**Figure 11.42**
An Easter lily bulb ready for planting in a standard pot

## GENERAL CULTURE

### Temperature

Root medium and air temperature are the most important factors in forcing an Easter lily crop. There are three different temperature phases involved in forcing this crop.

1. *From the start of forcing to emergence date*
Root medium temperature should be held between 60° and 65°F. This will promote rapid, healthy root and shoot development.

2. *From shoot emergence until flower buds are visible*
The recommended night temperature range is between 55° and 65°F. Development of flower buds is in progress. This development can be hindered by high night temperatures. Therefore, night temperatures should never exceed 70°F.

3. *From visible bud date until flowering*
Night temperatures should be maintained between 60° and 65°F.

### Watering

In the early stage of forcing, when the bulb is rooting, the root medium should not be allowed to dry out. Once the shoots have emerged, the surface of the root medium can become dry between irrigations to help prevent root rot diseases. Many growers used spaghetti tube irrigation systems to reduce labor costs. They tend to avoid subirrigation systems like capillary mats and ebb and flow benching because these systems are likely to produce excessively tall plants.

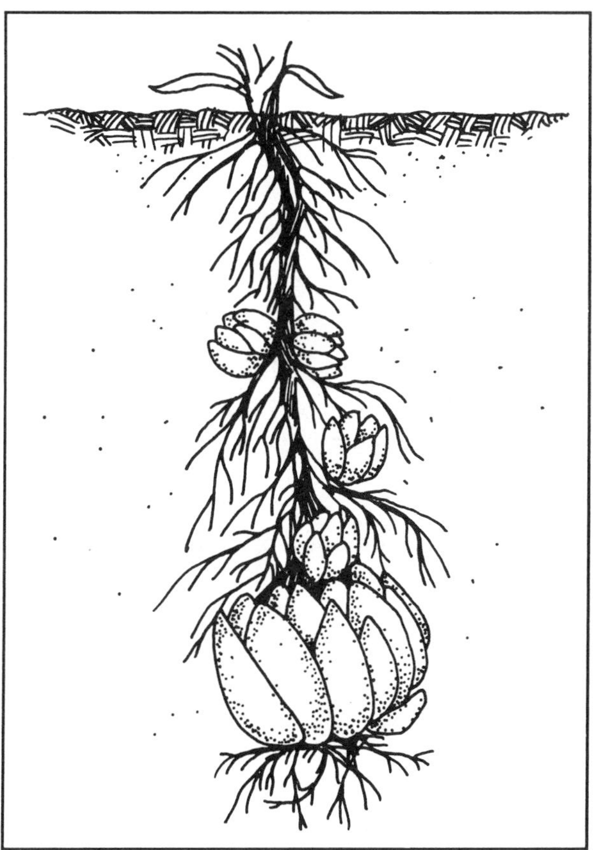

**Figure 11.43**
Roots forming along the stem help anchor lily plants.

## Nutrition

Adequate nitrogen helps to maintain good green foliage and improve the overall appearance of the plant. The best nutritional program is to inject 200 ppm of both nitrogen and potassium at each irrigation for soil-based root media and 250 ppm for soilless root media. Weekly applications of a complete fertilizer at 2 pounds per 100 gallons of water is recommended when injection is not available. Osmocote® can also be mixed uniformly into the root medium to supply nitrogen and potassium. For all nutritional programs, a small amount of leaching should be allowed after each irrigation. This will prevent soluble salts from building up in the root medium and damaging the roots.

## Lighting

Research has shown that lighting Easter lily shoots upon emergence is a good substitute for cooling the bulbs on a day-for-day basis. For example, a shipment of bulbs that was commercial case-cooled received only 35 days of cooling instead of 42 days (six weeks). When the lilies emerged, they were given special lighting for 7 days (42–35 days). The results were the same as if the bulbs had received the full six weeks of cooling.

To light Easter lilies upon emergence, standard mum lighting is installed overhead. (See Chapter 4, page 88.) The crop is lighted from 10:00 p.m. to 2:00 a.m. with incandescent lamps that provide at least 10 footcandles of light at crop level.

Only light of full intensity will produce a crop of the highest possible quality. The glazing must be kept clean so that it will transmit the maximum amount of light.

## Height Control

When height control of a crop is necessary, chemical growth retardants can be used. The most popular is A-Rest®.

### *As a drench*

Prepare a solution of 4 fluid ounces of A-Rest® per 16 gallons of water. When the shoots are 6 to 8 inches tall, each pot receives 8 fluid ounces of this solution two times (with one week between applications).

### *As a spray*

Prepare a solution of 0.5 pint A-Rest® and 3.5 pints of water. Spray this half gallon of solution on 100 square feet of bench area two times, one week apart, when the shoots are 6 to 8 inches tall.

A more effective means of height control is to use a 0 or slightly negative DIF. Avoid using a large negative DIF because the lily leaves will curve downward, making the plant look droopy. (See Figure 9.4, page 172.) Since lilies are forced during the winter and early spring when cool day temperatures are common, implementation of DIF for height control is usually easy.

## Spacing

Proper spacing of the Easter lily crop is very important for crop quality and for adequate air circulation that helps prevent diseases. The recommended spacing for lilies grown from bulbs up to 8 inches in circumference is 6 x 8 spacing, or three pots per square foot. For larger bulbs, the crop will need more space - about 7 x 8 inch centers between pots.

When the crop is spaced properly, light will be able to penetrate each plant and prevent stretching. Air will circulate through the crop and eliminate "wet spots," reducing the occurrence of root rot disease.

## Scheduling

Scheduling an Easter lily crop can be a challenge for several reasons. Because of the variation in the date when Easter falls, different growing conditions may be encountered each year. Rate of plant development is affected by maturity of the bulb when harvested, the cooling temperatures used and their duration, and the cultural practices used during forcing. The importance of **accurate crop scheduling** cannot be overemphasized. An Easter lily crop that is not ready for Easter is almost worthless.

Whether growers have their bulbs cooled by an outside source or cool the bulbs themselves, there are schedules available from lily bulb suppliers and industry sources such as the Ohio Florists' Association.

**General guidelines** for scheduling are as follows:

1. Aim for the crop to come into bloom one week before Easter - Palm Sunday.
2. Set aside six weeks for cooling. If CTF is used, allow an additional three weeks for rooting the plants in pots before cooling.
3. Plan on 110 to 115 days for the properly cooled bulbs to force into bloom in the greenhouse.
4. Add up all those numbers of days and **count back** that many days from Palm Sunday. Now you know when you will need to receive the bulbs.
5. At eight weeks before Easter, aim at a shoot height of 4 to 6 inches for the plants.
6. To have buds visible at seven weeks before Easter, keep night temperatures at 60°F. To have buds visible at six weeks, maintain a night temperature of 65°F.

Monitoring the progress of the Easter lily crop is very important, and comparing the development of the plants to published schedules. If development needs to be slowed down or speeded up, temperatures can be adjusted accordingly. See Figure 11.44 for a sample growing schedule for a CTF Easter lily crop.

## Pests

The two primary pests of Easter lilies are aphids and bulb mites. Aphids damage Easter lilies by feeding on the foliage and excreting honeydew onto the plant. The result is deformed growth, black sooty mold on the foliage, and a crop that is ruined in appearance. Bulb mites feed on the bulb scales, causing serious damage to the bulb. The damaged bulb tissue allows disease organisms to become established.

Control of both pests is done by application of registered pesticides at label rates by a licensed pesticide applicator. IPM methods should be implemented to help prevent aphid infestation. Bulbs should be inspected upon receipt for symptoms of bulb mite infestation.

## Diseases

Root rot, a fungal disease caused by *Pythium* and *Rhizoctonia*, is the primary disease that affects Easter lilies. It causes roots to rot and turn brown (while healthy roots are white). Overwatering is the main cause of this disease, because wet root media promote the establishment of the disease organisms.

To prevent the occurrence of root rots:

1. Use pasteurized soil.
2. Allow the surface of the root medium to dry between irrigations.
3. Use only fungicides that are labeled for Easter lilies. Apply them as a drench monthly.

If root rot does become established, isolate the affected plants from the rest of the crop. Gently knock the root ball of each plant out of the pot. Then set the plants back lightly into the pots. Give them a light watering until new

**Figure 11.44 SAMPLE GROWING SCHEDULE FOR A CTF EASTER LILY CROP**

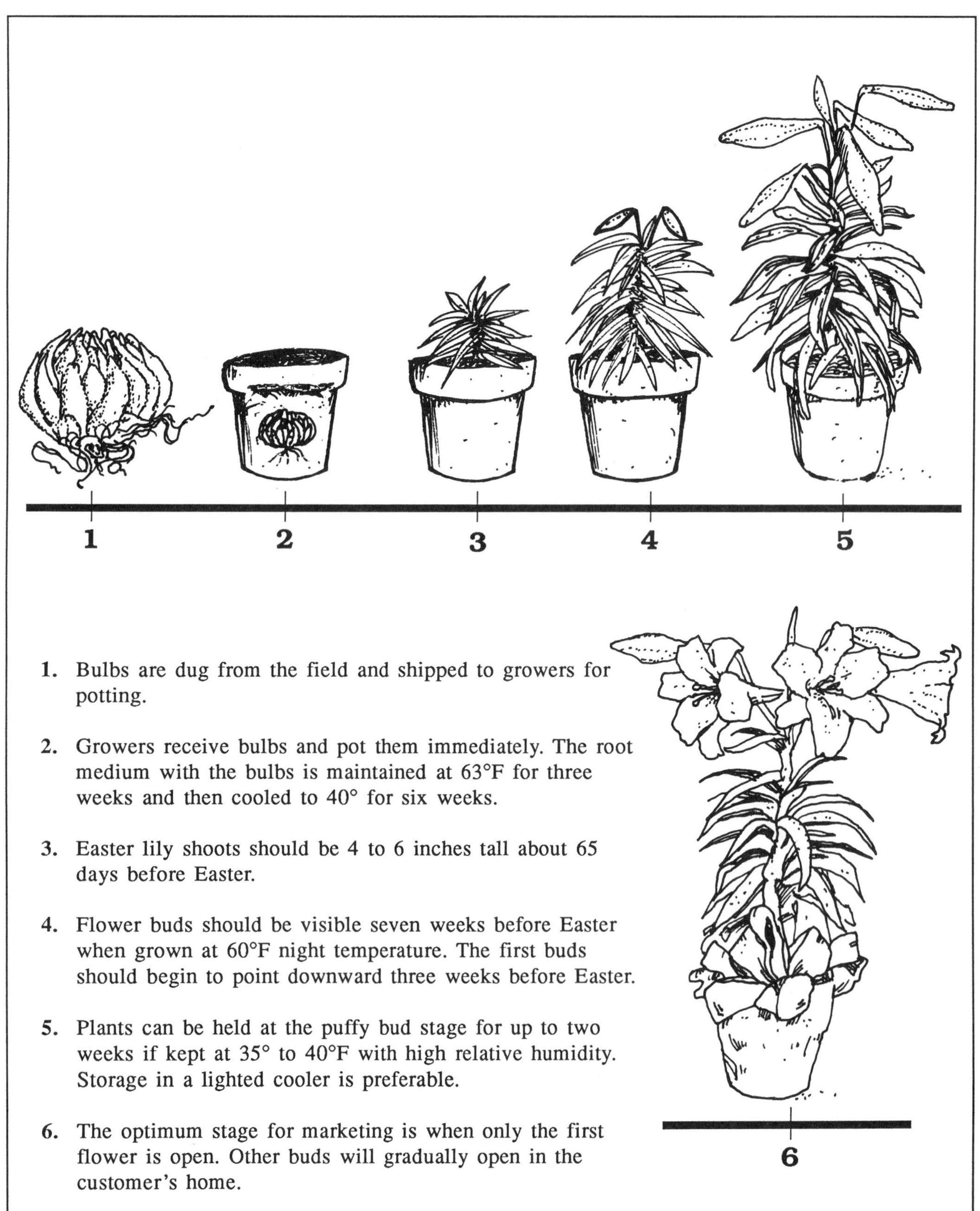

root growth is evident. These practices will discourage the growth of the fungal disease organisms. The roots will have a chance to dry out somewhat and produce new, healthy growth.

### Holding the Crop in Cold Storage

Sometimes, part or all of an Easter lily crop that has come into bloom too early has to be kept in storage. Plants may be stored at the stage when the first flower bud looks puffy and white (Figure 11.45). The plants should be irrigated first, then placed in a 35° to 40°F cooler, either lighted or in the dark. Easter lilies can be stored up to two weeks in this puffy bud stage. The root medium should be checked periodically and irrigated before it completely dries out. When the lily plants are removed from cold storage, they should be given an hour or two to warm up slowly in the headhouse. They should ***not*** be placed directly into a warm, sunny greenhouse. A slow warming will reduce water stress considerably by keeping the foliage from warming up faster than the root medium. (Cold roots do not take up water very well.)

## MARKETING

An Easter lily should be sold when the first flower is open. Usually, the pots are covered with colorful foil and decorated with an attractive ribbon. As the flower buds open, the pollen-bearing anthers inside should be removed as soon as possible (Figure 11.46). Anthers produce an abundance of yellow pollen, which can fall onto the petals and discolor them. Also, removal of the anthers prolongs the life of the flower.

As stated previously, Easter lily sales in 1990 ranked this crop fourth in flowering potted plant production. Ohio is a major Easter lily-producing state. Its 1990 ranking was fourth in the country at $2.4 million wholesale value.

---

**Figure 11.45** Easter lilies at the white puffy-bud stage can be placed in cold storage.

**Figure 11.46** Flower parts of an Easter lily with the anthers labeled

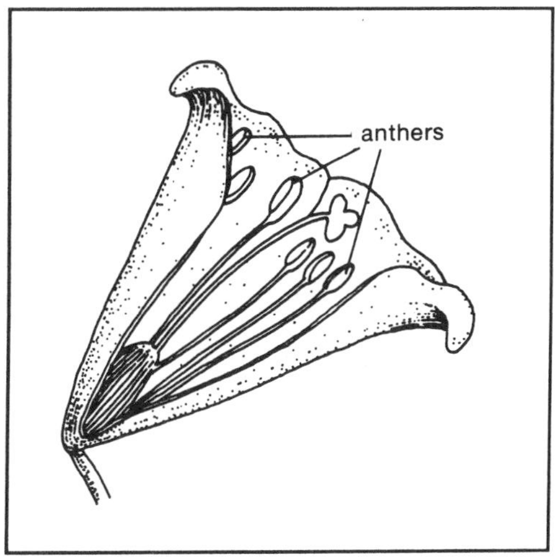

## EASTER LILY REVIEW

This review is to help you check yourself on what you have learned about Easter lily production. If you need to refresh your mind on any of the following questions, refer to the page number given in parentheses.

1. What is the scientific name of the Easter lily? *(page 261)*

2. What are the two most popular Easter lily cultivars? *(page 261)*

3. Why do Easter lilies have to be cooled during production? *(page 262)*

4. At what temperature and for how long must Easter lily bulbs be cooled? *(page 262)*

5. List the four cooling methods used for Easter lily bulbs. *(pages 262-263)*

6. Which Easter lily bulb cooling method is most commonly used? Why? *(page 263)*

7. What type of pot is best to plant Easter lily bulbs in? *(page 264)*

8. For a constant feed program, what is the recommended ppm of nitrogen and potassium to be applied to an Easter lily crop growing in a soilless root medium? *(page 265)*

9. If Easter lily bulbs are not cooled for the required period of time, what can be done upon shoot emergence to substitute for the missed cooling time? *(page 265)*

10. How can DIF be used to control the height of Easter lilies? *(page 266)*

11. Why is scheduling Easter lilies more difficult than scheduling other potted flowering plants? *(page 266)*

12. What is the main disease of Easter lilies? How can it be prevented? *(page 267)*

13. At what stage of their development can Easter lilies be stored in a cooler to keep them from blooming too early? *(pages 268-269)*

14. Why should the anthers of an Easter lily be removed? *(page 269)*

# CHAPTER 12

# MINOR POTTED CROPS

## Competencies for Chapter 12

As a result of studying this chapter, you should be able to do the following:

1. Give the scientific name of each crop.
2. Describe the major cultural guidelines for five minor flowering potted plants.
3. Describe the major cultural guidelines for foliage plants.
4. Identify each crop by its distinctive flowering and foliar characteristics.
5. Name the minor potted crops with the highest wholesale value in your state.

## Related Science Concepts

1. Examine plant development.
2. Determine cultural needs of minor potted crops.
3. Describe the effects of environmental conditions on crop growth and quality.
4. Describe the processes of acclimation and hardening of Florida-grown foliage plants for indoor use.
5. Implement IPHM strategies.
6. Implement IPM strategies.
7. Examine techniques of plant propagation.

## Related Math Concepts

1. Apply basic operations to whole numbers, decimals, and fractions as they relate to minor potted crops.
2. Apply basic operations to ratios and percents as they relate to minor potted crops.
3. Apply mathematical concepts and operations to minor potted crops.
4. Read, interpret, and construct charts, graphs, and tables related to minor potted crops.

## Terms to Know

acclimation
corm
phylloclade
succulent

# INTRODUCTION

In Chapter 11 we discussed three major flowering potted crops. In this chapter are several other potted crops that are not as major, but still merit discussion.

- ☆ African violets
- ☆ Cineraria
- ☆ Cyclamen
- ☆ Holiday cacti
- ☆ Kalanchoe
- ☆ Foliage plants

African violets are close behind Easter lilies in wholesale value. They flower year-round in the home with little care. Cineraria and cyclamen are produced in abundance during the spring for Valentines' Day, Easter and Mother's Day. These two plants produce very showy flowers that last several weeks in the home.

Holiday cacti are very popular during the Thanksgiving, Christmas, and Easter holidays. They come in a wide variety of colors and bloom year after year in the home with a minimum of care. Kalanchoe is another colorful flowering plant that is produced year-round. The flowers last up to one month in the home. Kalanchoe plants are quite tolerant of harsh home conditions.

Potted foliage plants are found in nearly every household and office building in the United States. Foliage plants not only improve the appearance of a room, but actually purify the air, removing pollutants and adding oxygen. We will now get into a brief discussion of the cultural guidelines for producing each of these crops.

---

**Figure 12.1** African violet in bloom

# AFRICAN VIOLETS

The African violet *(Saintpaulia ionantha)* is one of the best-known, most popular house plants in the United States. Its colorful flowers bloom almost constantly throughout the year. The flowers are borne in large clusters that fill the center of the plant (Figure 12.1).

African violets may be propagated by leaf cuttings or from seed. Production time from seed is approximately ten months. Production time using leaf cuttings is roughly four months to produce a blooming crop.

African violets are usually produced in 3- or 4-inch pots using a soilless root medium. The root medium must have excellent drainage and aeration; its pH should be between 6.0 and 7.0. Watering can be done either by capillary mats (Figure 12.2), ebb and flow, or overhead watering. With overhead watering, however, water temperature **must** be no more than 5 degrees (F) cooler than the air temperature. If the water is colder, it will produce white spots on the leaves. African violets are best fertilized on a constant feed basis. Since this crop is quite sensitive to high soluble salts levels in the root medium, 100 to 200 ppm of nitrogen should be applied at each irrigation. (The lower end of this range is preferred.)

**Figure 12.2**
African violets irrigated by capillary mats

During the summer (and year-round for some cultivars), light intensity on African violet plants must be reduced, because the leaves burn easily in high light intensities. The light intensity should be reduced by 75 to 80 percent to achieve the low light levels (1,500 footcandles) that are ideal for this crop. Day temperatures for African violets should be around 75°F and night temperatures near 70°F.

Cyclamen mites, aphids, thrips, and mealybugs are the most common pests of African violets. These pests are controlled by IPM procedures and wise use of the appropriate pesticides. Powdery mildew, *Botrytis* blight, and crown and root rots are the primary diseases that affect African violets. Following proper cultural procedures and implementing IPHM procedures during production will usually prevent these diseases from becoming established.

# CINERARIA

Cineraria *(Senecio* x *hybridus)* is a cool temperature crop that is produced mainly for sales from Valentines' Day through Easter. This plant has a large, colorful flower cluster in the center of the plant, surrounded by large leaves (Figure 12.3). The many flower colors include white, lavender, blue, red, pink, and multiple colors.

**Figure 12.3**
The large flower cluster of cineraria

Cineraria are started from seed sown in August and on into October for January through April sales. Some growers prefer to purchase started plants at a later date to avoid the labor and space required for seedling germination and growth. Approximately six months are required to produce a finished crop of cineraria started from seed. Four to five months are required for a cineraria crop produced from started plants.

The root medium that is used should be well drained with good aeration and good water-holding capacity. The pH for a soilless root medium should be 5.5 to 6.0. Cineraria are potted in either 4- or 6-inch azalea pots; for the mass market, 4-inch pots are very profitable. A constant feed program of 100 ppm of both nitrogen and potassium is recommended.

For the first four to six weeks after transplanting, night temperatures should be 62° to 65°F for rapid vegetative growth. After this period, the crop must be exposed to cool temperatures for flower bud development and blooming. The night temperature should be lowered to 45° to 50°F for a minimum of four weeks and preferably six weeks. Day temperatures during this time should be no higher than 60°F. Cineraria grow and flower best when given full light intensity, especially during the winter months.

The major pests of cineraria are whiteflies, aphids, and thrips. IPM strategies should be implemented during production, as these pests, in a matter of days, can "explode" into huge populations on this crop. Powdery mildew and *Botrytis* will attack cineraria if air circulation is not adequate and/or the foliage is wet during the night. Viral diseases also affect cineraria, resulting in streaking of the foliage and flowers. Thrips can spread these viral diseases, so control of thrips is very important in disease prevention.

## CYCLAMEN

Cyclamen *(Cyclamen persicum)* is another cool temperature crop that is grown mainly for sales from Christmas to Easter. Cyclamen grows from a corm and produces an abundance of colorful flowers that are borne above the foliage (Figure 12.4). A wide variety of flower colors is available, including red, white, pink and lavender.

**Figure 12.4** Cyclamen plant grown from a corm, blooming in a 6-inch pot

Cyclamen can be grown either from seed or from purchased, well-established small plants. The crop is commonly grown in either 4- or 6-inch pots. Production time for 6-inch pots from seed takes about nine months; from started plants, blooming will begin in about six months. Crops produced in 4-inch pots are mini-cyclamen (Figure 12.5). Their production time from seed is seven to eight months, and from purchased starter plants, five months.

Cyclamen should be grown in a moist, light, well-drained root medium. The pH should be 5.5 to 6.0 for soilless mixes. Cyclamen should be kept moist, but never wet nor totally dried out. The crop should be watered in the morning so that the foliage will be dry before evening. Leaves that remain wet during the evening are very susceptible to foliage diseases. Once the crop is established after transplanting, apply 150 to 200 ppm of nitrogen. Then reduce the amount of nitrogen to no more than 100 ppm during the time when the plant has from 15 to 40 unfolded leaves. Too much nitrogen applied during this stage of development (when flower buds are actively forming) will delay flowering.

Cyclamen should be grown in night temperatures of 50° to 55°F to promote heavy flowering once the transplanted seedlings or plants have become established. Warmer night temperatures can be used to speed up the crop, but flowering may be decreased. The root medium temperature should be maintained below 65°F.

**Figure 12.5** A crop of mini-cyclamens growing in 4-inch pots

Gibberellic acid is a growth regulator that accelerates cyclamen flowering by two to five weeks (depending on the cultivar). Gibberellic acid should be applied approximately 150 days after sowing the seed, when the plants have 10 to 12 fully developed leaves. A 10 ppm solution of gibberellic acid is prepared and sprayed **lightly** on the new growth just above the corm. Always follow label directions for best results.

Cyclamen are susceptible to cyclamen mite, aphid, spider mite, and thrips infestations. These pests all feed on the foliage and/or flowers, disfiguring them. Control of these pests is accomplished by IPM strategies and by well-planned insecticide applications.

Crown rots and root rots are two common diseases that affect cyclamen. Crown rot is characterized by rotting flowers and leaves that are often covered by the gray growth of the fungus mold, *Botrytis*. The fungi *Pythium* and *Rhizoctonia* cause root rots, which ultimately kill the plant. These diseases can usually be controlled using the IPHM techniques of proper watering, adequate air circulation, maintaining dry foliage, and others.

## HOLIDAY CACTI

Three major types of holiday cactus are on the market today: Thanksgiving cactus *(Schlumbergera truncata)*, Christmas cactus *(Schlumbergera bridgesii)*, and Easter cactus *(Rhipsalidopsis gaertneri)*. Easter cactus is the newest of the three cacti for production in the United States. All three plants naturally produce a profusion of showy flowers in the home around the time of the holiday for which they are named. Flower colors include red, white, peach, lavender, dark purple, and orange.

These holiday cacti are all similar in appearance, especially the Thanksgiving and Christmas cacti. An easy way to tell these two cacti apart is to examine the phylloclades (stem segments). (See Figure 12.6.) The edges of the phylloclades of Thanksgiving cactus are **toothed or pointed**; those of Christmas cactus are **rounded**. The phylloclades of Easter cactus are more elongated than the other two cacti. They also bear easily visible tufts of brown "hairs" along the two edges and the ends of the phylloclades.

Holiday cacti are propagated by cuttings taken from stock plants. Scheduling guidelines are published in industry literature. In general, the *Schlumbergera* species require eight to twelve months from propagating cuttings to a finished crop, depending on when cuttings were rooted. Easter cactus requires 12 months to produce a finished crop, starting with propagation.

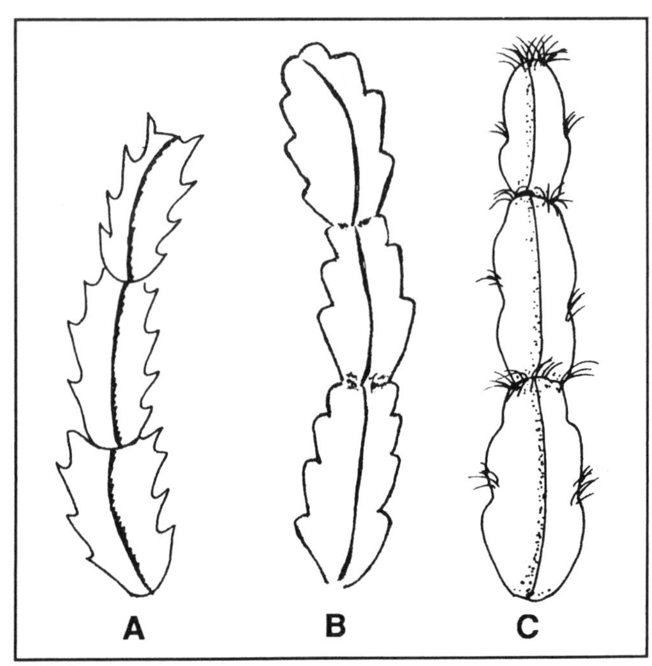


**Figure 12.6**

Three types of holiday cactus can be differentiated by the shape of the phylloclade:
**A)** Thanksgiving cactus
**B)** Christmas cactus
**C)** Easter cactus

The root medium (typically a Peat-Lite soilless mix) must have excellent aeration and drainage, since these cacti are vulnerable to root and stem rots. The pH of the root medium should be 5.5 to 6.0. Generally, three or four rooted cuttings are planted in a 4-inch pot for greenhouse production. The *Schlumbergera* species are relatively light feeders, requiring only 100 to 150 ppm of nitrate nitrogen once a week. Fertilizing should be discontinued one month before flower buds start to develop. Easter cactus should be fertilized with 300 to 500 ppm of nitrogen every two weeks during the summer and once every four weeks during the rest of the year.

Holiday cacti will flower in response to two environmental conditions: long nights and cool temperatures. *Schlumbergera* should be grown in night temperatures of 55°F to start flower bud development. Easter cacti respond best at temperatures between 47° and 53°F for flower bud formation. If cool night temperatures are not possible, holiday cacti will bloom when exposed to long nights of 12 hours or more. Many growers combine cool nights (60°F) and long nights to obtain the maximum number of flowers per plant.

Three to four weeks after flower buds start to develop, they will become visible. The plants will be in full bloom eight to ten weeks after the start of flower bud development. Research has shown that the use of benzyl adenine, a growth regulator, on *Schlumbergera* will increase the number of flowers produced after flower buds have started to develop. This chemical is applied as a spray at the rate of 100 ppm two weeks after the start of long nights.

Holiday cacti are usually little affected by insect pests, though sometimes mealybugs and scale can be a problem. It is important to examine plants carefully and periodically for signs of infestation.

The major diseases of holiday cacti are root and stem rots. These fungal diseases strike when plants are kept too moist or contaminated root media are used. These diseases can be avoided by allowing the surface of the root medium to dry between irrigations. Also, steam pasteurization should be done for all soil-based root media and any soilless root media that are contaminated.

## KALANCHOE

Kalanchoe *(Kalanchoe blossfeldiana)* is a colorful potted crop that can be scheduled for year-round flowering, like chrysanthemums. These plants are succulents with thick, dark green, fleshy leaves. The multiple, showy flower clusters come in many colors, including red, pink, orange, and yellow (Figure 12.7).

Kalanchoes are propagated by cuttings. Growers start new crops by purchasing rooted cuttings (liners) from specialist propagators. It is very difficult to grow stock plants yourself and to get disease-free cuttings from them. Let the specialist propagator do the job for you!

**Figure 12.7**

Kalanchoes produce multiple flower clusters that are accentuated by dark green, glossy leaves.

Cuttings are planted in either soil-based or soilless root media. The root medium should have excellent drainage and aeration. The pH for soil-based mixes should be between 6.0 and 6.5, and the pH for soilless mixes from 5.5 to 6.0. Kalanchoes typically are produced in 4- or 6-inch azalea pots.

Kalanchoes should be grown at night temperatures of 65° to 68°F; the day temperature should be 75° to 78°F. The root medium should be kept consistently moist for the first two weeks after transplanting so that the cuttings will get established rapidly. Then you will find that this crop does not have as high a water requirement as most other potted crops. Once established, the crop should be watered only when the surface of the root medium dries out. Avoid overhead hose watering, since this can cause stem and crown rots and powdery mildew. Spaghetti tube and capillary mat systems are recommended.

Kalanchoes should be on a constant feed program with respect to nutrition. With less frequent irrigations, fertilizer concentration must be increased to make up for this. Apply 300 to 400 ppm of both nitrogen and potassium until one week before the start of long nights. After that, apply 150 to 200 ppm of both of these elements. Reducing the amount of fertilizer during flower bud formation results in more flowers per plant.

For kalanchoes grown in 4-inch or smaller pots, pinching is generally not needed to produce a full-looking plant. For pots 5 inches and larger, if needed, pinch the cuttings to fill out the pot. Make a soft pinch, removing the top one-half inch of the stem two to three weeks after potting.

Kalanchoes, like chrysanthemums, are long-night plants with respect to photoperiod and flowering. Kalanchoes need at least 13 hours of darkness a night, with 14 or 15 hours preferred. Long nights should be implemented until flower buds show color. Photoperiodic black cloth is usually used from March 1 until October. Missing any long nights will delay the crop. Scheduling of this crop is also similar to chrysanthemums in that the crop is first given a period of short nights so it can attain sufficient height. Then, long nights are applied to bring the crop into bloom. Schedules are available from industry literature and suppliers of kalanchoe cuttings.

When grown during the fall and through until late spring, kalanchoes should receive full light intensity. HID lights are recommended for use in parts of the country that experience long periods of cloudy winter weather. During the summer, the light intensity may cause leaves to scorch. Therefore, apply 50 percent shade over the crop to protect the plants in summer.

The main pests of kalanchoes are aphids, which affect the stems and flowers. Other pests are mealybugs and whiteflies. Careful inspection of the plants should be done for early detection of pests. Also, be sure to implement IPM procedures to prevent many problems before they arise.

Powdery mildew and crown and stem rots are the primary diseases of kalanchoe crops. All these diseases occur because of improper irrigation practices. Powdery mildew develops on foliage that is wet during the night. Crown rot and stem rot occur when the plants are overwatered. Therefore, keep the foliage dry and water the crop only when necessary. Also, steam pasteurize soil-based root media and implement IPHM practices in the greenhouse for preventive measures.

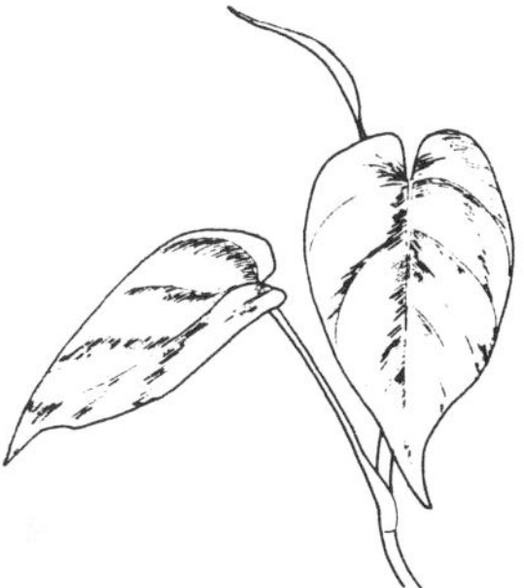

# FOLIAGE PLANTS

## States and Statistics in Production

Foliage plant production is big business in the United States. The wholesale value of foliage plants totalled $512 million in 1990 - a 5 percent increase over the previous year. Foliage plant production is third behind bedding plants and potted flowering plants in wholesale value. The wholesale value of foliage plants in Ohio was $11.6 million in 1990. This ranked Ohio fifth behind Florida ($280.8 million), California ($109.2 million), Texas ($21.5 million), and Hawaii ($13.1 million). Ohio's wholesale production value for foliage plants increased by 10 percent from 1989 to 1990.

These data show us that over half (55 percent) of all foliage production in the United States in 1990 occurred in Florida. Together with California, these two states accounted for 76 percent of all foliage produced in the United States during 1990.

The reason is simple. Foliage plants are tropical in nature. Both Florida and California have the warm climate suitable for outdoor foliage production. Their investment in greenhouse structures is practically non-existent. They can use simple, inexpensive shade structures instead. Compared to these southern states with their warm climate, there is only minor foliage production in the northern states. (Ohio ranked fifth in foliage production in 1990, but accounted for only 2 percent of the nation's total wholesale value.)

Therefore, our discussion of foliage plants will focus on production practices used in Florida. Foliage plants are produced in huge quantities in central and south Florida. The two largest production centers are Apopka (near Orlando) and Homestead (near Miami) (Figure 12.8).

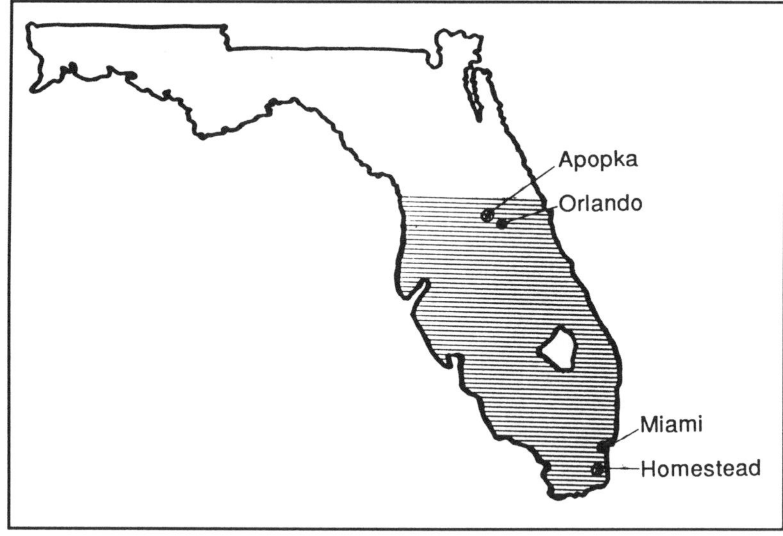


**Figure 12.8**
Foliage plant production in Florida occurs mostly in the southern half of the state.

## Use of Foliage Plants

Foliage plants are used primarily for interior decoration (Figure 12.9). Most homeowners have at least one foliage plant decorating the home. Nearly all office buildings, hotel lobbies, and malls are decorated with foliage (Figure 12.10). To add color to an installation, interior plantscapers use foliage plants with colorful foliage and/or showy flowers. They place colorful floral arrangements in strategic areas to add contrast and beauty to the installation (Figure 12.11). Interior plantscapers also rotate seasonal plants in their installations throughout the year; for example, potted mums in the fall and poinsettias at Christmas.

**Figure 12.9**
A spathiphyllum plant produces large white flowers even under low light intensities.

**Figure 12.11**
Floral arrangement used by an interior plantscaper to add color

**Figure 12.10** Foliage plants are used to decorate **A)** office buildings, **B)** hotel lobbies, and **C, D)** malls.

A

B

C

D

## Production

### *Vegetative Cuttings and the Root Medium*

Most foliage plants are produced vegetatively by cuttings or by air layering (Figures 12.12 and 12.13). Cuttings and air layers are taken from stem sections or stem terminals of large stock plants. They are then planted in a well-drained root medium that is high in organic matter. Various combinations of peat, bark, vermiculite, and perlite or sand are used. The root medium for most foliage plants should have a pH between 5.5 and 6.5. Growing containers range in size to 30 gallons and even more.

### *Shade Structures*

Some foliage crops are grown outside in full sun with no overhead cover (Figure 12.14). However, most crops are grown in simply-constructed shade houses, typically covered with saran that blocks 50 percent or more of the sun (Figure 12.15). While some of these structures are quite large for production of large foliage plants, most foliage is produced in shade structures averaging 10 feet in height (Figure 12.16). Foliage plants should be grown at night temperatures of 65° to 75°F and day temperatures not over 95°F.

**Figure 12.12**
Rooted air layers of weeping fig being planted. Note the holes prepared in the growing pots.

**Figure 12.13**
Rooted corn plant cutting *(Dracaena fragrans* 'Massangeana') showing new top growth.
*(Courtesy of Mike Fulton, ATI, Wooster)*

**Figure 12.14**
Ponytail palms *(Beaucarnea recurvata)* produced in full sun

---

## *Acclimation*

Foliage plants must be shaded during production in Florida if they are to be **acclimated** (adapted) to indoor growing conditions of low light intensity. Most foliage growers in Florida do produce light-acclimated foliage plants. Plants that are not acclimated during production will shed a significant amount of leaves when placed in a low-light situation. The result will be inferior-looking plants and panicked customers!

Sometimes an interior plantscaper purchases from a grower plants that have not been acclimated. The interior plantscaper will then have to acclimate the plants in a specially designed greenhouse or holding area (Figure 12.17).

**Figure 12.15 A**
A large shade house for production of large foliage plants. Inside are **B)** and **C)**.

**Figure 12.15 B**
Queen palms *(Arecastrum romanzoffianum)*

**Figure 12.15 C**
Weeping figs *(Ficus benjamina)*

**Figure 12.16**
Braided, variegated weeping figs in production in a 10-foot-high shade house

**Figure 12.17**
A holding area with HID lights for acclimating Florida-grown foliage to low light levels

### *Fertilization*

Fertilization should emphasize nitrogen for vegetative growth. Recommended rates are 150 ppm of nitrogen, 25 ppm of phosphorus, and 100 ppm of potassium. Constant feed is most often used, though many growers use slow-release fertilizers applied to the root medium after potting. Ideally, growers should stop fertilizing their foliage crops before shipment in order to further acclimate the plants to indoor conditions.

### *Boxing and Shipping*

Foliage that is shipped from Florida to interior plantscapers in Ohio is boxed (small plants) or sleeved (large plants) for protection during shipment (Figure 12.18). Trucks that are used for plant shipment should be environmentally controlled in order to keep plants warm in cold weather and cool in hot weather. When the plants arrive at the interior plantscaper's greenhouse, they are unsleeved, inspected for damage and insect infestations, and cleaned (Figure 12.19).

**Figure 12.18**
Foliage plants sleeved and ready to be loaded on trucks for shipment

**Figure 12.19**
An interiorscape worker cleaning foliage plants that have just arrived from Florida

## Plants in the Interior

### *Maintenance Tasks after Installation*

Once foliage plants are installed in an interiorscape, they must be maintained by technicians on a regular schedule. Their duties include watering; fertilizing; inspecting plants for pests, diseases, and other problems; removing yellowed foliage; cleaning foliage; and pruning.

### *Pests*

Major pests of foliage plants are aphids, spider mites, mealybugs, and scale (Figures 12.20 and 12.21). With plants located in public places, the best pest control methods are to use pest-free plants, follow strict sanitation procedures, and provide ideal cultural conditions to keep the plants healthy.

**Figure 12.20**
Mealybugs on schefflera
*(Brassaia actinophylla)*

**Figure 12.21** Scale and mealybugs on a fig tree *(Ficus benjamina)*

Treatment of a pest infestation should be done when people (the public) are not present (e.g. in the evening). Only pesticides that are labeled for interior foliage plants should be used.

### *General Cultural Requirements*

The main disease of foliage plants is root rot, caused by overwatering. Since most foliage plants grow very little in an interior environment, they do not need frequent watering. Technicians must be trained to recognize when the root medium needs water and to water only then. The optimum time for most species is when the top inch or two of root medium is dry. Of course, the root medium itself should be formulated to promote good aeration and drainage.

Improper watering also causes leaf drop and yellowing of leaves. This further emphasizes the importance of technicians who are properly trained not only to do the watering, but to know the water requirements of many types of foliage plants.

The very slow growth rate of most foliage plants indoors means that very little fertilization will be needed. Most foliage plants are fertilized lightly only two or three times a year, depending on their environment. See the **Foliage Plants Table** at the end of this chapter for general cultural requirements and recommendations for many common interior foliage plants. The information provided should be helpful to any new interior plantscape technician.

### *Common Species and Variety of Uses*

The most popular foliage plants are listed in Table 12.1. Dracaena, pothos, figs, dumbcanes, and palms account for nearly 40 percent of the foliage produced in Florida. See Figure 12.22 for some of the interior plants that are most commonly used in interior plantscape installations.

Another use for foliage plants indoors, but in ***smaller*** sizes, is in terrariums and dish gardens (Figure 12.23). These small foliage plant groupings are available from retail florists, or they can also be made at home. Terrariums and dish gardens are miniature landscapes created with living plants that are easily cared for by the homeowner. Like large foliage plants, terrariums and dish gardens add interest and beauty to any room.

Finally, foliage plants are popular because they not only add beauty and a soothing effect to the commercial and home environment, but also actively remove pollutants from the air. Thus, the air in an environment supporting foliage plants will be of better quality. Also, because plants release water vapor into the air, that air will not be so harsh and dry during the winter months (provided the plant installation is large enough). Heating systems dry out the air and cause discomfort for some people. Plants help to replenish some of this lost moisture. Foliage plants also visually "smooth out" stark construction features such as corners and large, blank walls.

**Table 12.1**

Commonly used foliage plants in interior plantscapes

| Common Name | Scientific Name |
|---|---|
| Dracaena | *Dracaena* spp. |
| Pothos | *Epipremnum aureum* |
| Weeping figs, other figs | *Ficus* spp. |
| Dumbcane | *Dieffenbachia* spp. |
| Palms | *Chamaedorea* spp. |
| | *Chrysalidocarpus* spp. |
| | *Howeia* spp. |
| | *Phoenix* spp. |
| | *Rhapis* spp. |
| Chinese evergreen | *Aglaonema* spp. |
| Spathiphyllum | *Spathiphyllum* spp. |
| Philodendron | *Philodendron* spp. |

There are many cultivars of these species.

**Figure 12.22**
A few of the plants used by indoor plantscapers

**A.** Nephthytis *(Syngonium* spp.*)*

**B.** Dracaena *(Dracaena fragrans* 'Massangeana')

**C.** Dumbcane *(Dieffenbachia maculata* 'Rudolph Roehrs')

**D.** Split-leaf philodendron *(Monstera deliciosa)*

**E.** Rubber plant *(Ficus elastica decora)*

Figure 12.22 *(continued)*

F. Silver queen aglaonema *(Aglaonema commutatum* 'Silver Queen')

G. Schefflera *(Brassaia actinophylla)*

H. Red-edge dracaena *(Dracaena marginata)*

I. Norfolk Island pine *(Araucaria heterophylla)*

J. Heartleaf philodendron *(Philodendron scandens* subsp. *oxycardium)*

Figure 12.22 *(continued)*

K. Kentia palm *(Howeia forsterana)*

L. Triangle palm *(Neodypsis decaryi)*

M. Janet Craig dracaena *(Dracaena deremensis* 'Janet Craig')

**Figure 12.23**

Retail florists use a number of small foliage plants in terrariums (left) and dish gardens (right).

**Foliage Plants Table** General requirements of some commonly grown tropical foliage plants

| Common Name | PLANT USAGE | | | | | LIGHT REQUIREMENTS | | | | WATER | | | FERTILIZER | | | |
|---|---|---|---|---|---|---|---|---|---|---|---|---|---|---|---|---|
| | Floor Specimen | Table Specimen | Dish Garden | Terrarium | Hanging Basket | Full Sun | Bright Indirect Light | Diffused Light | Shade | Heavy | Medium | Light | 6 mo. | 4 mo. | 2 mo. | 1 mo.[1] |
| Aglaonema | X | X | | | | | | X | X | X | X | | X | X | | |
| Amaryllis | | X | | | | X | X | | | Water sparingly till flower stem appears | | | Fertilize once a month for three months after flowering[1] | | | |
| Aralia | X | X | X | X | | X | X | | | | X | | X | X | | |
| Asparagus fern | | X | | | X | | X | | | | X | | | X | | |
| Baby tears | | X | | X | | | X | X | | X | | | | | X | |
| Begonias | | X | X | X | X | | X | | | | X | | | | X | X |
| Bromeliads | | X | | | | X | X | | | | | X[2] | X | | | |
| Browallia | | | | | X | X | | | | | X | | | | | X |
| Cacti | | X | X | X | | X | X | | | | | X | X | | | |
| Caladium | | X | | | | | X | | | X | X | | Fertilize once a month only during active growth[1] | | | |
| Croton | X | X | | | | X | X | | | | X | X | | X | X | |
| Dieffenbachia | X | X | X | X | | | X | X | X | | X | X | X | X | | |
| Dracaena | X | X | X | | | | X | X | X | | X | X | X | | | |
| Episcia | | X | | X | X | | X | | | | X | | | | X | X |
| Fatshedera | X | X | | | | | | | | | X | | | X | | |
| Ferns | | X | | X | X | | X | X | | X | X | | X | X | | |
| Ficus | X | X | | | X | | X | X | | | X | X | | X | | |
| Fittonia | | X | | X | X | | X | X | | X | X | | | | X | X |
| Grape ivy | | X | X | | X | | X | X | X | | X | | | X | X | |
| Hibiscus | X | | | | | X | | | | | X | | | X | | |

| | | | | | | | | | | | | | | | | |
|---|---|---|---|---|---|---|---|---|---|---|---|---|---|---|---|---|
| Hoya | | X | X | | X | | X | | | | | X | | X | | |
| Ivy | | X | X | X | X | X | X | X | | | X | X | | X | | |
| Jade plant | | X | X | X | | X | X | | | | | X | X | X | | |
| Moses-in-the-cradle | | X | | | | | X | X | | | X | | | X | | |
| Nephthytis | | X | X | X | | | X | X | | | X | | | X | X | |
| Norfolk Island pine | X | X | | X | | | X | X | | | X | | | X | | |
| Parlor palm | X | X | X | X | | | X | X | X | | X | X | X | X | | |
| Pellionia | | X | | X | X | | | X | | X | X | | | | X | |
| Peperomia | | X | X | X | X | | X | X | | | X | X | | X | | |
| Philodendron | X | X | X | | X | | X | X | X | | X | | | X | X | |
| Pilea | | X | X | X | X | | X | X | | X | X | | | | X | |
| Pothos | | X | X | | X | | X | X | | | | X | | X | | |
| Prayer plant | | X | X | | X | | X | X | | | X | | | | X | |
| Sansevieria | | X | X | | X | X | X | X | X | | X | X | | X | | |
| Schefflera | X | X | X | | | X | X | | | | X | X | | X | X | |
| Shrimp plant | | X | | | | | X | | | X | X | | | | X | |
| Spider plant | | | | | X | | X | X | | | X | | | X | X | |
| Swedish ivy | | X | | | X | | X | X | | | X | | | | X | X |
| Velvet plant | | X | X | X | X | X | | | | | X | | | | X | X |
| Vinca vine | | | | | X | X | X | | | | X | X | | | X | |
| Waffle plant | | X | | X | X | | X | X | X | X | X | | | | X | |
| Wandering Jew | | X | X | X | X | | | | | | X | | | | X | |
| Zebra plant | | X | | | | | | X | | X | X | | | | X | |

1 Omit during midwinter. 2 Bromeliad "cup" must be kept filled with water at all times; medium should be dry.

*Part 2 follows on the next page.*

**Foliage Plants Table** General requirements of some commonly grown tropical foliage plants **PART 2**

| Common Name | TEMPERATURE | | | HUMIDITY | | | INSECT OR DISEASE PROBLEMS | | | | | PROPAGATION | | | |
|---|---|---|---|---|---|---|---|---|---|---|---|---|---|---|---|
| | Warm | Average | Cool | High | Medium | Low | Spider Mite | Scale or Mealy-bug | Disease | Fluoride | Cultural Problems | Division | Stem Cutting | Leaf Cutting | Seed or Spore |
| Aglaonema | X | X | | | X | X | | X | | | | X | X | | |
| Amaryllis | X | X | | X | X | | | | | | | X | | | Bulb |
| Aralia | X | X | | X | X | | X | X | | | | | X | | |
| Asparagus fern | | X | X | | X | | X | | | | | X | | | X |
| Baby tears | X | X | | X | | | | | X | | Must remain moist. | X | | | |
| Begonias | X | X | | X | X | | X | | X | | | X | X | X | X |
| Bromeliads | X | X | | X | X | | | | | X | | X | | | |
| Browallia | | | X | X | X | | X | | | | Needs plenty of light. | X | X | | X |
| Cacti | X | X | | | X | X | | | | | | X | X | | X |
| Caladium | | | X | X | X | | | | X | | Needs dormancy period. | | | | Tuber |
| Croton | X | X | | | X | | X | X | | | Full sun essential. | | X | | |
| Dieffenbachia | X | X | | | X | X | | X | | | X[1] | X | X | | |
| Dracaena | X | X | | | X | X | X | | X | X | | | X | | |
| Episcia | X | X | | X | X | | | X | | | Avoid using cold water on foliage. | | X[2] | | |
| Fatshedera | X | X | | | X | | | | | | | | X | | |
| Ferns | | X | X[3] | X | | | | X | | | | X | | | X |
| Ficus | X | X | | | X | | X | X | | | | | X | | |
| Fittonia | X | X | | X | | | | X | | | | | X | | |
| Grape ivy | X | X | | | X | | X | | | | | | X | | X |
| Hibiscus | X | X | | X | X | | | X | | | Full sun; overwatering causes leaf drop. | | X | | X |

| | | | | | | | | | | | | | | | |
|---|---|---|---|---|---|---|---|---|---|---|---|---|---|---|---|
| Hoya | X | X | | | X | X | | X | | | | | X | | |
| Ivy | | X | X | | X | X | | X | | | | | X | | |
| Jade plant | X | | X[3] | | X | X | | X | X | | | | X | | |
| Moses-in-the cradle | | X | | | X | | X | | | | | X | X | | |
| Nephthytis | X | X | | | X | | X | | | | | X | X | | |
| Norfolk Island pine | | X | X | X | X | | X | | | | | | X | | X |
| Parlor palm | X | X | | | X | | X | X | | X | | | | | X |
| Pellionia | X | X | | X | X | | | | | | | | X | | |
| Peperomia | X | X | | | X | | | | | | | | X | X | |
| Philodendron | X | X | | | X | | | | X | | | | X | | |
| Pilea | X | X | | | X | | | | | | | | X | | |
| Pothos | X | X | | | X | | | | X | | | | X | | |
| Prayer plant | X | X | | | X | | X | | | X | | X | X | | |
| Sansevieria | X | X | | | X | X | | | | | | X | | X | |
| Schefflera | X | X | | | X | | X | X | | | | | X | | X |
| Shrimp plant | X | X | | X | X | | X | | | | | | X | | |
| Spider plant | | X | | | X | | | | | X | | X | X[2] | | |
| Swedish ivy | | X | | | X | | X | X | | | Sensitive to overfertilization. | X | X | | |
| Velvet plant | X | X | | | X | | | X | | | | | X | | |
| Vinca vine | X | X | | | X | | | X | | | Seasonal availability. | X | X | | |
| Waffle plant | X | X | | X | X | | | | | | | | X | | |
| Wandering Jew | | X | | | X | | X | X | | X | | | X | | |
| Zebra plant | X | X | | X | | | X | | | | Water carefully; needs humidity. | | X | | |

1 Excessive leaf drop due to excessive water; toxic effect from plant juices. 2 Cut off entire offset or runner. 3 Plants do not thrive at higher temperatures.

*This table was developed by D.C. Kiplinger and A.W. Welch; additions by R. W. McMahon*

## CHAPTER 12 REVIEW

This review is to help you check yourself on what you have learned about the production of several minor potted crops, including foliage plants. If you need to refresh your mind on any of the following questions, refer to the page number given in parentheses.

1. Give the scientific name along with the common name of each flowering crop discussed in this chapter. *(pages 273-277)*
2. Which crops discussed in this chapter may be started from seed? *(pages 273-275)*
3. What is the recommended ppm of nitrogen to be supplied to an African violet crop on a constant feed basis? *(page 273)*
4. Give the production time required for African violets started from leaf cuttings. *(page 273)*
5. Culturally, how are cineraria and cyclamen similar? *(pages 274-275)*
6. During what parts of the year are cineraria and cyclamen produced? *(pages 274-275)*
7. Outline the recommended nutritional program for cineraria. *(page 274)*
8. What effect does gibberellic acid have on cyclamen? *(page 275)*
9. From what structure do cyclamen produce leaves and flowers? *(page 275)*
10. What are the three types of holiday cacti? *(page 276)*
11. What is the phylloclade of a holiday cactus? *(page 276)*
12. How are holiday cacti propagated? *(page 276)*
13. What do holiday cacti require in order to bloom? *(page 277)*
14. What are the major diseases of holiday cacti? *(page 277)*
15. By what method are kalanchoes propagated? *(page 277)*
16. What should the night temperature be for kalanchoes? *(page 278)*
17. At which concentration of nitrogen (in ppm) should kalanchoes be fertilized on a constant feed basis? *(page 278)*
18. What is the photoperiodic requirement of kalanchoes with regard to flowering? *(page 278)*
19. What are the major diseases of kalanchoes? Identify the preventive measures to be taken for these diseases. *(page 279)*
20. Where are most foliage plants produced in the United States? *(page 279)*

21. What are the most common propagation methods of foliage plants? *(page 281)*

22. Why do foliage plants have to be acclimated before they are placed in a home or office building? *(page 282)*

23. Name two methods of fertilizer application for the production of foliage plants. *(page 284)*

24. How are foliage plants shipped from their production areas to Ohio? *(page 284)*

25. List the major pests and diseases of foliage plants. *(pages 284-285)*

26. Why are foliage plants fertilized very lightly once they are placed in an interior environment? *(page 286)*

27. List the five most popular types of foliage plants. *(page 286)*

28. ***Large*** foliage plants are used in homes and public places. What are two different uses for ***small*** foliage plants? *(page 286)*

29. What benefits do people obtain from having foliage plants in their homes and work environments? *(page 286)*

# CHAPTER 13

# CUT FLOWER PRODUCTION

## Competencies for Chapter 13

As a result of studying this chapter, you should be able to do the following:

1. Identify five common cut flower crops grown in the U.S.A.
2. Give the scientific name of each of these cut flower plants.
3. Name any cut flower crops in your state.
4. Describe general cultural guidelines for cut flower crops.
5. Describe the importance of support for many cut flower crops.
6. Recognize the most common problems (diseases, pests, etc.) of each cut flower crop studied.
7. Describe post-harvest handling of cut flower crops.

## Related Science Concepts

1. Describe and name different floret arrangements in flowers.
2. Examine plant development.
3. Describe the effects of greenhouse environmental conditions on cut flower growth and quality.
4. Determine cultural needs of cut flower crops.
5. Describe photoperiodic manipulation in relation to cut flower crops.
6. Implement IPHM strategies.
7. Implement IPM strategies.

## Related Math Concepts

1. Apply basic operations to whole numbers, decimals, and fractions as they relate to cut flower crops.
2. Apply basic operations to ratios and percents as they relate to cut flower crops.
3. Apply mathematical concepts and operations to cut flower crops.
4. Read, interpret, and construct charts, graphs, and tables related to cut flower crops.
5. Read thermometers.
6. Set thermostats.

## Terms to Know

calyx
cyme
ethylene
rhizome
sepals

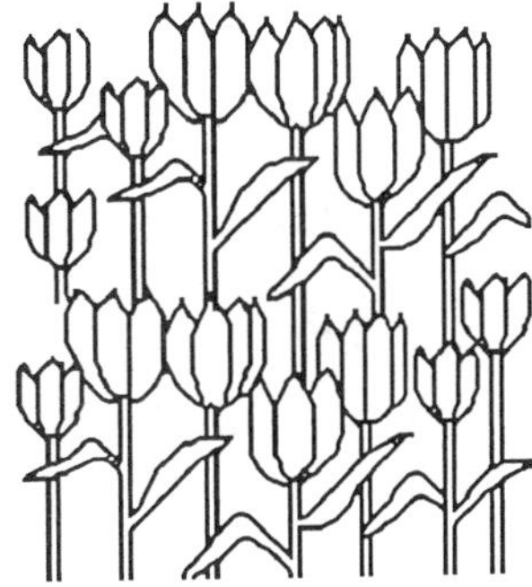

## INTRODUCTION and STATISTICS

Cut flower production in the United States during 1990 had a total wholesale value of $503 million. This was a rank of fourth behind bedding plants, potted flowering plants, and foliage plants (in order of decreasing wholesale value). According to the USDA's *Floriculture Crops 1990 Summary:*

1. Roses had a wholesale value of $200.3 million, or 40 percent of the total cut flower wholesale value,
2. Carnations (standard and miniature) were second with $57.8 million (11.5 percent of the total cut flower wholesale value), and
3. Chrysanthemums (standard and pompon) were third with a wholesale value of $38 million.

As we learned in Chapter 1, nearly two-thirds of all cut flowers sold in the United States are imported from other countries. Cut flowers are not subject to Quarantine 37 (which bars potted plants from entering this country from abroad). Many of these exporting countries, like Colombia, can grow high quality plants with minimal labor and overhead costs. In the U.S., these imported cut flowers can then be sold at prices that are below domestically grown cut flower crops, even with air freight charges figured into the price.

Thus, imported cut flowers are forcing domestic cut flower growers to streamline their production procedures to cut down on costs. Some of these techniques are:
1. use of greenhouse automation,
2. more efficient scheduling,
3. better use of growing area, and
4. better irrigation and fertilizer management.

In addition, some cut flower growers are no longer growing **common** cut flower crops like carnations and roses, as these are largely imported. Rather, they are "filling niches" by supplying cut flower crops that are not in competition with imported flowers. These are flowers in demand in the local area, but not supplied by outside sources.

This chapter will familiarize you with some specific cut flower crops and supply you with general guidelines for growing these crops.

---

## ROSES

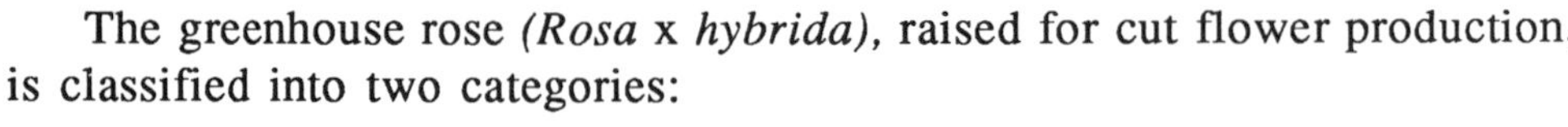

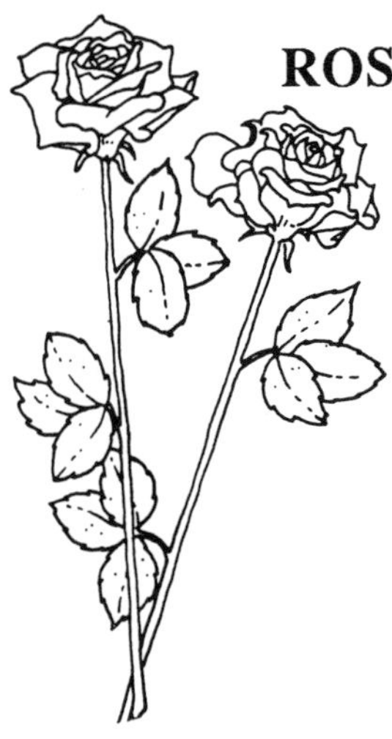

The greenhouse rose *(Rosa* x *hybrida),* raised for cut flower production, is classified into two categories:

***1. hybrid tea roses***
These roses develop one large terminal flower per stem (Figure 13.1.) Any lateral buds that develop are removed as soon as possible.

***2. floribunda or sweetheart roses***
The blossoms are smaller than those of hybrid tea roses (Figure 13.2). Floribunda roses may be disbudded to produce larger terminal flowers, or the

**Figure 13.1** Hybrid tea rose

**Figure 13.2** Floribunda or sweetheart rose with lateral buds intact

lateral buds may be allowed to bloom. This will result in a spray of flowers on each stem.

According to the USDA's *Floriculture Crops 1990 Summary,* 83 percent of all roses grown and sold in the United States during 1990 were hybrid tea roses. The remaining 17 percent were floribunda roses. The most popular rose colors are red, followed by pink, yellow, and white cultivars.

Greenhouse roses are grown in ground benches which typically run the length of the greenhouse. Rose growers frequently apply a mulch over the root medium to conserve moisture and reduce soil compaction. Rose plants need this culture because they are in production up to ten years before they are replaced by a new crop. Most rose crops are irrigated by a system that does not wet the foliage. A type of perimeter system is most widely used.

Roses are extremely susceptible to powdery mildew, a fungal disease that covers the leaves with a white, powdery growth (Figure 13.3). Moisture on plants favors powdery mildew development. Red spider mites and aphids are the two most serious pests of cut rose crops.

**Figure 13.3** Powdery mildew on rose leaves

Rose flowers are harvested when the petals are just beginning to unfurl (Figure 13.4). This degree of unfurling varies somewhat among cultivars. Rose flowers are graded by the length of the stem, placed in a floral preservative solution, and stored in a cooler until they are sold.

**Figure 13.4**
Rose flowers ready for harvesting

**Figure 13.5**
Bench of roses that have just been cut back

Since they gradually keep gaining in height during production, rose plants must be cut back once a year to control their height (Figure 13.5). This is usually done after Mother's Day, since the demand for roses during the summer is low.

## CARNATIONS

Carnation *(Dianthus caryophyllus)* production for use as cut flowers in the United States has greatly declined since 1971. Cut carnations imported from other countries (especially Colombia) have taken over the market, comprising nearly 80 percent of all carnations sold in the United States in 1990. In 1971, only 5 percent of the carnations sold in this country were imported. As a result, cut carnation production has been limited mainly to California and Colorado, states that have the best climate for carnation production. The domestic grower who wants to compete with growers of imported carnations must provide ideal growing conditions, automate as much as possible, and implement efficient growing methods.

Cut carnations are classified into two groups: **standards** and **miniatures**. Standard carnations have one large terminal flower with all lateral buds removed (Figure 13.6). Miniature carnations have smaller flowers. All the lateral buds are usually allowed to bloom as a spray (Figure 13.7). The terminal flower bud, which opens first, is usually removed to enhance the appearance of the spray. Popular colors include red, pink, white, purple, and variegated.

Carnations are grown in ground beds in either a one- or two-year rotation. Better quality is obtained from a one-year rotation, but less money is invested in cuttings in a two-year rotation. Rooted cuttings are purchased from specialist propagators and planted **very shallow** to prevent root and stem rots

**Figure 13.6**

A standard carnation flower. Label indicates where to make cut on the stem when harvesting.

**Figure 13.7**

A miniature or spray carnation flower. Label indicates where to make cut on the stem when harvesting.

(Figure 13.8). The cuttings are irrigated by ooze tubes or a similar system that will not wet the foliage.

Carnations require cool temperatures for optimum quality. Night temperatures should be from 50° to 55°F and day temperatures 10 degrees warmer. Carnations also require high light intensities. Thus, for carnation production in the summer, cooling equipment is a necessity.

Standard carnation flowers are ready for harvest when the petals are expanded so that the flower is semicircular in shape. If carnations are to be

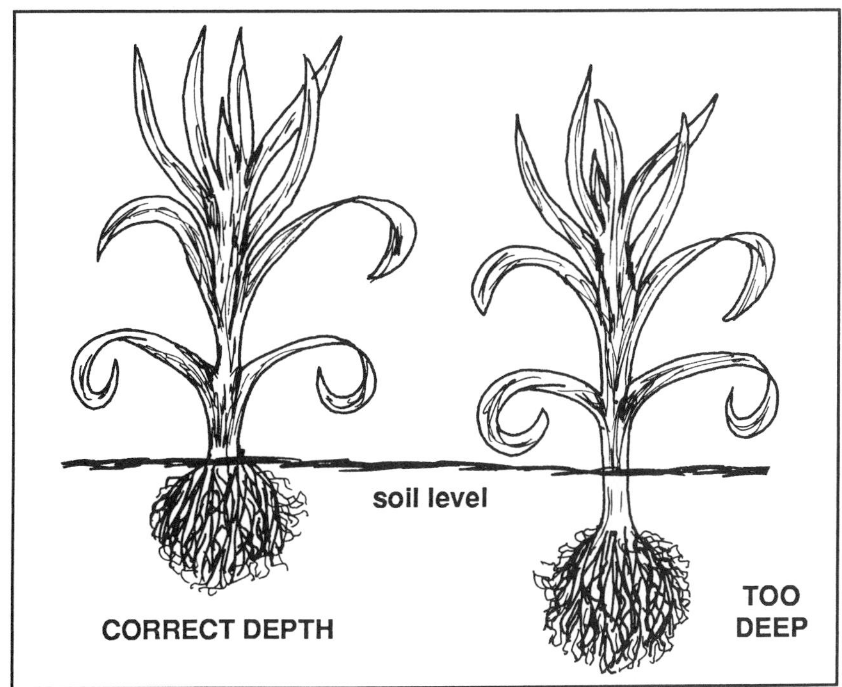


**Figure 13.8**

Carnation seedlings should be planted very shallow.

shipped long distances, the flowers can be harvested when approximately one-half inch of the petals is showing above the green sepals, or **calyx** (Figure 13.9). Miniature carnations are harvested when two flowers are fully open and the rest of the buds are showing color. When the stem is cut for harvest, several pairs of leaves must be left beneath the cut so that new blooming stems will develop. Carnations are graded by stem strength and length and flower size.

The main problem of carnations is **splitting of the calyx**, which results in a misshapen flower (Figure 13.10). Some cultivars are more susceptible to splitting than others. This splitting is caused by sudden temperature fluctuations. The main pests of carnations are spider mites and aphids. Stem and root rots and *Fusarium* wilts are the most serious diseases of carnations.

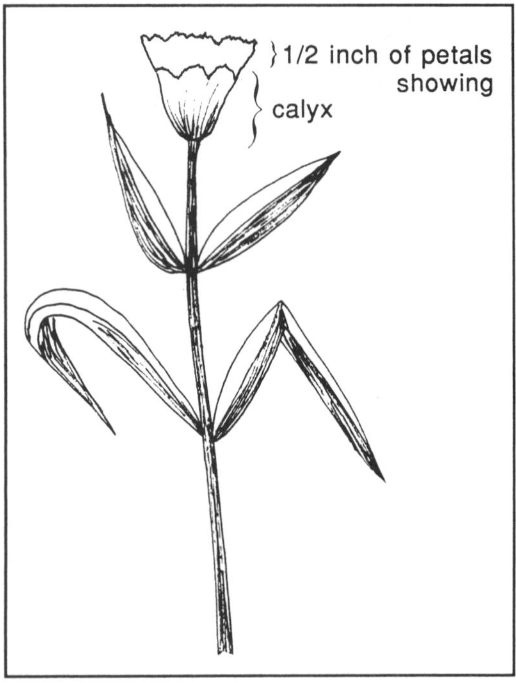


**Figure 13.9**
A carnation ready for harvesting in the bud stage (bud cut carnations)

**Figure 13.10**
A carnation with a split calyx

## ALSTROEMERIA

Alstroemeria (*Alstroemeria* sp.) is a cut flower crop that is very popular in Europe and is rapidly gaining popularity in the United States. The flowers are clustered on the stem in an arrangement known as a **cyme** (Figure 13.11). Many flower colors are available, including bronze, orange, pink, red, and yellow.

Alstroemeria plants reach heights of 6 feet or more, so this crop is best suited for ground benches (Figure 13.12). These plants grow from fleshy rhizomes which are obtained from specialist propagators. The rhizomes are planted quite deep, since they can grow to 12 to 14 inches below the root medium surface.

As with most cut flower crops, the foliage of alstroemeria should stay dry during irrigation. An irrigation system like a perimeter system or ooze tubes should be used for this crop (Figure 13.13). Such systems will help prevent foliar diseases.

A unique characteristic of alstroemeria is its high nutritional requirement. The crop flourishes when provided as much as 600 ppm of nitrogen twice a week. This amount of nitrogen would adversely affect most other cut flower crops.

**Figure 13.11**

Alstroemeria flower cluster borne in a cyme

**Figure 13.12**

An alstroemeria crop in production with plants over 6 feet in height

**Figure 13.13**

A recently planted crop of alstroemeria. The irrigation system, a plastic pipe with nozzles, applies water only to the root medium.

For alstroemeria to bloom, the rhizomes must be kept cool in a root medium temperature of 40°F for four to six weeks (depending on the cultivar). After receiving this cold treatment, the plants are lighted from 10 p.m. to 2 a.m. with standard mum lighting to speed up flowering. As long as the root medium temperature does not exceed 60°F, the plants will bloom continuously for two to three years. Then they tend to lose vigor and decrease flower output. It is then time to dig up the rhizomes, divide them (discarding the older portions), and replant them.

Alstroemeria flowers are ready for harvesting when the first flowers in each flower cluster (cyme) begin to open. Alstroemeria are graded by both the number of flower clusters per stem and by stem length.

Generally, alstroemeria are not susceptible to insect pests. However, aphids and whiteflies can become a problem during warm weather. The only significant disease problem is leaf mottling, caused by a virus. This problem can be prevented by proper greenhouse sanitation and use of culture-indexed plants from specialist propagators.

## FREESIA

Freesia *(Freesia refracta)* is another European cut flower that is becoming popular in the United States. The plant grows from a corm that is planted in ground benches. The leaves of freesia are similar to those of gladiolus, and the lily-like flowers are both colorful and very fragrant. Each flower consists of many florets on a spike that is usually perpendicular to the rest of the stem (Figure 13.14). In other words, the spike is on a horizontal plane. Freesia flower colors include white, yellow, blue, pink, and red.

**Figure 13.14** Fragrant freesia flowers

Freesia corms should be purchased from a specialist propagator, since this plant is very susceptible to viral diseases. The corms are planted 2 inches deep in ground benches - 80 to 100 corms per square yard. When the plants have started to grow and have developed three or four leaves, the root medium temperature must be maintained at about 55°F. Thus, planting should be done in the fall, from September to December, when these cool soil temperatures are easier to maintain. Freesia may also be grown from seed. But production time will be an additional three months compared to crops started from corms.

Freesia flowers are ready for harvesting when the first floret opens. Long-term storage is not recommended, since freesia flowers are easily damaged by ethylene.

The main pest of freesia is aphids. The serious disease problem is viral diseases, as mentioned previously.

## SNAPDRAGONS

The snapdragon *(Antirrhinum majus)* is grown from seed, unlike most other cut flower crops. The popularity of this cut flower is once again increasing after peaking in the 1950's. The most popular flower colors are white, pink, and yellow for year-round sales. Red and bronze-colored cultivars are popular in the fall.

Snapdragons are divided into four groups based on their optimum photoperiod and temperature requirements. These four groups collectively cover the entire year, so, with careful cultivar selection, quality snapdragon flowers can be produced year-round.

The snapdragon flower is composed of many florets arranged vertically on a spike (Figure 13.15). The lowest floret opens first, followed by the next highest floret, until all the florets have opened.

Snapdragon seed can be started either in plug trays or standard flats. In flats, no more than 1,000 seeds or half a seed packet should be sown per standard flat. When the seedlings have developed their first set of true leaves, they are transplanted from the flat to the ground bed. Plug seedlings may be transplanted when two or more sets of true leaves are visible.

Snapdragons are grown at night temperatures of 50° to 55°F. Day temperatures ideally should be no higher than 60°F. However, transplanted seedlings at first should be given somewhat warmer temperatures (around 60°F at night) to help them become rapidly established.

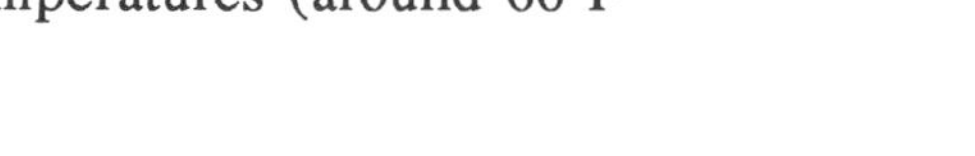

**Figure 13.15** A bench of snapdragons

It is extremely important to keep the flower spikes **vertical** during development. If they are allowed to fall over, the tip will bend upwards, causing a **permanent bend** in the spike. This ruins the appearance and quality of the plant. The spikes should be supported with a series of welded wire meshes aligned vertically over the bench.

Snapdragon spikes are ready for harvesting when the lowest one-third of the florets have opened. Leaves are stripped off the lowest one-third of each stem, and the spike is placed in a solution of floral preservative. Again, the spikes ***must*** be kept in a vertical position during storage so that the tip of the spike will not bend. Snapdragon flowers are graded by the length of the spike and stem.

The main pests of snapdragons are aphids, thrips, and whiteflies. The primary diseases of snapdragons are damping-off during the seedling stage and *Botrytis* during production.

# GENERAL CULTURAL GUIDELINES

## Root Media

Root media for cut flower crops are usually soil-based, since most crops are produced in ground benches. The root media must have good drainage and aeration, yet allow for good water and nutrient-holding capacities. Usually, growers amend field soil with sphagnum peat moss, vermiculite, perlite, or other ingredients. Steam pasteurization of the root medium should be done after ***every*** crop.

Before planting, the root medium should be analyzed using soil tests and amended according to the recommendations made by the soil testing laboratory for the particular crop to be raised. For most cut flower crops, the soil-based root medium should be maintained at a pH of 6.0 to 6.5.

## Watering and Nutrition

Nearly all cut flower crops should be watered with a system that does not wet the foliage. This will help prevent foliar diseases like *Botrytis*. Watering systems such as ooze tubes and perimeter irrigation are most commonly used.

Fertilizers are typically applied on a constant-feed basis. Fertilizer injectors inject concentrated amounts of fertilizer stock solution directly into the water lines. For most crops (except alstroemeria), 200 to 250 ppm of both nitrogen and potassium is recommended. Ammonium nitrogen fertilizers should not be used during the winter because cold root media hinder the conversion of ammonium nitrogen to nitrate nitrogen. As a result, ammonium levels rising in the root medium may become toxic to the plants. Superphosphate, which supplies phosphorus, is mixed into the root medium before planting. The rest of the essential elements are supplied by micronutrient fertilizer mixes, dolomitic limestone, and other root medium amendments.

## Temperature

Several cut flower crops, like carnations, alstroemeria, and snapdragons, are cool temperature crops. Night temperatures should be kept in the low to mid 50°s(F) and day temperatures approximately 10 degrees warmer. For crops like roses, night temperatures should be maintained around 65°F and day temperatures 10 degrees warmer.

## Light Intensity

Most cut flower crops produce the best quality flowers when grown under full light intensity. However, sometimes in summer, when light intensity is very high, it may be necessary to reduce light intensity. Light intensity levels that are too high can cause petals to burn or scorch. Obviously, the quality of the flowers would be seriously affected. Growers then must make a choice:

1. Apply shading compound to the greenhouse glazing,
2. install shading curtains overhead, or
3. place saran over the ground benches.

Reducing light intensity by 50 percent is often done to prevent flowers from scorching. Even at 50 percent light intensity, plants still receive sufficient light intensity for maximum rates of photosynthesis and subsequent growth.

### Support

Most cut flower crops grow to heights of several feet. Thus, because flowers with long, straight stems are wanted, support must be provided for cut flower crops during production. The most common method of support is a series of welded wire fabric grids installed over the crop (Figure 13.16). Grid size can vary, but 8 x 8 inch square grids are most commonly used. As the plants grow, three or more series of grids are usually installed over the ground bench and spaced 12 to 18 inches apart. The grid supports the plants as they grow up through the squares with long, straight stems.

**Figure 13.16**
A welded wire fabric grid on a recently planted crop of roses. As the crop grows in height, additional wire grids will be placed over the crop at 12- to 18-inch intervals.

## HARVESTING

Harvesting procedures for cut flower crops vary with the crop being grown. Usually, flowers are harvested just as they are beginning to open (like roses) or when only a few florets are open on a spike (like snapdragons). Some crops (like carnations and cut mums) are harvested when the flower buds are showing color. This stage of development is best for flowers being shipped long distances. Bud-cut flowers are less likely to be damaged during shipment than flowers that are fully open.

When the flower stem has been cut, the leaves are stripped from the lowest third of the stem. Leaves that are submersed in water will rot and shorten the post-harvest life of the flowers. The stems are then recut under water to keep air bubbles from entering the stem and blocking the **xylem**, the water-conducting tissue of the stem. The stems are placed in a warm floral preservative solution, because a warm solution is rapidly absorbed by the stem. The cut flowers are then stored at 35° to 40°F until they are sold.

## Post-harvest Handling

Cut flowers that have been harvested are graded and bunched. Grading varies from one cut flower crop to the next: length of stem, stem strength, flower diameter, number of flowers per stem, or combinations of these are used. Cut flowers are bunched by the dozen or in groups of 25, depending on the crop. The bunched cut flowers are then often sleeved for protection during shipping (Figure 13.17).

Floral preservative is mixed into the water for holding cut flower crops after harvesting. Floral preservative helps to prolong the life of the cut flowers and to preserve their original quality as long as possible. A food source for the flowers is included in the floral preservative along with an ethylene-inhibiting agent. Ethylene is a gas that causes flower petals to fall off prematurely and prevents flower buds from opening. Carnations and freesia are especially susceptible to the effects of ethylene.

**Figure 13.17**

Roses in bunches sleeved for shipment

## CHAPTER 13 REVIEW

This review is to help you check yourself on what you have learned about the production of cut flowers. If you need to refresh your mind on any of the following questions, refer to the page number given in parentheses.

1. Name four commonly grown cut flower crops. *(page 298ff)*

2. Give the scientific name of each of these four plants. *(page 298ff)*

3. What was the wholesale value of cut flower production in the United States in 1990? *(page 298)* In your state?

4. What effect do imported cut flowers have on the production of cut flowers in the United States? *(page 298)*

5. What is the difference between hybrid tea and sweetheart roses? *(pages 298-299)*

6. Why is it important that the irrigation system for cut rose crops never wets the foliage? *(page 299)*

7. At which stage are roses usually ready for harvesting? *(page 299)*

8. How are roses graded after they are harvested? *(page 299)*

9. What are the two categories of cut carnations? *(page 300)*

10. What percentage of all carnations sold in the United States in 1990 were imported? *(page 300)*

11. Where are most carnations grown in the United States? *(page 300)*

12. In what range of night temperatures should carnations be grown? *(page 301)*

13. Describe the procedure for harvesting the two categories (forms) of carnations you named in question 9. *(pages 301-302)*

14. What is splitting of the calyx? How can it be prevented in a carnation crop? *(page 302)*

15. What is the cyme of an alstroemeria? *(page 303)*

16. How does an alstroemeria crop differ from other cut flower crops with regards to nutrition? *(page 303)*

17. What is the main requirement of alstroemeria crops in order to bloom? *(page 304)*

18. For alstroemeria to bloom continuously, what root medium temperature is required? *(page 304)*

19. At which stage of flower development are alstroemeria flowers ready for harvesting? *(page 304)*

20. How are alstroemeria flowers graded? *(page 304)*

21. What is the main disease problem of alstroemeria? *(page 304)*

**Chapter 13 Review** *(continued)*

22. What underground structure do freesias grow from? *(page 304)*

23. Describe the freesia flower. *(page 304)*

24. At which stage of flower development is the freesia flower ready for harvesting? *(page 304)*

25. How are snapdragons propagated? *(page 305)*

26. What are the criteria for classifying snapdragons into four groups? *(page 305)*

27. Describe the snapdragon flower. *(page 305)*

28. Give the recommended night and day temperatures for a snapdragon crop. *(page 305)*

29. Why must snapdragon flowers be kept vertical during development in the greenhouse? *(page 305)*

30. At which stage of development are snapdragon flowers ready for harvest? *(page 305)*

31. What are the main pests of snapdragon crops? *(page 305)*

32. What is the most common method of applying fertilizers to cut flower crops? *(page 306)*

33. How are cut flower crops typically supported in the bench? *(page 307)*

34. Why should cut flowers be re-cut under water before they are placed in a floral preservative and stored? *(page 307)*

35. What is ethylene? How does it affect cut flower crops? *(page 308)*

36. What can be done to prevent or lessen the effects of ethylene on cut flower crops? *(page 308)*

## REFERENCES


Ball, Vic, *Ball Redbook,* 15th edition, George J. Ball Publishing, West Chicago, IL, 1991

Boodley, James W., *The Commercial Greenhouse,* Delmar Publishers, Inc., Albany, NY, 1981

Ecke, Paul, Jr.; Matkin, O. A.; and Hartley, David, E., *The Poinsettia Manual,* 3rd edition, Paul Ecke Poinsettias, Encinitas, CA, 1990

Feilner, Veronica, *Greenhouse Operation and Management* (student reference), University of Missouri-Columbia, Columbia, MO, 1990

*Greenhouse Grower,* Meister Publishing, Willoughby, OH

*Grower Talks,* George J. Ball Publishing, West Chicago, IL

Larson, Roy A., *Introduction to Floriculture,* Academic Press, New York, NY, 1980

Laurie, Alex; Kiplinger, D. C.; and Nelson, Kennard S., *Commercial Flower Forcing,* 8th edition, McGraw-Hill, New York, NY, 1979

Nelson, Kennard S., *Flower and Plant Production in the Greenhouse,* 4th edition, Interstate Publishers, Danville, IL, 1991

Nelson, Paul V., *Greenhouse Operation and Management,* 4th edition, Prentice Hall, Englewood Cliffs, NJ, 1991

Ohio Cooperative Extension Service, *Tips on Growing Bedding Plants,* 2nd edition, The Ohio State University, Columbus, OH, 1989

Ohio Cooperative Extension Service, *Tips on Growing Poinsettias,* The Ohio State University, Columbus, OH, 1988

Ohio Cooperative Extension Service, *Tips on Growing Zonal Geraniums,* 2nd edition, The Ohio State University, Columbus, OH, 1991

Ohio Florists' Association, Floriculture Crops: *Chemical Use Booklet (A Guide for Insecticide, Miticide, Fungicide, Growth Regulator, and Herbicide Application),* Bulletin No. 735, Ohio Florists' Association, Columbus, OH, 1991

USDA (United States Department of Agriculture), National Agricultural Statistics Service, and Agricultural Statistics Board, *Floriculture Crops 1990 Summary,* Washington, DC, 1991

Voigt, Alvi O., *Flower Marketing Information Newsletter,* The Pennsylvania State University College of Agriculture and Cooperative Extension Service, June 1991

| | |
|---|---|
| **A-frame** | greenhouse frame that with its sidewalls and even-span roof forms the letter "A" in outline. |
| **A-Rest®** | chemical applied to greenhouse crops to control height. |
| **acclimation** | preparing a plant grown outdoors for indoor environmental conditions by regulating factors such as light, water, and temperature. |
| **acidity** | condition of the root medium or water with a pH of less than 7.0. |
| **acrylic** | rigid plastic used to cover greenhouses; often used in double-layer form. |
| **aeration** | penetration or infiltration of air in a substance such as a root medium. |
| **aeroponics** | growing plants in air by spraying nutrients periodically onto the roots. |
| **alkalinity** | (with regard to water quality) the concentration of calcium carbonate and magnesium carbonate in water. |
| **amendment** | any substance mixed into a root medium that improves one or more of its physical properties. |
| **apex** | the main growing point of a plant |
| **apical dominance** | growth of a plant exclusively from the apex because of the presence of an auxin that inhibits the growth of lateral buds beneath the apex. |
| **aquifer** | underground soil layer that contains enough water to be a potential source of water for a greenhouse operation. |
| **asexual** | in plants, the vegetative rather than the sexual stage of development. |
| **aspirated chamber** | box equipped with a fan that moves air through it. |
| **azalea pot** | pot with height three-quarters of the diameter of the pot. |
| **B-Nine®** | chemical applied to greenhouse crops to control their height. |
| **bacterial blight** | disease affecting foliage and flowers that is caused by bacteria. |
| **bedding plants** | plants that are started under precisely controlled greenhouse conditions and sold in spring to customers for planting outdoors. |
| **biological control of pests** | use of a beneficial predator or parasite organism for the control of a pest organism. |
| **biotherm** | bottom heating system of a greenhouse bench comprised of a series of black plastic tubes through which hot water circulates. |
| **blackleg** | disease of geraniums caused by the fungus *Pythium* that attacks and blackens the base of the stem. |
| **Bonzi®** | chemical growth retardant used to control the height of various floriculture crops. |

| | |
|---|---|
| ***Botrytis* blight** | fungal disease characterized by water-soaked spots on the foliage, dark and wilted flower petals, and gray mold growing on various plant parts. |
| **bract** | petal-like modified leaf of a plant |
| **British Thermal Unit (Btu)** | measure of heating efficiency in fuels; the amount of heat required to raise one pound of water one degree Fahrenheit. |
| **broadcasting seed** | sowing bedding plant seed uniformly by scattering seed across germination media in flats. |
| **buds breaking** | lateral buds beginning to sprout and grow after the apex has been removed by pinching. |
| **buffering** | making additions to root media or water to offset pH changes |
| **bulb pan (pot)** | pot with height one-half of the diameter of the pot |
| **calibration** | procedure used on a fertilizer injector to verify the accuracy of its performance. |
| **calyx** | protective covering of the flower bud |
| **capillary action** | movement of water upward through tiny "tubes" in the root medium. |
| **capillary mat** | irrigation system for potted plant crops that consists of a water-absorbent mat that supplies water to the crops through the drainage holes of the pots. |
| **capillary pore** | small space in a root medium that is capable of holding water and oxygen. |
| **cation exchange capacity (CEC)** | measure of the ability of a root medium to attract and hold nutrients for plant use. |
| **cellulose** | complex chemical compound in the cell wall of plants that gives the plant its strength. |
| **chlorophyll** | green pigment in plants that is responsible for photosynthesis |
| **chlorosis** adj. **chlorotic** | yellowing of leaves from lack of chlorophyll |
| **cold frame** | small structure composed of side walls and a transparent top in which bedding plants are started from seed in early spring; no heat except that of the sun is provided. |
| **combustion** | burning of a substance such as a greenhouse fuel. |
| **compaction** | condition of a root medium in which the particles are pressed together and little air is present. |
| **complete fertilizer** | fertilizer containing nitrogen, phosphorus, and potassium. |
| **composted** | advanced decomposition of root medium components carried out under controlled conditions. |
| **condensation** | formation of water from water vapor on surfaces that have been cooled due to falling greenhouse temperatures. |

*(continued)*

**conduction** transfer of heat through solid objects

**constant feed** method of fertilizer application in which low concentrations of fertilizer are applied at each irrigation.

**controlled temperature forcing (CTF)** preferred method of cooling Easter lily bulbs for scheduling purposes.

**corm** modified, underground, solid stem consisting of nodes and internodes from which a flowering plant grows.

**cotyledon** food storage part of a seed that provides nourishment for the seedling.

**crown buds** disorder of mums in which flower buds form but never develop, usually in response to improper photoperiod.

**cultivar** group of plants that have been genetically developed, with one or more unique characteristics that are passed on to the next generation.

**culture-indexed cuttings** specially-produced cuttings that are free of viral and other diseases.

**curtain wall** non-transparent lower portion of sidewall in an even-span greenhouse.

**cyathia** inconspicuous yellow flowers of poinsettia

**cyclic** repeated at regular intervals

**Cycocel®** chemical applied to greenhouse crops to control their height.

**cyme** cluster of many small flowers in a whorled arrangement, making up a globe-like flower head.

**damping-off** fungal disease that commonly attacks germinating seedlings, killing them.

**decomposition** the process of breakdown of soil components by chemical and physical means.

**dibble** blunt object used to make holes in the root medium into which seedlings or cuttings are planted.

**DIF** (abbreviation for "difference")
manipulation of plant height of a crop by regulating the difference between day and night temperatures (DT - NT).

**disbud mum** mum flower form with one small flower per stem

**disinfectant** chemical substance applied to surfaces to eliminate harmful organisms.

**disk florets** individual flowers or flower parts in the center of a composite flower (like a chrysanthemum flower).

**DNA** deoxyribonucleic acid, the basic genetic "building block" of every living cell.

**drip gutter** small V-shaped strip of metal under mist lines and greenhouse gutters that collects and drains away water dripping from them.

| | |
|---|---|
| **eave** | part of the greenhouse where the roof and sidewall join together. |
| **ECHO** | Environmentally Controlled Hanging-basket Operator - a watering system. |
| **ecosystem** | balanced interaction of all organisms with their environment, in a particular location. |
| ***Encarsia formosa*** | small parasitic wasp used for biological control of whiteflies. |
| **energy conservation** | procedures implemented in the greenhouse to reduce the amount of heat lost from the structure. |
| **environmental** | having to do with the surroundings and influencing factors such as air, water, and land (and including plants and animals). |
| **EPA** | Environmental Protection Agency |
| **ethylene** | colorless, odorless gas that causes distorted plant growth and flower drop from plants. |
| **evaporative cooling** | greenhouse cooling process that removes heat from the air by changing water from the liquid to the gaseous state. |
| **even-span** | greenhouse design with two roofs of equal lengths and angles joined at the peak or ridge. |
| **excelsior** | shredded aspen commonly used in pad cooling systems. |
| **fertilize** | to add nutrients in known amounts to a root medium. |
| **fertilizer analysis** | the three numbers of a fertilizer label that correspond to the percent weight of nitrate, phosphate, and potassium salt. |
| **fiberglass** | greenhouse covering made from a mixture of acrylic plastic and glass fibers. |
| **finishing plants** | the final phase of plant production in which plants become salable. |
| **floriculture** | growing and marketing of bedding plants, flowering potted plants, cut flowers, and foliage plants. |
| **fluorescent lamp** | low wattage, tube-shaped, electrical lamp used for limited supplementary greenhouse lighting. |
| **foliage plant** | plant grown mainly for its foliage and commonly used to decorate building interiors. |
| **foliar** | having to do with leaves |
| **foliar analysis** | determination of the nutrient content of a plant by running tests on selected leaves in a laboratory. |
| **footcandle** | measure of light intensity one foot away from a lighted candle. |
| **footer** | foundation for a greenhouse or other permanent structure. |

*(continued)*

**fossil fuel** fuel such as coal and oil that is formed in the earth from fossilized remains of organisms.

**fumigant** chemical applied to a greenhouse as a fog or smoke to control pests and diseases.

**fungicide** chemical applied either to plant foliage or the root medium to control pathogenic fungi.

**gable** the area of a greenhouse above the height of the eave.

**genetic** the biochemical basis of heredity in a plant cell contained in its nucleus in the form of DNA.

**geometric design** design shaped like a circle, square, triangle or modification of one of these.

**germination** emergence of the root from a seed

**glazing** transparent covering material for greenhouses that allows sunlight to pass through

**greenhouse** artificially heated structure that is covered with a transparent glazing and high enough for a person to stand in.

**greenhouse range** two or more greenhouses situated at the same location

**ground bench** exposed area of root medium at floor level

**growing medium** (plural, **media**) substance in which a plant is grown

**growth regulator** chemical applied to plants that affects one or more growth processes.

**headhouse** service building of a greenhouse

**heat exchanger** device used to transfer heat from its source to a distribution pipe for heating a greenhouse.

**herbicide** chemical which kills plants

**High Intensity Discharge (HID) lighting** most commonly used form of bright supplemental lighting (like high-pressure sodium lamps) in the greenhouse industry.

**high-pressure sodium lamp** type of HID supplemental greenhouse lighting that produces light of high intensity.

**honeydew** sticky excretion of insects that feed on plant sap

**Hozon®** fertilizer injector that works by a simple siphon mechanism

**hydroponics** growing plants with water as a root medium

**incandescent lamp** lamp that produces light by a white-hot metal filament; used for photoperiodic lighting.

**infestation** colonization of a plant by harmful insects

**infrared** type of invisible thermal radiation that does not affect plant growth.

**injector** device that injects precise amounts of concentrated fertilizer into irrigation lines.

**inorganic** not originating from living organisms

**Integrated Pest Management (IPM)** a combination of four methods for the control and prevention of insect pest infestations in the greenhouse.

**Integrated Plant Health Management (IPHM)** a combination of four methods for the control and prevention of diseases that affect greenhouse crops.

**intermittent mist** applications of tiny droplets of water at frequent, regular intervals.

**internode** section of a plant stem between two nodes

**interveinal** area between the veins of a leaf

**irrigation** process of applying water to greenhouse crops

**leach** to saturate the root medium with 10 percent more water than needed for irrigation.

**leaf orientation** the angle at which leaves are held from the stem

**life cycle** the different sexual and asexual stages that complete the life of a plant or animal.

**light transmission** passage of light through a greenhouse covering

**liners** small starter plants usually potted in 2 1/4-inch pots

**long-night plant** plant which requires a period of darkness longer than a certain number of hours in order to express a growth response.

**louvers** movable overlapping strips of metal installed in greenhouse walls to let outside air into the structure.

**macro-elements** elements essential to healthy plant growth, in relatively large amounts

**microbe** a microscopic organism

**micro-elements** elements essential to healthy plant growth, in minute amounts

**nematode** small worm-like organism that commonly feeds on plant roots

**nitrate** nitrogen in the form of a compound that is utilized by plants

**node** area of a stem from which leaves, flowers, and branches arise

**non-capillary pore** large space in a root medium that will not hold water

**non-tunicate bulb** form of bulb with separate fleshy scales surrounding the central bulb stem, and no paper-like tunic on the outside.

*(continued)*

**oedema** physiological disorder (notably in ivy geraniums) characterized by raised, corky areas on the underside of leaves, in response to high levels of moisture in the root medium.

**organic** originating from living organisms

**parasite** organism that obtains its nutrients by living off another living organism.

**pasteurization (soil)** heating soil by steam at 140°-160°F for 30 minutes in order to kill harmful organisms.

**peat pellet** compressed disk of sphagnum peat, moistened and used for germinating seeds.

**peninsula** raised benching arrangement consisting of a series of benches projecting out from a common bench.

**perimeter** outer walls or edge of a greenhouse or bench

**pesticide** one of a class of chemicals used to control insect pests, disease organisms, and plant height.

**petiole** stem of a leaf

**pH** measure of acidity or alkalinity in water or soil

**photoperiod** length of time in light and darkness experienced by an organism in a 24-hour period.

**photosynthesis** process of food manufacture in green plants by which carbon dioxide and water are converted into sugar and oxygen in the presence of light.

**phylloclade** flattened stem segment of a holiday cactus

**pistillate** containing the female parts of the flower

**plant hardening** process of preparing a greenhouse plant for outside growing conditions through decreased fertilizer and water applications.

**plug growth stages** four definitive stages of plug seedling growth from germination to transplanting stage.

**plug tray** tray (typically the size of a standard flat) made up of many cells fused together; used for germinating bedding plant seed.

**pollutant** introduced substance that is usually harmful to the organisms living in that environment.

**polyethylene** film plastic used for covering greenhouses; lasts up to three years.

**polyvinyl fluoride** film plastic used for covering greenhouses; lasts up to ten years.

**pompons** spray mums characterized by small globular flowers

**pore space** area between individual particles of a root medium

**porous** physical condition of a substance in which air and water readily pass through it.

**powdery mildew** fungal disease characterized by white powdery growth on plant surfaces.

**ppm** parts per million, a measure of very small concentrations in volumes of liquid.

**predator** organism that feeds on other organisms

**primed seed** seed that has been partially germinated

**propagation** the process of increasing the population of a plant species

**proportioner** device used to inject precise amounts of concentrated fertilizer into irrigation lines. (See *injector.*)

**purlin** greenhouse framing which connects the trusses

***Pythium*** fungus that causes several plant diseases

**Quarantine 37** policy enforced by the U.S. Animal and Plant Health Inspection Service restricting imports of potted flowering plants from other countries into the United States.

**quonset house** film plastic greenhouse with a roof shaped like a semi-circle.

**radiation** loss of heat from a greenhouse by direct transfer of heat from the inside to the outside without warming the air.

**ray florets** the (usually) larger, strap-like individual flowers or petals around the edge of a composite flower like a chrysanthemum.

**refined seed** seed that has been sorted by physical characteristics

**relative humidity** amount of water contained in the air at a given temperature expressed as a percent of the total amount of water the air can hold at that temperature.

**rhizome** underground stem

**rockwool** synthetic root medium resembling fiberglass insulation

**root medium** any substance in which a plant is grown

**rooting hormone** chemical applied to the base of cuttings that enhances rooting.

**runoff** drainage of excess greenhouse irrigation water into the soil beneath.

**saran** synthetic woven fabric used to reduce light intensity

**sash bar** greenhouse framing which holds glazing panes in place

**scouting a crop** visually inspecting a crop for pests

**seeders** machines used to sow seed in plug trays

**seedling** young plant that has just sprouted from a seed

*(continued)*

| | |
|---|---|
| **sepals** | individual sections of the outer covering of a flower bud. |
| **side post** | part of the greenhouse frame which supports the truss in an even-span greenhouse. |
| **sleeving** | the process of placing plastic or paper around harvested cut flowers or potted plants to cover and protect them during shipment. |
| **slow-release fertilizer** | fertilizer applied to a root medium that is released slowly over a period of several weeks to several months. |
| **"soft" pesticide** | pesticide that is relatively harmless to the environment |
| **soft pinch** | removal of the uppermost one-half to one inch of a plant stem to promote lateral branching. |
| **soilless media** | root media that contain less than 20 percent field soil by volume; most soilless root media contain 0 percent field soil. |
| **soluble salts** | dissolved chemicals such as fertilizer nutrients in the water. |
| **solubridge** | instrument used to measure the soluble salts concentration in root media. |
| **spaghetti tubes** | system of irrigation for flowering potted plants consisting of small black tubes tipped with either plastic or lead water breakers placed in each pot. |
| **splitting** | physiological disorder of poinsettias in which flowers form prematurely, vegetative by-pass shoots form, and a misshapen plant results. |
| **spray mum** (also, **pompon mum**) | mum flower form with several small flowers per stem |
| **staminate** | containing the male parts of the flower |
| **standard mum** | mum flower form with one flower more than four inches in diameter per stem. |
| **standard pot** | pot with height equal to the diameter |
| **sterile** | free of any living organisms |
| **sterilization** | process of killing all living organisms |
| **stock tank** | large covered container that holds a concentrated fertilizer solution. |
| **stomata** | tiny openings or pores in leaves through which carbon dioxide and water vapor pass. |
| **succulent** | plant with thick fleshy leaves, adapted to survive in a dry environment. |
| **supplemental lighting** | additional lighting supplied to greenhouse crops most commonly in the form of high pressure sodium lamps. |
| **target pest** | pest singled out for "control" in a pest control program |
| **target ratio** | specified ratio(s) of a fertilizer injector |

**temperature regime** 24-hour temperature changes implemented per day during crop production.

**thermostat** device which controls the heating and cooling equipment in a greenhouse.

**topography** physical characteristics of the land

**truss** greenhouse framing, comprised of rafters, struts, and chords, that supports the weight of the roof in an even-span or uneven-span greenhouse structure; in quonset greenhouses, framing composed of pipe bent into an arc.

**tunicate bulb** form of bulb with continuous fleshy scales surrounding the central bulb stem and covered by a brown, paper-like tunic.

**turgid** plant condition of "crispness" of stems and leaves

**ultraviolet (UV)** type of light which causes most plastic coverings to darken and become brittle.

**uneven-span** greenhouse design with two roofs of unequal length and angle joined at the ridge.

**vegetative** referring to the foliar parts of a plant; i.e. its stems and leaves; also, asexual.

**ventilator** small movable section of the greenhouse roof or sidewall used for ventilation.

**viscosity** measure of how easily a liquid flows

**water boom** irrigation device consisting of a long water distribution pipe with water nozzles spaced at regular intervals along its length.

**water breaker** attachment at the end of an irrigation hose that reduces the pressure of the water as it is applied to greenhouse crops.

**water-holding capacity** ability of a root medium to retain water for plant use

**weighted leaf** device used to control the frequency and duration of intermittent mist systems.